INTEGRA SALUTES ROBERTO

For over a century, Integra's team of banking professionals has been committed to helping Western Pennsylvania's communities and businesses succeed. It is with this same spirit that we remember and recognize the achievements of the great Roberto Clemente. Integra salutes Roberto's unselfish dedication to excellence and dignified leadership during his eighteen seasons with the Pirates.

A Book Review

This review was written by Taylor Scott for Pittsburgh's Point *maga-zine. A native Pittsburgher, Scott has lived elsewhere the past 32 years. He is sports editor of the* Boca Raton (Fla.) News.

Who said you can't go home again? Each time Jim O'Brien comes out with a book, I am home again, and this is true of *MAZ And The '60 Bucs.*

His two previous books that I have read, *Doing It Right* and *Whatever It Takes,* both about the NFL Pittsburgh Steelers, did the same thing. That has always been the uniqueness of O'Brien. He puts you in Pittsburgh.

The person out there, away from Pittsburgh, all he knows is Bill Mazeroski's home run in the bottom of the ninth that beat the New York Yankees in the '60 World Series.

But that was only one climatic hit in a season. There were more reasons to celebrate. O'Brien tells you why.

No, not in hits and runs and base stealing and pitching and pinch-hitting. That isn't what the book is all about.

It's about Pittsburgh as much as it's about the 1960 Pittsburgh Pirates.

Before the likes of Barry Bonds and his ilk and whatever has hap-pened to sports today, athletes were a part of the city. You feel that when you read the book.

It isn't the mini-biographies of players that grabs you. It's the feel-ing that these guys *were* Pittsburgh.

It's why baseball fans throughout the nation hurt when the Dodg-ers left Brooklyn. God made some things the way they are supposed to be: The Dodgers belong in Brooklyn.

The 1960 Pirates were 1960 Pittsburgh.

And that's why O'Brien wrote the book.

The 1960 Pirates were as right for Pittsburgh then as the NFL Steelers were for the '70s.

Read this book and you travel through Pittsburgh. You smell it, you feel it, you experience it. Woven throughout is a city and its people and its culture.

That's what you get from O'Brien. And you like it.

BOOKS BY JIM O'BRIEN

COMPLETE HANDBOOK OF PRO BASKETBALL 1970-71
COMPLETE HANDBOOK OF PRO BASKETBALL 1971-72
ABA ALL-STARS
PITTSBURGH: THE STORY OF THE CITY OF CHAMPIONS
HAIL TO PITT: THE SPORTS HISTORY OF
THE UNIVERSITY OF PITTSBURGH
DOING IT RIGHT
WHATEVER IT TAKES
MAZ AND THE '60 BUCS
REMEMBER ROBERTO

REMEMBER ROBERTO

Clemente Recalled by Teammates,
Family, Friends and Fans

By Jim O'Brien

Author Jim O'Brien revisits the wall that remains from Forbes Field.

Copyright © 1994 by Jim O'Brien

James P. O'Brien — Publishing
P.O. Box 12580
Pittsburgh PA 15241
Phone (412) 221-3580

First printing, May, 1994

Manufactured in the United States of America

Printed by Geyer Printing Company, Inc.
Pittsburgh PA 15213
Typography by Cold-Comp
Pittsburgh PA 15222

ISBN 0-916114-14-7

To order copies directly from the publisher, send $24.95 for hardcover edition and $14.95 for softcover edition. Please send $3.50 to cover shipping and handling costs. Pa. residents add 6% tax to price of book only. Copies will be signed by author per your request. Discounts available for large orders. Contact publisher regarding availability of earlier books in *Pittsburgh Proud* series.

Contents

7

*"A nation reveals itself
not only by the men
it produces but also by
the men it honors,
the men it remembers."*
—John F. Kennedy

Acknowledgements

This is the sixth book in my "Pittsburgh Proud" series and, as always, I had great assistance and support from many special people in writing and publishing this tribute to Roberto Clemente.

I want to thank all the members of the Pirates family who invited me into their homes and offices and shared their time and stories. Special gratitude is extended to Vera Clemente and Roberto Jr. and Luis for their gracious cooperation.

No one helped me more than Sally O'Leary of the Pirates public relations staff, who was always there when I needed a name, some statistics, a telephone number and, most of all, a pleasant smile. She is an angel.

Jim Lachimia and Jim Trdinich of the Pirates public relations and publicity office had open doors over a two-year period, and were always generous with their help.

David Arrigo, the Pirates official team photographer, continued to be an MVP, and other Pirates marketing officials, such as Steve Greenberg, Mike Gordon, Kathy Guy and Rob Ondo, offered their support. Club President Mark Sauer gave his blessing.

Richard B. Kantrowitz, a former classmate in high school and college who serves as treasurer of the Roberto Clemente Foundation, and Jana Halloran Phillips of the law firm of Kirkpatrick & Lockhart, helped with legal clearances and served to establish a viable relationship with the Roberto Clemente Foundation. The same was true of Alicia Berns of Pro Star Management, who represents the Clemente family's commercial interests. I want to help them with their mission.

I am appreciative of special permission granted to me to reprint articles about Roberto Clemente that first appeared in *The New York Times, New York Daily News, The Daily News* in McKeesport, *The Pittsburgh Press* and *Post-Gazette.*

Special thanks to Barbara Potter, a professional writer and neighbor, and my oldest daughter, Sarah O'Brien, a second-year pre-med student at the University of Virginia, for their proof-reading assistance. The ready reference service and photographic archives of the Carnegie Library of Pittsburgh were invaluable.

Special assistance was provided by Judy Kelly and Jacob Brody of the public relations staff of Mayor Tom Murphy. Thanks to Mayor Murphy for his introductory message in this book.

Gayland Cook and John Williams of Integra Bank Pittsburgh have been especially supportive of my book projects — Integra's theme of "for times like these . . ." is certainly appropriate to what I am doing — and Integra has provided a base on which to build a library about accomplishment and sports successes in Western Pennsylvania.

I wish to thank these patrons: Aeriss, Inc., Arco Chemical, L.D. Astorino & Associates, Ltd, Architects, Babb, Inc., Baierl Chevrolet, Blue Cross of Western Pennsylvania, Bowne of Pittsburgh, Christopher's Restaurant, Continental Design and Management Group, Daniell-Sapp-Boorn Associates, Inc., Eat'n Park Restaurants, E-Z Overhead Door &

Operation Service, Ernst & Young, Bill Few Associates, Frank B. Fuhrer Wholesalers, The Gustine Company, F.E. Harmon Construction, Inc., Hawthorne Sports Marketing, H.J. Heinz, Local Chevrolet/Geo Dealers, Mascaro Inc., Merna Corp., Miles, Inc., North Side Bank, Nortim Corp., PNC Bank, Reed Smith Shaw & McClay, Sargent Electric Company, TRACO, Westinghouse Electric Corp., Wheeling-Pittsburgh Steel Corp.

I wish to thank the following for their continued support: Dennis Astorino, Bill Baierl, Eugene J. Barone, Walt Becker, Michael Berlin, Tom Bigley, Jim Broadhurst, Dave Brown, John Bruno, Everett Burns, Ray Conaway, Carole Cook, Joe DeGregorio, John Fadool, Richard E. Farrell, Mike Fetchko, Gregory W. Fink, Patrick Fleming, Barbara and Ted Frantz, Bob Friend, Lloyd Gibson, M. John Gaurneri, Frank Gustine Jr., Bill Haines, Darrell J. Hess, James D. Hesse, Dave Jancisin, Andy Komer, Ron Livingston, Robert Lovett, Laura Madonna, Jack Mascaro, Del Miller, Carl R. Moulton, Thomas H. O'Brien, Ron Parkinson, Christopher Passodelis, Jack Perkins, Alex Pociask, Bill Priatko, Bob Randall, Jim Roddey, Ed Ryan, Bob Scott, Tom Snyder, Stanley M. Stein, Dick Swanson, Roy Werner and Earle Wittpen.

Special thanks to Tom Mariano and Pittsburgh Trane, Jay A. Miller and Richard J. Nesbit of Sutersville Lumber Co., Clark Nicklas of Vista Resources, Steve and Charlie Previs of Waddell & Reed Financial Services, W. Harrison Vail and Three Rivers Bank.

Pittsburghers who took tremendous pride in producing this series of books are Ed Lutz of Cold-Comp Typographers and Stan Goldmann, Bruce McGough and Tom Samuels of Geyer Printing. All the work on this book was done in Pittsburgh, and that is a point of pride.

—Jim O'Brien

Selective Bibliography

Baseball's 100, A Personal Ranking of the Best Players in Baseball History, by Maury Allen (Galahad Books), 1981.

Clemente! by Kal Wagenheim (Praeger Publishers), 1973.

Cult Baseball Players, edited by Danny Peary (Simon & Schuster), 1990.

Five Seasons, A Baseball Companion, by Roger Angell (Simon & Schuster), 1972.

I Had A Hammer, by Henry Aaron with Lonnie Wheeler (Harper Collins Publishers), 1993.

Kiner's Korner, by Ralph Kiner with Joe Gergen (Arbor House), 1981.

The Pittsburgh Pirates — An Illustrated History, by Bob Smizik (Walker & Company), 1990.

The Pirates — We Are Family, by Lou Sahadi (Times Books), 1980.

The World Champion Pittsburgh Pirates, by Dick Groat and Bill Surface (The Coward-McCann Sports Library), 1961.

Who Was Roberto? A biography of Roberto Clemente, by Phil Musick (Doubleday), 1974.

Willie Stargell, An autobiography by Willie Stargell and Tom Bird,

Dedicated to the memory of
Roberto Clemente
and to his family
and his fans
who loved him

Illustration by Tom Mosser

Foreword

The name Roberto Clemente evokes timeless memories of magnificent play on the baseball field. But my father was much more than a baseball player. He was a man with humanitarian vision — a dream of a better life for all children through sports and education.

His dream was first manifested in 1974 with the creation of the Roberto Clemente Sports City in Puerto Rico. Hundreds of thousands of children have benefited from its sports and educational programs.

I wanted to continue my father's dream in a place that was close to his heart — Pittsburgh. My father always gave his best on the field because of his love for the city and its people. My family and I share that affection and wanted to give something back to the Pittsburgh community for all it has given to us.

We established the Roberto Clemente Foundation to provide children in the Pittsburgh area with the opportunity to learn, enjoy and participate in sports of all kinds in order to instill in them the qualities of responsibility, character and leadership. The Foundation will emphasize the importance of education through supplemental tutoring and will rehabilitate local parks, playgrounds and ballfields.

I was fortunate enough to know my father for at least a short time and to learn more about him from those who loved him. After reading this book, I hope that you will get to know my father a little bit better and share his dream of a better life for all children.

Roberto Clemente Jr.

City of Pittsburgh
Office of the Mayor

Remembering Roberto Clemente...

Forbes Field opened to the public on June 30, 1909, the year Halley's Comet, the brightest of all recurring comets, lit the night sky. Forty-six years later, Pirates fans got to experience another astral phenomenon of sorts — Roberto Clemente's arrival in Major League Baseball. His star would burn bright for eighteen seasons.

The analogy fits Clemente for a number of reasons. His on-field heroics stood out not just as those of an exceptional baseball player, but as movement itself, transcendent of sport, team standing or any particular game situation. Clemente seemed to travel the field along a different median, known only to him and baseball.

To watch Clemente run bases, field a line drive or throw a runner out was to see grace restored.

Of course, these are the recollections of an adult. As a ten-year-old boy watching Clemente take the field for the first time, I sensed only that I was part of a privileged moment. In that sense, Clemente helped a generation or more of young people understand that life could be, at times, exceptional.

Clemente challenged people off the field as well. As one of baseball's first Puerto Rican superstars, Clemente embodied change, both for the game of baseball and in the culture at large. He faced and fought his way through real barriers — language, perception and prejudice.

Again, he proved to be a model for others, determined, direct and tempered by the responsibilities that came with being Puerto Rico's most famous citizen.

Clemente's sudden and tragic death on Dec. 31, 1972 was no less remarkable in its impact. I recall the enormous outpouring of grief among the people of Pittsburgh, and the feeling that our new year did not begin until months later when our grief began to subside.

As we prepared as a city to honor Roberto Clemente in the summer of 1994, these memories and more all converged into one. Although it was his many gifts as an athlete that first captured our attention, we later came to love Clemente as a human being, a man of great courage, humility and heart.

That love, between man and a city, will forever remain a part of Pittsburgh.

Tom Murphy
Mayor of Pittsburgh

Roberto Clemente Jr. and Mayor Tom Murphy meet at the launching of Pittsburgh's "Look At Us Now" campaign at the City-County Building.

Preface
Setting the scene in the summer of '62

My education in the daily newspaper business truly began in the summer of 1962 when I went to work on a summer internship as a city-side reporter at *The Pittsburgh Press*. As a sophomore at the University of Pittsburgh, I had been named the sports editor of the student newspaper, *The Pitt News*, the first sophomore to be so honored, and had won a *Wall Street Journal* scholarship for the princely sum of $500 that I would get in addition to my weekly salary of $85 for a summer's work. I thought I had died and gone to heaven.

I had worked at *The Press* on Friday evenings as a junior and senior at Taylor Allderdice High School, as a copy boy in the classified ad department. It was my door opener, and I frequently wandered from my work station to the desks of reporters and the sports writers, to watch them at their work, to run and get a coffee or something for anyone who asked. I got to know everyone who had a byline in the newspaper, and the people in the engraving shop and the press room. It was a wonderful world.

It was a great internship that I had in the summer of '62. I would come to realize this a year later when I had a terrible internship experience at the *Philadelphia Evening Bulletin*. Leo Koeberlein, the assistant managing editor of *The Press* back then, really put me to work and gave me great assignments and even let me write columns which they ran on the same page as those of nationally-syndicated giants in the industry. It was heady stuff. In Philadelphia, they had me scratching horses in the race listings, and working the overnight shift.

For starters at *The Press*, I was sent around town to spend a day with each of the regular beat reporters, such as the one at the police station, City Hall, labor, the court house, et al.

I remember one morning being led into a room at the City Morgue where I witnessed the autopsy of a woman who had been found dead in one of the city's streets a few days earlier. Her knees were all scraped up, I recall, and parts of her body had turned purple. She had brown hair. She lay naked on a slab in a very cool room at the morgue.

An assistant coroner cut her with a scalpel from one side of her stomach to the other, and then up each side to her armpits, and simply lifted her chest in one large flap back toward her neck. Her breasts came back to her chin.

That's when I knew this job would be different.

I covered the opening of the Police Circus at Forbes Field, and was invited to a party on the eve of the opening held by all the circus performers. They were from all over the world, and so was the food they offered. It was an international party.

I went there with Al Herrmann and Don Stetzer, two photographers from *The Press* and my older brother, Danny. We had a great time. I remember we were taking a leak against the outside of the wall at Forbes Field when lions roared in a nearby cage, scared the hell out of us and nearly sent us running through the wall. Danny got a date with a beautiful woman who performed in the high-wire act. Her father, who was the "catcher" in the high-wire act and looked like a strongman from Bulgaria, accompanied them as a chaperone on a day at Kennywood Park.

I assisted on the coverage of the U.S. Open at Oakmont where Jack Nicklaus knocked off Arnold Palmer in a playoff.

I covered a riot at Western Penitentiary that lasted a week, and ran on the front page of the paper the entire period. Several prisoners, all black, climbed to the top of a water tower in the prison yard and remained there to protest conditions at the prison.

I watched the activity from the rooftop of a nearby warehouse, along with photographers from *The Pittsburgh Press*. I called in every so often to a facile rewrite man named John Place, whom I still bump into on occasion at his neighborhood pub, Atria's, in Mt. Lebanon. I scooped the *Post-Gazette* a few times that week, much to the chagrin of their blustery crime reporter, Vince Johnson, who had once covered the Pittsburgh Pirates, but was pulled off the beat for upsetting too many of the players with his controversial reports.

Several days into the protest, when it was obvious that the rioters were getting tired and suffering from lack of food and exposure to the elements, some thought they were about to give up and return to their cells. I remember a newsman at Channel 11 hollering up to the rioters, "Stay up there! We're getting the word to Harrisburg about your plight! Stay up there!" Even then, Channel 11 was after exclusives.

I remember that same newsman standing atop the same warehouse where I perched myself each morning to remain the rest of the day, and waving his arms — like the director of the Pittsburgh Symphony Orchestra — to get the prisoners who were in the yard on a lunch break to start carrying on. On cue, the prisoners started shouting and waving their arms — the way sports fans do routinely these days whenever they see a TV camera or any kind of camera focused their way — and supposedly protesting at large as the Channel 11 cameras caught the action for film at 11. Only this wasn't a ballgame.

Unreal, I thought then. They think they're making a movie or something. The prisoners were mere props, part of another TV sitcom. And this was long before "Inside Edition" and "Hard Copy" and the rest of the TV tabloid journalism.

I will never forget some words of advice that were given to me as I sat in front of an old battered typewriter at the police station. A veteran police reporter told me, the latest cub reporter:

"Don't concern yourself with police reports about colored people, or stuff that goes on in The Hill or Homewood, where somebody is just stabbing somebody else, or crap like that. Just ignore it. And if one of them kills another one, hold it to a graph. Our readers don't care."

17

This was in the summer of 1962.

It was 15 years after Jackie Robinson had broken the color barrier in baseball by playing for the Brooklyn Dodgers.

The Pirates had just come back from spring training, where Roberto Clemente and Willie Stargell and Alvin O'Neal McBean and Bob Veale and Donn Clendenon had been required to stay in separate housing accommodations and eat in different restaurants than the rest of the team throughout the South because they were black. This was the year the New York Mets came into being. It wasn't that long ago.

This was the same year that Mal Goode, a Pittsburgher who had befriended Jackie Robinson, Clemente, Henry Aaron and Willie Mays, broke another color barrier, at age 54, by becoming the first black TV network news correspondent.

This was two years after Clemente had contributed, as much as anyone on the team perhaps, to the Pirates winning the World Series over the mighty New York Yankees, winning the seventh and deciding game at Forbes Field on a home run by Billy Mazeroski in the bottom of the ninth inning.

It's no wonder Clemente found the going tough when he first came to Pittsburgh. He had the gall to think he was as good as anyone else. Imagine that.

Beano Cook, sports information director at Pitt in the early '60s, was a strong influence on student writers on *The Pitt News*, left to right, Stan Stein, Bob Smizik, Jim O'Brien, Marvin Zelkowitz and Art Fleischner. Stein and Fleischner became attorneys, Zelkowitz a pediatric neurologist and Smizik and O'Brien became sportswriters. Cook became a TV network publicist and then a TV college football analyst.

"Goodbye, Norma Jean
Though I never knew you at all
You had the grace to hold yourself
While those around you crawled

They crawled out of the woodwork
They whispered into your brain
They sent you on a treadmill
And they made you change your name

It seemed to me you lived your life
Like a candle in the wind
Never knowing who to cling to
When the rains set in

Now I would have liked
To have known you
But I was just a kid
Your candle burned out
Long before your legend ever did

— Written and sung by
Elton John
"A Candle In The Wind"
About Marilyn Monroe

Roberto Clemente acknowledges cheering after doubling for his 3,000th hit on September 30, 1972.

Roberto Clemente
The Great One

Roberto Clemente

"In a way, I was born twice."

He was always a heroic figure, a sleek, compact-muscled man who could do it all on a baseball field, whether it was Forbes Field, Three Rivers Stadium or some distant outpost in this country or his native Puerto Rico. It took awhile for Pirates fans to truly appreciate him, and it took his untimely death in an airplane crash in 1972 to properly focus attention on his marvelous feats, both on and off the playing field. Real fame came to Clemente late in life, and more so when he was gone.

Roberto Walker Clemente came to the Pirates in 1955, brought here by Branch Rickey, and he played 18 summers — sometimes spectacular summers which stretched into falls, and found the Pirates winning the World Series — and he set the standards for Willie Stargell, Dave Parker and Barry Bonds to push toward in later days.

He was something else, something special, an athletic marvel. Sometimes he was hard to understand, and to fathom, but this may have added to his mystique more than anything else. Clemente cried out to be loved, to be lauded, to be cheered, to be crowned as one of the game's greatest players.

He came from Puerto Rico, but Clemente became a big part of Pittsburgh. "In a way, I was born twice," Clemente said when he was honored in special ceremonies on July 25, 1970 at Three Rivers Stadium, his night at the ballpark. "I was born in 1934 and again in 1955, when I came to Pittsburgh. I am thankful I can say that I live two lives."

He didn't live either of them long enough, however.

Clemente was killed in an airplane crash on December 31, 1972, one-and-a-half miles off the shores of San Juan, Puerto Rico, attempting to fly relief supplies to earthquake victims in Managua, Nicaragua.

His image was such among his good friends and teammates that one of them, Manny Sanguillen, fully expected Clemente to come walking out of the water, and return to play for the Pirates. It's the stuff of television movies.

Clemente was with the Pirates so long, yet he was gone too soon, leaving behind his wife, Vera, and their three children, as well as his many admirers. He left us with many cherished memories.

The rule requiring a ballplayer to be retired five years before becoming eligible for Baseball's Hall of Fame was waived, and Clemente was enshrined during ceremonies in the summer of '73 at Cooperstown, the sleepy and picturesque little community in upstate New York where Abner Doubleday supposedly invented the game of baseball. Clemente became the first Hispanic inducted into the Hall of Fame.

Clemente became an overnight sensation with his sterling performance in the 1971 World Series. He led the Pirates to a comeback championship series victory over the favored Baltimore Orioles as only he could. He hit .341 for the season and .414 for the World Series.

The Pirates dropped the first two games of that Series in Baltimore, but bounced back to win the next three, then dropped the sixth game, so the Series was squared at three games apiece. Clemente had hit a home run in that sixth game, but it wasn't enough as the Orioles prevailed, 3-2.

In the deciding seventh game, Clemente gave the Bucs a 1-0 lead with his second home run of the Series. It was also the 14th consecutive World Series game in which Clemente had hit safely. He had a hit in each of the seven games when the Pirates won the World Series in 1960. He was only the second player ever to pull off that feat.

The Pirates won the seventh game, 2-1, and Clemente became a national sports hero. He was 37 years old at the time, and felt that such recognition had been long overdue. He felt neglected. "How come they call Pete Rose in Cincinnati Charlie Hustle?" asked Clemente. "I hustle just like Pete Rose and they don't call me nothing."

One thing they did call him was a hypochondriac, but again he felt it was undeserving. He was a thoroughbred. People generally conceded that he was a hitter of great consistency, a runner with blazing speed and that he had an arm of pure gold.

He joined baseball's elite on September 30, 1972 — during the last season with the Pirates — when he doubled against New York's Jon Matlack to become only the 11th player in baseball history to get 3,000 hits. He hit .312 that year.

At the close of the '70s, Clemente remained the Pirates' all-time leader in games played, at-bats, hits, singles, total bases and was second to Honus Wagner in runs-batted-in. He later was bumped to third in RBIs by Stargell.

He won 12 Gold Glove awards, batted over .300 in 13 different seasons, and was selected to 12 All-Star Games. He led the league's outfielders in assists five times, tying a major league record. He had back-to-back 5-hit games against the Los Angeles Dodgers on August 22-23, 1970.

He was the National League's MVP and Player of the Year in 1966 when he batted .317 and had 119 RBI.

Even after he died, he was still an inspiration to the Pirates. Stargell spoke of him often, missed him dearly. When Manny Sanguillen came through with a game-winning performance in the 1979 World Series triumph, he said he did it in memory of Roberto Clemente. He was a positive influence on Al Oliver and Dave Parker. He was a hero for Orlando Merced, from a different generation, who grew up in the same community where Clemente lived in San Juan, Puerto Rico.

"You know all about him," said Baltimore's Brooks Robinson, himself a Hall of Famer, during that 1971 World Series. "But in real life he's even better."

Clemente's Major League Record

Year	G	AB	R	H	2B	3B	HR	RBI	BA
1955	124	474	48	121	23	11	5	47	.255
1956	147	543	66	169	30	7	7	60	.311
1957	111	451	42	114	17	7	4	30	.253
1958	140	519	69	150	24	10	6	50	.289
1959	105	432	60	128	17	7	4	50	.296
1960	144	570	89	179	22	6	16	94	.314
1961	146	572	100	201	30	10	23	89	.351
1962	144	538	95	168	28	9	10	74	.312
1963	152	600	77	192	23	8	17	76	.320
1964	155	622	95	211	40	7	12	87	.339
1965	152	589	91	194	21	14	10	65	.329
1966	154	638	105	202	31	11	29	119	.317
1967	147	585	103	209	26	10	23	110	.357
1968	132	502	74	146	18	12	18	57	.291
1969	138	507	87	175	20	12	19	91	.345
1970	108	412	65	145	22	10	14	60	.352
1971	132	522	82	178	29	8	13	86	.341
1972	102	378	68	118	19	7	10	60	.312
18 yrs.	2433	9454	1416	3000	440	166	240	1305	.317

CHAMPIONSHIP PLAYOFF RECORD

Year	G	AB	R	H	2B	3B	HR	RBI	BA
1970	3	14	1	3	0	0	0	1	.214
1971	4	18	2	6	0	0	0	4	.333
1972	5	17	1	4	1	0	1	2	.235
3 yrs.	12	49	4	13	1	0	1	7	.265

WORLD SERIES RECORD

Year	G	AB	R	H	2B	3B	HR	RBI	BA
1960	7	29	1	9	0	0	0	3	.310
1971	7	29	3	12	2	1	2	4	.414
2 yrs.	14	58	4	21	2	1	2	7	.362

Roberto Clemente Jr. gets "hooked" by young fan near "A Tribute To Roberto" exhibition at 1994 Piratefest.

Piratefest
A Tribute To Roberto

Fans swarm to Clemente family

Some of The Great Ones were there. Roberto Clemente, of course. And Arnold Palmer. Paul and Lloyd Waner. Honus Wagner. Mario Lemieux. Ralph Kiner. Willie Stargell. Forbes Field. They were all on canvas or celluloid.

The images were mixed. Some were paintings and prints by Tom Mosser, the multi-talented young man who doubles as one of the nation's finest sports artists and as the Pirate Parrot — the wonderful mascot who delights children and adults alike with his antics at Three Rivers Stadium. Others appeared on enlarged photographs, black and white. The Steelers seem to have lost favor with Pittsburgh sports artists, and were noticeably absent at this exhibition.

The images persist. Anybody who has pulled for the Pirates, past or present, and anybody who cares about sports in Pittsburgh and western Pennsylvania, and anybody who thrilled to the hits, catches and throws of Roberto Clemente would have enjoyed this multi-image scene and the carnival-like atmosphere.

This was the 5th annual Piratefest, a three-day extravaganza for the fans hosted by the Pittsburgh Baseball Club at the Expo Mart exhibition hall in Monroeville, about ten miles east of Pittsburgh on Route 22.

Pittsburgh was in the midst of its coldest winter in history, with record low temperatures and record high snowfall. It was relatively warm this weekend of January 28-30, also Super Bowl Weekend for followers of the National Football League, though there were some snow flurries in the air.

Piratefest provided the perfect relief for those suffering from cabin fever, and eager to get out for a change. It signaled that spring training wasn't that far off, nor was the 1994 All-Star Game that would be hosted by the Pirates at Three Rivers Stadium.

Stories were circulating that the financially-struggling Pirates were for sale, and no one seemed sure whether this was good news or bad news. But this was not a time to worry about such things. That was for attorneys and accountants to contend with; baseball fans are always optimistic in January. The Piratefest is a modern-day, multi-image presentation of what used to be called the Hot Stove League. In short, it sparks stories and thoughts about baseball, a break from basketball and hockey and football dominating the day's sports conversations. This particular winter was also marked by daily diatribes about the Olympic ice skating whodunnit scandal involving Tonya Harding and Nancy Kerrigan. The story about the attack on figure skating favorite Kerrigan during pre-Olympic competition had captured the nation's attention.

25

So baseball fans by the thousands toured the seemingly endless exhibition hall, checking out the paintings, prints and photographs, picking up the latest baseball paraphernalia at the Pirate Clubhouse Store, taking their chances at various baseball-related contests and raffles. There was also a Collectors' Corner, with baseball and sports cards, balls, memorabilia and more for sale. Admission to the Piratefest was $7 for adults and $3 for senior citizens and children, a boost from the year before, but increased ticket costs have become a baseball tradition, too.

There were cages to test one's pitching skills and hitting skills. Clinics for future Pirates were provided by Pirates coaches Rich Donnelly and Ray Miller. KDKA Radio had its mobile unit there for remote broadcasts by Goose Goslin, Susie Barbour, Fred Honsberger, Rick Bergman, with Lanny Frattare and Pirates players and officials sitting in as guests to talk baseball.

Some of baseball's biggest hits, such as "Take Me Out To The Ballgame" and "Talkin' Baseball" provided background music, and the voice of the venerable Bob Prince doing Pirates' baseball broadcasts lent a nostalgic, often eerie, touch to the activities.

One of the most popular sites was a simulated Forbes Field, and fans filled the green bleachers to hear about baseball from Pirates manager Jim Leyland and general manager Cam Bonifay, who were interviewed over the p.a. system by Frattare.

There was one somber note. At one of the autograph booths, a large photo was posted in memory of Harvey Haddix, who had appeared at such autograph sessions the previous two years. Haddix, who had been the winning pitcher in two of the games in the 1960 World Series and had pitched 12 innings of perfect baseball before losing to the Braves in one of baseball's most famous games back in 1959, had died at age 68 from emphysema on January 8.

Present-day Pirates and Pirates of the past were there to sign autographs for anyone willing to wait in line for their prized signatures. Leyland was joined by Kevin Young, Jay Bell, Steve Cooke, Al Martin, Tim Wakefield, Jeff King, Randy Tomlin and Andy Van Slyke.

There were 11 Pirates from the past who had represented the team in All-Star Game competition who were also signing autographs at a different booth. They were Manny Sanguillen, Dave Giusti, Steve Blass, Al Oliver, Bob Friend, Chuck Tanner, Bob Veale, Vernon Law, Dock Ellis and ElRoy Face. Gene Alley was also scheduled to sign, but was a late scratch.

His place was taken by the Clemente family, and no one complained. The Clemente family was not originally scheduled to sign autographs, but as soon as they appeared at the Expo Mart they were surrounded by adoring fans who sought their signatures.

Vera Clemente, the widow of the late Pirates' star, and their two oldest sons, Roberto and Luis, were there. The youngest, Enrique, chose to remain at home in Puerto Rico. The Clementes are a handsome family. They were as popular as any attraction at the Piratefest.

Their friendly manner and non-stop smiles set everyone at ease.

They were quick to accommodate all requests for autographs and photographs, and their warmth drew fans in from out of the cold. The Clemente clan had a magnetic appeal for all in attendance.

The featured display at the 1994 Piratefest was labeled "A Tribute To Roberto." It was billed as the most comprehensive tribute ever to the greatest Pirates player of them all. The Great One. The Pirates official team photographer Dave Arrigo and the Director of In-Game Entertainment Mike Gordon had arranged this collection in an attractive walk-through museum in testimony to Clemente's celebrated career.

It featured Roberto's actual World Series rings, awards like the Gold Glove, uniforms he wore in his one year of minor league ball in Montreal and in the winter league in Puerto Rico, as well as his No. 21 Pirates uniform. They were all on loan from the Clemente family. There were hundreds of black and white photos showing Clemente in action and posing alongside teammates through the years.

There were Clemente calendars and videotapes for sale, and images of the Pirates' All-Star rightfielder were everywhere one looked. Billboards around Pittsburgh and TV commercials had created a Clemente clamor in the city.

The Clementes were overwhelmed by the warm response to their visit. Roberto Jr. had been in Pittsburgh for several weeks, meeting with the new mayor, Tom Murphy, and other civic and corporate officials to get the necessary backing and financing for a project to properly memorialize his father. He had come here to establish a foundation in his father's memory, to start and develop an inner-city youth baseball program, the kind of initiative his father would have approved of, and to make sure his father was properly honored. Roberto Jr.'s efforts had drawn a rave review in *The New York Times*.

For the fans, Vera and Roberto Jr. and Luis were the closest they could get to the revered Roberto Clemente.

Pittsburgh Pirates

Roberto's Achievements

- 11th player to record 3,000 hits

- First Hispanic player elected to Baseball Hall of Fame

- 1966 National League MVP

- 12-time National League All-Star

- Five-time NL leader in outfield assists

- Earned four National League batting titles

- Thirteen .300-plus seasons

- Four 200-plus hit seasons

- Hit safely in all 14 World Series games in which he appeared (.362)

- Won 12 Gold Glove Awards

- All-time Pirates leader in
    - Games (2,433)
    - At-Bats (9,454)
    - Hits (3,000)
    - Singles (2,154)
    - Total Bases (4,492)

- Named to the Pirates All-Time Team in 1987

Roberto Clemente is a banner subject at Three Rivers Stadium in summer of 1994.

DAILY ⊡ NEWS
NEW YORK'S PICTURE NEWSPAPER ®

. 54. No. 164   Copr. 1973 New York News Inc.   New York, N.Y. 10017, Tuesday, January 2, 1973*   WEATHER: Sunny, breezy and

AIR CRASH KILLS
BUCS' CLEMENTE

Baseball
Great Dies o
Mercy Missi

Roberto Clemente holds son Enri
and greets wife, Vera, and sons Ro
erto Jr. (c.) and Luis at Shea St
dium, Sept. 25, 1971. Bucs' star w
honored by local Puerto Rican fan
You didn't have to live in Pittsburg
to know Roberto was something sp
cial. Clemente died Sunday when h
plane crashed in sea near San Jua
Puerto Rico. He was on mercy flig
to aid Nicaragua earthquake victim

*Stories on page 2;
other pictures centerfold*

NEWS photo by Dan Farrell

PR llora a Clemente

...mos un Suplemento
...o a la memoria del ídolo
...ecido. Roberto Clemente,
...tras páginas centrales.

El Nuevo Día/Luis R. Ramos

...ctar el hit número tres
...olver a su posición en el
...d, todavía el público
...aba aplaudiéndole.

Inmediatamente que Doña Vera pudo pasar el túnel que en el parque de Three River conduce del terreno al club house a los peloteros, la gentil esposa de Roberto Clemente lo hizo para la felicitación cariñosa.

"The lads that will die in their glory and never be old."

—A. E. Housman's "To An Athlete Dying Young"

Vera's Vigil
She searched the waters in vain

"She, too, is a champion."

Once she was young and beautiful. She had the brilliant dark brown hair and matching dark brown eyes. Her name was Vera Cristina Zabala. She met Roberto Clemente in her early 20s at a drug store in their hometown of Carolina, Puerto Rico. She was a secretary for a local bank. She knew he was good at baseball, though she had never attended a game. "I had heard his name here and there," she said. They started dating, they fell in love, and they were married. They lived happily, but not ever after. During the nearly eight years they were married, she and her husband were a handsome couple.

All was good in their lives. Then Roberto was killed in an airplane crash off the coast of San Juan on New Year's Eve, 1972. Everything changed.

Vera, at age 32, stood in a roped-off area called Piñones Beach, at the nearest land point to where the airplane carrying her husband and others had crashed. Now it was New Year's Day, and she watched search efforts. The Coast Guard was out there, the Coast Guard cutter Sagebush, searching the area. At night, flares would light up the skies and there were search lights on the water. There were six U.S. Navy divers. Vera stood there, for a week-long vigil, looking through binoculars. One of Roberto's teammates and best friends, Manny Sanguillen, joined the Coast Guard in its search efforts, and went into the water himself several times in futile attempts at finding his friend.

When Vera returned home, and met and spoke to visitors and the media, she seemed under control. A family member told a UPI newsman, "She, too, is a champion."

Of her three children, she had told only Roberto Zabala Jr., who was 7, what had happened to her husband and his father, as the other boys — Luis Roberto, 5, and Roberto Enrique, 4, also called Lusito and Ricky — were thought to be too young to understand.

She was there for several days watching the search operations. They were diving at her request to recover the body of her husband and his fellow travelers. There were four others on the plane. The water was about 120 feet deep where the plane went in. There was a surface and air search. Rescue efforts were hampered by a choppy sea and murky waters.

Bits and pieces of the wreckage would surface here and there. Vials of medicine, apples, bits of wreckage, a single grapefruit, life jackets, luggage, a single shoe, a pair of new gray slacks, boxes filled with supplies would surface and wash ashore or float with the tide. A major part of the plane was found at the deepest point, about a mile-and-a-half off shore. There were no bodies inside. Later, the pilot's body was found.

Then a second body was spotted, but divers couldn't go near it. The waters were so rough, they feared they would be swept against the rocks. Some debris indicated the plane had been on fire before it hit the water. It was later determined that the plane was not in the best shape, was underserviced, and overloaded with supplies. It simply wasn't up to the strain.

A Navy expert said that the longer the delay in recovering the bodies the less likelihood there would be of finding any remains. "They tend to disintegrate in salt water," he said. Then, too, there were sharks in the water.

The trip had been delayed because of mechanical problems. Reports later indicated the plane wasn't properly loaded, that the supplies shifted when the plane was heading into the sky. The plane developed engine problems once airborne. It was a four-engine propeller-driven DC-7 airplane. It took off from San Juan International at 9:15 p.m. It was in the air about five minutes before it fell into the ocean.

According to an official at the airport control tower, the plane took off normally and then banked to the left as prescribed in the flight plan. Then the plane suddenly disappeared from the radar screens.

According to an eyewitness, the plane was on top of the water for awhile, and then disappeared.

It was later learned that Federal Aviation Officials had attempted to close down the operation of the airplane's owner at an earlier period because he was thought to run an unsafe and illegal operation. It was said he didn't conduct required safety inspections and proper maintenance.

The city of Managua in Nicaragua had been nearly leveled by an earthquake on December 23. Roberto Clemente had headed a relief effort in his native Puerto Rico and had collected tons of supplies to take there to help the victims.

Clemente had insisted on making the trip himself because he had heard that supplies were getting into the hands of profiteers, and not the people who needed them the most.

Clemente's body was never found. This only added to the distress of his family and friends. He could not have a proper Catholic burial.

An ecumenical service was held at Hiram Bithorn Stadium, where Clemente had played in Puerto Rico's winter league. It was also the headquarters for Clemente's campaign to collect materials for the earthquake victims in Nicaragua.

Puerto Rican Governor Rafael Hernandez Colon at his inauguration on Tuesday, January 2, said Clemente had been "a glory" for his native land.

"The hearts of all of us are in sorrow," the governor told the thousands massed before the white marble steps of the Capitol overlooking the ocean.

President Nixon said, "He sacrificed his life on a mission of mercy." Nixon sent a $1,000 contribution to the Roberto Clemente Memorial Fund. Nixon would later present Mrs. Clemente with the first Presidential Citizens Medal, a specially-coined medallion, in ceremonies at The

White House. She would be accompanied by Willie Stargell and Manny Sanguillen.

A mass was said on January 4 at San Fernando Roman Catholic Church, where Vera and Roberto had been married on November 14, 1964. This was in Carolina, where the sugar cane fields his father had worked in were located, about 15 miles from the coast line. "We got a report in the middle of the mass that a body had been found," Vera told me during my visit to her son's apartment in Robinson Township on February 1, 1994, "but it was not Roberto. But there was real confusion."

Roberto's death could have been avoided, his family felt. Vera had objected to her husband about flying to Nicaragua. She was afraid, she said, that the plane might be overloaded. Casually, her husband told her, "When your time comes, it comes. If you are going to die, you are going to die."

He had told friends from Pittsburgh not to visit him during the holidays. Roberto said he was too busy to see them. He had not even opened his Christmas presents.

Upon his death, Mrs. Clemente was given $100,000 from a life insurance policy that all major league ballplayers had at the time. She received immediately a $1,049 per month pension for life. She received an additional $65 a month for each of the children.

At the home opener of the 1973 season, Vera wept as she accepted her husband's uniform, and his 12th Gold Glove award. Mrs. Luisa Clemente, Roberto's mother, was there, too. Vera stood tall, in the image of her husband. It was the first time the Clementes had come to Three Rivers Stadium without their dad. There was a crowd of 51,695 for the occasion.

"For me, he's still alive."

A month after her husband's death, Vera Clemente spoke to a group of American writers about her experience in dealing with this tragic setback in her life and her family's life.

"For me, he's still alive," she said. "You see, all his clothes are in the same place. I just think he left on one of his trips and is coming back. . ."

She was still living in a beautiful home on a hillside in Rio Piedras, with a breath-taking view of metropolitan San Juan. It has a moat in front of the main entrance and it has twelve rooms. It was often referred to as "the house on The Hill."

"But it feels empty," said Vera Clemente, as she looked at large pictures of her husband that were hung on the walls in the living room.

She was doing her best to answer the thousands of sympathetic letters and cards that had come in. She was doing her best to console her three children.

"Roberito, the oldest one, has been reading a whole lot about his father since this thing has happened, and now he wants to be a ballplayer more than ever before," she said, calling her son by his nickname.

"You know, I have never told this to anybody before, but Roberto Jr., or 'Roberito,' as his father and I called him, said what did happen would happen.

"The night my husband tried to fly to Nicaragua, I knew I would get home late from the airport, so I took the children to my mother's house in Carolina (Puerto Rico). I told them they were going to stay overnight and Roberito said to me, 'Mommy, is the earthquake finished?' I told him it was, and he asked me, 'Is Daddy all right?' I said yes, he was, and then I left for the airport.

"Later, my mother told me when she was fixing Roberito's bed, he said to her, 'Grandma, Grandma, Daddy is leaving for Nicaragua, and he's not coming back. The plane is going to crash! He's not coming back to us. I know it. Call Mama and please don't let him go!'"

Vera Clemente continued. "My mother says now she was thinking of calling me at the airport, but it was late, and you know how it is — Roberito is only seven years old — so she never called."

Coincidentally enough, Clemente's father had a similar premonition. He had a dream in which he saw his son's plane crash.

There were newspaper clippings on a table detailing her husband's death, which had been sent to her from all over the world. "Whenever I start to read one of these articles, it brings tears to my eyes all over again," said Vera Clemente.

"I begin to remember . . . how we met . . . it was inside a drug store in Carolina and Roberto asked me if I was from the neighborhood because he had never noticed me before . . . I remember our first date. We went with friends to a ball game in San Juan. I had never seen a baseball game before. It rained and the game was canceled. . .

"I remember everything, even how Roberto would tell me he traveled so much by airplane that it scared him sometimes. He told me he was on one plane that nearly hit another one, and how he had a narrow escape going to spring training last year. . ."

Clemente was not alone in his concern. One of his teammates, Dick Groat, for instance, has always been a bad traveler on airplanes. Groat grips the seat in front of him on the slightest dip or turbulence.

"You know, the plane was supposed to leave at 4 o'clock in the morning," said Vera. "It didn't get off until 9:15 at night. There was a lot of trouble with the plane.

"At 3:30 in the afternoon, after numerous delays, I fixed Roberto's lunch and went to the airport with him. I had to meet some friends flying in later that afternoon from Allentown, Pennsylvania to stay with us. Roberto turned to me and said, 'If anything else happens, I'm going to postpone this flight until tomorrow.'

"At 5 o'clock, I kissed Roberto goodbye. The plane seemed ready to leave. Then I went to meet my friends. Their plane was delayed. Then it took an hour to get their luggage. A rainstorm hit and we were stuck at the airport another half-hour.

"I remember I got home at 20 minutes to eight. When I raised the garage door, the phone was ringing. Just as I picked up the receiver,

I heard the other party hang up. The thought struck me: 'Could this be Roberto calling? No, it couldn't be. He's halfway to Managua by now.'

"A little after midnight, my niece called and told me about the crash. I said, 'Oh, no, it's not possible. Roberto already is in Nicaragua.'

"Only the pilot's body was found. I found only a black briefcase of Roberto's. It was empty and tattered. And a brown sock. 'Was he wearing this sock?' I asked myself, 'Or did it fall out of his suitcase?' I hoped it might have come from his suitcase.

"And I still think of that telephone call that I didn't reach in time and Roberto Jr. coming to me and saying, 'Mama, I told Grandma we shouldn't have let him go. I knew he would be killed.' "

Vera Clemente thought back to that night when her husband said goodbye to her for the last time.

"The lady (maid) in our house here had to leave us that day," she recalled. "Just before Roberto got into the airplane, he said to me, 'The first thing I will do when I get back is get you someone to help you with the house. There is too much in it to do by yourself. Now don't worry about me. It is New Year's Eve and I don't want you to stay by yourself. Go over to your family's house and be with them for the New Year.' " Vera Clemente could talk no longer. She paused to regain her composure.

"He wanted to do so much more," she went on, wiping away the tears. "He wanted to see his project — Sports City for the kids — finished. He had not really lived his life yet. The whole thing is like a dream to me. I keep thinking he is coming back. I know he's not, though."

She said she was keeping busy and trying to carry through her husband's plans. She showed visitors a trophy room full of Clemente's memorabilia. There had been newspaper reports that visitors to the home during that time had stolen some of Clemente's mementos, but that report was later denied by family members.

"Roberto loved his trophies," Vera said. "There are others in closets upstairs and just this week we received a big carton of trophies which came from Roberto's 3,000th hit. I haven't had a chance to open it.

"Roberto was proud of his trophies — not so much because of himself but because of the recognition he thought it brought Puerto Rico and Latin ballplayers.

"He was a very unselfish man, not vain at all. His life was devoted to helping others. He got a lot of rings. They're all in a drawer. We tried to get him to wear his 1971 World Series ring. He did for a week, and then went back to an old ring he liked — the one he got in an All-Star Game. I forget which." That's understandable. Roberto Clemente competed in 12 All-Star Games.

"It's something always inside you."
— Vera Clemente

Two years after her husband's death, Vera visited Miami to attend ceremonies to dedicate a park in the memory of Roberto Clemente. She was still in mourning.

"It's the same," she told Janet Chusmir, a staff writer for *The Miami Herald*. "You live an empty life. It's hard to explain. You never forget. It's something always inside you."

She said her main concern was her children. She wanted to raise them the way her husband would have wanted. "The right way. To be religious, to be respectful to other people, to be educated, to be good citizens."

She said she and Roberto got along fine because they had similar lifestyles and interests. "I was a quiet person," she explained. "We had the same likes and dislikes. I didn't like parties. He never liked to go here and there. He liked to stay at the house in his pajamas and watch TV."

Only two weeks before the earthquake, they ended a month's stay in Nicaragua where Roberto was managing a Puerto Rican baseball team. "He really liked it there in Nicaragua," said Vera. "He liked to talk to the poor people. He used to tell me it was the same way Puerto Rico was years ago.

"We felt so bad, like someone from our family died, when the earthquake came. So, he started collecting supplies and he went. . ."

She said it was her mission to keep his memory alive. "Everything he did in baseball," she said, "he was Puerto Rican. He was Puerto Rican in his heart."

Pittsburgh Pirates

Vera Clemente cries during Opening Day ceremonies at Three Rivers Stadium in 1973 as Bob Prince and Pirates GM Joe L. Brown present her with Roberto's 12th Gold Glove Award.

Roberto and Vera Clemente are all smiles on plane returning team from Baltimore after Pirates won 1971 World Series.

Vera Clemente and sons Enrique, Roberto Jr. and Luis at special ceremonies in her husband's honor at Three Rivers Stadium.

Pittsburgh Pirates

Roberto Clemente and his family, above, at Pirates Father-Son Game, and Vera with children and Roberto's mother after his death.

Pittsburgh Pirates

President Nixon presented a special medallion in honor of Roberto Clemente at ceremonies at The White House attended by, left to right, Willie Stargell, Vera Clemente and Manny Sanguillen.

Former Pennsylvania Governor Hugh Scott stands behind President Nixon at ceremonies to pay tribute to Roberto Clemente.

Enrique, the youngest of the three Clemente children, kisses photo of his father at memorial service.

Monty Irvin

Vera Clemente accepted husband's Hall of Fame plaque at ceremonies at Cooperstown, N.Y. She was flanked by two other inductees, Warren Spahn, at left, and Monte Irvin.

Warren Spahn

ROBERTO WALKER CLEMENTE
PITTSBURGH N. L. 1955-1972
MEMBER OF EXCLUSIVE 3,000-HIT CLUB. LED NATIONAL LEAGUE IN BATTING FOUR TIMES. HAD FOUR SEASONS WITH 200 OR MORE HITS WHILE POSTING LIFETIME .317 AVERAGE AND 240 HOME RUNS. WON MOST VALUABLE PLAYER AWARD 1966. RIFLE-ARMED DEFENSIVE STAR SET N.L. MARK BY PACING OUTFIELDERS IN ASSISTS FIVE YEARS. BATTED .362 IN TWO WORLD SERIES, HITTING IN ALL 14 GAMES.

Vera and Roberto Clemente
at home in Rio Piedras.

Edwin Morgan/The Pittsburgh Press

Vera Clemente
Roberto's Wife

"I feel like he is with us always."

Vera Clemente was charming. She could not have been more cordial or cooperative. Whenever I called her on the telephone, in Puerto Rico or in Pittsburgh, she always talked to me with great enthusiasm, eager to share stories about her late husband Roberto Clemente. She was always upbeat, an absolute trill in her Latin voice, always inviting. Sometimes apologetic. "You must excuse my English," she'd say every so often. She needn't apologize; she speaks English just fine.

It was more of the same when I saw her several times at the Piratefest, the winter celebration of baseball that was highlighted by a "Tribute To Roberto" photo and memorabilia exhibit at the Expo Mart in Monroeville the last weekend in January, 1994. And when I visited her on the first day of February and talked to her for nearly two hours at an apartment in Robinson Township shared by her son, Roberto Jr., and his wife of two years, Zulma.

The apartment/condominium complex, off Campbell's Run Road enroute to the Pittsburgh International Airport on the Parkway West, is called McKenzie Place and is the sort that attracts young marrieds. It is a more modern version of the apartment complexes, like Pennley Park in East Liberty, where Vera and her husband lived when Roberto was the rage of Forbes Field. Or Chatham West in Green Tree, where they lived when he was playing for the Pirates at Three Rivers Stadium.

During our conversation, she smiled a lot. She never grew melancholy, or seemed on the verge of tears, though she spoke at length of her late husband. She seems at peace with that, and her role as a spokesperson on his behalf.

There was a sense of *deja vu* during my visit. When my wife Kathie and I were married in August of 1967, we moved into the Pennley Park Apartments, located at the intersection of Penn Avenue and Negley Avenue, and counted the Clementes among our neighbors. Kathie was then a social worker at Presbyterian-University Hospital in nearby Oakland, and I was the editor/co-publisher of *Pittsburgh Weekly Sports*.

I reminded Vera that Roberto had a dark green Lincoln Continental with RWC on a vanity license plate affixed to the front bumper back then, and that other Pirates such as Alvin O'Neal McBean, Matty Alou, Jose Pagan, Manny Mota and Juan Pizarro also lived at Pennley Park. I recalled seeing them play ball with their kids on the grassy areas amid the apartments.

I did not mention to Vera that just before I got married and moved into the Pennley Park Apartments that her husband had leveled a million dollar lawsuit against me for a stupid story I had written as a 20-year-old student in *Pittsburgh Weekly Sports*, a quixotic tabloid I published on a shoestring with Beano Cook. He was then the sports information director at Pitt, and he prodded me to write the story about an alleged fight in the Pirates' clubhouse between Clemente and Willie Stargell. "This will make us," Cook cried. That's all I needed to hear. Cook, more recently a college football analyst for ESPN, had come up with the information from a ballpark usher who had gotten it secondhand. Talk about impeccable sources. There had been a fight; we just had the wrong combatants. Stargell also sued me, with the assistance of an attorney who was a subscriber to our newspaper — ouch! — to the tune of $750,000.

I think I made about $3,000 that year. Kathie was making about $8,000. We had a pre-nuptial agreement that I had two years to see if I could make a living publishing *Pittsburgh Weekly Sports*. She agreed to carry me financially for two years. The following year I would accept an offer to cover the Miami Dolphins for *The Miami News*. We left Pittsburgh in 1968 and didn't return until 1979, spending nine of those years in New York where I worked for *The New York Post*. We missed out on some of the best years in Pittsburgh sports history, when Pittsburgh became known as "The City of Champions."

Now I realize, more than ever before, considering the closeness of the Clemente-Stargell relationship, how outrageous that report was that we ran in *Pittsburgh Weekly Sports*. But there was no malicious intent, and the suit was settled with a printed apology on our part. I never held a grudge. No one ever thought I was worth as much as Clemente and Stargell did. They made me look like a millionaire to my school chums. In time, Stargell become one of my favorites. I just wished I could have gotten to know Clemente as well.

And now his wife and I were reminiscing and smiling about those days at Pennley Park. Now we were both in our early 50s. Life takes some strange twists. . .

Among the many photographs I viewed with Vera were some showing her and Roberto playing with their first-born son, Roberto Jr., on the carpet of their living room at Pennley Park, and some showing Vera very pregnant with the second of their three sons, Luis Roberto. Their third son was Roberto Enrique. At the time of this interview, Roberto Jr. was 28, Luis, 27 and Enrique, 24.

Vera laughed aloud, shrieking sort of, when she saw the one of her in a maternity dress, cooking at a stove in her kitchen at Pennley Park. She called to her daughter-in-law, Zulma, who was also very pregnant with her and Roberto Jr.'s first child. Zulma was due to deliver on July 28, a day before her birthday. Roberto Jr. had a 5-year-old daughter, Christina, by an earlier marriage. There are six framed photographs of Christina decorating the wall in the dining area of the apartment at McKenzie Place.

I asked Vera to identify family members and friends who appeared in photos with her husband. She had never seen some of them before, and asked if I could get her copies. "I'd love to have these," she said. "This one was during the night they had for Roberto at Three Rivers Stadium when the whole family, Roberto's parents, were there."

Vera Clemente, 1994

Jim O'Brien

"I never expected to be married to a famous person."

It was another cold day during the coldest winter in Pittsburgh history and, at first, I was tempted to dress casually for my visit with Vera. But I thought better of that, and wore a sports coat, dress shirt and slacks, and it's a good thing I did. I sensed that Vera would be well dressed for my visit and she didn't disappoint. She is a classy woman.

She wore mostly black, a jersey, slacks and shoes, and a silver-gray jacket with black trim on the wide lapels. There was an ornate gold cross at the end of a gold necklace. Her dark brown hair was well-coiffured, and her make-up subtle but stunning. She is still a beautiful woman, dark-eyed, with the kind of complexion that models would envy.

Like many of us, however, she has put on weight since she first appeared in Pittsburgh. She was always sturdy in stature, never slender. It's the face that draws your attention, though. There is an absolute glow to it. It reminded me that Roberto Jr. had likened his mother to a saint for the way she has comported and carried herself since she lost her husband.

She frequently referred to her husband's death in an airplane crash off the coast of San Juan, Puerto Rico as "the accident," as we chatted at length. Occasionally, she would turn and say something to Zulma, who had streaked dark hair and wore an orange-red maternity dress and orange-red lipstick, and they would have an animated, excited exchange in Spanish.

I was able to recognize a word or two, and wished I were able to understand and speak Spanish. Roberto Jr. and Luis lapsed into Spanish a few times when we talked earlier at the Radisson Hotel in Monroeville. I grew up on a street in the Hazelwood section of Pittsburgh where everyone else was Italian, and when they spoke in Italian we always thought it was because they wanted to say something without us knowing what they were saying.

I had taken a year of Spanish at Taylor Allderdice High School, and two years of Spanish at the University of Pittsburgh. Actually, I took three years of Spanish at Pitt because it was the only course I ever had to repeat during my student days in the early '60s. For me, going to Spanish class was like going to the mill or coal mines. I sweated a lot in Spanish class. When I said a few elementary words in Spanish, Vera was kind enough to smile, and call Zulma's attention to my effort. They were amused.

In advance of our visit, I had anticipated that I might find it difficult to interview Vera. Our previous exchanges had been brief, and she had smiled in response to many of my remarks. She had been pleasant, for sure, but I didn't know how she'd handle an extensive interview. I had no idea she spoke English so well, only occasionally hesitating to find the right word to express herself. "How can I say. . .?" she would say from time to time. Sometimes I filled in the void, and she nodded, and seemed pleased with my assistance.

Teenie Harris, Courtesy of the Pittsburgh Courier Photographic Archives

ra Clemente is pregnant with Luis at
nley Park Apartments in East Liberty.

Roberto holds Enrique.

Pittsburgh Pirates

Pittsburgh Pirates

Roberto Clemente's family joins him on his night at Three Rivers Stadium in
July, 1970.

Above a cream-colored mantel in the room was a large portrait of Roberto Clemente, keeping watch over the room. Wherever the Clementes set up shop, there are always likenesses of Roberto on the walls.

"I was shy when I was a little girl," said Vera. "I never expected to be married to a famous person, and to be traveling and talking to so many people.

"When I first met him I was 23 and he was 30. My father would tell me how many days and how many hours he was permitted to see me in any week." She smiled at how strict and concerned her father was about her courtship. "Everything was different then," she added.

Another airplane mystery

History repeats itself: The front page of the *Pittsburgh Post-Gazette* carried several stories that caught my attention the day I visited Vera Clemente. The city's current superstar, Mario Lemieux of the Penguins, had back problems again and would continue to be sidelined when he had hoped to return to action. Lemieux had little to say to sportswriters most of the season, and seemed to be at odds with them, though most of them had treated him with kid gloves. None of them, unlike some fans, had yet labeled Lemieux a malingerer. The Pirates were possibly for sale, and KBL, the local sports cable channel, and Penguins owner Howard Baldwin were among those interested in purchasing the franchise and possibly Three Rivers Stadium as well. A local editor-publisher revived a Pittsburgh mystery when he called a press conference to say he was seeking first-hand information about what really happened to a B-25 bomber that disappeared into the Monongahela River on January 31, 1956. The plane had plunged into the water between the Homestead High Level Bridge and the Glenwood Bridge, near our home. I remember my father coming home and talking about it. He crossed the Glenwood Bridge on the way to and from work every day at Mesta Machine Company in West Homestead. That was the same year I went to work at the local newspaper as the sports editor, and began my career in journalism. I have always thought the plane mystery — they never recovered the plane and some suspected that our government removed it in the dark of night for some furtive reason — would make a good book. What was on that plane?

"I always loved Pittsburgh."

"I feel very happy to be back here," said Vera. "I always loved Pittsburgh. The Piratefest was a success. I really feel good to be here. I talked to many people. They were remembering scenes with Roberto. Certain things he did. Telling me different anecdotes and stories. It was really nice."

The following day she would make an appearance at the Shaler Area Middle School in the suburbs just to the north of Pittsburgh. She talked to students who were reading books to raise money for the Clemente statue fund. The goal of the school project was to raise $10,000. She would be a big hit.

She also spoke of seeing some of Roberto's former teammates like Manny Sanguillen — "he is special" — and Bob Veale, Al Oliver, Bob Friend, Steve Blass and Vernon Law, among others. And she telephoned the family's good friend, Phil Dorsey, at his daughter's home in Pittsburgh.

Vera would be coming back to Pittsburgh in July for ceremonies to be conducted at the unveiling of a statue in her husband's memory that was tied in with the 1994 All-Star Game at Three Rivers Stadium. She said many people in Puerto Rico wanted to come, too, and share in the celebration.

"I feel very happy that they're building a statue," she said. "At first, I was concerned. I say to my sons, 'What if it don't look like him?' Luis and Roberto say it's coming out beautiful (they saw a clay model before it was cast in bronze). In Puerto Rico, there are two statues of him in San Juan."

She had seen renderings showing what the statue would look like, and she had also seen the statues of Pirates Hall of Famer Honus Wagner and Steelers owner Art Rooney that were already standing outside the Stadium. Rooney and two of his players, John Brown and Preston Pearson, had represented the Steelers at the memorial service for Roberto Clemente that was held in San Juan. I had to smile when I learned about Rooney going to the funeral. Art Rooney never missed a good wake.

Was there a difference between the way Roberto was viewed in Pittsburgh and in San Juan?

"In Puerto Rico, the people still love him, and he's a big man; they never forget him," she said. "Every time it's a special anniversary, they commemorate it on radio and TV. He's still on everyone's mind. There are many books, and the students there write reports on him.

"Here, they show much more, not only in Pittsburgh, but throughout the United States. They dedicate schools, gymnasiums, ballfields, community centers and playgrounds in his honor. Last year, I went to Holyoke, Massachusetts, where they had a program in his honor, and gave me an award. They named a street after him there, and the mayor proclaimed it Roberto Clemente Week. I am invited to come to the States two or three times a year to attend some kind of dedication ceremonies in his name.

"Next week, I am attending a banquet honoring him and myself at Trenton, New Jersey. There are over 30 schools, 40 or more ballparks or playgrounds named after him. There's a new school building in Rochester, New York. In Ann Arbor, Michigan, they've had a school named after him for many years — I didn't even know about it — and they're renovating it, and want me to come to ceremonies to mark the completion of the work."

53

While touring Pittsburgh during this visit, Vera had seen a huge billboard honoring her husband at a busy intersection in the West End — "We were shocked; it's beautiful," she said — and TV promotions with highlights of her husband playing for the Pirates. Videos about her husband had sold out at the Giant Eagle stores.

At The Galleria, an upscale indoor shopping mall in the South Hills, she had seen portraits and photos of her husband in window displays. Everywhere you looked in Pittsburgh, Roberto Clemente was looking back at you.

"His mother's last name was Walker."
— Vera Clemente

I asked Vera to verify the names of her husband and sons so that I had them straight. I had heard that her husband's real name was originally Roberto Clemente Walker. She nodded. "That's the way his name is said in Puerto Rico," she explained. "His father's last name was Clemente, and his mother's last name (or maiden name) was Walker. In Puerto Rico, we say the mother's name last."

I had also heard that all three of their sons were named Roberto. She said their first child is named Roberto Jr., the second Luis Roberto, and the third Roberto Enrique. "After Roberto passed, I was looking at some documents about Roberto, and I saw him registered as Roberto Enrique Clemente Walker. He never used the name Enrique. I didn't know that was his name. My baby has the same name — Roberto Enrique — as his dad."

I mentioned that the famous boxer George Foreman had five sons all named George. "I have a brother named Orlando," offered Vera, "and he had four sons named Orlando."

"He was a special person."
— Vera Clemente

Looking back to January, 1973, Vera said, "The whole month of January, our house was full of people from the United States, the Dominican Republic, Venezuela and places like that. They had to keep the road closed that led to our house. People came from everywhere to see me, to see us.

"They were still searching for the plane at the time. I was busy for a few months after that trying to get things straightened out. Then it was just us.

"When Roberto was alive, we had many, many friends who used to come to visit us, especially during the holidays. Many came from Pennsylvania. Only a few kept coming. The others disappeared. Maybe they didn't want to bother us.

54

Roberto Clemente's parents, Melchor and Luisa, pay visit to Pittsburgh.

Vera Clemente stands out in the crowd at Three Rivers Stadium.

"I had a dream that Roberto was coming back home. He used to say, 'Don't open the door. When I disappear they disappear. When I disappear they don't even come to see how my kids are.' In my dream, he was upset that we were all alone."

I told Vera that I thought she was a beautiful woman. She had been a widow for 21 years. Her son Roberto had told me only a few days earlier that she had never expressed any interest in dating or marrying another man. Why not?

"For me, he was such a good husband and father, and a good man," she replied. "He was such a special person to me. I never thought of another man in my life.

"He always was saying he was going to die young. He says, 'You'll marry again.' I'd say, 'No, you can be sure, I will never marry anyone else.' I just — for me — I feel like he is with us always. He was a special person. I loved him so much and admired him a lot."

I wanted to know what life was like for Vera these days in Puerto Rico.

"I'm always busy," she said. "We're still living in the same house, and I am at the Sports City at least six days a week. I leave the house at 7:30 or 8 in the morning, and I'm there till 6 o'clock in the afternoon, and sometimes into the evening."

Sports City, or Ciudad Deportiva, in San Juan was something that was very important to Roberto Clemente. He had a mission to do something special for the young children of Puerto Rico to enrich their lives.

"We have many programs," she said. "We have seven baseball fields, four professional tennis courts, a swimming pool with ramps for the handicapped, we have a running track, volleyball and basketball facilities. We are building dormitories, and we'd like to build a museum as well.

"We get much of our support from the government and private corporations, but we are trying to become more self-sustaining. We are looking at a hotel, a golf course and a marina to bring in income.

"We have a staff of 30 most of the time, and close to 50 in the summer. We have 1,200 kids at summer camps in two different sections."

Are the children taught about Roberto Clemente?

"We have videos and books there, and he is talked about," said Vera. "My role has changed there. I've been president of the board. Last year I became the executive director, and am involved in the day-by-day operation, to make decisions and to push projects."

She said the Sports City was incorporated in 1973, less than a year after Clemente was killed. It is located on 234 acres. It started with baseball fields being put in during the summer of 1976. "Nothing was there before," said Vera, "and now it is such a lively place."

There is a statue of Roberto Clemente at the entrance, and another statue of him at the Roberto Clemente Coliseum in downtown San Juan.

Roberto Clemente

SPORTS CITY

Pittsburgh Pirates

a Clemente and Pedro Barez-Rosario, the original executive director of the Roberto Clemente rts City, stand before statue at entrance to sports complex in Puerto Rico.

"The way he died was the way he lived."

What does she want the children of Puerto Rico and Pittsburgh to know about Roberto Clemente?

"I think he was a very good baseball player, but the biggest thing is . . . as a person . . . as a human being. They should remember that part of his life. The important thing is the tremendous kind of person he was. He was always caring for others, and the way he died was the way he lived."

With the Pirates, for instance, she said Roberto was always pushing for the wives to be more involved in team activities, and road trips. "He was always defending the wives when someone said they couldn't go to this or that," said Vera. "He also wanted to share everything with the lesser players."

Yet he did not want her to stay more than a week during spring training. "He wanted to concentrate on his training," said Vera. "I understood."

When he had an off-day during the season, Clemente chose to stay home with his kids. "He'd get five or six invitations to dinner, but he wanted to be home with us," said Vera. "He'd have all those invitations for us to go out, but I'd be home cooking instead. He wanted to be with just me and the children.

"There were things he liked to do when he had the time. He made ceramics and artwork. He made lamps. He was learning how to paint china. He could play the harmonica, and we had a Hammond organ he liked to play. He'd play popular music. He'd play hymns for the church. He wrote poems. He had a chiropractor's license. He helped a lot of people. He had old people come to our house, and he'd help them. He saved people from having to have surgery. He was always trying to do something. He couldn't sleep well at night so he'd get up and do some of those things.

"He didn't like to go out much, or spend time with strangers. Some people in Puerto Rico thought he had a superior feeling, or that he thought he was better than them. Like stuck up. He didn't sit down at bars drinking. He'd have one or two beers in a social setting, and that was it. I never saw him drunk. I never saw him smoking.

"He didn't want the children to have everything easy. He wanted them to suffer and to work hard. He liked people who had to work hard, the way his dad did, working in the sugar cane fields back in Carolina. Or someone who was a taxi driver."

It was interesting to learn that Clemente was a chiropractor. One of his dear friends during his days in Pittsburgh was a chiropractor from McKees Rocks named Dr. Chuck Murray, who came to visit him in Puerto Rico, and provided him with relief from the back problems he was plagued with throughout his life, the result of an auto collision early in his ball-playing career.

"Once Roberto made up his mind, nothing could stop him," Murray had said after the death of his friend. "If you knew him, it was go, go, go."

Murray was planning on visiting the Clementes during the Christmas holidays in 1972. "Stay home," Roberto advised him. "I am too busy to entertain you."

I asked Vera how her children dealt with a life without their father.

"They were so little when Roberto died," she said, looking somber for the first time since she started talking about her husband. "Soon after his death, when they had something on TV about him they'd walk out of the room and go out and play. When they grew up, they became more interested in remembering him."

About four years after the death of their father, the Clemente children, Vera said, wanted to know more about their father. "What they liked to do was hear the tapes. There were interviews with Roberto, special programs after he died. There was one with Bob Prince (former Pirates announcer) and some of the players talking. I have tapes, records, films. Sometimes the children would play those things, and I feel so sad.

"Roberito, he kept listening and replaying it. I hid the tapes, but he found them again. I remember about a month after the accident he hide and read all the newspaper clippings. I found him in the back of the house reading about it . . . I have Roberto's uniforms and sometimes Roberito would use some of the stuff from baseball. Sometimes he'd put on his sweatshirts and they were so big. I tell him, 'Roberito, that's too big for you,' but he wanted to wear it.

"Roberto Jr. wanted to play baseball. I used to have to wait till he fell to sleep to take his uniform off and wash it," she recalled. "He and Luis used to play in two different baseball tournaments, one after the other. Enrique played one year. He didn't care for it.

"It was difficult for them to be baseball players. They have the same name as their father, a famous baseball player. The three of them look like him in different ways. It's been difficult for them.

"It was toughest on Ricky. He is very shy. Sometimes he didn't want to be recognized as a Clemente. When he was 12 or 13, he didn't want people to know who he was. Ricky looks more like Roberto than any of them. Plus, he has the same exact name — Roberto Enrique.

"When Roberto Jr. was signed by the Phillies, as soon as he went to training they were comparing him to his father. There was too much pressure." Roberto Jr.'s fledgling baseball career came to an end in 1991, ironically enough, because of back problems.

I mentioned that Enrique, or Ricky, had remained behind in Puerto Rico rather than fly to Pittsburgh for the Piratefest and the tribute to his father. "He doesn't like to fly," she said.

"Every year after Roberto died, beginning in 1973, we spent the summers in Pittsburgh. We bought a home in Green Tree. For a few years, they didn't want to go back to Puerto Rico when the summer was over. At first, we stayed for three months. Then two months. Then, as they got older, we stayed less and less in Pittsburgh. Their closest friends were in Puerto Rico."

Now Roberto Jr. was planning to remain in Pittsburgh and develop a youth baseball program in the inner-city in his father's memory. "Roberto thinks there's something to be done in Pittsburgh; I'm proud of him," said Vera. I asked Zulma how she liked the cold weather and snow of Pittsburgh. "I like it," she said. "It's too hot in Puerto Rico."

Luis and his wife, Olga Beatriz, have a three-year-old son, named Luis Roberto Jr., and they were expecting a second child in April. They were living in Miami, where Luis was employed in customer service by American Airlines. He flies a lot, and has no problem with it. Enrique remained in Puerto Rico, where he also works at the airport, for the Port Authority, despite his personal aversion to flying.

"Luis Roberto is a very active three-year-old," said Vera. "He's left-handed, and he runs fast. He's always talking about his grandfather. He speaks English very clearly. He says he wants to be strong, like his grandfather. He knows about his grandfather. If he sees just a shadow of his figure, or part of a picture, he notices. He knows it's his grandfather. And, ah, the Pittsburgh Pirates, they are his favorite team."

"I try to be good every day."

I asked Vera about the cross she was wearing on her necklace, and whether she went to church and prayed for her husband since religion was reported to have been important to him.

"I visit church regularly, and not only the Catholic church," said Vera. "I might go to the Baptist church as well. Because I am Catholic I don't stay away from other churches. I am ecumenical. There's only one God. Every year we have an ecumenical service for Roberto. We have a priest and a minister at the service.

"Every day I try to do what I can do for others. I try to be good every day. The church is close to us. To be in church every day and to criticize people is wrong. I always pray before I go to bed, and then when I wake up I pray. And, yes, I pray for Roberto."

Vera also prays before she gets on an airplane. She travels to the U.S. mainland often in her role as the wife of Roberto Clemente. "I'm afraid to fly, but I do it," she said. "I'm afraid. Sometimes it's worse. I think of so many scenes. One time Roberto and I were flying to the Dominican Republic and back, and we had to return to the airport because the plane had an equipment problem. That was scary. I don't want anything to happen to me. I want to live longer."

She laughed when she said that last line, probably so she wouldn't cry.

"I'm getting old," she said, "and, yes, I wanted Roberto to be with me when our children were growing up. There's always that empty space. But I keep busy. I don't sit down to think too much. I keep busy. I don't want to be sad. So I do things."

Remember Roberto
Broken dreams

"We just all sat around
and no one said anything."

Beth Painter
Butler

"I was born in 1959, and I was only a year old when Maz hit the home run. But Clemente's death was one of my strong early memories. I remember my mother woke me up very early on New Year's Day and told me Clemente had been killed. I didn't believe it. I cried and cried. We'd been to a playoff game; it was the last time I saw him play. When I was going through some of my stuff recently, I found a boxscore from the '72 season. Clemente had a couple of hits in that game."

Mike Komlos
Ambridge

"I taught elementary school for 18 years so I am always interested in the way people treat children. I remember as a kid going to Forbes Field with the Knot-Hole Gang. I remember this incident when I was 11. I remember that Jerry Lynch always signed autographs for everybody, but he made everybody line up orderly. Roberto Clemente came out carrying suits in both hands. He said, 'No can sign. Both hands full.' My dad was aggressive, and he took the suits out of Clemente's hands and held them for him, and Clemente stayed for a half hour and signed autographs. I also remember a hot dog stand near the bleachers. Their mustard was the best I ever tasted in my life. I'm still searching for it."

Maggie Craig
Chicora, Pa.

"We were too young for the Kennedy thing, so we'd never experienced any of the assassinations. I was born in 1960, so we hadn't experienced winning that World Series, either. We lived on a farm outside of Parker, Pa., about 65 miles north of Pittsburgh. I was one of ten children in the Kaufman family. My dad was a chemist, and we raised beef on our farm. We heard over the radio that Clemente had been killed. I was 12 years old at the time. We all went out to the barn, which was kinda our meeting place. It was really weird. We just all sat around and no one said anything. It was a shock. It was sad."

Maggie Craig was one of ten Kaufman children on the family's farm in Parker, Pa. back in 1972 when Roberto Clemente was killed in an air crash. The Kaufmans included, left to right front row, Bill, Jim, Maggie, Edward and Raymond, back row, Madeline, Kathleen, Rie, Paul and Tom. Upon learning of Roberto's death, they retreated to the barn in the background at left and sat in silence.

Jim Riley
Latrobe

"I had tryouts with the Pirates in 1957 and 1958. There were five of us at this one tryout at Forbes Field. I was trying out as a catcher and Clemente was there, I remember. Clemente was on base and he tried to steal on me. I dusted him. I was more shocked than he was. I was a senior at Latrobe Area High School, and I was playing American Legion ball and dreaming of being a big league ballplayer. I weighed only 150 pounds and they wanted big dudes. Branch Rickey told me I was too small. But throwing out Clemente is something I'll always remember. I also hit the ball off the scoreboard. I thought it was a home run, but they said it was a double. I came up short all the way around that day."

63

Happy trails to you
until we meet again.

— Roy Rogers

Orlando Merced
Clemente's Neighbor In Rio Piedras

"This is right field.
This is where he played."

Only a Hollywood screenwriter would dare to come up with a story like that of Orlando Merced.

As a little boy, Merced lived across the street from the Great Roberto Clemente in Rio Piedras, a suburban community on the hill in San Juan, Puerto Rico. At age 6, Merced accompanied his father when he went to pay his respects to the Clemente family after Roberto was killed in an airplane crash off the nearby coast.

He grew up with Roberto's sons, Roberto Jr., Luis and Enrique, played ball with them, had the run of the Clemente house, with all its trophies, plaques, mementos, photos and baseball memorabilia attesting to the Hall of Fame career of their late father.

None of the Clemente boys made it to the big-time as a baseball player, Roberto Jr. getting the farthest as a minor leaguer during a short stay in the Philadelphia Phillies organization, giving up the ghost because of back problems in 1991.

But Orlando Luis Merced not only made it to the major leagues, but he made it with the Pittsburgh Pirates and in the summer of 1993 he became the regular right fielder for the Pirates. He led the Bucs in batting and finished ninth in the National League with a career-high .313 batting average.

The year before, in his first full season in the major leagues, Merced made 11 starts in right field, seeing more action at first base, and it was then he realized that he was, indeed, playing in the same place once occupied by his boyhood hero.

The Pirates were playing the Mets on June 6, 1992, and it marked the first return of Bobby Bonilla, who had played right field in previous years with some distinction, but abandoned the Bucs for bigger money with the Mets, and left a bad taste with Pirates fans, as Barry Bonds would later do.

"The fans were throwing a lot of quarters for some reason," said Merced. "I looked back to the stands and I saw Clemente's name and number there. It flashed through my mind like a picture — the way he played — and I realized, 'Hey, this is right field. This is where he played. This is what it's like.' It was a good feeling."

Merced may be making good money these days, but he can remember when such coins were a little more difficult to come by as a kid in Puerto Rico, even though his parents were rich by comparison to most families. So he picked up $1.50 worth of quarters that June night at Three Rivers Stadium and pocketed them.

After the 1993 season, there were great expectations held out for Merced. No one in the Pirates organization looked at him as somebody who could play right field or hit the ball like Clemente, but he was pretty good in both respects, and that was good enough for them and the fans.

For Merced, it's good enough just to be playing the same position as his idol.

"It's very special," allowed Merced, who was 27 at the start of the 1994 season, and just coming into his own as a major league baseball player. "There's not another right fielder who won 12 Gold Gloves and played right field the way he played. I'm not saying I will play that way, but it is a dream come true. It's something in front of me that pushes me to be better."

There's something behind him, though the memories are a little foggy, at first, that account for the special relationship to right field and the Clemente legacy.

He was six years old, just a few months younger than Roberto Jr., when several hundred people gathered in the darkness of the early morning, January 1, 1973, at Roberto Clemente's big house across the street from his home.

Adults were holding handkerchiefs to their eyes, crying aloud and whispering details about the airplane crash in which Roberto Clemente had been killed only hours before.

Orlando Merced was riding in a car with his family, returning from a New Year's Eve party, when they were shocked to hear the news of the airplane crash and that Roberto Clemente had been lost. With his father, Orlando went to the Clemente home that morning.

"It was very sad," Merced recalled. "I saw people cry, so I cried. I didn't know what death was about, but I understood that a super, super star had passed away. It hurt."

Today, Merced and his wife Lori and their two children, Natalie and Orlando Jr., live in Ocala, Florida, near Orlando and Disney World. It only makes sense, with that same knows-no-shame Hollywood script writer, that Orlando Merced would live outside Orlando, Florida. His mother lives there, too, and a sister lives in Tampa.

When the Pirates played the Miami Marlins at Joe Robbie Stadium in mid-June, 1993, there was a Merced-Clemente reunion of sorts. Orlando had to come up with 40 tickets to take care of everybody who was there to see him.

Clemente's second son, Luis, was living in Miami, as was Orlando's older brother, Sydney. Orlando's father, uncle and friends were flying in from Puerto Rico. They were all getting together to cheer for Orlando.

Merced was in the midst of a wonderful dream-come-true season and was becoming one of the most popular Pirates.

It had been an amazing season for Merced, who as a child had run around the Clemente home with Luis and Roberto Jr. and Enrique, playing kids' games among the trophies and awards that filled the Clemente's basement gameroom.

At the time of the visit, Merced was second in the league in hitting with a .364 batting average. His average during his first three seasons were .208, .275 and .247.

Orlando Merced

David Arrigo

Merced was giving most of the credit to two coaches on Jim Leyland's staff, hitting instructor Milt May and outfield coach Bill Virdon, for the progress he had made. Merced was always quick to shoot down anyone who wanted to make comparisons with Clemente. He knew he couldn't win at that game.

"I don't think I'll ever be able to equal his accomplishments," he told Amy Niedzielka, a sports writer for *The Miami Herald.* "He played 18 seasons. I would have to play 40 seasons to do that."

By the way, to take this incredible tale to its extreme, Merced is named after Orlando Cepeda, a contemporary of Roberto Clemente. Merced's mother was a big fan of Orlando Cepeda, himself a long-time Hall of Fame candidate after a distinguished 17-year-career, mostly with the Giants, Cardinals and Braves.

Consider this: here was a kid named after Cepeda who played with the sons of Clemente, using major league baseballs, gloves, bats and uniforms brought home by Clemente.

"It was not a big deal to us," Merced remembers. "We would even throw his bats, leave them outside in the rain. I only have one picture with his signature, and that was given to me by Steve Blass. He couldn't believe I never had anything signed by my neighbor. I wish I had an idea of what was going to happen."

It's mind-blowing stuff.

"It was just a dream I had when I was a kid," Merced said. "But I never, ever thought I would have a chance to do that. It's something to make me feel very proud.

"I dreamed about playing for the Pirates. I dreamed about playing right field. I dreamed about being just like him."

When he talked about his early struggles of playing in right field, he sounded like a disciple of Clemente. "I'm going to be the best I can be, hustle, play hard, play smart and win," said Merced. "I know I can do more."

Virdon won a Gold Glove himself as a center fielder for the Pirates, playing next to Clemente for ten years. He believes Merced can only get better. "He has pretty good hands, and he runs pretty good," said Virdon. "Most of it is going to be getting used to it, judging the ball. But that just comes from playing and working at it."

Vera Clemente had hoped to see one of her sons playing for the Pirates someday. She has called to congratulate the kid across the street. "She's very happy for me," said Merced.

So is Orlando. "I'm a major leaguer," he said, "and playing on the same team as Roberto. It's a dream come true."

David Arrigo/Pittsburgh Pirates

Orlando Merced became a happy fellow after adhering to advice offered him by two of the Pirates coaches, Milt May and Billy Virdon, in dark jackets to his left on Pirates bench. They helped him with his hitting and his play in the outfield.

David Arrigo/Pittsburgh Pirates

Members of the Pony League team of Puerto Rico meet one of their heroes, Orlando Merced, when visiting Pittsburgh while competing in Pony League World Series at Washington, Pa. in August of 1991.

Bob Purkey
The Pride of Mt. Washington

"If you asked Clemente who gave him the most trouble, he'd say me."

It was fast closing in on 1:30 a.m. and Bob Purkey was pitching the game of his life. He was in the midst of striking out Roberto Clemente, a Hall of Famer. He struck him out on three pitches, three well-planned pitches that went against the book on how to pitch to The Great One.

"Hey, if you're gonna tell a story," Purkey would say the day after, "why not tell one where you're the star?"

Purkey, a pretty good story-teller, had been entertaining a half dozen people at our table in the dining area of DaLallo's, an Italian restaurant-bar in Bethel Park where Purkey has had his own insurance agency since he retired from baseball in 1966. It's located in the suburbs about 12 miles southeast of Pittsburgh and Three Rivers Stadium.

Purkey had pitched for his hometown Pittsburgh Pirates from 1954 to 1957, then the Cincinnati Reds from 1958 to 1965, before returning home for one last hurrah in 1966.

This was a Friday night, October 22, 1993, and DaLallo's, just down Fort Couch Road from South Hills Village, was full of people, wall to wall, following high school football games in the neighboring communities of Bethel Park and Upper St. Clair.

Purkey was pitching for the Reds when he was relating his story of the success he usually had when facing his good friend Roberto Clemente. After he departed the Pirates, Purkey came up with a new pitch — a knuckleball — and it made him most effective with the hard-hitting Reds.

He had his best season, with a 23-5 record in 1962, and he had the highest winning percentage (.821) in both leagues.

"I made my living on the inside," explained Purkey, in setting up his story. "We were playing the Pirates this one day at Forbes Field, and we had a heated battle and we had received some warnings from the umpire about throwing at batters. I was going out on the field this one inning and I walked past Jocko Conlan, who was umpiring behind the plate. I told him, 'I'm going to be throwing the ball inside to Clemente. I'm not trying to hit him. I'm trying to get him out.' I didn't like people who reached into my refrigerator and took out a ham or chicken. I was going to do whatever I had to do to keep him from taking food from my family. It was that simple: a law of self-preservation.

"I threw a ball six inches off the inside corner. Then I threw the next one a foot off the inside corner. Then I threw the next one a foot and a half off the inside corner and I got him out. He swung at all three pitches and he missed all three pitches.

"I just kept coming in on him. I knew he knew I was going to come inside and that he'd adjust. But I was going to stay inside, and keep jamming him more and more.

"Everyone else thought, because of how far back in the box Clemente stood, that it was best to throw him outside. But he could lash out and hit it there and send it to right field. I had been around Roberto enough in Pittsburgh to know how to pitch to him.

"I don't know what the hell it was, but I had a lot of success against him.

"Roberto and I were very close. If you asked Clemente who gave him the most trouble he'd say me. I don't know why, but I had luck with him. He batted under .200 against me. You could look it up, I suppose.

"When I was with the Reds, we remained good friends. I had a bad shoulder once when I was with the Reds, and he wanted to send me to see his doctor in Puerto Rico. His name was Doctor Garcia, I think. He offered to fly me there at his expense. What makes that crazy is, first of all, I was pitching for the Reds. And I got him out regularly. Yet he tried to make me well again. That's how much he liked me."

Purkey hurt his right arm in spring training in 1963. "I was so eager to get going because of the year I'd had the season before," recalled Purkey, who slipped to a 6-10 record the year after he went 23-5.

Purkey was between pitches, between stories. But he warmed up fast with a change-of-pace offering.

"One day Clemente comes out swinging three bats like he did, to limber up. He saw me and he started smiling. He said, 'Hey, Purk, you pitching today?' I said I was. He said, 'I'll tell you what, Purk, you're not going to get me out today.' I said, 'Why not?' He said, "I'm not going to play today.'"

Purkey laughed at his own story. When he laughs his already-thin eyes appear to close completely above his puffy cheeks. They become mere slits. Purkey was 64, but looked more like 50, when we spoke and probably felt like he was 25 as he pretended to be pitching a baseball across our table.

Laughing just as hard at his story, though surely she has heard it hundreds of times before, was Joanie Purkey, his wife of 41 years. They had met on Mt. Washington, where both grew up, and where Purkey had first gained fame as a fine pitcher at the local Olympia Field. She was a student at Mt. St. Mary's High School and he at South Hills High School when they first got sweet on one another. Both schools are long gone from the Pittsburgh scholastic scene, but the Purkeys remain popular on the Pittsburgh landscape.

Once it was their custom to dine at Tambellini's when it was located on Southern Avenue on Mt. Washington. They still go to Louie Tambellini's relocated restaurant on Route 51. But they like to go to DaLallo's on Friday night.

It is my custom after home football games at Upper St. Clair High School to go to either Eat'n Park or King's for an ice cream sundae or pie with coffee. Good friends Alex and Sharon Pociask invited me to join them and some friends of theirs at DaLallo's this time, however, and it was a stroke of good fortune.

Sometimes you get lucky as a writer. As soon as I entered DaLallo's, I spotted Steve Blass, a broadcaster for the Pirates who had been a big star for them as a pitcher when they beat the Baltimore Orioles to win the World Series in 1971. I had seen Blass earlier in the evening sitting in the stands on the 50-yard line with his good friend and neighbor, Dave Giusti, who won Fireman of the Year honors as a standout relief pitcher for the Pirates in that same 1971 season. Giusti had gone home halfway through the game. Giusti had gone to the game to check out the team's quarterback, Mike Tomko, also a good baseball player, who was a neighbor of his.

Jim Render's Upper St. Clair team had crushed Canon-McMillan of nearby Canonsburg to keep their unbeaten streak (8-0) intact. Upper St. Clair was the No. 2 rated team in Western Pa. in the top football division, just behind North Hills. One of those two teams figured to win the WPIAL Quad A title. Upper St. Clair was the defending champion, and had won the WPIAL as well as the Pennsylvania title in 1986. (They would lose to North Hills in the Quad A Final at season's end.)

Among those celebrating the latest victory was Steve Furness, a defensive lineman (1972-80) on the Pittsburgh Steelers' four Super Bowl teams, and the defensive line coach for the Steelers. He had several reasons to feel particularly good. The Steelers had won four straight games, following two season-opening setbacks, and the team's defensive unit was suddenly — and prematurely — drawing comparisons to the Steelers of the '70s. They had been especially impressive the previous Sunday when they really dominated the undefeated New Orleans Saints, 37-14. Furness and his wife, Debbie, were also delighted because their son, Zack, a junior lineman, had started and played well for Upper St. Clair that same evening. (There was no reason for Furness to fear that he would be fired by Bill Cowher at season's end, one of the scapegoats for a frustrating season.)

Then, at the far end of the barroom, I spotted Purkey. Sometimes it gets scary when you are writing a book. It has been my experience that suddenly people you hadn't thought about, but would make sense in such a book, start popping up in front of you wherever you travel.

After the usual greetings, I got Purkey aside and posed a question to him: "Did you know Roberto Clemente well?" No sooner had I asked the question, and Purkey responded in a positive manner, that I saw Roberto Clemente looking over Purkey's shoulder. It was spooky, and it was still a week away from Halloween.

This requires a little explanation. Directly behind Purkey, just over his right shoulder, was a framed photograph showing Clemente in the company of Danny Murtaugh, his manager with the Pirates when they won the World Series in 1960.

I told Purkey I would call him to get together to talk about his relationship with Clemente. I had no idea at the time that Purkey would later be joining us, and entertaining us with his ball-playing stories in the next room.

Around 1 a.m., Purkey was standing up in our midst, and animatedly relating how he got out the great Roberto Clemente. His knuckleball never danced so much.

"He's still unique."

The next night, the Toronto Blue Jays came from behind to beat the Philadelphia Phillies, 8-6, in the sixth game to win the World Series. They did so on a three-run homer by Joe Carter in the bottom of the ninth inning.

It was only the second Series that ended on a home run. Bill Mazeroski won the 1960 Series for the Pirates with a home run off Ralph Terry in the bottom of the ninth.

So Mazeroski's name was back in the news again, and ESPN and other networks were showing vintage film of Maz's 1960 home run again, and his name was mentioned early in most reports of the 1993 World Series.

"It's funny how that happened," pointed out Purkey, "but Maz is still the only one to do it in the seventh game of the World Series. So he's still unique."

On Sunday, the Steelers suffered a 28-23 setback to the Browns in Cleveland. This silenced the Super Bowl talk and the comparisons to the Steelers of the '70s for awhile.

"He did a lot for his home people."

Purkey graduated from South Hills High School in 1947. During the summer, he pitched for the Mt. Washington Merchants, a sandlot team managed by Joe Roeb. They played their home games at Olympia Field, near his Duquesne Heights neighborhood. Back then, people in the neighborhood liked to boast about Eddie "Eppy" Miller, who grew up on Mt. Washington and played shortstop 14 years (1936-1950) in the major leagues, with Cincinnati, Boston, Philadelphia and St. Louis. "He was a good one," Purkey pointed out.

There was a late model black Cadillac Sedan de Ville that belonged to Bob Purkey parked alongside a two-story gray building on Brightwood Road in the heart of Bethel Park. It's the home of Bob Purkey Insurance Agency. Purkey has built up quite a business through the years. Purkey is a popular fellow, and people like doing business with him, and his equally likable insurance sales associate, Tom O'Malley Jr. His father, Tom O'Malley Sr., a retired advertising sales executive of *The Pittsburgh Press* and the mayor of Castle Shannon, had grown up and played baseball with Purkey on Mt. Washington.

To see Purkey's office, a visitor would think Purkey had played professional golf rather than baseball. Pictures and trophies abound relating to golf, a game he plays to a 12 handicap. "I had a great day

David Arrigo/Pittsburgh Pirates

Bob Purkey participates in 1993 Pirates Alumni golf outing.

Pirates and Reds have reunion under the stands at Forbes Field in '60s: from left to righ
Dick Stuart, Bob Purkey, Smoky Burgess, Vada Pinson, Jerry Lynch, Leo Cardenas an
Joe Christopher.

Roberto Clemente congratulates
Bob Purkey after Pirates
pitcher hit grand slam
home run at Forbes Field.

Pittsburgh Pirates

yesterday," he said. "I shot an 81 at Valley Brook — 38 and 43."

He is still welcome as a former Pirate at many civic events, and is invited to participate in a lot of fund-raisers. "I play 15 to 20 charity golf events a year," he said with more than a hint of pride. "It gives me a chance to play every top country club in the area, from Firestone to Oakmont, from Fox Chapel to Sewickley, Churchill, St. Clair and Valley Brook.

"It gets me out of the office on Mondays during the summer golf season. It's good for business, it's good for charity, and it's good for me."

Purkey is a people person. Always has been, always will be. "Here's what I used to do when I was playing for the Reds," he said. "I stayed at home here, rather than in the hotel where the Reds were staying when they were playing in Pittsburgh. I'd sit on the back of the batting cage when the Pirates were taking their practice swings. I'd talk to them, fraternize, I guess. I liked to talk to them because they were all my friends. The other uniform didn't come into play until the umpire said, 'play ball.'"

One of the players he enjoyed teasing the most was Roberto Clemente.

"He had his own style of playing," Purkey recalled. "You had to look at him. Sometimes you looked at him in awe, even when he first came up, because of his abilities.

"The thing I remember about him is that he didn't run. He galloped. He just didn't run. He sorta had a gait about him. He was a good player, in every respect. He was well-built, strong in the forearms, and he was a handsome guy. Striking."

I asked Purkey about the stories that Clemente came into a clubhouse that wasn't particularly friendly, at first, one that was slow to warm up to him. I had read where he had few real friends on the team, that he kept to himself, that none of the Pirates went out of their way to welcome him, and make him feel at home.

"He may have felt that way," said Purkey. "I don't think the guys treated him any differently than they did any other rookie. Any rookie has to prove himself with the ballplayers who are there."

Why did Purkey feel like he was a close friend of Clemente?

"Probably because we just respected each other. I had no problem with Clemente. We got along well, right from the start. We both recognized it fast. I didn't have any adverse feelings about him being on the club.

"I didn't have much experience playing with black ballplayers, on any level. I'd come to the team in 1954, the same year as Curt Roberts, the first black to play for the Pirates."

I mentioned that Clemente had complained more than once about the treatment Roberts received from many of the Pirates, like they made fun of him, or told jokes at his expense.

"That could have been a sign of the times," said Purkey. "I've always been able to get along with anyone. I take a person at face value. I don't care what color, race, religion a person is. I don't care.

"When I went to Cincinnati, I had no trouble with Frank Robinson or Vada Pinson. I never had a problem with black players."

Did Purkey have any idea of what Clemente was doing away from the ballpark, the way he tried to help so many people, especially children, who were less fortunate?

"He kept a lot of that stuff to himself," said Purkey. "What he did off the field, and for people, you didn't hear much about because he didn't broadcast it. That was him. He did a lot for his home people."

Did Clemente change his demeanor as he continued to play for the Pirates?

"When he first came up, he wasn't the Clemente of later years, which is not unusual. Most people are the same way, as they mature. At first, Clemente was tough to get to know. He became more comfortable later on. It wasn't just a matter of language. He changed when he realized everyone wasn't out to take advantage of him."

How did he account for the continued interest in Clemente among younger fans, many of whom never saw him play.

"The media hasn't let him die," opined Purkey. "I think they also respect the way he died — trying to help the victims of an earthquake in Nicaragua. I think that has a lot to do with it."

"It was too much for his heart."

When I was interviewing various former Pirates who had played with Roberto Clemente, it struck me how so many of them have had to deal with their own difficulties, deaths of loved ones, their own setbacks, their own tragedies. They had compassion for the Clemente family because they had to deal with grief of their own. To the public, they may appear as something special, something from a different world, because they wore the uniform of the Pirates and other big league teams, but they bleed when you prick their skin, and they are, indeed, very human.

Bob and Joan Purkey lost their son, Bob Jr., at age 18, in the prime of his young athletic life. He died while challenging himself, and his heart, in some student craziness in a swimming pool in Colorado.

Young Bob was a prize pitcher for the Gulf Coast Community College baseball team in Panama City, Florida — the same team that Bill Mazeroski's son Darren coaches these days.

"They went to play in a tournament in Grand Junction, Colorado," recalled his father. "They were swimming in the hotel pool. They were seeing who could swim the longest underwater. He won. He came up gasping for air. He was suffering from fibrillation."

That's a muscular twitching involving individual muscle fibers acting without coordination, a very rapid irregular contraction of the muscle fibers of the heart resulting in a lack of synchronism between heartbeat and pulsebeat.

"He suffered cardiac arrest. He couldn't handle being without air for so long. It was too much for his heart. He never came out of it. We had an autopsy. Dr. Finegold, the Pirates team physician, later explained to me what happened. Bob was born with a thread-like blood vessel leading to his heart. He'd had a steak dinner just before he went swimming. That, along with the high altitude of Colorado, the pressure of the water, and Bob's congenital heart problems combined to be too much for his system. There was not enough oxygen getting to the brain. Even so, if they had the kind of emergency medical services we have today, Bob would probably still be alive. He was too long without any kind of treatment on the way to the hospital."

The baseball field at Bethel Park High School was named in honor of young Bob Purkey shortly after his death in 1973. Many people mistakenly think the ballfield is named in honor of his father, the former Pirate. "We're always correcting people on that," said Bob Sr.

"Our son had a 30-0 pitching record during the regular season over a four-year period at Bethel Park High. He lost some games in playoffs and championships, but he had quite a career. Joanie and I were so proud of him. He was a great kid. It's still a problem for Joanie and me."

The Purkeys have a daughter, Candy Holland, 35. She has two sons, Ross, 9, and Brian, who was born December 10, 1993, a month after my visit to Bob's office. "We're grandparents twice," said Bob, "and we sure love those boys."

Bob Purkey Jr. in uniform as a pitcher for Gulf Coast Community College baseball team in Pensacola, Florida, prior to his death. The baseball field at Bethel Park High School was named in his honor.

Bobby Del Greco
Still on The Hill

*"Clemente grew up the hard way
so he liked the little people."*

T
he way he was rubbing the baseball, and by the look on his grizzled face, Bobby Del Greco may have appeared to a casual observer as if he were pitching in the playoffs, if not the World Series. His motions and manner seemed that serious. His square jaw was set firmer than the one on Honus Wagner's statue on the other side of the wall at Forbes Field.

But this was batting practice prior to a Pirates game at the old ballyard in Oakland in the late '60s, and Del Greco was going to throw his hardest pitch to Roberto Clemente. The Great One had been getting to Del Greco, giving him the business about having a bum arm and being washed up, and Clemente must have forgotten that you could give it to Del Greco only so long before you got his goat. After all, Del Greco had grown up nearby in The Hill district, and had come up the hard way. He has always been a nice guy, but you could only push him so far. Then The Hill in him took over. Being competitive, no matter the game or activity, was in the blood.

"The kids in my neighborhood were mostly Italian, Lebanese and black, with a few Irish kids mixed in," said Del Greco. "We got along fine, but we did a little fighting, too." It was important to defend one's honor.

So the right-handed Del Greco reared back and fired the ball as hard as he could. And he plunked Clemente on his left shoulder.

Clemente jumped around in the batter's box for awhile as if Del Greco had given him a hot foot. Clemente protested in an exaggerated theatrical manner, as only Clemente could, as if he had been mortally wounded. They could probably hear him hollering at the nearby Presbyterian-University Hospital on the campus of the University of Pittsburgh. Clemente's outcry might have put the emergency room team on alert.

Then Clemente got back in the batter's box. "C'mon, Greek," Clemente said in that sing-song Spanish accent of his. "What are you doing out there? Can't you get the ball over the plate? C'mon, get the ball over the plate. Get the ball over and don't hit me. Don't hit me anymore. Please. Let me get my hits and get outta here."

"Then I'd throw it over the plate," said Del Greco with a grin, "and he'd hit a line drive, or maybe he hit one over the wall. I can't remember. But he hit me pretty good.

"Those guys would try to jack me up. They'd holler stuff like, 'Why don't you move up ten feet? Maybe you can get something on the ball. You can't throw hard from the rubber. C'mon, move up!' They'd get me riled up. I'd try to throw the ball harder, and I'd get wild. I hit them a few times, and they hit me a few times, too. Thank goodness I had that protective screen in front of me most of the time.

"Every once in a while I'd try to throw the ball by them. When I was pitching against Clemente or some power hitters, people like Willie Stargell and Dave Parker and Al Oliver, I'd try to bust one in on them every once in awhile to keep them on their toes. To have some fun. Remember Richie Zisk? I'd do that with him, too. In the late '60s, and early '70s, I had a pretty good arm. I could always throw the ball in pretty hard when I was an outfielder. Those guys were tough to pitch to. In the end, they always beat me. But they were supposed to hit me. That's what I was getting paid to do."

Bobby Del Greco is still a recognizable name among long-time Pirates fans. His face, even with the salt and pepper sprinkled throughout his mustache and the hair on his head, is a familiar one, especially on The Hill where he grew up and where he delivered the *Post-Gazette* and then *The Press* for ten years as a truck driver, and in Brookline and Baldwin Township, where he has lived ever since he first played for the Pirates.

I was having breakfast with Del Greco at an Eat'n Park Restaurant on West Liberty Avenue in the heart of Dormont, a community near his home and just south of Pittsburgh that once boasted one of the area's best sandlot baseball teams. Several customers greeted Del Greco as they passed him. He looked up from his "Breakfast Smile" special — two eggs over easy with crisp bacon, home fries and white toast and decaffeinated coffee — to respond with a smile and a wave. He was still a popular fellow in his home town.

He was still pitching batting practice during the summer of 1993, his 25th year in that role, only now he was only pitching to the pitchers. They had someone with a stronger arm giving the hitters a more honest test. At 60, Del Greco had to give way to stronger arms.

Del Greco was glad he was still wearing a Pirates uniform. He was glad he still got a chance to get out there on the field at Three Rivers Stadium. Baseball has been his whole life. He had driven a truck for the daily newspaper for 27 years altogether, but that was a job, a way to pay the bills. He had retired from that job four months before our meeting, taking advantage of a buyout after a long strike had unbelievably buried *The Pittsburgh Press*. Baseball had been in his blood since he could throw a ball on Bedford Avenue, in the same neighborhood that is now the upper parking lot of the Civic Arena.

Del Greco was a second generation Italian. His father had worked at Frank & Seder Department Store, and a buck was tough to come by at their home on Bedford Avenue. He got his nickname "Greek" from Sam Narron, the Pirates' bullpen coach from North Carolina, who served on Danny Murtaugh's staff in the late '50s and early '60s. Narron could never get Del Greco's name right, for whatever reason, so he said, "I'm just gonna call you Greek from now on." And it stuck.

Baseball people don't come any nicer than Narron, so Del Greco gave in to the new nickname, and learned to live with it. His parents never cared for it, because they were proud of their Italian heritage.

Bob Del Greco

Bobby Del Greco took great
pride in wearing his
Pirates uniform,
and delivering
The Press for many years
in his old neighborhood.

Bobby was the youngest of eight children of Catherine and Nick Del Greco. He started school late, and was 16 by the time he left Epiphany Grade School near his home. He never went to high school, which I never knew until I talked with him for this book. He was an indifferent student at best, and was more enthusiastic about playing games at the Washington Park ballfield and recreation center across the street from Connelley Vocational High School. "We played all kinds of sports, and we played in the street, and went swimming when we could at Connelley. We just went from one sport to another," said Del Greco. "It was pretty tough living on The Hill in those days. We didn't have a lot of money. But we loved to play ball, whatever the season was."

His dad died when Bobby was in grade school, and Bobby never finished school. "When I got a little bonus, I quit school and went away to play ball."

Hall of Famer Pie Traynor signed him to play for the Pirates. Bobby remembers it was for a $500 bonus. "That seemed like big bucks to me then," he recalled. "I had been playing for a sandlot team that was sponsored by Mellon-Stuart Construction Company. I was playing ball every day. I had been playing ball with Tony Bartirome for years. I signed with the Pirates a year before Tony did.

"I didn't have a hero on the Pirates; I didn't pay much attention to them at the time. But I liked Frankie Gustine when he was playing for the Pirates. When I first met him after I was playing for the Pirates, he was such a gentleman. He gave me such a big lift; he boosted me. He'd say, 'Stick with it; you'll be fine.' He was a super individual. Around him, you didn't swear or get out of line.

"When I broke in with the Pirates in 1952 they had guys like Ralph Kiner, Gus Bell, George Metkovich, Bob Friend and Dick Groat. Groat came from Duke the same year I got my first look. They had Ed Fitz Gerald, Clyde McCullough and Joe Garagiola as catchers. The O'Brien Twins, Eddie and Johnny, came up the next year."

Del Greco was only 18 and he was the starting centerfielder for the Pirates during that 1952 season. The Pirates were a pretty bad team back then and lost a record 112 games.

"I was too young and, playing in my hometown, I was pressing too much. If I had a bad night, I'd take it home with me, which is bad.

"It was a real big thrill to become a professional ballplayer. To get off The Hill and to get away and see the towns and meet all the people was a real exciting experience. At the time I signed, I didn't realize it, but as I started through the minor leagues, I learned how lucky I was.

"I started out with Hutchinson, Kansas, which was a Pirates farm team."

I asked Del Greco what was the most distant place he had ever traveled from home before he signed with the Pirates.

"Probably Aspinwall or Etna," he said, without a hint of humor.

Del Greco saw action in 99 games for the Pirates in 1952, batting .217 in 341 plate appearances. He came back in 1956 and was batting .200 when he was traded to the St. Louis Cardinals. He hit two home runs in a Sunday game at Forbes Field. Frank "The Trader" Lane, the colorful general manager of the Cardinals, was in the stands, and agreed to a deal with Joe L. Brown the next day, May 17, 1956. Del Greco and pitcher Dick Littlefield were sent to the Cardinals for Billy Virdon. Only a year earlier, Virdon had been named the National League's Rookie of the Year. He went on to have a terrific career with the Pirates as a dependable hitter and one of the best centerfielders in the league.

"Virdon and I were both having terrible years," recalled Del Greco of the events leading up to that trade. "Lane came in to see me play and I hit those two home runs. The next day they made the trade and Virdon almost led the league in batting. He had a fantastic year."

Virdon, who rented Del Greco's home after the trade, finished with a .319 average, second only to Henry Aaron's .328. Del Greco, on the other hand, hit .214. He worked hard and managed to remain in the big leagues until 1965.

It was one of Brown's best trades, and one of the building blocks for the team that would win the World Series in 1960. Del Greco was an outstanding defensive player as an outfielder, but was a lifetime .229 hitter in his nine pro seasons. In addition to playing for the Pirates and Cardinals, he also saw duty later on with the Chicago Cubs, New York Yankees, Philadelphia Phillies and Kansas City Athletics.

Altogether, he played 666 major league games in the outfield, six at third base and one at second base.

I asked him how he felt at first, being a hometown boy, when he was traded away to the Cardinals.

"I felt a little hurt, a lot hurt. I had just hit two home runs the day before I learned I had been traded. But they had some great guys on the Cardinals, like Stan Musial and Ken Boyer, and they turned me into a Cardinal. When I first got there, I was still upset. But they made me feel at home in a hurry."

I mentioned to Del Greco that Ralph Kiner had described Musial to me this way: "He's like Frank Gustine with a better batting average." Del Greco agreed. "He talked to anybody," he said. "He never ran away from you. If he saw you out eating, he'd pick up the check. He was making big money and he looked after the little guys on the team. You could talk to Musial, just like you could talk to Clemente. If you were having some problems with baseball, they'd listen to what you had to say. They'd help you if they could.

"Kiner was great, too. When he got married to Nancy Chaffee, my wife got along well with her, and we went out with them a few times. Kiner picked up a lot of checks, too."

He still thinks of himself as a Pirate, however, and treasures his friendship with Groat, Frank Thomas and Bob Purkey, and looks forward to spending time with them at alumni golf outings and parties. He mentioned Dave Giusti, Steve Blass, Bruce Dal Canton and Ron Necciai as former Pirates he had golfed with the previous summer.

At such outings, the players talk about the past, and one of their former teammates that comes up for conversation often is Roberto Clemente.

Del Greco didn't play long with Clemente, but remembers the early impressions he had of him. "You knew right away that he had a lot of natural ability," said Del Greco. "He could run and throw; it was just a matter of putting it all together. Which he did. He was a super guy, a real laidback guy when he first came up, a real family man.

"I think Willie Mays was the best all-around ballplayer I'd ever seen. Clemente was right up there. He couldn't hit home runs like Mays did, but he did everything else as well. He could have hit more home runs and been a .290 hitter. If they told him to hit home runs, he could have. But he was a line drive hitter. Mays pulled everything. Overall, though, Clemente was as good as anyone who ever came along.

"I remember one day, in 1971, the year before Clemente was killed, I took my son George with me to a ballgame at Three Rivers Stadium. I threw batting practice, and George was in the dugout watching. I introduced him to Clemente and, right away, Clemente sat down and talked to him. He told my son that he had played with me — 'I know your Dad for a long time' — that we'd been teammates, that we were friends. He talked to him for about ten or fifteen minutes. It was one of my son's bigger thrills.

"Clemente first came up to the Pirates in 1955. When he first came up, he couldn't speak much English. He couldn't communicate well with people, but he made jokes and kidded as he got more comfortable with everyone.

"When I came back to the Pirates as a batting practice pitcher in 1968, I got to know Clemente a lot better. He was more established, and he was a team leader. It was Tony Bartirome who recommended me to be the team's batting practice pitcher. They were looking for someone, and he suggested my name. I'm grateful for that. It's been fun.

"Clemente would sit on the bench and kid the guys. He was great with the ground crew. He'd kid them all the time. When we were still at Forbes Field, he'd say the grass was too high, or the grass was too low, and he'd want them to build it up, cut it down, fix it up. He'd say, 'Fix up right field for me, please guys.' There were all local guys on the crew, like Steve DeNardo, who grew up in Oakland near the ballpark but lived in Brookline, like I did, when he got married. We all knew each other, and we all had similar roots, so we got along great. Clemente came up the hard way, too, so he liked the little people.

"I remember Clemente was always bringing his kids to the ballpark, in the last days at Forbes Field, and then at Three Rivers Stadium. He'd play ball with them. He'd hit the ball to them. He was always one of the first ones there. He liked to sit in the clubhouse or the dugout and just talk to people.

"He had changed a great deal from when he first came up. Back then, I think he was a loner, again because of the language. He stayed by himself. When we got a few Spanish-speaking players, he opened up a little. I remember Roman Mejias and Felipe Montemayor also came to the team in 1955.

"I never went out with him or ate with him. I was only with him for a few months before I was traded. But when I was with other teams, and we'd see each other, he always talked to me. He was always friendly.

"What I admired about him was that he always gave you a hundred percent when he was out there. He got better and better as the years went along. He never dogged it, and he played hurt, and always gave you a hundred percent, which a lot of people say he didn't. But I disagree."

Al Abrams was the sports editor of the *Pittsburgh Post-Gazette*, and wrote the most popular sports column in the city. Abrams was Lebanese and had lived in The Hill district when he was growing up. He wrote notes about local fighters like Charlie Affif, who grew up in the same neighborhood and was also Lebanese. And he wrote many kind and complimentary columns about Del Greco and Bartirome. "He always wrote nice things about us," said Del Greco. "He'd write stuff like 'these guys are from The Hill, and they had a rough time when they were kids and look how they made it.' He always made us look good. The writers aren't like that today. They seem like they want to make you look bad today."

Del Greco had been living in Baldwin Township for nearly 40 years when we talked. He bought a house there in 1953. He had been married for 40 years to Cathy Thomas, from Brookline, where they lived when they were first married. They had eight children. Only one of them pursued a professional baseball career, but Jimmy came up with a bad knee while playing baseball at Florida State University. "We've been lucky," said Del Greco. "Our kids have all made out OK."

When Del Greco went to work as a truck driver, delivering the daily newspapers, he was assigned areas in The Hill and in Brookline and Homestead.

"I'd go by my house every day on The Hill, only it wasn't there anymore," he said. "They tore it down when they built the Civic Arena. Every time I went by where Washington Park had been, I'd remember how Tony and I had played ball there. We used to shoot pool at the recreation center there. We lived there when we were kids. I'd get out of the truck every now and then, and spend a few minutes, just walking around by Connelley Vocational, or standing on Bedford Avenue, and reminisce to myself.

"Baseball took me off the streets in The Hill, and it taught me how to get along with people, to tolerate people, to be nice, not to be crazy and do things I shouldn't do, and to meet people who are really, really nice to you."

Most white people steer clear of The Hill, and have done so for many years. It has always been one of the black ghettos of the city. It is in a great location, with its nearness to Downtown and Oakland and the city's Strip District, but many of the homes there are downtrodden.

"It was always risky business, I guess," said Del Greco, "especially when I was taking papers up there at night. But I never had any real

85

problems. Many of the people knew me; they knew I'd been a professional ballplayer and they wanted to talk to me about that. But I worked up there, on and off, for about 15 years.

"But one of the reasons I decided to take the buyout and retire was because it was getting more and more dangerous on the streets in the city. You have drive-by shootings, and kids killing each other every day. It's routine now. I never had any problem getting along with black people. I always got along fine. But these kids today are different; these kids are crazy."

Del Greco was sitting in a truck in the parking lot next to the building that housed *The Pittsburgh Press* and *Post-Gazette* on New Year's Day, 1973. "I was dozing in my truck, waiting for the papers to be ready for pick-up," he recalled. "I had the radio on, but I was half-asleep. I heard on the radio that Roberto Clemente had been killed in an airplane accident in Puerto Rico.

"I couldn't believe it. I walked inside to see what the guys there knew about it. The guys didn't have any radio on. They said, 'Are you crazy?' But it was true, and they got it in the later paper. They put it in around 2:30 in the morning. It was a shock to everyone.

"At first, I didn't want to believe it. I thought maybe somebody was jagging around on the radio, and I didn't hear it right. The first thing that came to my mind was, 'How are they going to replace Roberto Clemente in right field? It will take two or three guys to do it.' In truth, they have never replaced him."

Bobby Del Greco, at left, and boyhood buddy Tony Bartirome flank Pirates hero Ralph Kiner in 1952, Kiner's last full season in Pittsburgh.

View from Bedford Avenue where Bobby Del Greco and Tony Bartirome played ball as kids. Connelley Skill Learning Center is at right, the USX Tower is in the center, and the Civic Arena at the left.

Tony Bartirome
He had Clemente's number

"Roberto was at his best
with people he trusted."

It's a long way from Bedford Avenue to Bradenton, Florida, but Tony Bartirome enjoyed the journey. He worked hard and paid his dues, and deserves relaxed days in the sun. Bartirome remembers where he came from, a tough, modest neighborhood in Pittsburgh's Hill District that was torn down to make way for the Civic Arena. His buddy Bobby Del Greco lived on the same street, just a block or so away, and they both realized boyhood dreams to play for the Pirates in the early '50s.

Neither played that long for the Pirates, but they made their mark because they were hometown boys, and everybody was rooting for them to succeed. Bartirome and Del Greco are both familiar to any long-time fans of the Pirates, way beyond what they ever achieved with bat or glove. They were two likable Italian kids from The Hill, and they had a local following. They came back to serve the Pirates after their playing days, and kept the flame alive for themselves and their fans.

Back at the beginning, in 1952 when he broke in the big leagues for his first and last season, Bartirome was a skinny kid, at 5-10, 155 pounds, with high cheekbones, and coal-dark hair. Suffice to say the face and waistline are much fuller now, but he looks like a guy who could still play softball with his buddies from Bedford Avenue.

After their playing days, Del Greco and Bartirome both came back to the Pirates, Bartirome as the team's trainer, beginning in 1967 and lasting till 1985, and Del Greco as a batting practice pitcher, a sideline to his regular job as a truck driver delivering the city's daily newspaper.

Bartirome was with the Pirates for two World Series championships, in 1971 and 1979. He went to Atlanta when Chuck Tanner was fired by the Pirates after the 1985 season and became manager of the Braves. When Tanner was canned on May 23 of his third season, Bartirome was also bounced, along with coaches Willie Stargell, Al Monchak and Bob Skinner by Bobby Cox. Stargell was re-hired at the end of the season in a different capacity.

Bartirome retired from baseball after the 1988 season. He could have gone to work for the New York Yankees as a traveling secretary, but the Yankees wanted him to move to New York and live there year round. Bartirome's wife didn't want to make the move, and that was the end of that. Bartirome stays in contact with the game he loves by living in Bradenton, where the Pirates conduct their spring training. Now that Major League Baseball has expanded to Florida with the Marlins, there's even more of an opportunity for Tony to stay in touch. He enjoys reminiscing with Charley Feeney, the former Bucs' beatman for the *Post-Gazette*, who winters in Bradenton. When I talked to

Bartirome over the telephone in November of 1993, he said he had just spent some time with Feeney as well as Ron Cook, a columnist for the *Post-Gazette*, who was vacationing in Florida. Tanner telephones him from time to time. "We all stay in touch," said Bartirome.

Bartirome enjoys talking to sports writers. Bartirome enjoys talking to anybody. He was born at Magee-Womens Hospital. "I wanted to be born at home so I could be close to my mother," jokes Bartirome. He grew up in a neighborhood where people sat on their porches and stoops, and talked to each other, and swapped stories, and might share a broadcast of the Bucs' games blaring from a radio. Bartirome is a people person. He is good company. He has never taken himself too seriously. There were blacks living in his boyhood neighborhood, and he had gone to school and played ball with blacks, so it was no big deal for him. He is an amusing, obliging fellow, which is why Roberto Clemente liked him. Bartirome would do anything for a guy he genuinely cared about.

No one in the Pirates organization spent more time with Clemente than Bartirome, unless it was Bartirome's predecessor in the trainer's room, Danny Whelan. Keep Clemente's reputation as a hypochondriac in mind. Clemente was very conscious of his physical well-being, or his myriad of physical problems, and spent considerable time in the trainer's room, getting rubdowns for his aching back, for instance, or having his neck, arms, wrists, knees, ankles, you name it, attended to regularly. Bartirome put enough tape on Clemente to mummify him many times over. Clemente could have had his nameplate on the whirlpool bath tub in the clubhouse. No one was more in touch with Clemente than Bartirome. No one sounds his praises more often. The feeling was mutual. Clemente loved Bartirome. Tony the Trainer just rubbed him the right way.

"He was one of the funniest guys I've ever been around in my life," said Bartirome for openers. "Some people think of him as serious and solemn, but they didn't really know him. He was at his best with people he trusted.

"In the trainer's room, he was always laughing. He always had something going on, playing little tricks. It was a pleasure to be around him."

Clemente and Bartirome both came from humble surroundings, which helped explain why they related to each other so well. After graduation from Connelley Vocational High School in 1950, Bartirome was signed by Pie Traynor for the Pirates. As a first baseman for the Bucs, Bartirome played in 124 games in 1952 and batted .220. He managed to set a club record by not grounding into a double play during the entire season.

That was, strangely enough, the only season he played for the Pirates. He was an outstanding minor league player for ten years before winding up his career as player-coach of the Bucs' Triple A Columbus (Ohio) farm club in 1963. He then served as trainer of the Columbus team for the next three years before re-joining the Pirates in 1967.

"We suffered through some lean times," said Bartirome. "We ended up sixth in '67 and '68 and third in '69. But things really started to fall in place when Murtaugh came back in '70. Then we won it all in '71."

Bartirome and John "Hully" Hallahan, who looked after the equipment and clubhouse, were credited for creating a comfortable and loose atmosphere for the Pirates. "A lot of them hang out in the training room, and it's just a laugh a minute," Bartirome said back in 1971. "Guys who came here through trades and the minors couldn't believe our clubhouse. They're just not used to laughing and jagging around." Hallahan, who started with the Pirates as a batboy for the visiting team in 1941, came from nearby Greenfield's "Four Mile Run." Clemente was more comfortable with the so-called "little people" of the Pirates.

"I lived at 1218 Bedford Avenue," said Bartirome, "and Del Greco lived at 1414 Bedford Avenue, up near Connelley Vocational (now called Connelley Learning Skill Center at 1501 Bedford). We lived right where the Civic Arena is. They tore our places down when they built the Arena."

In that regard, Bartirome and Clemente had more in common than might meet the eye.

"He never forgot where he came from, either," Bartirome said of Clemente. "His hometown of Carolina, Puerto Rico, was close to his heart. He was a poor kid, and he always wanted to do things to help the poor people back home.

"He may have grown up poor, but he had the appearance and attitude of a king. You could put him with 10,000 guys who looked like him, but he always stood out. He had that regal attitude and look.

"We were training at Fort Myers for the first time when Clemente joined the club in 1955. I had played for the Pirates in 1952, and then I was in the U.S. Army during the Korean War. I didn't go to Korea; I was assigned to Berlin, Germany where I spent two years in 1953 and 1954. So I came back in time to be there when Clemente came to the Pirates.

"I remember him wearing a uniform number something like 50 or 55, which they would give to rookies and first-year players. I had worn No. 5 when I played for the Pirates, but when I came back they gave me No. 21.

"I was cut from the squad in spring training. I had gotten hurt in training camp, and I came back to Pittsburgh for some treatment and rehab before I was reassigned to Brunswick, Georgia. When I got to Pittsburgh, Clemente kidded me, 'Hey, Tony, I got your number!' He went on to become one of the greatest players in history. And they have since retired that number. So I can tell people the Pirates retired my number, too."

Bartirome has cherished rings to prove he was with the Pirates when they won the World Series twice in the '70s, under Murtaugh and then Tanner. But he was also on the scene when the Bucs beat the Yankees to win the World Series in 1960.

iner Tony Bartirome rubs down Roberto
nente, above, and checks out Manny San-
len's eyes.

Tony Bartirome

Tony Bartirome flexes muscles as first baseman for
Pirates, and lines up with John "Hully" Hallahan,
Pirates' clubhouse manager.

"I'd just come home from Denver, where we won the American Association championship in 1960," said Bartirome. "The minor league playoffs were over before the big league schedule was completed. So I came back home — I still have a lot of relatives in Pittsburgh — and the Pirates were right in the middle of the World Series.

"I took my girl friend — her name was Carol and she was from Greensburg — with me to the seventh game of the World Series. It was the first baseball game she ever saw. Imagine that. She didn't know anything about baseball. I'm sitting on the edge of my seat the entire game, and she's not really into it that much. We had a box seat in the second tier. When Maz came to bat in the bottom of the ninth, I was nervous. As soon as he hit the ball, I wasn't too excited. I didn't know if it was going out or not. I saw Yogi Berra going back to the wall. I'm screaming, 'It's got a chance!' My girl friend shouts to me, 'What happened?' And then the ball went out over the wall, and we all went crazy. She's screaming at me, 'What's that mean? What's that mean?' What a first date, huh? What a way to introduce her to baseball. She sat in on history. We got married and we've been together ever since. She can appreciate now what it all meant."

"He wanted to be with the fans."
— Bartirome on Clemente

Bartirome remembers when he signed with the Pirates in the winter of 1966 to return to the team as its trainer for the next season. "I went to the Dapper Dan Dinner where Clemente was getting some kind of award," said Bartirome. "I saw him, and he told me he was glad I was coming back to the ballclub. That made me feel good."

Nellie King had told me that Clemente often went out to eat on the road with Bartirome, more so than he did with most of the ballplayers.

"He was that kind of guy," said Bartirome. "He kept to himself pretty much. He was not a loner, though. He was always having fun with people. Three or four times on a road trip, he'd take me out to eat. He especially did that when we got to San Francisco. He loved seafood. He loved an Italian dish called ciappino, which consisted of all shell fish. It was cooked in a bowl with tomato sauce, and you'd have to shell all the seafood, like shrimp, clams, calimari, crab claws and pieces of lobster. It was messy, but it was great. He always wanted to go get some of that stuff. We went to the movies a lot, too. He liked to go to the movies. When he had an evening off, he'd go somewhere with Manny Sanguillen and me.

"Clemente liked to be with the people. The day they won the World Series in 1960, Clemente left the clubhouse celebration, and went outside and went to celebrate with the fans. I'm told that the players held that against him. He wanted to be with the fans. There was some feeling that he should have been with his teammates, that his place was in the clubhouse.

"He had bad feelings about the MVP voting that year. He felt un-appreciated. He never wore the ring from that World Series. He wore an All-Star Game ring instead. He said he'd never wear that World Series ring."

Bartirome talks about Clemente's physique the way a sculptor talks about marble. After all, Bartirome dug his fingers into Clemente's muscles, and had a close-up look at the physical marvel on a routine basis.

"He took care of his body," Bartirome said. "God blessed him with a magnificent body, a beautiful body. He was accused a lot of being a hypochondriac. We were in St. Louis once, and a sportswriter confront-ed me and said, 'How do you deal with that hypochondriac?' I got mad. I said, 'How could you say that?' And we got into it pretty good. 'Hey, he played more games than Honus Wagner, or anyone else who ever played for the Pirates.'"

A check of the records reveals that Clemente averaged 135 games per season over 18 years, compared to an average of 127 games a year for 17 seasons for Mazeroski, and 112 games a year for 21 seasons for Willie Stargell. Clemente went to bat 408 more times in his career than did Wagner in a similar 18 year span, 1,527 times more than Stargell and 1,699 more than Mazeroski. Clemente played one more game than Wagner in his record-setting career.

"Clemente had many real physical ailments," said Bartirome. "He had a bad back because of an automobile accident before he first report-ed to the Pirates. He picked up other ailments because of how hard he played the game, all-out, all the time. What he was was a chronic com-plainer. It was always, 'My neck . . . or my back . . . or my leg.' At the same time, he was very meticulous. He took care of his fingernails and toenails. His personal hygiene was exemplary. He didn't smoke or chew, and he only drank a little, maybe some beer or some wine on special occasions. But not much."

I had been told by others that Clemente was among the many Pirates who took amphetamines ("uppers") routinely before games whenever the Pirates played on the west coast. The Pirates would fly from St. Louis or Chicago and get in late, and have to play an afternoon game against the Dodgers or Giants. Bartirome said none of the Pirates got hooked on them, or abused them, and that it was no big deal back then. No one knew much about the side effects at the time. Bartirome preferred to talk about how Clemente was careful about his physical well-being.

"He usually came to the clubhouse early so he could take his time in the training room and relax," continued Bartirome. "He was at his best about 20 minutes before we took the field. That was the funniest time of the day. All the strangers were out of the clubhouse; the media was gone. Everyone was more relaxed.

"He used to go at it with Giusti. They used to argue violently. You'd think they were killing each other, to hear them going on. But they loved each other. And Blass would be crawling under the training table, do-ing goofy stuff. It was some scene. It was better than going to the movies.

"He was special. I remember once Clemente called a meeting in the clubhouse. Back then, only the top three or four players on the team ever were offered any money, $300 or $400, to make any appearances, or do any promotions. Now they all participate. Clemente proposed that everybody on the team would share, that all the money would be put in a pot to be divided at the end of the season. All the players and coaches would participate, and so would the trainer and the clubhouse man. Clemente said it wasn't fair that only a few got the extra money. But we had one player on that team who'd been an All-Star with another team. He said everyone should keep his own money, that it should be every man for himself. And that was the end of that idea. But Clemente always wanted to share. He was always thinking about his teammates."

I asked Bartirome how he learned of Clemente's death on New Year's Eve in 1972.

"My wife and I were living in Irwin at the time, and we had just come back from a party. Phil Dorsey called about 3 a.m. He told me Roberto was killed. I couldn't believe it. It was too hard. Poor Phil. He's in a prison in Texas. He was as close to Clemente as anyone. When Clemente came to Pittsburgh in 1955, Dorsey was the first guy outside the team to meet him. They were inseparable. They used to go up to The Hill, places like the Crawford Grill where they had live music, and certain restaurants where they'd go. Clemente used to get his hair cut at a barber shop on The Hill.

"Clemente and I got to be close. He had a great sense of humor. The guy was as funny as any comedian in Hollywood. He was very leary of the media. He was misquoted a lot of times, and they made fun of the way he spoke. They made him sound like one of those Indians in the movies. This was a proud man, and this really got to him. He had fierce pride. He was proud of being a Puerto Rican. He was proud that he served in the military service here. He was proud that he was in the Marine Corps. He trained at Parris Island in South Carolina. That was the toughest kind of training soldiers had to go through.

"I remember this one time he was late getting to the dressing room when we were playing in San Francisco. He walks to his locker, and we tell him he better hurry up and get in uniform. He said something about how fast a guy could get dressed, something he had learned in the Marine Corps. He said, 'I'll be undressed and dressed in three minutes.' I bet him he couldn't do it. And I put the clock on him. That sonuvagun was in full uniform in less than three minutes.

"A lot of times he'd run out onto the field with his pants unbuttoned, or his glove on top of his head as he pulled at his belt. And he'd be hollering, 'Where's my glove? Where's my glove?' I'm telling you, he was a funny, funny man.

"There were plenty of times he shouldn't have played. Even at 38, he was playing full tilt. Never could anyone tell me they saw Roberto Clemente loaf. He ran out every hit, no matter how small the chance to beat out a throw. Roberto Clemente was always trying to beat you. He was a proud man."

94

Pennsylvania governor and former Pittsburgh mayor David L. Lawrence talks to Cleveland Browns star Jimmy Brown and U.S. Marine Roberto Clemente prior to Dapper Dan awards dinner.

Governor David L. Lawrence, left, and *Pittsburgh Post-Gazette* sports editor Al Abrams present Roberto Clemente with Sportsman of the Year award at 1962 Dapper Dan award presentation.

Alcoa sign atop Mt. Washington offered final farewell to Roberto Clemente. This somber note contrasts drastically with joy exhibited by Clemente, leaping toward teammate Dick Groat, after scoring ahead of Hal Smith on three-run homer that gave Pirates a short-lived 9-7 lead in eighth inning of seventh game of the 1960 World Series at Forbes Field.

Dave Giusti

He kept Clemente loose

*"A lot of things I found out
about Clemente and his generosity
were after he died."*

D
ave Giusti gives credit to Roberto Clemente for his becoming
a pitcher for the Pirates in the first place, and recalls Clemente's
compassion for people down on their luck and how Clemente
came to him on occasion to boost his spirits when he was not pitching
well. In short, Clemente was a caring individual.

Giusti was the player representative for the Pirates in the early
'70s, and he remembers how several of the Latin players would take
their complaints or inquiries first to Clemente, and how Clemente would
then relay them to Giusti, with a certain firmness to make sure they
would be heard. Clemente truly cared, and he was always helping others.

"And I didn't find out how much he really did for people until after he died," Giusti admitted. "Then people came out of the woodwork
to praise him and his efforts on behalf of people who needed help.

"Joe L. Brown, our general manager, told me that Clemente recommended that the Pirates get me," said Giusti. "I was going through a
difficult period as a starting pitcher for the St. Louis Cardinals back
in 1969 — I was struggling, and didn't have a good year. I was up for
grabs and I had become trade bait. Brown was looking at several pitchers who were available around the league, and he checked with
Clemente to see what he thought of them. Brown would do that, talk
to some of his players about talent around the league. He didn't have
a know-it-all attitude. That's one of the reasons why he was such a good
general manager.

"Over the years, beginning with when I was with Houston, I had
pitched fairly decent against Clemente. I'd had some success. Maybe
he took that into consideration. In any case, Brown told me Clemente
said to get me if he could."

Giusti, a starting pitcher while with Houston and St. Louis,
switched to the bullpen for Pittsburgh when he came in 1970. His 30
saves in 1971 led the league, and he saved two games for the Pirates
in the National League Championship Series against the San Francisco Giants and one in the World Series victory over the Baltimore Orioles.

Clemente, of course, was the star of that World Series, and captured the kind of attention and national recognition he had always
sought.

"It finally took a World Series," said Giusti, "for people to say,
'Hey, this guy is one of the greatest players ever to put on a uniform.'"

Giusti earned a B.A. and an M.A. in physical education at Syra-
cuse University. Baseball players with college degrees were still as rare
on the Pirates as they were when Dick Groat came to the club from the

Duke campus in 1952. Giusti was given a great deal of respect because of his college background, and because he was such a fierce competitor. Giusti gave his all, and his teammates recognized that.

Giusti still remembers vividly how he learned that Clemente had crashed in an airplane that was enroute with supplies to earthquake-stricken Nicaragua on New Year's Eve, 1972. Giusti was at a party hosted by Steve Blass, a good friend, neighbor and teammate, when Blass received a telephone call from Joe L. Brown with the bad news.

Blass and Giusti were living in Upper St. Clair — and they remain in the same homes today — and Brown lived in nearby Mt. Lebanon.

"It was about four in the morning," said Giusti. "I don't think we said anything to anybody about what we were told. We went right over to Joe Brown's home in Mt. Lebanon. There were just the three of us. It was so shocking. You just couldn't imagine that he was gone.

"The guy was absolutely in the prime of his playing career, of his life, and had a great season and led us to the playoffs, and had his 3,000th hit. And two months later he's dead. It didn't make sense.

"You could tell it hurt Joe Brown a lot. Joe was close with his players, unlike a lot of other front office bosses. He hung out with us, and talked to us a lot. He was into the players' heads and their families and their lives. He may have been in tears at one point. He was noticeably hurt about the situation.

"We tried to get as many of our people as possible to go to Puerto Rico for the funeral. A lot of the things I found out about Clemente and his generosity were after he died, like when we went down to Puerto Rico. People would come up to me and tell me that Clemente did this and that for them, or for their kids, or for someone they knew.

"Clemente was an absolute god in Puerto Rico."

"Ginny and I were both brought up in a conservative environment. We're happy with what we have."
— Dave Giusti

Giusti had been out in his backyard before my visit, raking leaves, tidying up his garden. "I love the outdoors; I like growing things," he said. "We have raspberries back there. There's a cherry tree, and there were three deer out there this morning. They come into our yard frequently."

We were standing in the dining room of the Giusti home. There were potted flowers at the base of the bay windows, dark red roses, pink and violet geraniums, hibiscus. Ginny Giusti, Dave's wife, likes to grow things, too. She even had ivy spilling down from corner cabinets, and crawling along the baseboard. It was all very green, shiny, and clean. "Ginny can grow anything," said Dave, with more than a hint of pride. "Ginny's got a green thumb. I'm just afraid that ivy is going to make its way upstairs, and strangle me in bed some day."

Dave Giusti gets 1971 Fireman of the Year Award from 1962 winner ElRoy Face.

Dave Giusti entertains former Pirates at alumni dinner at Churchill Country Club in 1993, and visits Roberto Clemente photo exhibition at 1994 Piratefest.

Giusti stood at the window and pointed out the boundaries of his lot, about three-fourths of an acre, with woods on the outskirts. It was just past one o'clock in the afternoon in late October and the foliage was still beautiful, though many leaves had already fallen. "I just raked that, and look at it already," Giusti said with a grunt.

Ginny had just left the house an hour earlier to go to work. She has a part-time position which she shares with a friend as a receptionist for a local physician. Dave was doing his best to keep busy, to make the transition into being a gentleman farmer of sorts.

Giusti had taken an early retirement six months earlier after working nearly 12 years for American Express. He had been the corporate sales manager for Western Pennsylvania, and dealt with travel-related services. There were four mock *Time* magazine covers hailing him as Man of the Year, with four different looking faces of Dave Giusti gracing the covers. "That's one of the reasons I was able to retire," said Giusti, just 54 and 17 years removed from his days as a major league pitcher. He had played 15 years in the majors, and was now drawing on a sizable baseball pension as well as a company retirement fund.

Giusti could afford to take it easy for awhile, and then decide what he ultimately wanted to do.

Giusti, Blass and Kent Tekulve, another Pirates pitcher who lives in Upper St. Clair, have all been careful with their money. They all have nice suburban homes, but nothing spectacular. They are not living in mansions. "I never saw any reason to be house poor," said Giusti. "People often overextend themselves in that area. Ginny and I were both brought up in a conservative environment. We're happy with what we have.

"We could have afforded a house three times this size, but we always liked this place. Now the girls are gone and we don't need anything bigger. We're just ten miles from the city. We have always had good neighbors, and we've always been comfortable here."

Just a few nights earlier, Giusti had gone to see the Upper St. Clair High School football team play Canon-McMillan, because he wanted to watch the home team's outstanding quarterback, Mike Tomko. Giusti does not go to many local games. In fact, he got kidded by his buddies about being there. "I'm not a spectator," he said. "I went because I've worked with Mike a little as a pitcher, and his parents have asked me to give him a little guidance as far as college and his athletic choices are concerned. The parents are super people. They're the kind of neighbors I'm talking about."

There were items on display in the Giusti kitchen calling attention to Dave's skills as a cook — he likes to fool around in the kitchen — and there were family photos on display everywhere one looked, including on the doors and the top of the refrigerator.

The Giustis have two daughters, both living away from home. Laura, 28, was in her fifth year of a doctoral program in clinical psychology at the University of Kansas in Lawrence, Kansas. Cynthia, 24, was teaching in Penn Hills, a suburb just east of Pittsburgh.

Giusti didn't have much baseball memorabilia on display in his family room/office. There were a few gold-plated bowls he had been awarded by the Dapper Dan organization, and a few knickknacks he'd picked up during his days in the big leagues. There was a prized plaque he had received as a participant in the 1973 All-Star Game in Kansas City. "That was a big thrill," he said.

There were decorative bats fashioned by his father, with the autographs of former teammates, on display on the wall, along with a framed photo of him with Willie Stargell, a going-away gift with a hand-written message from Stargell.

He didn't have a photo of him with Clemente. "I wish I did, but I didn't worry about stuff like that back then," he said.

Giusti learned woodwork from his father, and enjoys making knickknacks, serving bowls and tables, and such. He pointed out his handiwork. He also offered a strong home-made wine sent to him by his uncle. It had been made with grapes grown in Giusti's native upstate New York. "It's strong, all right, almost like a cognac," said Giusti, smiling when I coughed after taking a sip. "You have to sip it slowly."

I asked Giusti how he pitched to Clemente. "I pitched to him like I did with a lot of other guys," said Giusti. "I threw him fastballs away, and palm balls over the plate, and he'd be out in front of it. I'd sneak a fastball outside.

"I learned very early not to throw him inside."

I interrupted Giusti here, and mentioned that Bob Purkey had told me that same morning that he'd been successful pitching to Clemente because he kept coming inside on him. "Yeah, but Purkey had a knuckleball; that's different," said Giusti, not missing a beat.

"Everyone told me you gotta throw him low and away. He stood so far away from the plate, and deep in the corner. I got him out a few times with a fastball inside. But, once at Forbes Field in a critical situation, I did that and he hit a three-run homer off me.

"We seldom beat Pittsburgh when I was at Houston. But this is a game, in the mid-60s, we could've won. I went inside with a fastball — I'd gotten away with it before — and he went inside and outside, and hit it over the screen in right-center field. He taught me a lesson on that one. Overall, my pitching record against the Pirates was 8-7.

"I worried more about some other Pirates, more so than Clemente. He didn't kill me the way Willie Stargell or Donn Clendenon could. Clemente didn't stand out with that club. They had so many guys who could hurt you. But if you made a mistake with Clemente he was going to hit you hard. I was fortunate; he didn't hurt me that much. I'd hang a slider to guys like Clendenon and Dick Stuart and those guys hurt me a lot."

How did Giusti come to be comfortable with Clemente, or how did the relationship take root?

"It was a slow type of thing," conceded Giusti, "to be able to relate to him or to have conversations with him. I had a poor spring

101

training when I first joined the Pirates, and they made me a relief pitcher. I kept my mouth shut — I just wanted to stay with the ballclub — and I was reserved in that respect.

"I was doing middle relief the first few weeks. I started getting confidence and found my way with the guys in the clubhouse. I became the player rep for the club. That first year, by mid-season I felt comfortable, and I started to look into what Clemente was made of.

"A lot of guys would try to get Clemente to participate in things. Talking to other people, I learned that he really started to enjoy the players on the team at about that stage in his career. He could participate in the kidding around that went on, the foolishness. He'd been a small portion of it up until then. In the early years, he was not a participant at all, I was told.

"More and more, he was approachable. Just sitting down and talking to him. There was still such a sense of his being a super star, and he carried himself proudly, and he was a little standoffish at times. But he became more interested in his surroundings, in the players around him.

"He'd come to me once in a while, and ask me about different facets of the pension plan, for example, or about benefits. He'd say, 'Hey, you may want to bring this up at the next meeting.' Some of the Latin players like Jose Pagan and Matty Alou would go to him, and then he'd tell me what was on their minds.

"Clemente's problems with the press hurt his image, I think. Other than the people who adored him as a ballplayer, a lot of people were critical of him for one reason or another, feeling he sat down too quickly when he was hurting, stuff like that.

"He had this feeling of — not guilt, but something like that — because he wasn't able to speak the language real well. But the things he did for people, or for teammates, showed his true spirit.

"In 1971, when I was doing so poorly as a reliever, there was a period of two weeks or more when I didn't pitch well. He came over to me and talked to me for about ten or fifteen minutes. He talked about life in general, about family, and he tried to bring out the belief that baseball wasn't the end all in our lives, that we had to make sure we kept things in balance. He wanted you to make sure you kept them in the right order: like family and your wife. He wanted us to remember that these were the most important things. He didn't have to come over and talk to me, but he did.

"I lost a game one night and he stayed around, until it was just him and me and 'Hully' (clubhouse man John Hallahan's nickname, pronounced Hoo-lie). He did things like that.

"When I felt so bad after the last game of the 1972 playoffs, Clemente came over and talked to me. Everyone was down, but he got after all of us. He hollered, 'This is not the end of the world. We'll be back next season.' He told us to keep our chins up, to carry our heads high."

Here's what happened in Game 5 of the 1972 playoffs that Giusti was talking about: Giusti got the call to pitch in the ninth inning with the Pirates leading, 3-2, and just three outs away from winning the National League pennant again.

Giusti had been a successful closer in the third game. He combined with Nelson Briles and Bruce Kison in a 3-2 win in that one. But he was not equal to the challenge for the pivotal game. Johnny Bench was the first batter he faced, and Bench hit a home run over the right field wall to tie the score. Tony Perez and Dennis Menke both followed with singles, and Giusti got the hook.

Bob Moose came on to replace Giusti and faced Cesar Geronimo. Geronimo flied out to right, and on the play George Foster, running for Perez, raced to third. That made a big difference in the final outcome. Then Darrell Chaney popped up to short. The game was one out from going to extra innings.

But with Hal McRae at the plate, Moose threw a pitch that Giusti said hit the front of the plate, and skipped under catcher Manny Sanguillen's glove, and went all the way to the base of the screen. Foster scored from third on the wild pitch and the Pirates' season was over.

"Everyone remembers Moose's wild pitch, but I had let the game get away from us. I felt like the goat," Giusti said. Giusti always took losses hard.

He still does, even when he's playing platform tennis.

Bob Smizik captured the moment in this manner in his book, *The Pittsburgh Pirates — An Illustrated History*: "Giusti, always the team's hardest loser, was slumped at his stool in front of his locker. For so long it had been Giusti who railed at Clemente to bring him out of his shell. Now the roles were reversed.

"'Giusti! Damn you, Giusti! Look straight ahead! Pick up your head! We don't quit now! We go home and come back in February!'"

Steve Blass followed Clemente's lead and got after everyone. When the team returned to Pittsburgh from Cincinnati that night, everyone went to a party at the home of pitcher Bob Johnson in Upper St. Clair. It was the last time, for most of the Pirates, that they would ever see Clemente alive.

"I was with Clemente for three years," Giusti went on during my visit to his home. "He really enjoyed himself as a player when I was with him. He became more outspoken, and participated in the tomfoolery in the clubhouse. We could kid with him.

"He could put on his uniform in less than two minutes before a game, and come out on the field, buttoning his blouse and pulling up his pants. We'd make fun of him for doing that.

"He and Doc Finegold were good friends. They spent a lot of time together. Clemente was also close to our trainer, Tony Bartirome. He always had Bartirome rubbing his neck, or his shoulders, or his back, you name it. Tony would be working on his back, and Steve Blass and I would come in and get on them both.

"Steve said and did some funny things. Clemente would be on the training table, and Steve would sneak under the table. I always started some stuff with him, getting him involved, through Doc Finegold.

"Steve Blass's humor in the clubhouse was unmatched. He was a terrific mimic. Perfect. He could do Robert Kennedy. He could do Manny Sanguillen. He could do Roberto Clemente — not just the way he moved but the way he talked. Clemente loved it. Lots of other stuff. It all made for looseness and togetherness. Because of Steve, the clubhouse was never completely silent, even after a loss."

Dave Giusti used palmball as ace relief pitcher in early '70s.

Harry J Walker

Clemente had his most productive seasons when Harry Walker was Pirates' manager.

Malcolm W. Emmons

Roberto Clemente takes lead against Dodgers' first baseman Wes Parker.

Pirates Hall of Fame hitting instructor George Sisler speaks to Clemente.

Bob Skinner

ob Skinner, Bill Virdon and Clemente pose for picture at Fort Myers, Florida during spring
aining camp in late '50s.

Danny Murtaugh
A smart manager

Some quotes about Roberto

There was always thought to be a rift between Roberto Clemente and Danny Murtaugh, his manager. "Clemente's Clemente," said Murtaugh when asked about their relationship. "He's the best player I've ever seen. I'm old enough, I'm intelligent and I think I'm smart enough to get along with anybody on our ballclub — especially if he's a .350 hitter."

After Clemente's death:

"Two catches Roberto made stand out in my mind. Each came at the risk of great personal injury and each had a vital part in the winning of a pennant although they were 11 years apart. We were in a scoreless tie with the New York Giants in Forbes Field late in the 1960 season when Willie Mays tagged one. Roberto turned his back on the ball and raced back, knowing he could not avoid crashing into an unpadded wall. He still made the catch, saved the game and wound up with a dozen stitches in his chin.

"Late in a tie game with Houston during our present drive of 1971, Bob Watson hit one deep along the right field line. Two were out and the winning run was on its way home when Roberto tore across the field at full speed and made the catch as he crashed into the wall. He was knocked groggy, but still had hit a game-winning home run in the next inning. When he was approaching his 3,000th hit, I asked him if that would be the most important thing in his life. 'No, Danny,' he said. 'I have a project going in Puerto Rico for the underprivileged and I have made so much progress with the political men in our country that I'm beginning to think my dream will come true.' That's the Roberto Clemente I know who constantly thought of others instead of himself."

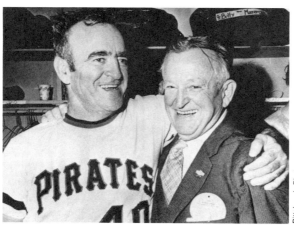

Danny Murtaugh
draws big smile
from Pirates owner
John Galbreath in 1971.

Pittsburgh Pirates

108

Nellie King
The Story-Teller

*"Latins are a very proud people.
Pride is what killed him."*

Nellie King can't help himself. He has to tell stories. King is an incorrigible raconteur. He can tell a story at the drop of a name, any name, and particularly about Pirates of the past. He takes great pride in knowing the likes of Elbie Fletcher, Carlos Bernier, Clem Koshorek, Dino Restelli, George Metkovich, Felipe Montemayor, Gene Freese and Toby Atwell. The list is nearly as long as the Pirates all-time roster, or King's still lanky six foot-six frame.

"Joe L. Brown never understood that when he fired Bob Prince — and me in the process — that he was tossing out a tie to the Pirates of the past, the team's tradition, its history," said King. "Prince was a link to Rosey Rowswell and all that. No one understood the story of the Pirates as well as Prince. It was by far the worst move Brown ever made."

Prince and King were the last Pirates broadcasters who could tell stories, who could swap yarns, who had a comic's timing, and knew instinctively where to start a story, and when to provide the punch line. It's an art form. Prince was, indeed, a Pittsburgh institution. One on one, they were animated in their conversation, enthusiastic in their story-telling. They commanded your attention. A Prince and a King can do that.

King was a pitcher for the Pirates from 1954 to 1957, and a broadcaster as a sidekick to Bob Prince for nine years from 1967 to 1975, and for a shorter spell during that same time with Jim Woods. They were a tough trio to beat. King began his radio career in 1960 with WSSH Radio in Latrobe, and then WHJB in Greensburg.

His radio career began the same season that the Pirates would win the World Series in 1960. He remembers taking his tape recorder to Forbes Field and interviewing players from the Pirates and Yankees before the Series started, and asking several of them who they thought would be the hero of the World Series.

"Most of them said Mickey Mantle or Roger Maris, or maybe Roberto Clemente or Dick Groat," recalled King. "But I remember that Harvey Haddix said he thought Bill Mazeroski would be the hero. When I asked him why, he said, 'I don't know. I just think he will be.' And, of course, Haddix was right on the mark."

King considered himself a close friend of Clemente. King's first full season with the Pirates was 1955, the same year that Clemente came to the team, and became a confidant of Clemente when he returned to the Pirates as a member of the KDKA broadcasting team. This prompted my visit to King's three bedroom split level red brick home in Mt. Lebanon, a suburb about ten miles southeast of Pittsburgh, in

Pittsburgh Pirates

early November of 1993. His yard was covered with fallen leaves, soaked flat from several days of snow and rain. King could only shake his head when he surveyed a task that awaited his attention.

He had retired a few months earlier, at age 65, after serving 18 years as the sports information director at Duquesne University. He planned to continue as coach of the school's golf team, and as a color commentator on radio broadcasts of Dukes basketball. His three daughters, Laurie, Leslie and Amy, all gained degrees from Duquesne during his stay there, and his wife, Bernadette Earl, took advantage of the tuition waiver for family members by obtaining a master's degree. She had recently resumed working in the mental health field.

No sooner had I stepped into the home of Nellie King than he started telling me a story. Bernadette was watching a CNN report on TV about destructive wild fires in California, and Nellie thought we would be better off retreating to the kitchen where he could tell stories till I ran out of ink or paper.

But before we left the family room, King told me a story about Dick Stuart.

"Stuart came to spring training with the Pirates in 1957," recalled King. "He had hit 66 home runs the year before in Lincoln, Nebraska in the Western Association, and he was up for a look-see. He didn't stick with the Pirates, but he certainly made an impression.

"We were playing the Cincinnati Reds in an exhibition at Tampa. Before the game, we were asked to sign some baseballs. Stuart signed in a spot on the baseball where the seams come closest together that was traditionally reserved for the manager or the star of the team.

"Not only did he sign there, but he added a star at the end of his name and wrote in '66' above his name. He has signed his name that way ever since. Some of the veterans on the team, like Dick Groat, were put off by Stuart's brashness. They were saying, 'Who the hell does this guy think he is? He didn't even play in Triple A last year.'

"So Stuart goes up to bat the first time. He connected and hit a ball that looked like a 2-iron shot in golf. It just took off low and kept rising. It went out over the outfield wall with room to spare. As Stuart was running around the bases, Groat and some of the other guys, told everyone on the bench not to acknowledge what Stuart had done. 'Don't pat him on the back or ass, or anything like that,' growled Groat. 'Don't show him any emotion.' So Stuart comes into the dugout and walks the length of it, and no one said anything to him. When he got to the end of the bench, he turned back and addressed all the guys, 'You don't have to say anything, boys. You're gonna see a lot more like that from Big Dick Stuart.' He always thought a lot of himself. He never changed."

Reporters were put off as well by Stuart's cockiness. They felt the same way when Roberto Clemente came to the team. Clemente knew he was good, and often voiced his belief that he was one of the best at what he did. He had great pride in his ability. He came from a different culture, and his confidence was misunderstood by most people he encountered in Pittsburgh.

King may have told the story about Stuart to show that all hot-shot rookies were treated the same way by veterans, that they were expected to be humble, and seldom heard from, that they were expected to respect their elders, and not stick out. They were not expected to blow their own horn.

"The biggest misunderstanding with Clemente was not that he was black, but that he was a Latin," allowed King. "We didn't understand Latins.

"Latins are a very proud people. Pride is what killed Clemente. He had such pride in everything he did. And he wanted everything he was associated with to be done right. He flew in that plane to Nicaragua because he had heard that the food and supplies were not going to the people who needed it the most. He wanted to make sure the relief effort for the earthquake victims was carried out properly. If Clemente was in charge of the relief effort, he would lead the effort. He was never an honorary chairman of anything.

"If somebody pays you a compliment in Puerto Rico, you accept it, and say 'Thank you very much,' and then you say why you are deserving of such a compliment. If someone told him 'You are one of the greatest ballplayers,' Roberto would smile and say, 'Thank you,' and then tell why he thought he was. He didn't understand that wasn't the way ballplayers in this country would handle it. In the United States, if a guy gives you a compliment, you play the humility game. 'Nah, I don't deserve that kind of praise.' Humble pie stuff. In Puerto Rico, you have to support what they said. He knew he was good. No one ingratiated themselves to people more than I did, so I know how to play the humble role. I had grown up in an orphanage, so I was always trying to please people, and be accepted.

"I don't remember a lot about Clemente in his rookie year. I saw him for the first time at spring training in 1955. But I was worried only about myself that spring. I was like a guy trying to learn how to swim. You don't see anyone else in the water. You're just trying to survive. Oh, I knew he had raw talent. He could run and hit and throw the ball. You could see that right away.

"He was focused on finding his place on the team, his place in base-ball. He used to tell me, 'My first year in the big leagues, I was so scared. I'd stand out in right field, and I was so scared. I couldn't see anything but the batter. I was so nervous. I wanted to make sure I didn't make a mistake. Little by little, I could see the first baseman, then the second baseman, and shortstop. Then I began to see the whole picture.'

"Clemente came up at a different time. In my first and second years with the Pirates, I remember that black players couldn't even stay at the Chase Hotel with the rest of the team when we played in St. Louis. It was that time. It was a white man's game. The Pirates had their first black player, Curt Roberts, in 1954. The Pirates signed him seven years after Jackie Robinson broke the color line with the Brooklyn Dodgers.

"Guys like Face and Mazeroski had almost an *animosity* toward Clemente. It upset them when he would sit out a game because of an injury or ailment. Maz always felt that Clemente, at 70 percent, could do more than Maz and most of the guys could when they were 100 percent. You couldn't keep Maz and Face out of a game, no matter how they were feeling, but Clemente was different. Even when Bill was in a batting slump, he felt he could help the team win with his work in the field. He came from a different background.

"Clemente, to me, was like an artist. Artistic people have greater sensitivities. They're different, whether you're talking about Van Gogh or Gore Vidal. They see, feel and hear things differently.

"Clemente's sensitivity was toward his body. It was his cathedral. At age 38, he was still in great shape. If he hadn't died, there's no doubt in my mind that he could have made good on his desire to play another four or five years. Why couldn't he? In 1972, he was playing for the best team in baseball, and on that team he had the best arm, was the best base runner, and was probably still the best hitter."

King wasn't just talking. Clemente had hit .312 that year, .341 the year before, and .350 the year before that. As sports writer Bob Smizik put it, "In the outfield he was still the master."

King said that Clemente kept a book on his injuries and ailments. "Prince and I went to Puerto Rico once to present Clemente with a silver bat, and to participate in a special recognition ceremony," recalled King. "Clemente told me about the log he kept. He said, 'I knew what part of my body would be weaker, and what I had to do during the off-season to correct that.'

"Roberto also tried to get Mazeroski to stay in baseball longer. Bill was having problems with his weight, and just thought he couldn't continue to fight the battle anymore. It was in his genes. His mother was very overweight, and Bill battled his weight from start to finish. Clemente told him, 'Cash is OK, and Stennett is OK, but you're still a better second baseman. You can come down to Puerto Rico with me and get in shape.' Bill told him, 'Roberto, I still think I can play, but I can't fight this weight thing anymore.' Maz had his own pride. But he didn't understand the pride thing with Clemente.

"Clemente was painting a picture every time he played. He didn't want to play unless he could perform at his absolute best."

Didn't he and Danny Murtaugh clash over this from time to time?

"Murtaugh and Clemente never really got along that well, but they had talks from time to time, and would reach truces. Murtaugh was pretty good at it, too. To be a good manager, I think you have to be a good father and a good card player. Murtaugh was both.

"I remember him telling us once, 'I'm not much for meetings. I am for sitting and watching, and some of the things I see I don't like.' He set the limits. He found out what guys could do. Good parents never put kids in a position where they'll be embarrassed.

"The biggest change occurred with our club after Branch Rickey and Fred Haney gave way to Joe L. Brown and Bobby Bragan. They got rid of the unhappy people on the Pirates. When I was there in 1954 and 1955, there were a lot of older guys who didn't want to help you. They were strictly out for themselves.

"Dale Long came to our team in 1955, and the following year he hit home runs in eight consecutive games, and personally lifted the team. He was one of the best leaders I have ever been around. He had more leadership ability than anyone I've ever seen on any team, even in the years I broadcasted. He was a real stand-up, out-front guy. I really admired him. He was like a Big Daddy to us. He changed the whole attitude inside the club. The attitude on the team had been, 'We're happy to be here.' He changed it to 'We can play with these guys. Let's go get them.'

"So the atmosphere wasn't the best when Clemente first came to the club. When Clemente flowered, it was when he got away from the 1960 championship team. I think there was a misunderstanding about him that stuck with him, as far as his willingness to gut it out and play when he had minor ailments or injuries. There was almost an animosity toward him because he didn't play under certain conditions. It was a bum rap on him. He was always trying to fight that image. Eventually, he was playing with guys who didn't know him from 1960. He became the club leader and the younger players looked up to him.

"He no longer had to put up with that doubt about his desire and dedication. It wasn't until 1969 that he and Maz got along well. Maz started to understand what he was talking about, and what he was all about.

"Murtaugh could never quite understand Clemente. When Murtaugh came back to the team after Larry Shepard was let go, to manage the team for the 1970 season, he had a meeting in the clubhouse with Clemente. 'We do not get along,' Clemente told him. 'I'll play for you. I'll respect you as a manager.' There were others who mocked Clemente as well whenever he took himself out of the lineup. I heard more than one remark where someone said, 'The super nigger isn't playing today.'

"Bob Prince didn't understand Clemente, at first, but then again Bob and I got off to a rocky start as well. He didn't like having a former jock joining him in the broadcast booth. He thought a professional radio broadcaster should have the job. I put up with that for awhile, but then he made me look bad once, and I told him if he ever did it again I'd punch him in the mouth. It was good that we cleared the air. After that, he changed in the way he treated me. I had been playing an obsequious role. That came from my childhood, being in an orphanage, feeling neglected as a kid, being alone is a tough way to grow up. I wanted to belong. I told Prince off because I decided I was either getting into the business in earnest, or I was getting out for good. We had a much better situation after that.

"Clemente was breaking new ground in Pittsburgh. He was breaking a different kind of ground than Jackie Robinson. In his last year, at age 38, Clemente was still playing first-rate baseball. Stargell looked up to him, and so did Al Oliver. Giusti was amazed with him.

"I'll tell you a story about Clemente that tells you the kind of exceptional guy he was. In 1972, after the World Series he had the season before, Clemente became a marketable person. People on Madison Avenue were taking aim at him.

115

Nellie King can get a laugh out of Steve Blass anyplace, but former Steelers coach Chuck Noll is a different challenge. King got a laugh out of everyone when he spoke at alumni gathering at Churchill Country Club, including, (from left to right) Bill Virdon, Bob Friend, ElRoy Face, Noll, Dave Giusti, Frank Thomas, Blass and Andy Kosco.

"Eastern Airlines got fascinated with him. They had a big luncheon in his honor in New York, and talked about investing in and promoting a Roberto Clemente City in Puerto Rico, helping Clemente to realize a dream to do something special for the kids, especially the poor kids, in his native land. He wanted to help the kids in the ghettos.

"Eastern Airlines hosted this event at the Marriott Hotel at the southern end of Central Park. I was talking to an ad executive at the luncheon, and I told him, 'If you use Clemente, you're not just getting his name. He'll get involved.' I sat with Clemente on the bus going to Shea Stadium that day. I told him what I told the guy from the ad agency. Clemente told me that the guy had gone to him later. 'It's funny, Nellie, the guy offered me an envelope,' he told me. 'This is a partial payment for your agreement with us.' Clemente turned it down. He said he told the man, 'I will take your check after you do everything you say you will do. Not until then.' He told me, 'Nellie, once they give you the check then they've got you by the balls.' That tells you about the depth of the guy. Other guys would take the check and run.

"When Willie Mays was traded by the Giants to the New York Mets, Clemente thought it was a tragedy. He thought it was awful that a man of Mays' stature would be swapped that way. Clemente told me he told Joe Brown, 'Do not ever try to do that to me. Do not ever trade me for money. If you do, I want 80 percent of the money and you take 20 percent. You are my agent. I want my share of it, if you ever try to sell me.' No one ever thought that Brown tried to trade Clemente at any time."

Nellie King is flanked by Vernon Law and ElRoy Face and young pitching prospects at Fort Myers, Florida spring training.

117

Love Letter
From Altadena

"Roberto was the only Pirate who would play pepper with me."

From Jim Rubel, a fan in Altadena, California:

This Pittsburgh-born and bred (Homewood) Pirates fan and 1957 Central Catholic High School grad enlisted in the U.S. Air Force to see the world and saw 3.5 years of a quartermaster camp at Fort Lee, Virginia.

I jumped up on the barracks chair after Ralph Terry threw a high slider for a 1-0 count. I yelled, "The only thing Maz can hit is a high fastball!" a moment before the Pirates became the 1960 World Series champions.

TV didn't cut away in the middle of the ninth inning. I watched Terry throw eight straight high warmup pitches to Johnny Blanchard who kept coming up out of his catcher's crouch to glove the ball. That set the stage for the best City of Pittsburgh party and celebration I ever missed.

Your book (*MAZ And The '60 Bucs*) changed my cherished opinion that Mickey Mantle made the greatest clutch base running play in World Series history to keep the seventh game alive. So much for historicity. . .

It was interesting to read Rocky Nelson's account that the Mick could have strolled into second. I had thought Mantle made a brilliant base-running play when he broke toward second, spun and returned under Rocky Nelson's tag at first base to keep the Series alive for the Yankees. Mick said he thought it was a line out. I had thought Rocky Nelson was maneuvering into a better throwing angle for throwing to second base for the tag-out and was surprised to learn Dick Groat wasn't covering! Where was Maz?

I'm discovering history is more reliable than it used to be. One major mystery remains: Why did kamikaze pilots wear helmets?

I'll never forget the wonderful summers in the 1950s I spent shagging fly balls and drinking free pop in the Pirates clubhouse with Pie Traynor and George Sisler who conducted the workouts. Sam Narron was a regular and Clyde McCullough, a keen judge of character, loaned me his catcher's glove after inquiring, "You won't steal my glove will you, kid?" I weighed almost as much as his glove.

A batting practice pitcher by the name of Smith would give me a ride to the ballyard from Braddock and Forbes Avenues. Roberto was the only Pirate who would play pepper with me. He would say, "Throw dee bull, keed!" I loved and admired him. I read where Clyde died in San Francisco a year or two ago.

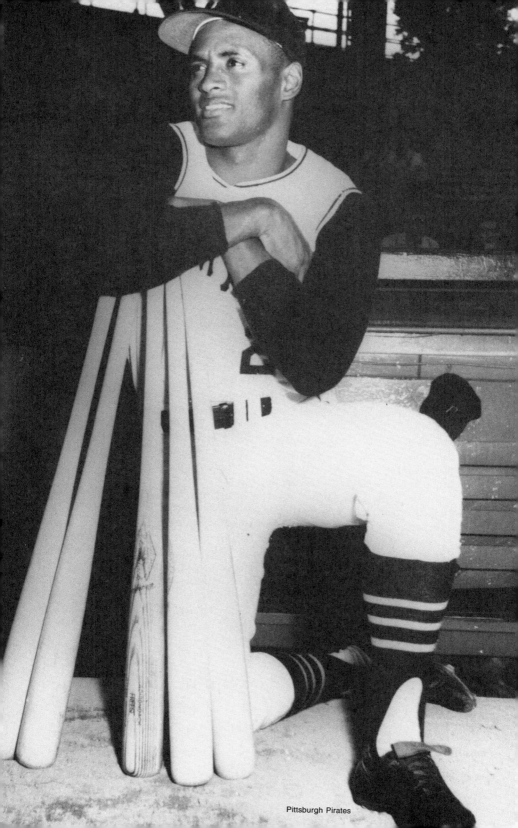

Pittsburgh Pirates

Joltin' Joe DiMaggio has his 56-game streak and I have mine. One season when the Pirates played 77 home games, I sneaked into or got an occasional pass to 56 ball games at Forbes Field. My dad knew Mr. Joe Dolan in the Pirates press cage who would write on whatever he could find, "Let this kid in." Signed, Joe Dolan.

Forbes Field forever: Forbes Field was my second home. To borrow from Thomas Boswell, *Washington Post* baseball writer, "There are two kinds of people in the world — those that go to batting practice and those that don't. Only the former have any chance of becoming anything significant."

The Homewood Knot-Holers developed sneaking into Forbes Field into an art form. We refined more ingenious (to us) ploys and mapped multiple devious routes into the show, and when our game plans were thwarted, we knew the gates opened to let you in for free in the seventh inning.

From the general admission right field stands, we discovered if we climbed 45 feet up a girder we could reach the roof behind the third tier. We could run across the roof to the back door of the men's room adjoining the third tier concession stand. That was our grand entrance and ticket to the field box and reserved seats.

I saw Pirate Ted Beard hit what I thought was a foul ball pop-up down the line that disappeared over the right field roof for a home run. I read about Babe Ruth's last home run that cleared the right field roof for the first time in Forbes Field history.

I wondered why a Pirate rookie was bouncing baseballs off the right field wall during the summer mini-camps conducted by George Sisler and Pie Traynor. That season I saw No. 21 run the opposite way on a ball that bounced off the wall near the 300 foot foul line. Clemente fielded the ball on one hop, whirled and threw a perfect knee-high strike to second base where the runner was tagged out while busy congratulating himself on his stand-up double.

Does anyone remember the Sunday "End Of The World Game" with the Cincinnati Reds at Forbes Field? Ewell "The Whip" Blackwell was pitching for the Reds when the skies darkened. The smell of smoke permeated Forbes Field. Soot rained down. The lights were turned on. Some fans panicked and bolted the ballpark. Having made nine First Fridays at Holy Rosary, I calmly remained until the ballgame was called.

The Pittsburgh Press and *Sun-Telegraph* both reported a forest fire in Canada was responsible for the acrid, yellowish smoke. Personally, I think a UFO crashed and burned in Schenley Park. They didn't have those U.S. Army Nike sites around Pittsburgh protecting our beloved Bucs, Steelers and Hornets for nothing.

Harold "Pie" Traynor

Joe DiMaggio

Clemente with The Yankee Clipper, Joe DiMaggio

Remember Roberto

*"I couldn't think of a better
role model than Clemente."*

Neil Capretto
Director of Treatment
Gateway Rehabilitation Center
Aliquippa, Pennsylvania

"I was born in 1955, Clemente's rookie season with the Pirates. On my birthday, my wife gave me a gift of his rookie card and his last card, and a big picture of him that is signed by him. But I think it's a print, not an authentic autograph. I do work with athletes with problems at Gateway. When I think of someone of the caliber of Clemente, and his maturity, and what a role model he was, it's quite a contrast to what I deal with at Gateway. I have two boys and I couldn't think of a better role model than Clemente. I looked up to those guys like they were larger than life. I think of Clemente and Maz, and the way they were is mostly lost today. I see guys with home problems, guys who are overwhelmed with problems. They're self-absorbed. They don't think the rules of life apply to them. People are always doing them favors, and they come to expect it, and depend on it. They get hooked on alcohol or drugs. They come in for tests and think they can beat the tests. They think they can get through without being caught because they're so superhuman."

Jim Perch
Pittsburgh

"I was a 16-year-old student at Keystone Oaks High School, and my mother was calling me and I couldn't figure out why. It was New Year's Day. There was no school. She told me Roberto Clemente was killed. I said 'that can't be.' I thought he wasn't in the plane, or that somehow they'd find him. But they didn't. And I went to my room and cried."

Frank Meleni, Jr.
Quality Control Inspector
Jefferson Boro

"My father was the fire chief's driver, and he used to drive the chief to ballgames at Forbes Field. Back in 1967 or 1968, my father managed to get one of Roberto Clemente's bats. I went to a special promotion at Hardee's on Route 51 and had Clemente autograph the bat. I remember it was a Louisville bat, and it was varnished half way down and then clear, just natural wood, at the bottom. It didn't have a head or knob at the end of it. It was just tapered toward the bottom of the bat like bellbottom pants. It had his number — 21 — written at the bottom of it with a black magic marker. I had it with me for a full year, and I brought it out to show it to everybody. Then, like a fool, I started using it to play in sandlot baseball games, and I broke it in half, and threw it away. What would it have been worth today if I had taken care of it?"

William Adams
Monroeville

"My daughter Dawn was 13 when he died. She went upstairs when she learned that Clemente had been killed in an airplane crash. She was crying when she came back downstairs. She brought her piggy bank with her. She got the money out and she asked me to write a check in the amount she had saved and send it to Clemente's fund for his Sports City in Puerto Rico. And that's what we did. She lives in Milwaukee now, and every time we go to Milwaukee she wants to go to a baseball game. It's kind of a ritual. She loved sitting out in the left field bleachers at Forbes Field and hearing the old guys talk about the past. She'd lean over the fence and look into the bullpen. You were closer to the players back then. That was the true beauty of Forbes Field."

Carnegie Library of Pittsburgh

Bullpens were located behind fence when Greenberg Gardens were located in left field at Forbes Field.

"Whenever death comes
to a public figure —
a politician, a movie star,
an athlete — it is always
shocking because they seem
to be a part of our lives
and when they die
a little of us seems
to die with them."
— Joe Falls
Detroit Free Press

Frank Thomas
He nearly became a priest

*"I was probably one of the greatest
agitators in the history of baseball."*

A light rain fell on the face of Frank Thomas as he surveyed what remains of the outfield wall of Forbes Field. He was standing like a sentry on the Schenley Park side of the center field wall, the side that is scarred by mostly indecipherable graffiti.

Thomas did not say anything about the graffiti or the rain. Maybe he did not even notice the graffiti or the rain. Perhaps he saw the scene the way it was when he played left field for the Pirates, from 1951 to 1958. It is easy enough to let one's mind drift back to those days when the ballyard was the big magnet in Oakland. After all, he had played ball in the rain before.

He pointed across what is now Clemente Drive, a street that runs from Bouquet Street to the Schenley Plaza, a street that runs through what was once the middle of the outfield at Forbes Field, a street that runs between the Joseph M. Katz Graduate School of Business and Forbes Quadrangle on the University of Pittsburgh campus, and he pointed to a marker on the sidewalk. "That's where the 406 foot marker was in left field," he said.

That, of course, is where he once worked, where he is best remembered for playing for the Pirates. He also played third base and first base for the Bucs. He later played for the Reds (including four games as a second baseman), the Cubs, the Braves — he would come back to play for the Cubs and Braves for second stints — the Astros and the original 1962 Mets under the master, Casey Stengel. He hit 34 home runs for the Mets that first year. "But I think of myself as a Pirate," he said as we stood by the wall.

That plaque on the sidewalk along Clemente Drive also marks the spot where Bill Mazeroski's home run sailed over the left field wall to win the 1960 World Series. It sailed over the head of Yogi Berra, as trivia experts recall. This was mid-November, 1993, and the ivy on the center field wall was drying up, turning burgundy, and its leaves dropping off for the winter. I had been there only a month before, joining about twenty-five fans who came out to the wall on October 13 to listen to a tape of the broadcast of that memorable 7th Game of the 1960 World Series. Back then, the ivy was green and gleaming in a mid-day sun.

Many Pittsburghers make frequent pilgrimages to what remains of the wall from Forbes Field, taking their children, just to remind themselves of their own youth, of earlier days in their lives, telling them what they saw when their eyes were as young as their children's. Going back to the wall takes them back to the best of days, and it was no different for Frank Thomas.

Frank Thomas stands on the clean side of wall that remains from Forbes Field. Other side is scarred with graffiti.

Frank J. Thomas

"I was in left, Virdon was in centerfield, and Clemente in right field," said Thomas. "That's a pretty good outfield. I was with Roberto for four seasons, 1955, 1956, 1957 and 1958, and he played his position well. He was a master at what he did.

"Clemente is going down in history as one of the all-time great Pirates. They are honoring him with a statue. I don't know if that's the right thing to do. We had some great ballplayers here, like Kiner, Traynor, the Waner Brothers, Arky Vaughan, and they only have a statue for Wagner right now. But it's a big business now, and it's going to be tied in with the All-Star Game. It'll be one big week of promotion. But the bottom line is that I was glad to have the opportunity to be one of his teammates. I played with one of the greatest in baseball.

"I had his son, Roberto Jr., with the Little Pirates. We were up in Phillipsburg for a doubleheader and I was coaching the team. He kinda dogged it in the first game, and had a bad attitude. In the second game, he came in as a relief pitcher and did well. I took him aside and said, 'Your dad wouldn't have liked what you did.' He apologized to the rest of the team for the way he acted. He was fine after that. I think he went five-for-seven in another doubleheader. I thought he was going to be a ballplayer. But he didn't quite make it. It's tough to be the son of a great ballplayer."

Did seeing the wall, and being out where the ballpark used to be, spark any special emotions or memories?

"Sure, it's where you spent the better part of your baseball career," said Thomas. "I spent some wonderful days out here, as a kid, a young fan, and when I played for the Pirates. I spent 11 years in the Pirates organization, out of the 18 1/2 I put in. I don't think you're ever fully appreciated in your hometown, but I had the best of both worlds. When I'd come back to Pittsburgh and play I'd get standing ovations when I was introduced.

"I'm happy I played when I played, because I think it's going down as the grandest era in baseball. We had only eight teams in each league. If you hit .220, you wouldn't be in the major leagues. It's a big business today. I guess it was a big business when we played, too, but we didn't realize it. We just loved to play baseball, and we enjoyed it."

Thomas stood ramrod tall at 6-3, and weighed 230, thirty pounds over his playing weight. At age 64, he looked terrific. There was a gleam in his hazel eyes and good color on his cheeks, an absolute glow. "I feel good," he said with more than a hint of pride. He had just come back from a one-week cruise with his wife Dolores on the Windward, a ship in the Norwegian Cruise Lines.

"We went to Aruba, Curacao, Tortola, St. John, St. Thomas and Virgin Gorda. I worked in the yard yesterday, and a few days before that, and that may have put some color in my face, too. It took me six times to clean up the neighbor's leaves that are in my yard," he said. It was a typical Thomas observation. Thomas has never been a particularly tolerant soul.

Thomas wore a gray tweed cap, the kind Ben Hogan popularized as a pro golfer, a blue windbreaker, gray slacks and white sneakers.

128

It was brisk this day, and there was a fine drizzle in the air, but it only seemed to put a shine on Frank's face.

He participates as an instructor at those baseball fantasy camps that have become popular, wherein middle-aged baseball enthusiasts spend a week or two (and a few thousand dollars) on vacation playing baseball with the ballplayers of their youth. Thomas goes on cruises with Norwegian Cruise Lines in a special program they have for Major League Baseball alumni. Frank mixes with the regular clientele who are eager to chat with a former baseball player.

He likes to play golf in charity golf outings throughout the area, and remains a popular figure in any foursome.

"He's very competitive, too," related Jeff Underwood, a friend of mine who played with Thomas in such a golf outing, "He came within a foot of sinking a hole-in-one when a car was the prize for sinking one. He went after it, no doubt about it."

"It's like somebody being deaf and they can't hear."
— Thomas on Clemente's communication problems

I asked Frank Thomas to come out to Forbes Field to reflect on his former teammate, Roberto Clemente.

When I asked Thomas to consider Clemente, and what he remembered best about him, he began by saying, "He always liked kids. I had one long conversation with him, and he told me what he wanted to do in Puerto Rico. He had this dream to build a special Sports City for the kids, especially the poor kids. I always talked to kids, and he was that type of person, too, so we had something in common in that respect. Maybe he recognized that, and maybe that's why he talked to me at length about what he wanted to do in his home country.

"He was a moody guy. He was very quiet. He had two strikes against him when he first came up. He didn't speak or understand English very well, and he was a loner. That guy (Phil Dorsey) from the post office — the one who got into trouble a few years ago for stealing and selling stamps — he was always with him.

"I think he was genuine in his thinking. He cared for people. But like I say, I only spent four years with him when he wasn't really into his own yet. He was a young kid trying to make a name for himself. I appreciated his talent. And he was dedicated. I always thought the best way to pitch to him was down the middle. Some pitchers liked to go inside on him, some liked to go outside, but I told our guys to go down the middle. He'd moan and groan when we'd get him out that way.

"He had a tough time relating to the guys. It's like somebody being deaf and they can't hear. Like my mother-in-law. It's tough talking to her. She's in a world all by herself. I can't remember Clemente ever sitting down with guys at a restaurant on the road. People asked him to do things, I know. Everybody wanted him to be like one of the guys. But back then it was just like it is today: the blacks stayed together and to themselves."

Thomas said he can recall when he played for New Orleans in the Pirates' organization that there were separate restrooms and water fountains for blacks and whites. "I can remember when we were in spring training and we'd be traveling through the South that the black players had to stay on the buses when we ate at certain restaurants," said Thomas, "and we'd bring food out to them on the bus. That all changed when the blacks started protesting and holding civil rights demonstrations. That all happened when we were playing ball."

How did Clemente react to that sort of treatment? "I never noticed," said Thomas. "I guess he figured that's the way it had to be. He just accepted it, I guess. It was tough for them, no doubt about it."

I asked Thomas if he ever went to a movie with Clemente, or did anything off the field with him.

"No," he said. "To be honest, I never saw him on a road trip. The only time I saw him was on the ballfield. To be honest, I don't even remember him being on the bus. Wherever we'd go, the Latin people would cater to the Latin ballplayers. They'd drive them around town, take them places, take them to the ballpark. Feed them. Entertain them. Maybe he always went out to the ballpark with his people.

"I think you'd get a better impression of Clemente if you asked the ballplayers who played with him later in his career, like Giusti, Blass, Friend and Maz. They could give you more meaningful comments. He was just a raw kid when I was with them. I could see the difference when I was playing against him."

I asked Thomas what his first impressions were of Clemente when Clemente originally came up in 1955.

"Just watching him play, his actions, right then and there you knew he was a pretty good little player," said Thomas. "I said the same thing about Henry Aaron when I first saw him. We were coming north from spring training and we stopped to play the minor league team in Jacksonville. We played his team and Henry hit four of the damndest line drives. I said, 'He'll be coming up to the majors real soon.' He was a second baseman then, in the early '50s.

"I just felt that the way Clemente and Aaron swung the bat, so quick, and the way they handled themselves, that they had it. They had God-given ability. They just had to work to bring it out.

"I played with both of them. I liked Roberto, but people ask me which one would you take if you had to make a choice, and I'd take Henry. He could hit the ball harder, with more power, and he hit a lot more home runs. Aaron ran just as well, and he could steal as many bases. He had just as good an arm as Clemente, but he wasn't as colorful as Clemente in that light. I'd love to have both of them on my team.

"In my opinion, Willie Mays was the greatest of them all. To me, he could beat you more ways than anyone else."

Thomas was with Milwaukee during the 1961 season when the Braves set a major league record by having four batters — Eddie

rank Thomas was a big hit signing autographs at 1994 Piratefest.

Mathews, Aaron, Joe Adcock and Thomas — hit home runs in consecutive at-bats. "It's the only time it was done; it's a record they can never take away from me," said Thomas.

What if some team has five batters in succession hit home runs?

"I was the first one to hit the fourth straight home run; that's what they can never take away from me," Thomas replied. "We did it in Cincinnati. I still have three records with the Pirates, too. I had the most home runs and RBIs as a first-year man — 30 home runs and 102 RBIs in 112 games my rookie season — and I had 35 home runs and 109 RBIs as a third baseman in 1958.

"It was when I came into the infield, playing at third and at first base, that I really came to appreciate Bill Mazeroski. I don't think the ball ever hit his glove when he made the double play. He may have softened it, but that was about it, and the ball would be off to first base before you could see it. He was the greatest. He hit 19 home runs one year, and could have done better in that department, but George Sisler got him to hit more to all fields. Sisler wanted to do that with me, too, but I told him I wasn't the same kind of hitter that he was. Clemente could have hit more home runs, too, if he wanted to concentrate on that. But he was more of a line drive hitter.

"I wanted to hit home runs. That's what I was paid to do. I was always looking for a fastball. I felt I could adjust to any pitch if I were looking for a fastball first. Carl Erskine threw me 17 curveballs, and I kept fouling them off, in this one game. Finally, he threw a fastball and I hit it out. He said, 'Don't you ever look for anything but a fastball?' I said, 'No.' And he said, 'I'll never throw you one again.'"

"Some people don't want to hear the truth."
— Frank Thomas

Thomas was not known to be a great diplomat during his playing days with the Pirates. He sounded off a lot, and had a long needle which he liked to inject into everyone around him. How did he treat Clemente?

"I liked everybody, but I got on everybody," said Thomas. "I was friendly with everybody, but I agitated all of them. I agitated Bob Friend to no end because he was a nervous guy. I still agitate him when I see him. I was probably one of the greatest agitators in the history of baseball.

"I'd say what I thought. I wasn't going to say it behind your back. I was always honest and truthful with people. Some people don't want to hear the truth. I'd say what's meant to be is meant to be, and I was called a fatalist.

"I used to get mad at Clemente in his early years with the team," Thomas continued. "He was a great ballplayer, and he had a great arm, but he did things that hurt the ballclub. He'd throw the ball over the head of the cut-off man to home plate. If he didn't get the guy, the hitter would get to second base instead of having to stop at first. That could lead to more runs. I was playing first base at times, and I'd holler to him, 'Throw the ball down!'"

Didn't Clemente have the ability to fire the ball in from right field to first base and catch a runner rounding the base too far, and pick him off?

"For sure," said Thomas. "I knew I had to be alive at first, because he'd be doing just that. He played the wall as well as anyone I'd ever seen. I saw Paul Waner play the wall well, too, when I was a little kid, but Clemente knew every nuance of that wall. That wall was unforgiving, too. It was not padded. I saw Lee Handley hit that wall and split his head open. Rickey made us wear hard hats all the time just so we wouldn't get hurt like that. That's why my first bubble gum card has a hard hat. I look like a fugitive from some other planet.

"Clemente was always very colorful. He played his best baseball when we played the Giants. He tried to outdo Willie Mays, and he did many times. He worked at being a great outfielder, just like Virdon worked at it to become the great center fielder he became. Billy does it now, as a coach. He knows how important it is for a young outfielder to have the ball hit to him again and again, until he knows how to react to every possible situation. He's working now to make (Al) Martin a better center fielder. I did the same thing."

Clemente was known to miss games because of various ailments, and some of his teammates criticized him for his unwillingness to play hurt. Did Thomas have a problem with that?

"No one believes you when you're hurt, anyhow," said Thomas. "Clemente was not my responsibility. I personally was always afraid to be out of the lineup. I was afraid to lose my job. An injury ended my career with the Pirates. When I had the bad thumb, Dr. Finegold operated on it in his office. Not at the hospital. And I never should have let him do it. It was never right after that. Joe Brown traded me with a bad hand to Cincy."

That trade may have been Brown's best effort in that regard, and it's unlikely the Pirates would have won the National League pennant and the World Series in 1960 without that trade.

On January 30, 1959, Brown dealt Thomas with Whammy Douglas, Jim Pendleton and Johnny Powers to the Reds in exchange for Smoky Burgess, Harvey Haddix and Don Hoak. Thomas was later in trades that involved former Pirates like Lee Walls and Gus Bell.

"My hand never healed," said Thomas. "I went from hitting 35 home runs in Pittsburgh my last year there to hitting 12 in 1959 at Cincinnati."

"They wouldn't let me bat right-handed because I was hitting the ball too far."
— Frank Thomas
in his seminarian days

Thomas took me to show me his boyhood home at 347 Lawn Street, over-looking the Monongahela River, and the new technology center operated jointly by the University of Pittsburgh and Carnegie Mellon University.

His home was a red-brick affair with aluminum awnings. The bricks had been painted over. There were a few slats missing from the awnings. It reminded me of my own boyhood home in nearby Hazelwood, just down the Monongahela River. Some of the bricks in the porch were coming out of place at 347 Lawn Street, and Thomas pushed against them, like it was still his home and he wanted to tidy things. There was a FOR SALE sign in the front room window. I suggested he buy it, and he just shrugged his shoulders and wagged his head. Like it was too late.

Thomas pointed to a window above the porch. "That was my room up there," he said. From there, he could see the orange glow in the sky at night when the blast furnaces were going full blast above the J&L Mill. The mill is missing from the landscape now. It had been leveled a few years earlier. I had watched as the rusty structures came tumbling down and a part of my youth went to ashes as well.

The street where Thomas once lived should be desirable real estate, with its sensational view of Downtown Pittsburgh, but it's a bleak, ill-be-gotten street, where it's tough to sell a house these days. Sports superstars Danny Marino and Bruno Sammartino grew up on a similar hillside, with a similar view, in nearby South Oakland.

"My dad, Frank, was the foreman in the laundry at Magee-Womens Hospital for 50 years. But no pension," said Thomas. "He could walk to work from here. The hospital is just two blocks away." The family name was Tumas when his dad came over from Europe and someone called him Thomas when he arrived, and he let it go at that. He didn't want to come off as a greenhorn. There was a Tumas Hardware on the South Side owned by Frank's uncle. He pointed to an area that was overgrown with weeds. "That was a little ballfield when I was growing up," he said. "That's where I first played baseball."

As I bid him goodbye, Thomas turned up the street. "Now that I'm here," he said, "I think I'll visit one of my old neighbors to see how she's doing. She's over 80 now, and I might not get the chance again."

Thomas was a student at St. Agnes Grade School, on Forbes Avenue just a few blocks from his home, when a Father Lucian of the Carmelite Fathers came to speak to the students about religious vocations. "I liked the dissertation he gave; I thought I might like to be a priest," Thomas said. "I went up to their seminary for the summer, and had a great time, playing ball, and decided I'd go there for high school."

The seminary was called Mt. Carmel College, and it was located in Niagara Falls on the Canadian side of the border. Jack Butler, who

The parents of Frank Thomas and his boyhood home at 347 Lawn Street in Oakland, just below the Boulevard of Allies by Magee-Womens Hospital, where his dad worked for 50 years.

would later be a Pro Bowl cornerback for the Pittsburgh Steelers (1951-59), was a classmate at the seminary. Butler, who lives in Munhall, has been the head of Blesto, the NFL scouting organization, since its inception in the early '60s.

"We had a helluva athletic team in our class, I'll tell you," said Thomas. "It was a tradition at the school for the sophomores to play the seniors in all kinds of sports on Thanksgiving Day, and we beat the seniors in everything."

To hear Thomas talk about his athletic prowess in the seminary reminds one of the movies about Babe Ruth, and how he was so much better than the other boys playing ball in the orphanage in Baltimore.

"They wouldn't let me bat right-handed because I was hitting the ball too far," recalled Thomas with a smile. "I used to pitch — I had a good arm — but, after awhile, they wouldn't let me pitch either. They said I could hurt someone. I went through high school there, and I was in the novitiate in Baltimore. I was 17 and I had my religious habit. It was brown, with a hood. I was Father Godfrey by name. I picked Father Blaise, but they gave it to somebody else. He's still a priest. Father Blaise McInerney.

"Butler went to the novitiate, too. He left in November and I left in January. It's amazing when you think that one of us became a professional football player and the other a professional baseball player. And, coincidentally, we both fathered eight children.

"I knew I had the talent to play ball, and I knew I couldn't play sports in the priesthood. I wanted to be a major league baseball player. They read all the letters that went in and out and they came across one I tried to sneak out, saying I didn't want to be a priest. My mother cried when she heard that. She wanted me to be a priest. Finally, I got called in and I told the head priest at the novitiate that I wanted to be a major league baseball player. That was in January of 1947. I signed a contract to play for the Pirates on July 23, 1947. It was like a miracle.

"I played for a sandlot team that was sponsored by a meat market. Mike Kudro was our manager. I played 41 games of sandlot baseball when I was asked if I wanted to play for a better team, the Little Pirates, which was run by George Speirs and Billy Fuchs. I played my first game for them in Fineview. I played left field and I went five for five.

"We played our ballgames down in Carnegie, which was Honus Wagner's hometown. They still talk about a ball I hit there, over the houses and everything. That was in 1947 when I played for them.

"Pittsburgh was after me, and so was Cleveland. George Susce, a coach for Cleveland (who also played for the Pirates in 1939), lived up the street from me. He talked to me about signing with the Indians. Roy Hamey, the general manager, offered me $1,500 to sign.

"My dad didn't go for that; he said I was worth a lot more than that. He was a Lithuanian from the old country, and he was stubborn. He knew Chilly Doyle, the sports writer, real well, and Chilly thought I had a lot of talent. The Indians offered me $3,100 to sign. My dad said to sign, but I said no, I wanted to play in Pittsburgh. I told the Pirates that my parents had $3,200 left to pay on their mortgage. I said, 'Pay it off and I'll sign.' And that's what I did. I played for the Little Pirates the remainder of the summer. I didn't want to report till the next season. I went to spring training in 1948 in Hollywood.

"The first day I didn't hit anything, and they wondered why anyone wanted to sign me. The next day I'm hitting the ball up in the stands routinely. They sent me to Tallahassee, Florida, in Class D, for that season."

"Josh Gibson gave me my first baseball."

"I used to walk to Forbes Field," said Frank Thomas, as we sat in his new Chevrolet SIO pickup truck when the rain began to fall harder. "Sometimes I'd climb the fence to get in. Sometimes I'd sneak in with the Knot-Hole Gang in the right field seats. I'd not only come to see the Pirates play, but also teams like the Homestead Grays in the black leagues. Josh Gibson gave me my first baseball. I saw him hit two home runs over the 457 foot mark."

Thomas turned and nodded toward the 457 foot mark that remains on the wall, right behind the flag pole, that was the deepest spot in the outfield. Gibson was one of the greatest performers in the Negro Leagues, and eventually was enshrined in Baseball's Hall of Fame when a special selection committee was chosen to honor such too-long overlooked ballplayers.

"He was a great hitter," Thomas said of Gibson. "I went down by the dugout and asked him to give me a ball, and he did."

I asked Thomas what ballplayers he particularly liked at the time, or looked up to when he was a youngster.

"I didn't look up to anybody," he answered quickly. "I didn't have any idols. The Pirates had players like Ralph Kiner, George Metkovich, Wally Westlake, Gus Bell. I'd be playing at Schenley Oval and then I'd come over here to the ballpark. The only one I ever met as a kid was Rip Sewell. That was ironic because I ended up playing for Sewell at Charleston in 1951. He recommended me to Branch Rickey."

At the time of our meeting, Thomas was retired nine years. He had worked for ICM School of Business for 18 years. He went out to high schools and did presentations to the students to recruit them to ICM. "I'd tell those kids who thought they wanted to be pro ballplayers, if you're lucky enough to play till you're 37, like I did, you still have 28 years till you retire at 65. You better prepare yourself. You better get an education in some area where you can make a living."

All in all, Frank Thomas did quite well for himself, and he and his family managed to overcome great personal tragedy.

He lives in a two-story, five bedroom house on a cul-de-sac in Ross Township. He said he started taking his baseball pension at age 52, and had been getting it for 12 years. "It's not as good as what they have today, but it's good enough." said Thomas. "I'm on Social Security; I started taking that at 62. My wife just started to take hers, too, at 62.

"I consider myself fortunate to have a good family. We had eight kids, and three of them completed college. They've all done well. Our baby, Mark, is studying for the priesthood. He graduated from Duquesne University, and now he's in his second year at Pontifical College Josephinum in Worthington, Ohio, near Columbus."

Frank and Dolores lost one of their children in a freak and horrifying accident on New Year's Day in 1974. Their daughter, Sharon, the third oldest, attended a New Year's Eve party along with her sister Patty at what was then the Sheraton, and is now a Holiday Inn, in Ross Township.

She was with a group that was stuck between floors in an elevator at the hotel. Two of the fellows onboard managed to pry open the doors of the elevator. They were successful in jumping from the elevator to the floor below. Sharon tried to do the same. She lost her footing when her feet struck the floor, and she tumbled backward into the elevator shaft, and fell 35 feet to her death.

"To this day, I don't understand why she jumped," said her father. "Maybe she had claustrophobia. She jumped and she hit the edge, and fell backwards. They did an autopsy on her; I still have a copy of it. They had all been drinking at the New Year's Eve party, and that may have impaired their judgment. She had a punctured lung, her one leg was about severed, and she had a big gash over her eye. I can still see her. It's hard to believe that will soon be 20 years ago.

"It was the biggest funeral I ever saw. She worked at Burger King, and they took care of everything. There were 350 cars in the funeral procession. It was at the Staab Funeral Home in West End."

This reminded me that when I attended the funeral mass for Steelers owner Art Rooney at St. Peter's Church on the North Side, I was seated directly behind Thomas in the middle of the church. Thomas turned and talked to me for a few minutes, and I remembered him telling me what a wonderful man Rooney was. "He came to my daughter's funeral, and he took his place in line about a block from the front door," Thomas told me at Rooney's mass. "There was snow on the ground, yet he went to the back of the line. That's the kind of man he was. He would never think to cut in at the head of the line."

When I brought up that day to Thomas, he smiled knowingly, and added, "Art was a great guy. He never passed you by. He always sought you out to say hello, and to offer a kind word. Joe Tucker was like that, too. I remember when I finished playing ball and was looking for a job, Joe told me, 'Don't sell yourself short. You weren't just a ballplayer; you were a great ballplayer.'"

A year earlier, Thomas remembers where he was when he heard on January 1, 1973 of the death of Clemente. It's an anniversary date that hits even harder at his home because of what happened to Sharon.

"I was at home, and I heard it on the radio," recalled Thomas. "I was shocked. It always hurts when it's someone you've known."

Thomas did not become a priest, but he attends mass regularly, and his Catholic religion remains important to him. "You have to believe in something," said Thomas. "If a person doesn't have faith, I don't know what else he has."

The Thomas family has a fun run at Shea Stadium during his days with the New York Mets. They are, from left to right, his wife, Dolores, Peter, Frankie, Maryanne, Frank, Joanne, Patty and Sharon. Paul and Mark came later.

Clubhouse celebration marked Ron Kline's 6-hit victory over Chicago Cubs in 8-2 win in June of 1956. Having fun with the Callery, Pa. crewcut pitcher were, left to right, Roberto Clemente, Dale Long and Frank Thomas.

Fantastic views Frank Thomas had from his bedroom window at his boyhood home in Oakland, overlooking the Monongahela River. To the right, above, the skyscrapers of Downtown Pittsburgh, to the left, area once occupied by J&L Steel, with mills in the distance in Hazelwood, the author's hometown.

berto Clemente and Bill Virdon routinely
lled balls out of the ivy and off the walls of
rbes Field. They were one of the outstand-
g outfield duos in the history of baseball.

Pittsburgh Pirates

Roberto Clemente carried one of the biggest bats in baseball and used it to get his 3,000th hit on September 30, 1972.

142

Joe L. Brown

"Misunderstood is the best
way I can explain him.
He was such a warm, fine,
human being and yet
I don't think he came across
that way because I think
he was shut off in his
relationship by a good many
people early in his career."
— Joe L. Brown
Pirates GM

Pirates general manager Joe L. Brown is flanked by, from left to right, Roberto Clemente, Bill Mazeroski, Bill Virdon and Frank Oceak.

Bob Friend
Clemente's clubhouse neighbor

"He was there, but he wasn't. . ."

Bob Friend's frown said it all. Friend, the former pitcher for the Pittsburgh Pirates (1951-65), was doing his best to come up with stories relating to Roberto Clemente, but he was struggling. For ten years, Friend and Clemente were next-door neighbors in the home team's cozy clubhouse at Forbes Field, and Friend feels that they always got along well. Yet it was obvious by the difficulty Friend was having in reflecting on Clemente that he never really knew him at all.

"I was talking to Dave Giusti and Steve Blass about Clemente recently," said Friend, who still had a frustrated expression on his face, "and we were saying that none of us had many photos showing us with Clemente. The club had asked us to look for some for a promotion they are doing in connection with the All-Star Game."

I knew first-hand that Giusti had none in his home, or family album, showing him with Clemente, because I had already visited him.

"It's kinda like he was there, but he wasn't," offered Friend, doing his best to explain himself. "I always asked the newspaper photographers, and our publicity office, for photos, but I have few showing me with Bobby."

Through the years, Friend has often referred to Roberto as Bobby as well as Roberto. It would suggest a certain degree of intimacy. Friend was in his fourth season with the Pirates when Clemente came to the club, but Friend admits that none of the veterans went out of their way to make Clemente more comfortable with his new surroundings. "But that wasn't unusual," Friend said. Friend faults Clemente more than anyone else that they didn't have a closer relationship. "He was a loner, he kept to himself," said Friend. "He wasn't an outgoing guy; he was kinda laidback. He was full of fun in the clubhouse, but he went his own way outside the ballpark."

He could not recall a time when they went to lunch or dinner together. Friend was fond of walking to the ballpark, in spring training and during the regular season, from whatever hotel where the team was staying. But he didn't remember ever walking with Clemente to the ballpark. Maybe their relationship wasn't much different from those enjoyed by people who work in the same office, but seldom see each other outside the workplace. Maybe I was being unfair to Friend with my persistent line of questioning regarding his relationship with Clemente. Neighbors in the suburbs or inner-city can get along fine, but not socialize, or share coffee and rolls in the morning. Today's ballplayers go their own way more than they did in Friend's playing days. Back then, ballplayers were much closer, and hung together. Roommates were often inseparable.

Friend remembers Clemente being close with Roman Mejias, another Latin ballplayer (1955, 1957-61). "Clemente was all by himself," said Friend. "I don't know who he ate with on the road . . . maybe Roman Mejias."

Since Friend dressed and undressed in the stall next to Clemente, he could offer some thoughts on Clemente's sartorial taste. "He was a good dresser, sharp and conservative," said Friend. "He bought good stuff, and wore it well. He had that great physique, so he always looked good, whatever he wore."

Friend did introduce Clemente to Phil Dorsey, a black man from Pittsburgh who was in the same Army reserve unit as Friend. Dorsey became Clemente's constant companion and confidant. They were pals throughout Clemente's career.

Dorsey, a postal worker, had gotten into trouble a few years earlier when he was one of several workers convicted of theft charges for stealing a large amount of stamps from a post office in Pittsburgh. He had served time in a federal prison in Big Spring, Texas. "It's a damn shame he got into that stink," said Friend. "He sure earned Clemente's trust and friendship. He did everything for Bobby. They went everywhere together, and Phil usually took care of the arrangements. Clemente really leaned on Phil. He was his go-between here. I'm so upset with what happened to him. He was a helluva nice guy."

Many Pittsburghers say the same thing about Bob Friend. There aren't many former Pirates as affable or as comfortable in conversation as Friend. He is also a former politician, serving two terms as controller of Allegheny County from 1967 to 1974. Once a Pirate, always a Pirate, and once a politician, always a politician. Friend is a glib fellow, and remains one of the most popular of Pirates.

He was a reliable right-handed pitcher, and pitched more innings (3,481) than anyone else in team history, even more than the venerable Wilbur Cooper and Babe Adams and Vernon Law, and took pride in never missing a start.

I had told Friend a few weeks in advance that I would be visiting him to talk about Clemente. So he had time to warm up, but he didn't have his usual assortment of pitches working for him on this particular morning.

More often than not, his response to my questions about Clemente was a pained expression, like he was back at Purdue University taking an oral exam for which he was not properly prepared.

Friend was in his huge, high-ceilinged office at Babb, Inc., an insurance brokerage that dates back to 1929. His office was on the second floor of a beautiful brownstone building on Ridge Avenue on the city's North Side, just across the street from Community College of Allegheny County's main buildings, right in the center of the campus, a few blocks from the Pirates' present home at Three Rivers Stadium.

The street was once home to the city's millionaires when the area was known as Allegheny, and was a city separate from Pittsburgh. It's in Art Rooney's old neighborhood. The brownstone was a baronial mansion originally owned by William Penn Snyder (1862-1920), who was associated with Henry W. Oliver in developing the Lake Superior iron ore area, and he also owned the Shenango Furnace Company. William Penn Snyder III serves as chairman of the board of nearby Allegheny General Hospital.

It's a magnificent building with a rich heritage, a point of pride to Babb's principal owner and president, Ron Livingston. The building is full of heavy brass doors, beautiful stained glass windows, wood paneling, grand staircases and state rooms, a bank-size vault, a garage where horses and buggys were once stored, and a French ballroom in the basement with sparkling chandeliers that remains intact as a showcase as much as anything else. "It's something when you consider that the Olivers, Carnegies, Fricks and Mellons once moved across that ballroom floor," said Russell Livingston, Ron's son and the executive vice-president of the firm. His brother Ron has a similar role.

To me, it looked like an area that would be better put to use as a basketball court. "We thought of removing the chandeliers and doing just that," allowed Livingston. "But it's too beautiful, and this is a historic landmark building, and we are not allowed to alter it much."

Babb bought the building in 1969, and moved its offices there from Downtown. Friend has been with the insurance firm since 1976.

He was two weeks away from his 63rd birthday — on November 24 — when we met at his office. He and his wife Pat lived in Fox Chapel. They had two children and two grandchildren. Their daughter Missy, 33, lived in Costa Mesa, California, and had two children of her own. Their son, Bobby, had been married just over a year, and was in his third year on the Professional Golfers Association (PGA) tour.

"Pat was the team nurse for Dr. Finegold when I was playing for the Pirates," said Friend, "and Roberto always claimed he fixed me up with Pat. He took credit for putting us together. But that wasn't really true. Branch Rickey promoted our marriage more than anyone. Rickey liked his ballplayers to be married. He called me a matrimonial coward."

There are family photos about Friend's office. There are photos and plaques and baseball memorabilia displayed in the room, which contains a couch, coffee table and even a rocking chair given him by the Pirates. It's formal and sort of stuffy. The likes of Babe Ruth, Al Kaline, Jim Bunning, Red Schoendienst, Enos Slaughter are pictured here and there. There's a framed scroll attesting to Friend's one-time position as county controller. There's a museum look about the place.

I asked Friend for his first impressions of Clemente.

"He had the great physique," said Friend. "He was a good-looking guy. He had one of the greatest arms we ever saw. He was a little erratic throwing the ball in from the outfield early on, but he showed it off often, and became unbelievably accurate with his throws. He picked guys off first base, and I saw him throw out guys from deepest right center. He'd hit the plate on the fly with his throws.

"He was quiet and pleasant, no cockiness, when he came to the Pirates. We dressed in a corner of the clubhouse at Forbes Field; he was in the next locker. We had a great relationship. We were not that close, but there was respect for one another."

The Friend family in 1964: Pat and Bob with baby Bobby and Missy. Pat had been a nurse for Pirates team physician Dr. Joseph Finegold when she and Bob began dating.

Bob with son Bobby, a touring golf pro

Bob Friend takes his turn at the mike at Pirates Alumni affair at Churchill Country Club.

Friend insisted he never saw or was aware of Clemente scratching himself from the lineup when he didn't feel up to playing. "I've read about that stuff, but it must have come later in his career," said Friend. "I never saw that."

He did see a stormy blow-up between Clemente and Danny Murtaugh, the manager of the Pirates. "I thought Bobby was out of line in this instance," recalled Friend. "They didn't come to blows or anything like that, but it got pretty hot."

Friend recalled that the rest of the Pirates team was out on the field at Forbes Field, preparing for a doubleheader that day with the Los Angeles Dodgers. He said that he and John Hallahan, the clubhouse man, and Danny Whelan, the team trainer, were the only people in the room.

"It was about twenty to one on the clubhouse clock, and Clemente hadn't arrived yet," said Friend. "The team was taking batting practice. I was in the clubhouse because I was set to pitch the second game. When I saw Clemente coming into the clubhouse, I hollered to him, 'Roberto, you better get your ass out there!' Roberto said to me, 'I know. I slept in.' At that moment, Murtaugh came charging up to Clemente. 'Where the hell you been?' Murtaugh screamed at him. Roberto responded, 'I got sick last night. I couldn't get up.' And Murtaugh shouted, 'Don't take your clothes off. You're not playing today.' It went back and forth like that, one shouting at the other. There was a lot of heat in the room. They went at it pretty good. 'You don't like me; you never have!' Clemente cried out. Murtaugh hollered back, 'Put your clothes on and get the hell outta here!' Roberto was really hurt about that. He was upset that Murtaugh didn't want to listen to him explain what happened to him. Eventually, they patched things up, but it was never a warm relationship.

"It was a real blow-up, but it never hit the paper. Clemente didn't talk about that incident to reporters, but he frequently told them that Murtaugh didn't like him.

"Bobby always came to me and told me how Murtaugh was against him. I tried to tell him he was wrong, but he just wouldn't believe me. Really, Danny was on Bobby's side all the way, but Clemente didn't understand. He did more for Bobby than Bobby realized.

"But Bobby was right about some of the writers being against him. They hurt him more than anything, especially about that hypochondriac image. Bobby was one of the greatest players I ever saw, but he was the type who had to be encouraged by everyone."

Weren't there players who were critical of Clemente, over his health problems and his constant complaining about his various ailments? Weren't some of the guys cold toward him? I had read articles about strained feelings among some of the players in regard to Clemente.

"He was a loner, I'm telling you," said Friend. "I don't remember him turning off people. I was with him for ten years, and I didn't see a gang against Clemente or any rift between him and the other players.

148

Former Pirates from 1960 championship season appear at autograph signing session in 1990, including, from left to right, Joe Christopher, Earl Francis, Smoky Burgess, Harvey Haddix and Bob Friend. Bob and Pat Friend prepare to board the Mississippi Queen.

He had his way about him, but we realized that we needed this guy on our side if we were going to succeed. What galled Clemente was that he felt he didn't get the recognition he deserved.

"He publicly complained about the competence of our team doctor, Dr. Finegold. He had this Doctor Garcia and a Doctor Busó looking after him in Puerto Rico. The players all liked Dr. Finegold — Joe was a good guy — so that didn't go down well with many of the players. After Clemente would complain to him about something, Finegold would tell him, 'Here, Roberto, take two aspirin and you'll be all right.' Clemente didn't think Finegold could help him.

"Some of his comments after the '60 Series, when he complained about not getting his due in the voting for the most valuable player in the National League, rubbed some guys the wrong way."

Dick Groat won the award, and Don Hoak was second in the balloting. Vernon Law, the Cy Young Award winner, also finished ahead of Clemente, who was eighth in the voting by the Baseball Writers of America. Who did Friend feel should have won the award?

"I think it was Groat. Groat was consistent, and he hit .325, and he was there all the time. We were five games in front when he broke his wrist and missed a few weeks at the end of the regular season schedule."

I told Friend I felt that the players on the Pirates should have been more sensitive to Clemente's situation, and that some of the more mature players should have reached out to Clemente.

"I think it was one-sided," said Friend. "If Bobby had reached out, I think the guys would have been glad to be more involved with him. Nobody was going to do it on their own. Nobody really embraced him. Initially, they recognized that he was a loner-type guy.

"I got along real well with Roberto. I was a real agitator, and I'd nail someone's shower shoes to the floor, stuff like that, and Clemente got a kick out of it. He enjoyed a good prank. He got along well with Hoolie, our clubhouse guy (John Hallahan), and our trainer, Danny Whelan.

"I used to tease him about his place in baseball history. I'd tell him about the greatest outfielders I ever saw, and his eyes would light up. Then I'd tell him they were Joe DiMaggio, Mickey Mantle, Ted Williams and Willie Mays. And he'd get riled up. He'd say, 'You'll forget all about them by the time I'm through. I'll make you forget about all those guys.' In truth, Clemente wasn't far behind Mays as far as ability was concerned. It wasn't until the World Series with Baltimore in '71 that Clemente finally received the recognition that he had long deserved."

I asked Friend what he would tell his pals if he were to return to his hometown of West Lafayette, Indiana, or at Purdue University, where he was the eighth member of his family to get his degree.

"I'd tell them I like him very much," said Friend. "He's got a great personality. He's one of the greatest ballplayers I've ever seen. He's very bright, and very honest."

Friend thought Clemente could be self-deprecating as well as his more-celebrated demands to be properly acknowledged.

"I was going to the Dapper Dan Dinner one year at the Hilton," said Friend. "I was walking from the parking garage to the Hilton. I had been out of baseball for a year, and hadn't seen him for a year."

Friend's full name is Robert Bartmess Friend. The Bartmess is his mother's family name. Clemente often called him by his middle name. Clemente was batting about .360 when Friend came upon him that night.

He said to me, 'Bartmess, you quit too early. You could still be pitching. The pitching is so weak. I'm gonna play another ten years.'

"Now how many guys would say that? He was hitting about .360 at the time, but he was cutting down his own performance by saying the pitching wasn't as good as it used to be. Clemente kept in great shape, and he could have played until he was 45.

"I think the way Clemente played, running out every hit, and running recklessly into the wall, he realized he needed some time off and he took it. So many times, I saw him catch balls that went into the gap and he'd personally keep the other guy from getting that extra base. For a pitcher, that was something that was really appreciated. An average outfielder many times will give up the extra base. Often that's the difference between winning and losing.

"At Forbes Field, we had one of the toughest right fields to play in baseball. Clemente could play the ball off that cement wall. Clemente would cut off the ball before it could get to the wall; he'd hold it to a single and keep it from being a triple.

"He looked so unorthodox at the plate. He was always gyrating, and his ass would fly out, and he'd fall down when he swung and missed. Somebody like Don Drysdale would knock him down. He'd get up and hit a line drive. The knockdown didn't bother him. It looked like it would, with all the gyrations he went through.

"His greatest hitting performances were at Wrigley Field. He didn't hit as many home runs as some of the big hitters of his day — like Aaron, Mays and Frank Robinson — but he had good power, and I saw him hit the centerfield scoreboard many times in Chicago. He got pumped up whenever we played in Chicago. He'd get four hits, a few doubles, a triple, you name it. Wrigley Field brought out the best in him.

"He was popular in New York. There were always people waiting for him when we'd arrive at the hotel in New York. But he had a lot of friends in New York; I think some of them came up from Puerto Rico. I'm sure Roberto picked up the tab for most of them. If he had played in New York, he would have been so popular with the people, especially the Latin-American people. He was so proud of his heritage. And he'd have gotten the same kind of acclaim as Mays and Mantle did because they played in New York. But he loved Pittsburgh and its people, and always said he didn't want to play anywhere else."

Frank Robinson

151

Pittsburgh Pirates

Bill Virdon
A tough bird

*"He was the greatest all-around
ballplayer during my era."*
— Virdon on Clemente

*Bill Virdon returned to Pittsburgh in 1992 as a coach on Jim Leyland's
staff. He has played, managed and coached the Pirates and has always
been a popular figure in Pittsburgh. Virdon's friendship with Clemente
dates back to 1956 when Virdon was traded to the Pirates by the Cardinals in exchange for Bobby Del Greco and Dick Littlefield. Virdon and
Clemente were teammates for ten years before Virdon turned to coaching. Three years later, in 1972, Virdon was named manager of the Pirates
to replace the retiring Danny Murtaugh. He would be Clemente's last
manager.*

"What was it like to play ball next to Roberto Clemente?" I asked
Bill Virdon. "I can't say anything bad about it," replied
Virdon. "Nothing to my left side went undone. I knew if some-
thing went that way it would be taken care of."

"What sort of relationship did you have with Clemente?"

"We were friendly. There was a respect," answered Virdon. "He
was one of the best in the business."

"Why did it take so long for Clemente to gain acceptance as a truly
outstanding baseball player?" I asked.

"I think there were reasons for Clemente not being accepted as
a hero when he was playing for the Pirates. When he came up he was
19, right out of Puerto Rico, and he was not familiar with American
ways. There was a language barrier at first. He wasn't sure what was
expected of him. He was criticized for his ways. As he aged and matured,
he came a long way and did what was expected of him.

"At first, I don't think he had an idea of what it would be like for
him in the major leagues, especially coming from a small Spanish-
speaking island. He had the reputation of complaining about hurts all
the time, but you can look at the record and he was there."

"What was your reaction to his death?"

"I couldn't believe it. It was like a nightmare. It was a tough way
to start a new year.

"I don't know how you can think of baseball in Pittsburgh without
Roberto Clemente," Virdon went on.

"I don't think there's been anyone better in baseball. He could play
every phase of the game excellently. I've never seen anybody who could
play the game as he had during his last three years. He was 38 his last
season. He could do more things than a lot of 30-year-olds could do.

154

"I've never seen an individual who retained his physical abilities for so long. He was the greatest all-around baseball player during my era. He could do more things than anybody I've ever seen.

"He loved baseball. Baseball was his life. He gave much more to baseball than he took away from it no matter how much money he made."

Clemente was killed on his third trip to Managua. "It was typical of Clemente," said Virdon. "He made it a point to go entirely out of his way to help others. He was a very warm, friendly, happy and willing person. Somebody who was always willing to help somebody in need."

Bill Virdon is flanked by fellow outfielders Roberto Clemente and Willie Stargell.

ElRoy Face
Always a carpenter at heart

"He wasn't my kind of guy."
— Face on Clemente

ElRoy Face was never a fan of Roberto Clemente. Never was, never will be. Forgive Face if he didn't get caught up in all the hoopla about raising money to build a statue to honor Clemente. Face, for sure, participated in a few fund-raising activities with the Pirates alumni — he seldom misses any of their outings — but his heart wasn't in the spirit of contributing to the "Statue for Roberto" fund. He was simply having a good time with old friends and former teammates. If Clemente was coming along for the ride, that was all right with ElRoy.

"If I went along with all the praise he gets," offered Face, as frankly as possible, "I'd be a hypocrite. Because it's not my true feelings. I didn't look up to him as a person. He was a great ballplayer, when he wanted to play, but as a person — from my view — he wasn't my kind of guy. I'll probably get shot for saying that, but that's the way I feel."

These strong words were racing through my mind as I drove away from Face's apartment in North Versailles Township, 15 miles east of Downtown Pittsburgh, just past Forest Hills on Rt. 30. The sun had just gone down, and the sky was a dark blue, laced with black and gray. The sky was framed by the George Westinghouse Memorial Bridge, once heralded as having the longest reinforced concrete span of any bridge in the world, looming high in the sky to my left. It was a beautiful, if brooding portrait of a special Pittsburgh landscape. I divert here, but this was a breath-taking view. This bridge, on Rt. 30 in North Versailles, spans Braddock Avenue in Turtle Creek, and is a gem of a bridge in a city of bridges. It opened in December of 1932, 61 years earlier, and it remains an engineering and architectural marvel. I wondered how many men, coming and going to work, ever appreciated the wonder of this spectacular span.

I traveled through the towns of East Pittsburgh, where my father-in-law and his father both worked at the Westinghouse Electric plant for nearly 40 years. The plant had since been abandoned by Westinghouse. It was once the company's showcase plant, but it had become a dinosaur. I passed through Turtle Creek, Pitcairn and Wilmerding, depressed towns where steelworkers and railroaders once held sway, where men were respected for putting in an honest day's work and for the amount of sweat on their brows, and I kept thinking about Face's fury. All these years . . . still smoldering. His deep-seeded resentment toward the powers-that-be that denied him what he thought was his rightful reward was still evident.

When these towns were bustling, the workers looked upon Face as one of their favorites. He was a little guy with a big heart, who was willing to work every day, if necessary. After Face had pitched seven or eight days in a row, Danny Murtaugh would tell him not to come out to the ballpark that night, to take the night off, to rest his right arm. But Face would show up anyhow and, often, Murtaugh would call on him to come in out of the bullpen. Once Murtaugh told the pitchers prior to the start of the season that he didn't want them having sex the night before they pitched. Face put up his hand. "Hey, Skip," he said, "how do I tell the wife that I'm shut out for the season?" Face was only serious when he went to the mound. Then he was all business. The sight of Face coming in from the bullpen boosted everybody's spirits, Pirates announcer Bob Prince often observed. That's why the workers in East Pittsburgh and places like that could identify with him. Back in 1960, Face would have been far more popular in Pittsburgh's mill towns than Clemente.

In 1959, Face had posted an unbelievable 18-1 record. In the 1960 World Series, Face had three saves and was nearly the winner in the seventh and final game.

And Face would often show up in the same bars where the workers went for a shot and beer, and belly up to the same bars. He was one of them.

Clemente would claim their favor at a later date. Nowadays, one of those stars in the dark blue sky overhead is surely his.

The fires burn deep in Face's belly. The same fires that helped him be such a fierce and determined competitor and a bullterrier out of the bullpen made it difficult for him to comprehend a Clemente, who had a different approach to his craft, who came from a different culture, who spoke a different language.

Face felt that Clemente would sit out games for the slightest of reasons — "if he had a bellyache" — and that he was a showboat, often trying to do something sensational rather than what was prudent. He thought he was standoffish from the rest of the team. Face was critical of Clemente on several counts. In short, Face simply didn't care for Clemente. This may disappoint those who feel differently about Clemente, but credit Face for being honest about his feelings.

Face doesn't hide his feelings very well. Face, for instance, feels that he belongs in the Baseball Hall of Fame. Most of his teammates and many other baseball observers feel that Face and his teammate Bill Mazeroski were among the best at what they did, and that they deserve to be enshrined. Neither of them ever garnered enough votes in the 15 years they were on the ballot to be so honored. Face was among the first premier relief pitchers in the game, a fearless fireman. Mazeroski is best known for hitting the home run that won the World Series in 1960, but he gained admiration among his colleagues more so as a peerless second baseman. Mazeroski masks whatever feelings he has on the subject, seldom discussing it. It is not a subject he raises. He doesn't brood about it.

Face's frustration over the slight is obvious. He appears bitter, though he denies it. "I don't really care anymore," he says. But he doth protest too much.

"I know what I did; I had a pretty good career. I put in 15 1/2 years in the major leagues, 22 in pro ball. I know what I accomplished." Did he think there was still any chance he could be so honored? "I'm not dead yet," he said with a smile.

He also felt that Clemente should have had to wait the normal five year period after his playing career was over to be so enshrined. By special acclamation, however, Clemente was voted into the Baseball Hall of Fame within a year after his death. "They should have waited," said Face. "His children were too young to appreciate the significance of the honor." One has to wonder whether Face was genuinely concerned about Clemente's children, or whether he was just being critical of the special consideration rendered to Clemente.

Face took exception as well to the Pirates organization spearheading a drive to raise funds for a statue to honor Clemente. It was scheduled to be unveiled at the Major League All-Star Game at Three Rivers Stadium in July of 1994.

"It's all business," said Face. "It's all part of the All-Star Game business. It's all part of the show."

Then Face volunteered other thoughts he had been harboring on the subject. "I don't believe if Clemente were still alive that there'd be a statue. It's the way he died.

"I think, in my mind, Stargell did as much for the city of Pittsburgh, for the team, and the organization. He deserves a statue as much as Clemente does for the contributions he made here. That's my feeling. Stargell mingled more with the public, and he mingled more with his teammates, and he was more of a positive influence all the way around."

Yet Face was among the Pirates alumni who had agreed to participate in summer-long activities to promote the event. Begrudgingly perhaps, Face would be a part of the All-Star promotion.

Face had attended an alumni holiday party at the P.A.A. in Oakland on Thursday, November 9, the night before our meeting, and was reassured by several of his former teammates that he, indeed, deserved to be in the Baseball Hall of Fame. It's a rite of such get-togethers, like complaints about their pensions, or lack thereof. They tell Mazeroski the same thing, and he shrugs them off. Bob Purkey's wife, Joan, was one of those who told Face her feelings on the subject. "She said I should be in the Hall of Fame," said Face. "She said, 'I think you deserve to be there.' I told her I have a living will at home that calls for me to be cremated when I die, and that my ashes are to be spread over the ballfield at Cooperstown. That's how I'll get to the Hall of Fame. She said, 'You're morbid.'" Face smiled at his own story.

I asked Face if he remembered where he was when he learned that Clemente had died in an airplane crash on New Year's Eve of 1972. Again, somewhat strangely, a smile.

"I was sleeping," he said.

He was living in Penn Hills at the time with his first wife, Jeanne Kuran, who was from Pittsburgh and to whom he was married for 25 years, and their daughter Michelle, then 17, who woke him up to tell him the bad news about Clemente.

158

Face remembered his reaction to Michelle's wake-up call. "I said, 'Better him than me,' and then I rolled over and went back to sleep." It sounded harsh. Face chortled at his own story. It did not leave a pleasant impression.

Face was a carpenter most of his adult life. He carried a carpenter's union card during his entire pro baseball career. He went to work as a carpenter at Mayview State Mental Hospital. He retired from there in 1992 after 11 years on the job. "My whole family was full of carpenters — my grandfather, my father, my brothers — we all belonged to the carpenters union," said Face. They came from Stephentown, N. Y., about 20 miles from Albany, where it gets real cold in the winter, but the work never stops. You just keep hammering. Occasionally, even the best of carpenters strikes his thumb with a hammer, but he doesn't take the rest of the day off. He may lick his wound, or wave his thumb in the air while swearing. But he doesn't go home. He just keeps hammering away.

"I don't remember my father not going to work unless he was really ill, or really injured," offered Face. "There were a lot of times he didn't feel like working, but he went to work, anyhow. The only two times I can remember him not going to work was when he had an appendectomy at 45; he nearly died. Another time he tore the cartilage in his leg, and he was on crutches for awhile. I was raised that you were responsible to get a job done, and to do your best to do it right."

This may provide some explanation for Face's criticism of Clemente's work ethic. Face was not alone among the Pirates of the '60s who questioned Clemente's courage or attitude toward playing the game. Many in the media wondered aloud about Clemente's tolerance to play with pain, or when he simply didn't feel right. Clemente was called a malingerer by many early in his career. Some say it was another case of stereotyping Latins or blacks, or both. Fair or not fair, the criticism was there. Later in his career, Clemente was cited for his hustle and courage and consistency.

Face was sitting at a dining table off the kitchen of his two-bedroom apartment on the second floor of a two-story unit in North Versailles when I interviewed him for the second time in 11 months. His apartment was above a similar apartment leased by Charley Feeney, who covered the Pirates for over 20 years (1966-86) for the *Pittsburgh Post-Gazette*.

The trees were bare in the woods off the deck of the Face apartment. There were some tennis courts directly below. There was a deep culvert, and a black road, below that. "Sometimes you can see deer out there," offered Face. "And lots of small animals and birds. It's nice in the spring, summer and fall."

The apartment was modest and crammed with all kinds of collectibles. Face had many of his awards and plaques attesting to the greatness of his baseball career displayed about the apartment. His wife,

Roberta, called "Bo" by everybody who knows her, had quite a collection of ceramic cardinals, and paintings of cardinals, crowding the living room area. It was like being in an aviary. I hadn't seen so many feathered friends in a room since Alfred Hitchcock's (1963) movie "The Birds" when Tippi Hedren and Rod Taylor were terrorized by large bands of hungry birds. Bo loves birds, and she's absolutely crazy about cardinals. "Joe Torre gave her a Cardinals jacket," Face said.

Face had a Cardinal of his own in his wallet. It was a clipping from a 1976 issue of *Baseball Digest*, in which Stan Musial, the Hall of Famer from the St. Louis Cardinals and a big Pittsburgh favorite because he came from nearby Donora, listed his all-time baseball team. Face had Musial sign his name to it to certify it.

Musial's all-time team included Bill Terry, first base; Rogers Hornsby, second base; Honus Wagner, shortstop; Eddie Mathews, third base; Henry Aaron, leftfield; Willie Mays, centerfield; Roberto Clemente, rightfield; and as pitchers he picked Bob Gibson, Tom Seaver, Christy Mathewson, Grover Cleveland Alexander, Warren Spahn, Sandy Koufax, ElRoy Face and Clem Labine.

"I saw Musial at Nemacolin Woodlands at a golf tournament for Del Miller's Adios race, and asked him to sign it," said Face. "Musial beat me a couple games, but I had a good career against him."

The mention of Musial prompted Face to tell one of his favorite stories. "I had pitched 21 scoreless innings in relief, and I was going against the Cardinals in extra innings in St. Louis. I threw Musial a forkball down and away and he put it on the roof in right field to beat us. Danny Murtaugh walked by me in the clubhouse and said, 'Relief pitcher my ass!' "

Face has a ready storehouse of such stories, some that make him look good, others that humble him. He keeps things balanced better in that respect than he does his recollections of Clemente.

There is a limited print on display in the guest bedroom of the Face's apartment that portrays the Pirates' all-time baseball team. Clemente is among those portrayed in it, so Clemente is, in a sense, in Face's home, like him or not.

The Pirates All-Time team includes manager Danny Murtaugh, left-handed pitcher Harvey Haddix, right-handed pitcher Vernon Law, relief pitcher ElRoy Face, catcher Manny Sanguillen, first base Willie Stargell, second base Bill Mazeroski, shortstop Honus Wagner, third base Pie Traynor, outfielders Roberto Clemente, Paul Waner and Ralph Kiner.

"There are only 12 prints, and mine is number 10 of 12," offered Face. "They are signed by the artist."

Above the bed, there was a framed cover from *Sports Illustrated* in which Face was heralded as the greatest relief pitcher in baseball.

As I moved about the apartment alongside Face, I couldn't resist sizing him up. He's about 5-7 1/2, about an inch smaller than I am. I always excused myself as being too short to be a good athlete as a kid, and it blows my mind to find out that Face and Harvey Haddix, two giant-killers in that 1960 World Series who both made baseball history in 1959, were even smaller.

I mentioned to Face that I was surprised by how many young people, who never saw him play except in videos, hold Clemente in the highest esteem. They absolutely revere him. Some still write reports about him for school assignments. "I love Clemente," many of them have told me.

"That's because of all the praise he still gets from the media," said Face.

"Talk to Groat about him; it's not just me. Clemente had the ability, no doubt about it, but he was, for instance, always trying to show off his arm. He was always trying to throw out runners at the plate or at third, instead of throwing the ball to the cut-off man and preventing the hitter from taking the extra base. Instead of having runners at first and third, and still having the chance to get a double play, you'd have runners at second and third and no chance to get the double play. It makes it a lot tougher on the pitcher.

"He wouldn't throw the ball down where Groat could grab it as the cut-off man or let it go if he thought Clemente's throw could get the lead runner out. Clemente had a strong arm, but he was always trying to show it off. Early on, he used to throw the ball into the stands, but he got more accurate as he went on. He made some great throws and got some guys out, but there were more times he didn't get the guy.

"Little things like that. As a player you realize the significance of such things. The fan just sees him getting a guy out at home plate. But he did that two out of ten times. It looked great to the fans, and it was great for the Pirates if he got someone out like that. But more often than not he was putting more pressure on the pitcher."

It had been a difficult year for Face, and it might have contributed to his sense of disenchantment with a lot of things. His mother, who was 84, had a heart attack in February. His oldest brother, Joe, died at age 66. His Dad, also Joe, had died three years earlier. His youngest brother, Leonard, was dying from emphysema, and had only one lung. Face pointed toward his wife, Bo, and said, "Her mother passed away on the same day I got a call about my brother being hospitalized."

Face was smoking cigarettes as we spoke, and the remains of several others filled an ashtray on the table. My father, who looked a lot like Face, had died from emphysema and pneumonia, the results of smoking and drinking too much. My wife is a social worker in the oncology unit at Allegheny General Hospital and is always telling me tales of men and women who had lung cancer because of heavy smoking habits. "How can you keep smoking," I asked Face, "when your brother and Harvey Haddix both have emphysema from smoking like you do?" Face smiled, and said, "Because I can't do it after I'm dead."

Again, Face chortled.

"I enjoy a cigarette after a meal, or with my coffee," continued Face. "My dad smoked a pipe and chewed tobacco, and it was his heart that gave out on him."

162

Two of the grittiest little guys ever to fire a baseball, Harvey Haddix and ElRoy Face, check out record book published by *The Sporting News.*

ElRoy Face

oking fun at Bobby Shantz, the smallest pitcher on the staff in 1961, are, left to right, anager Danny Murtaugh, ElRoy Face and Harvey Haddix.

Face had been enjoying the company of his youngest granddaughter, Alyssa, who was two-and-a-half years old. The Faces had been baby-sitting. Then Bo's son, Bill, 33, who lives in nearby North Huntingdon, came to pick up his daughter. Alyssa gave ElRoy several hugs and kisses. "She really loves her grandpap," said Bill. The feeling was mutual. This was a different side of Face from the one that was so critical of Clemente. Face has nine grandchildren altogether, seven girls, two boys. He said he enjoys being a grandfather.

Face was looking forward to going to Bradenton, Florida January 9-16 to serve on the teaching staff at the Pirates' Fantasy Camp, where middle-aged would-be ballplayers spend a few thousand dollars to participate in a make-believe baseball training camp with some of their favorite Pirates of the past. He would turn 65 on February 20.

When I introduced Clemente into the conversation, I could tell that Face wasn't warming to the subject. He was a reluctant participant in the early part of our conversation, I could tell easily enough. I had been told that Face wasn't that close to Clemente. Then again, I didn't think that made him much different from most of the Pirates who had been teammates of Clemente. Face seemed uncomfortable with Clemente as a conversation topic, like he'd gotten some tobacco bits on the tip of his tongue.

"There wasn't too much contact with Clemente off the field; just at the ballpark," said Face. "He was pretty much by himself, a loner. We were never close."

"Who were you close to?" I asked Face.

"Maz and I were close," he responded. "Don Hoak was my roommate. He lived in Roulette, up in Potter County. It was east of Coudersport, near Port Allegheny, deer country. I went deer hunting with him a few times. I did things with Jim Pagliaroni and Dick Schofield. We'd get Harvey Haddix, and Bob Skinner and Bill Virdon, and there'd be six or seven of us, and we'd go out to dinner together. I associated with all of them.

"Once in a while, we'd get together and have a party. Anybody who wanted to go along could join us. Hal Smith came once in awhile, anybody who felt like going."

"What about Clemente?" I asked. "Didn't you ever ask Clemente if he wanted to come along?"

Face gave me the same pained expression as his Pirates teammates did when I posed this same question.

"He didn't hang around with us much," said Face. "He was always with Earl Francis, or Gene Baker or Joe Christopher. He had other friends. There were always people from Puerto Rico or other Latin countries wherever we traveled. He was just more of a loner."

"What was he like as a teammate?" I asked.

"He was all right," said Face. "He did his job, same as the rest of the guys. I don't think I really knew him, not like all the other guys."

Clemente was upset after the 1960 World Series because he felt that he deserved to be named the National League's Most Valuable Player that season. He never wore his World Series ring. Instead, he wore an All-Star Game ring, which he felt was a better acknowledgement of his ability. Dick Groat was voted the MVP by the baseball writers that season.

"I'd have to say Groat was the MVP," said Face, when asked whom he thought truly deserved the award. "Clemente didn't come into his own until later in the '60s. He was a good ballplayer, but he wasn't the main reason we won that year. Hoak was valuable to that team, pumping everyone up. Vernon Law and Bob Friend were very important to that team.

"Man for man, the Yankees were a better team. We just had a team that never gave up. Everything jived together that year. On paper, you'd have to say the Yankees were the better team. We never lost four in a row that summer, and we came back to win when we were trailing going into the late innings on more than 20 occasions."

What was it about Clemente that rubbed Face the wrong way?

"If a guy is getting paid to play, he should be out there," responded Face. "You don't sit out because you've got an upset stomach. Another guy who will tell you the same thing is Groat.

"I was never really that fond of Clemente as a person. He was a great ballplayer. He was a good man to have on your team, with lots of ability. But aside from that, we had little in common.

"You had a job to do, and you didn't let things keep you from doing your job. One night in Philly, our trainer Danny Whelan told Danny Murtaugh that I had a temperature of 102 degrees. Murtaugh told Whelan to keep me in the clubhouse. 'If I need him, I'll call him out,' Murtaugh told Whelan. 'And he called me.' I mentioned that Haddix was sick the night he pitched the 12 perfect innings in Milwaukee in 1959, and Face merely nodded.

"In 1959, when I went 18-1, I cut my hand and had to have stitches. I missed some games, but I came back, with the stitches still in my hand, and pitched. I still had scars. I had dropped a glass in a sink, and tried to grab it, and cut myself. I was out ten days. There was a story in the papers that Clemente had pulled a knife on me in an argument and had cut me. It never happened. We never got into any kind of fight.

"I was never a fan of Clemente the whole 14 years we were around each other. But it didn't affect me. I knew he had the ability to play his position. I didn't let my personal feelings affect my approach. In all the years I played with him, as a person, he just wasn't my kind of person. Clemente and I never had a disagreement. But we never got close together, either. We talked and associated with each other in the clubhouse. I guess he was something of a hypochondriac, and he wouldn't play unless he felt perfect.

"Hell, Hoak cut the webbing between his toes on a steel ladder at a swimming pool party, and he didn't miss a game. His socks were soaked with blood, but he played a doubleheader the next day. He had a different ability to stand pain. Some guys can stand more pain than others. I never wanted to miss a turn because somebody was always in the wings, wanting to take your job.

"Clemente was a great ballplayer. He could hit, run and throw. He was a great ballplayer, one of the better ballplayers I ever saw. Willie Mays was the best; he could beat you more ways than anyone else. As a ballplayer, whenever he wanted to play, there were few who could compare with Clemente. He had God-given talent and ability."

All the Pirates of the past say that. How about ElRoy Face? Didn't he, too, have God-given ability?

"I know I did," said Face. "I was gifted with a good arm."

Face was on the small side, just 5-7 1/2, 155 pounds, yet he always looked so confident, downright cocky, whenever he came to the mound, no matter the difficulty of the situation.

"I always felt I had eight guys behind me to help me get them out," said Face, "and the batter was all by himself."

ElRoy Face takes the ball from starter Vernon Law as, from left to right, Smoky Burgess, Don Hoak and Danny Murtaugh look on from the mound.

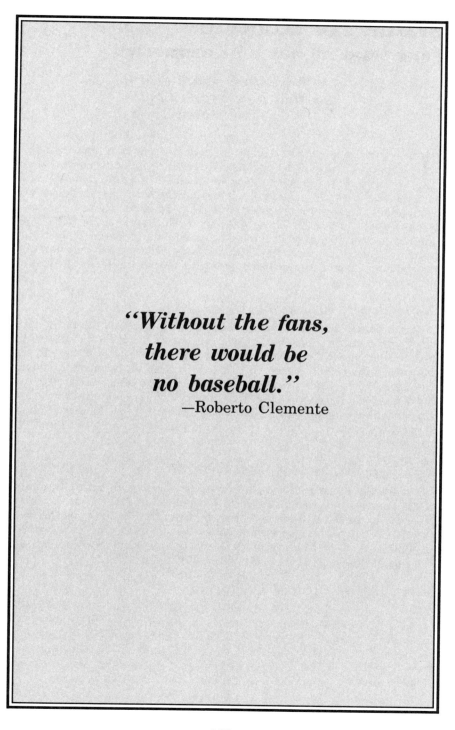

*"Without the fans,
there would be
no baseball."*
—Roberto Clemente

Statue For Roberto
Fans send money and memories

"Part of my youth died
on that New Year's Day!"
— Robin Bryer

T he Pittsburgh Pirates collected money from fans and friends of Roberto Clemente, as well as civic leaders and local corporations, to build a statue in memory of the Hall of Fame baseball star, perhaps the Pirates' all-time greatest performer. The response was tremendous. The amounts varied from $1 to $10,000. There were many checks for $21, or $21.21. There was one for $521 and one for $210. They came from over 40 states, and from Canada, Guam, Tokyo, Puerto Rico and England. Often, the checks and money orders were accompanied by brief notes. Some are reprinted here with the permission of the Pirates publicity office:

Robin Bryer, Westerville, Ohio

"I regret that I cannot make a larger donation to this effort. Roberto was far more than a baseball player. He was a hero! Part of my youth died on that New Year's Day. However, the happiest day of my life was this past June (1993) when we had our first child, a son. After being shot down on the first twenty or so suggestions on a name, I took a stab and offered the name Roberto. A gleam appeared in my wife's eyes and she consented enthusiastically. My son's full name is Roberto Richard Bryer. I will teach my son to be proud of his name and often I will tell him of the man for whom he is named."

Rick Bennett, Kansas City, Missouri

"As a transplanted Pittsburgher, I am happy to give a small amount to the statue fund. I can't begin to tell you what No. 21 meant to me growing up. I used to take the streetcar from Braddock to see the Bucs play in Forbes Field. I have many pleasant memories of sitting in the bleachers. He was taken from us at a young age, but his memory will live on. All the best from a homesick Pirates fan."

Susan Reeve, Benicia, California

"Here is my contribution and I wish I could send more, but the economy and job market are shaky. I am a big Pirates fan and also an A's season ticket holder. I have great hopes of coming to Three Rivers for the dedication in 1994. In 1971, I was in England where I was born and grew up with a father who played cricket. I married an American and learned about baseball and about The Great Roberto."

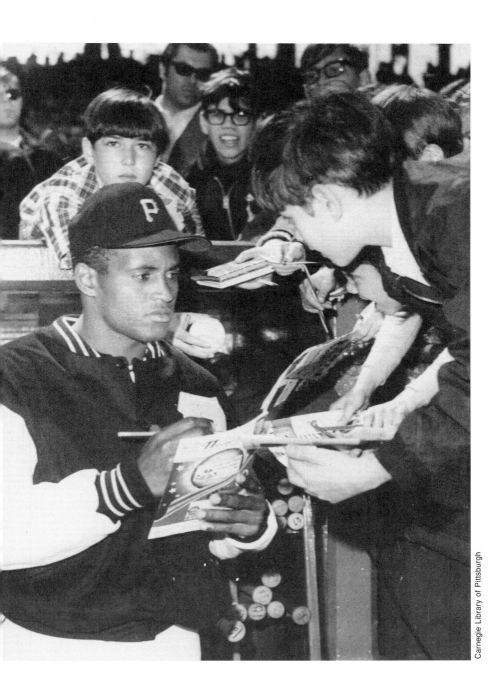

Murray Marlier, Kittanning

"With a tear in my eye, I enclose a modest check toward the statue for Roberto. I grew up a few blocks from Forbes Field. Born in '48, I was a perfect age to follow The Great One's career. No one played with more intensity. In my mid-20s, I cried unashamedly that New Year's Day. Thank you, Roberto!"

Bob Maisel, Ellicott City, Maryland

"Although I remember Roberto as a great player when I covered him for our newspaper (*Baltimore Evening Sun*) in All-Star Games or against the Orioles, I didn't get to know him personally. So, along with Roberto, this check is more for Joe Brown and Danny Murtaugh, two class guys who were good to an out-of-town sportswriter from Baltimore! Say hello to Joe. I hope Danny has to wait awhile to get his hello!"

Charles D. DeCarbo, Brightwaters, New York

"I grew up in western Pennsylvania and played Little League ball against Bruce Tanner (Chuck's son) and cried my eyes dry for two hours when The Great One died in the tragic plane wreck that awful New Year's Eve. Since his death, I moved to Stow, Ohio; went back to Pennsylvania for college (Slippery Rock University); then trekked to Texas as a sports writer for nine years. I attended a Pirates Fantasy Camp (1991) to fulfill that childhood dream. I hope my numerically designated donation ($21.21) helps in honoring my favorite Pirate of all time. I can't wait to come back home to see the statue."

Mary Kyper, West Brownsville

"Enclosed is a small donation for the statue for Roberto, who is my baseball hero. I am a senior citizen and would like to leave a memento to my grandchildren that I was, in fact, a small part of the statue. I do commend you for doing this in his memory. God bless."

Charles Teese, Pittsburgh

"I am writing on behalf of a nine-year-old boy from Binghamton, New York, who attended a game recently with his father and me. As a youngster, the father idolized Roberto Clemente. He was excited that, so many years after the tragedy that took Roberto away, his son, Tim, wanted to make a contribution to the statue fund. Tim had only one dollar. He was all excited about giving his donation to some official at the Stadium, but none of the Stadium staff he approached could tell him what to do with his dollar. One disappointed young baseball fan left the Stadium that night. This is a small story, I know, however, it is one I wanted to share. And enclosed is Tim's dollar."

Adam Poole, Connellsville

"I am 11 years old and play the majors in Little League. My Uncle B, who takes me to many Pirate games, told me about the wonderful man and player you are honoring with a statue. I saved up some money from cleaning for my uncle's business. Usually, I buy Game Boy tapes, but I want to send $20 to the statue fund."

Bob Conaway, Morgantown, West Virginia

"I am pleased to donate to the Clemente statue. I wish I could afford more. Roberto provided a great childhood for me as a baseball fan. I've said for years that the City of Pittsburgh or someone should erect a statue of him. I thank you for the chance to aid in its construction."

T.D. Stuck, Swanton, Maryland

"It's not a great deal of money, but I felt I had to send something. The Pirates have been my family's team since as long as I can remember."

Stephen Kehayes, Phillipsburg, New Jersey

"As a boy attending Bucco games at Forbes Field in the '60s, I have vivid memories of Roberto's spectacular play in right field. He was a man of unparalleled character and abilities. Arriba, Roberto!"

Alan Kalish, Philadelphia

"Fine people like Clemente should be preserved in our memories forever!"

Garry Brown, New York, New York

"One for The Great One. Your organization honors me by allowing me to honor Roberto. I can't think of a more gratifying or just thing to do. He was of the highest character. His greatness on the field was exceeded only by his caring and sacrifice off the field."

Richard Montgomery, Bethel Park

"Among many fond memories of my youth in Pittsburgh was listening to Pirates games on the radio with my family. My mother loved Roberto more than any other player. She always got terrifically excited whenever he was mentioned. I'm sorry that she didn't live to see this tribute to her favorite. Please recognize this contribution in memory of her."

Phil Caponegro, Brooklyn, New York

"Roberto was a great ballplayer and a great human being. Accept this small donation to help in your effort. I'm sorry I cannot send more, but these are very tough times for a lot of us."

Tom Plevin, Uniontown

"On July 14, 1993, my wife Karen passed away after a six-year battle with cancer. Although she did not understand baseball well enough to appreciate the playing skills of Roberto Clemente, she did appreciate his humanitarian personality and philanthropic display to people who were less fortunate. We make this contribution in her memory."

Bernardine Ratesic, McKeesport

"I loved Roberto and admire what he did, but this is all I can afford. Good luck and God bless. I admire what you're doing."

William Dertinger, Jr., Staten Island, New York

"While I am too young to have seen Roberto play, I have seen many documentaries that mention him. I have also read books about the man. I wish there were more players and men like Roberto, who both on and off the field could be looked up to by children as a role model. I regret that I can only donate $20, but I am a recent graduate who has not yet begun to work."

John and Mary Burgess, Pittsburgh

"My wife and I will always remember the excitement and intensity that Roberto brought to the game and the dignity that he brought to all athletics. He was the complete baseball player. More importantly, he was a noble man."

Mark Maranowski, Pittsburgh

"My younger brother and I, along with my father and grandmother, went to a Sunday afternoon game at Three Rivers Stadium in September of 1972. We found our seats, but my brother and I decided to go to one of the gates to get some autographs before the game. When we got there a long line had already formed. We had no idea which two players would appear to sign autographs in a few minutes. Bob Johnson and Roberto Clemente appeared in full uniform and took their seats at the table. When our turn came, I remember placing our yearbook in front of Roberto for him to sign. He graciously signed two pictures (one for my brother and one for me) along with our yearbook. After he had signed the yearbook, I remember saying 'thank you.' He looked up at me from across the table with a great big smile on his face. It's a moment I will always remember. Three months later he was killed in the plane crash."

Kim School, Kernersville, North Carolina

"I salute everyone involved in the fund-raising as well as Roberto and his family."

Betty McIntyre, Finleyville

"I am on disability so I can't give much, but every dollar counts. It's a great way to remember Roberto."

Mal Goode
The Dean of Black Broadcast Journalism

"He had a special ingredient.
He was hard to understand, but
he was some kind of human being."
— Goode on Clemente

Mal Goode moved among giants in his heydey. And he has the pictures to prove it, twenty-one albums worth, according to his wife, Mary. I scanned these albums and scrapbooks, which also contain testimonial letters, during a December, 1993 visit to the home of the Goodes, just off Frankstown Road in Penn Hills, a suburb five miles east of Pittsburgh. The Goodes had moved back to Pittsburgh that August after living 32 years in Teaneck, New Jersey. One of their daughters, Rosalia Parker, an attorney, and her family lived at the end of the same street in Penn Hills.

Goode appeared in photos along with the likes of South African black leader Nelson Mandela, former Attorney General and U.S. Senator Bobby Kennedy, civil rights leader Rev. Jesse Jackson, UN Secretary General U Thant, President Jimmy Carter, President Gerald Ford, George Bush before he became President, NAACP leader Roy Wilkins, former Cleveland mayor Carl Stokes. He also knew Dr. Martin Luther King, and regrets that he never had his photo taken with him. "There were so many times. . ." said Goode, shaking his head. "I wish I'd had somebody snap a picture somewhere along the way. I should have had all kinds of photos."

He settled back into a long couch, and closed his eyes, as if to seal the memories of time spent at the side of Dr. King. Anybody seriously interested in black history, or American history for that matter, would be wise to spend a day in the living room of Goode's comfortable red-brick home. He has been featured reflecting on his career on a WQED-TV special. His stories sometimes wander as much as his wavy gray hair, but he is a fascinating fellow. He brightened an otherwise gray, rainy day.

There were also times in his distinguished broadcast, journalism, public speaking and statesman career that Goode moved among Giants and Dodgers and Braves and particularly Pirates. And Roberto Clemente was among the latter. While he has photos showing him with Jackie Robinson, who broke the color line in baseball with the Brooklyn Dodgers in 1947, he does not, unfortunately, have a photo of him with Clemente.

At age 85, and two months away from being 86, Goode had led quite the life. He had grown up in Homestead, and made his mark as a radio broadcaster there at WHOD and in Pittsburgh at KQV, been affiliated in several roles with the *Pittsburgh Courier* back in 1948, when it was the largest black newspaper in the country. The *Courier* had clout in those days, with 17 regional editions and a national circulation of 400,000, and had extolled the excellence of black, or "tan" athletes, long before the popular press. Goode was a much-respected civil rights activist long before it gained this nation's headlines ("I was out there before Dr. King came on the scene.") Goode's was a non-violent protest and call for improved conditions and acceptance. He held many posts in Pittsburgh early in his professional career where he worked with young people — his favorite job was being in charge of the boys' program at the YMCA ("to us, it meant Young Men's Colored Association," he kidded) — and had a hand in improving housing, recreation and living conditions for blacks. He was Dr. King's kind of guy.

Mal mixed easily, and spoke softly, and warmly, for the most part, but he could get his points across, and he was not hesitant to protest angrily when it was appropriate. "You weren't going to call me nigger and walk away with it," he said, and nodded to affirm that declaration.

Goode said he had a fine relationship with Joe L. Brown, the general manager of the Pirates. Goode says Brown often consulted with him about the affairs of the black and Latin ballplayers on the Pirates because Brown trusted his judgment on such matters, and because Goode was a confidant of those players. Goode borrowed some money from Brown on one occasion to help finance a business venture. "I'd rather borrow from Joe Brown than from a bank,". said Goode with a grin.

In 1962, Goode's friend Jackie Robinson tipped him off to a broadcast opportunity at the American Broadcasting Company (ABC). Robinson had reprimanded officials at ABC about the lack of blacks other than doormen and elevator operators in their operation, and prompted change in that respect. Robinson came to Pittsburgh to speak in McKeesport, and Goode picked him up at the airport. "That's when Jackie told me to get in touch with the people at ABC," said Goode. "He thought they were about to do something."

Goode was one of 38 black men who auditioned for the position. He got the job and became the first prominent black network news correspondent. Like his friend Jackie Robinson, he had broken an important color barrier. He was 54 at the time.

The Goodes left Pittsburgh and bought a home in Teaneck, New Jersey that had been owned by Elston Howard of the Yankees. They became close friends. Howard, the first black ballplayer with the Yankees, had played against the Pirates in Pittsburgh in the 1960 World Series, and was the American League's MVP in 1963.

Born in White Plains, Virginia on land given to his paternal grandparents at the time of the Emancipation Proclamation, Goode takes great pride in being considered "the dean" of black professional broadcast journalism in America. I had met Mal Goode when I was a student at the University of Pittsburgh, his alma mater as well, back in the mid '60s. I was too young to appreciate his accomplishments then. He was quite a public speaker, though, and had an aura about him.

"My grandfather galvanized all of us," recalled Goode. "He had been a slave. He didn't want us to feel like we were better than anybody else, but he didn't want us to think anybody else was better than us."

Mal Goode listens
as Jackie Robinson
tells a story.

Goode still had an aura about him, though he was in failing health. This time around, I realized I was in distinguished company, and was in awe of the distinguished company he had kept. The purpose of my visit, however, was to learn more about Clemente from someone who knew him well, and had befriended Clemente and several of the pioneer black ballplayers in Major League Baseball back when friends in foreign cities were a welcome sight to the likes of Robinson, Willie Mays, Monte Irvin, Hank Thompson, Henry Aaron, Willie McCovey, Bill Bruton, Wes Covington and Juan Pizzaro.

Mal and his wife, the former Mary Lavelle, to whom he had been married for 55 years at the time of my visit, had often hosted those great baseball stars at the dining table of their home in the Homewood section of Pittsburgh.

"Sometimes we'd have as many as eight of them at our house, three or four from the Pirates, and three or four from the Braves or Giants or Dodgers," recalled Goode. What scenes they must have witnessed. Learning about this situation was a real revelation to me. I never knew there were such gatherings. Too bad Goode hadn't taped their conversations.

Then again, those future Hall of Famers came to the Goode home because they were comfortable there — Mary had both a warmth and inner strength about her, it seemed to me in my short stay — and Mal was a Goode guy in more ways than one, someone who recognized and sympathized with their special circumstances and the enormity of their challenge. He, too, had spent much of his life proving that he was as good as the next guy. "If I hadn't been black," said Goode, the consummate opportunist and promoter," I'd have been a millionaire."

As he put it, "You can't understand or appreciate what it was like being a Negro — no one called us black back then — 35 years ago. There were so many doors closed to us." But he clinged to something his grandfather often said: "It won't always be this way."

Mal Goode came up the hard way. During his days at Homestead High School and at Pitt, he followed his father to work in the Homestead mills of U.S. Steel. He worked there at night, doing janitorial work in the general offices, while attending school and for five years, as well as working at a men's clothing store in Pittsburgh in a menial capacity, after his graduation from Pitt during the Great Depression.

"My father worked in the open hearth No. 4," said Goode. "It's all torn down now, sad to say. He got to be a first helper; that's as high as a black man could go in those days. He was paid $12 an hour as a first helper. He trained many a man who ended up with better jobs, who made $24 an hour. He worked 12-hour shifts. He got to know Andrew Carnegie. He helped set a record for production of steel in a 24-hour period — him and some Polish fellow — and Carnegie gave them an award. It was a box of cigars. My dad didn't smoke. His name was Billy Goode. Everyone at U.S. Steel and in Homestead knew my dad."

His dad and mother, Mary Goode, were a plus in Mal's life as well as that of his sister, Mary Dee. The two of them worked at the same time at WHOD in Homestead in the early '50s, and were thought to be the only brother-sister radio team in the nation.

176

Henry Aaron   Willie Mays

Jackie Robinson

The Goodes have six children, all of whom attended college, with five of them graduating, often with distinguished academic records, and the other with three years of college.

He believes blacks have to get back into their churches, that everybody can benefit by hearing the preachers, by praying to God for guidance and blessings. "My father always had us kneeling, thanking God for what he'd given us."

Goode is concerned that today's young blacks aren't as well off as he and his sister were. "Today, many black youngsters don't have a home at all, not a real home," he said. "The family is broken down; especially the black family. The kids have nobody to guide them; they have no father. I know now that I came up well. I never heard my father speak back to my mother. I grew up in a rich home. My father knocked me down when I raised my voice to my mother. He'd say, 'If you get to the point where you don't want to hear from your father, or you don't want to hear from your mother, well, there are hinges on that front door.' And he meant it. I had a home where the children had an example, a model at home. It was Dad, or Father, or Pop. There were six of us children and after we had all graduated from college, we got together and paid off our parents' mortgage. We had a six-room house on 12th Avenue in Homestead. Today, there are too many broken homes, or homes where mothers and fathers don't speak to each other. I hope that will change."

Change is one thing Goode has witnessed on a first-hand basis. Shortly after he had been hired at ABC, he covered the Cuban Missile Crisis as well as UN debates. He covered the Democratic and Republican national conventions of 1964 and 1968 as one of ABC's floor reporters. He also covered James Meredith's Mississippi March against discrimination in 1966 and was the only black network reporter covering the funeral of Dr. King when he was assassinated in Memphis in April, 1968. One month later, he was ABC's man on the Poor People's March from Marks, Mississippi to Washington, D.C. He covered Operation Breadbasket with Rev. Jesse Jackson in Chicago.

Mal Goode had truly seen it all.

"Pittsburgh was Mal Goode's town. He was like our godfather."
— Henry Aaron

It was when he was working at the *Pittsburgh Courier* that Mal Goode got to know Clemente. "I had a press pass, and I used to go to Forbes Field an awful lot; I'd go in and out of the clubhouse, and we took a liking to each other," said Goode. "The Dodgers, Giants and Braves were the first ballclubs to have many blacks, and I'd pick up three or four and bring them out to our home in Belmar Gardens in Homewood; it was a new development I'd helped to build in 1952. My wife would fix dinner for them.

"We'd have Jackie Robinson, Monte Irvin, Hank Thompson, Willie Mays, and many were the times we had Henry Aaron. He mentions me in his book."

As if on cue, Mary handed me a copy of Aaron's book, *I Had A Hammer*, and there were paragraphs circled in red ink on pages 136 and 137. It had been personally autographed to him by Aaron.

In his book (Harper Collins Publishers), written with Lonnie Wheeler, Aaron spoke of being third in the MVP balloting in 1958 behind Ernie Banks and Willie Mays, after Aaron had won the MVP award in 1957.

"It was company that I enjoyed being in," wrote Aaron. "The three of us, along with Frank Robinson and Roberto Clemente and several others, were starting to develop a little National League fraternity of black players. To start with, our names always seemed to run together in the league leaders, but we had a lot more in common than that. We were a small group in a big league, and we understood that we had to stick together. Whenever we were in a new town, we would meet up with the black players from the other team. If we were in New York, or later San Francisco, we looked up Mays. In Chicago, it was Ernie. In Pittsburgh, we would all gather at the Crawford Grill, which had been an old Negro League hangout.

"Pittsburgh was Mal Goode's town. Mal was a local media guy who had a radio show and worked with the *Pittsburgh Courier*, and he was like our godfather. All the black players went to Mal's house when they were in Pittsburgh. If we had a day game on Saturday, we'd all meet at Mal's afterwards and he and his wife would serve up a big dinner that we'd eat out on the lawn. It was a black neighborhood and people would come off the streets and sit around and eat with us. We felt at home there. We'd tell Mal our problems and he'd tell us about Jackie Robinson and Joe Louis. Now and then he'd take us to an NAACP meeting. Later on, Mal became one of the first black network correspondents, covering the United Nations for ABC-TV. But he never lost touch with his ballplayers. Mal probably had more Hall of Famers at his house than anybody alive. He took care of us."

After I had read those passages, I looked up and regained eye contact with Mal. He was smiling proudly. Aaron's book certified what he'd been telling me. Just in case there was any doubt. I had visited Aaron at his home in Atlanta at the height of his career, to interview him for a cover story in *SPORT* magazine. I offered some personal observations about Aaron to Goode.

"I'll tell you what stands out most about Aaron," Goode has said. "I don't know where he got the idea, coming from Mobile, Alabama, but Henry Aaron believed innately that he was as good as anybody. He'd let you know right now if there was any indication that somebody was trying to discriminate against him. If you went to a counter and somebody was slow giving service, he was sensitive about it. He'd say, 'When you gonna wait on me?' Mays was timid about that sort of thing, but not Henry Aaron."

Goode picked up where he had left off in our conversation prior to Mary handing me Aaron's autobiography.

"There were things they could tell me about what was going on on the team," said Goode. "Clemente told me personal things, things that were bothering him. The Giants were in town and he was at our dining table along with some of the Giants. He called me 'Mellie.' He said, 'They say the black ballplayers are criticizing me for not fraternizing with blacks. They say I don't want to be Negro. Look at me, Mellie. Look at my skin. Mellie, what else I gonna be?'

"I can see him now, like he was talking to me right now. He was shook up. He had a special ingredient. He was hard to understand, but he was some kind of human being. He was so great. I'm glad they're going to honor him.

"Back in 1960, when Maz hit the home run to win the World Series, they voted Dick Groat the MVP of the National League. By no stretch of the imagination should that have happened. There was no question about it. Clemente should have been the MVP."

Goode and Bill Nunn, Jr., the sports editor and columnist for the *Pittsburgh Courier*, often accompanied Clemente to the Crawford Grill, a popular restaurant and music spot in Pittsburgh's Hill District. It was on Wylie Avenue, near where the Civic Arena now stands. "I'd take him to the Crawford Grill," said Goode, "The food was great, so was the music, and you couldn't get in the place."

He sounded a little like Yogi Berra there ("Nobody goes to that restaurant anymore. It's always crowded.").

I asked him if ballplayers like Aaron and Clemente created any kind of stir when they stopped in bars and restaurants like the Crawford Grill. "They were just mingling," said Goode. "People were tickled to death to see them. And they paid their own way."

Goode continued talking about Clemente. "If you ever saw him play, you know he was one of the greatest ballplayers ever," said Goode. "If you ever saw him throw the ball from right field to third base or home to get a runner . . . when you think about it, you know you saw greatness.

"Look what happened when Mazeroski hit the home run. He became an instant hero. But who had the most to do with winning the World Series? When you think how they got through the seven games . . . Clemente was the man who made the key plays."

Of course, it should be pointed out that a player's performance in the World Series does not figure in the balloting for league MVP honors. The balloting is done before the World Series. Then, too, Mazeroski was not the MVP in the 1960 World Series. Bobby Richardson, the second baseman for the New York Yankees who set Series hitting records, gained that honor, a rarity in that he was on the losing side.

Goode thought the media didn't understand Clemente that well, and that sportswriters weren't always fair in their coverage. He mentioned Al Abrams, the sports editor and columnist of the *Post-Gazette* back then, and Les Biederman, the baseball beat writer and columnist for *The Pittsburgh Press*.

"Abrams didn't have a prejudiced bone in his body," said Goode. "He was a nice guy, and he'd grown up in the Hill District. He was fair to Clemente, I thought. I think Biederman was more of a conservative. He told writers around the country that Groat was the better MVP candidate. Clemente didn't care much for him.

"I didn't just know Clemente as a great ballplayer. I knew him as a human being. The only thing that amazed me was from time to time the press wasn't fair to him.

"During that 1960 season, for instance, it was always Dick Groat and Don Hoak and the guy (Dick Stuart) who couldn't play much at first base; and he wasn't a great ballplayer. But they got precedence over Clemente.

"Unfortunately for us, the first black (Curt Roberts) Pittsburgh had on its ballclub wasn't a great ballplayer. With Clemente, at least we could brag about a black ballplayer being on the team."

"He still does pretty good."
— Mary Goode

Goode said, "I was doing a lot of speaking then at schools. I got around pretty good. I had an opportunity to tell them what it was like to be a Negro in America, and things they didn't know about achievement by Negroes. I'd say, 'Who invented the traffic light?' The man was from Cleveland, just 120 miles away."

Goode paused and turned his attention to his wife. "Mary, what was that man's name?"

Mary shook her head. "I'm 82, and I don't know why he thinks I still remember this stuff," she said. "It was Garrett Morgan."

"That's right," said Mal, not missing a beat. "It was in 1923."

Mary interjected, "Mal had a seizure this past year, and it's affected him a little bit. He has some memory lapses. But he still does pretty good."

A month after my visit to the Goode home, I had the opportunity to watch an hour-long PBS offering on WQED-TV, done as a project by Howard University, of Goode reflecting on his distinguished career.

It was done in 1991, and Goode appeared more vibrant and sure of himself, sitting on the porch of his home in Teaneck, and being interviewed by Doris McMillon, a radio-TV personality in Washington, D.C. The stroke his wife had mentioned to me had obviously stolen some of his steam and self-assuredness, and the clarity of his story-telling ability.

There were clips showing him interviewing Malcolm X and Stokely Carmichael, two angry young black men who took a different approach than Dr. King for calling for change and civil rights for black people in America. White America, naturally, was very uncomfortable with Carmichael and Malcolm X.

Talking about Malcolm X, Goode said, "We used to quarrel quite a bit. He preached 'Hate Whitey.' I told him, 'One kind of hate is no different from another, Malcolm. That's not the answer.' His philosophy was not right."

181

There was also a clip showing Goode standing in the foreground of the Ebenezer Baptist Church in Atlanta at the funeral service for Dr. King. "The body of Dr. Martin Luther King has come home for the last time," intoned Goode.

"Certain people make their mark, but die too young."

I asked Goode to explain why so many young people were so fascinated with Clemente.

"The killing of President Kennedy made his family even more a focal point of interest in this country," said Goode, "and I think that happens with a lot of young stars in sports and in the music and entertainment field. Certain people make their mark but die too young. Like Bobby Kennedy and Dr. King.

"As far as Clemente is concerned, he stood for something. He was a decent human being. He was just a nice human being. He voiced his opinions on behalf of himself and other black athletes. He could have been an even more effective spokesman if he had been more familiar with the English language, but he wasn't always sure what was the right word to use. He is really appreciated in Puerto Rico. There are so many things there named for Roberto Clemente, like playgrounds and libraries. I'm glad they're going to have a statue for him here in Pittsburgh. Perhaps he can be a positive influence on the kids here, too."

From the Goode family album

Mal Goode in early days at WHOD in his hometown of Homestead.

182

*The one constant
through the years
has been baseball.*

*Baseball has
marked the time.*

*This field, this game,
is part of our past.*

*It reminds us of all
that once was good
and could be again.*
—"Field of Dreams"

"Field of Dreams"

184

Reflections on Forbes Field
Days in the bleachers

"You were never in a hurry to get home."

Daniel L. Bonk
Wexford

Dan Bonk is a civil engineer at the Michael Baker Corporation in Coraopolis who serves on the ballparks committee of the Society of American Baseball Research. He enjoys poring over the design blueprints for Forbes Field which he discovered in the City of Pittsburgh files.

Pittsburgh Pirates baseball fans, between the 1991 and 1992 seasons, were subjected to a tease. The administration of Mayor Sophie Masloff proposed building a new publicly financed baseball-only stadium to be called Roberto Clemente Field, in honor of the late Pirates Hall of Fame outfielder. The proposal came as a shock to media and citizenry alike and was quickly embraced, surely, by every true baseball fan who ever bought a ticket at Three Rivers Stadium farther from the field than a box seat. Due to a variety of reasons, including a luke-warm reception from the general public asked to finance it, Masloff quietly but quickly withdrew the proposal.

Nevertheless, the city, 22 years after the opening of Three Rivers Stadium, effectively admitted that it inadequately serves its most routine function as the baseball home of the Pirates.

Clemente Field would have been both a step forward and backward — forward because it was conceived along lines pioneered in Buffalo in 1988 with the opening of Pilot Field, home of the Pirates' minor league franchise, and backward because such neo-classic design tries to recreate the ambiance, intimacy, and reduced scale of baseball's classic old parks in Chicago, Detroit, Boston and New York. Most ironic of all, Clemente Field would invariably been compared to the Pirates' home for five decades — Forbes Field, thought by many to have been the most classic of all. It was demolished in 1972 in the Oakland neighborhood, to bring professional sports Downtown — a general national trend which has contributed greatly to baseball's modern condition as a corporate, upscale entertainment of $40 million players and $100 family evenings.

Samuel Hazo, Upper St. Clair
Director and President
International Poetry Forum

From "The Pittsburgh That Stays Within You":
Lifelong residents of the city tend to measure the new against what preceded it and make their judgments accordingly. As a rule, Pittsburghers do not embrace the new just because it is new. They are more than casually conservative that way, and their ultimate criterion in

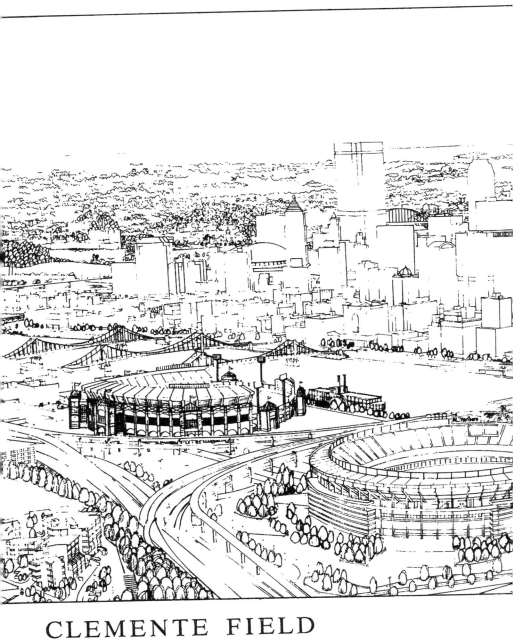

CLEMENTE FIELD

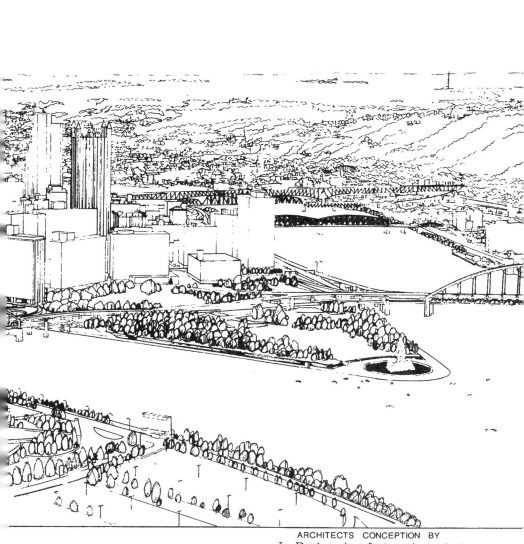

ARCHITECTS CONCEPTION BY
L. D. Astorino & Associates, Ltd.

evaluating the old against the new or vice-versa is to ask the sensible question, "Is it any good?" Take the case of Forbes Field, for example. Deep in tradition, it was where Pie Traynor and his championship team played, where Babe Ruth hit his 714th and final home run on May 25, 1935, where Ralph Kiner hit prodigious homers that made the Pirates interesting if not competitive in the forties, where no Pirate pitcher had ever thrown a no-hitter. Located at the edge of Schenley Park, Forbes Field was in the very heart of Oakland. On one side of it was the lush background of the park. But its real asset was that it was within blocks of restaurants, stores and trolley lines, and enterprising Oakland residents could make a quick dollar or two on game nights by allowing fans to park their cars in driveways and, occasionally, front yards, because of its location, you could go, as a leading Pittsburgh architect named Tasso Katselas (he was speaking with the stern authority of a fan) observed, to a baseball game on impulse. And many people did just that. They went to a baseball game because they suddenly felt like going to a baseball game. Why? Because it was possible, and what is possible eventually becomes factual. Torn down to make way for a complex of libraries and other buildings owned by the University of Pittsburgh, Forbes Field continues to haunt the new stadium built to take its place on the North Side. Many Pittsburghers will tell you that Three Rivers Stadium offers function without garnishes and color. Rand McNally rating or no Rand McNally rating, they insist that Forbes Field had the color and the ambience, and nothing anybody can say will change their minds.

Lee Gutkind
English Professor, Writer
University of Pittsburgh

Lee Gutkind grew up in Greenfield believing that Ralph Kiner, left fielder for the Pittsburgh Pirates, was the greatest man ever to live. He has written several successful books about the medical community in Oakland, notably Many Sleepless Nights, One Children's Place *and* Stuck In Time. *The following comes from his novel* God's Helicopter.

The third thing that happened to make the winter better was the arrival of the new kid from Florida whose name was Wier Strange. There's nothing more to report about this kid, except that he got Willie, Rip and Middlebaum thinking seriously about names.

"Why don't baseball players have dumb names?" said Middlebaum. *Ralph Kiner's not dumb. Pee Wee Reese, Gil Hodges, Gair Allie, Howie Pollett, Ted Kluszewski,* those are good names. I'd trade my Middlebaum name for any of those names in a minute."

"But they're baseball players," said Willie. "Only people have stupid names. You can't be a baseball player unless you have a name like Mickey Mantle, Whitey Ford, Vic Wertz."

"Yeah, and what about Duke Snider?"

"There's no better name in the world than good old Duke Snider."

188

"How about Richie Ashburn or Preacher Roe?"
"Or Branch Rickey?"
"I'd give my pitching arm to have a name like Branch."
"Which goes to show that the whole National League would be ruined if regular people with regular names played baseball."
"You mean like my uncle, Herman Gluck," said Middlebaum.
"Herman Gluck is a perfect example."

June and Rudy Gradisek
Center Township

"We used to sit in the bleachers, right behind third base. All five of us could get in, back in 1962, for $5. We went as a family, and later our son Rick went to all the games."

Bob Lesky
Weirton, West Virginia

"I remember the deep centerfield, and how they'd roll the batting cage out there and put it up against the wall. I'm sitting behind home plate with a glove in my hand. Meanwhile there's no way I'm going to catch a foul ball because there's netting overhead. I remember sitting sometimes in seats that had a blocked view. But it was still a joy to be there. I remember the scoreboard. That's when I got the fever and still follow the Pirates. We lived in Weirton. I was the oldest of nine children, and my dad took me to the games. I was born in 1949 and I was 11 in 1960 when the Pirates played in the World Series. I still miss Roberto. I still have feelings for him. Because he did everything on the baseball field that could be done. He'd stand deep in the batter's box and you still couldn't pitch him outside. He was a humanitarian, obviously. He was misunderstood because he was a Latin-American. He was just a joy to watch. It seems he played it just because it was a game."

Anonymous

"What I liked best about Forbes Field was that you were never in a hurry to get home."

Alan Byers, Lakeland, Florida

"My brother and I went to see the Pirates play the Cincinnati Reds at Forbes Field for a doubleheader on Easter Sunday, April 17, 1960. The Buccos won the first game, 5-0. In the second game, the Reds led 5-0 going into the bottom of the ninth inning. Hal Smith hit a three-run homer and Bob Skinner followed with a two-run blast to win the game. My brother and I raced onto the field to celebrate. By that time, the Reds were running to their dugout. One of them grabbed hold of my brother and threw him to the ground. It seemed like the whole team was trampling on him. We were laughing and jumping around, and couldn't believe how the game had ended. We read in the paper the next day how their manager, Fred Hutchinson, broke everything on his way to the locker room."

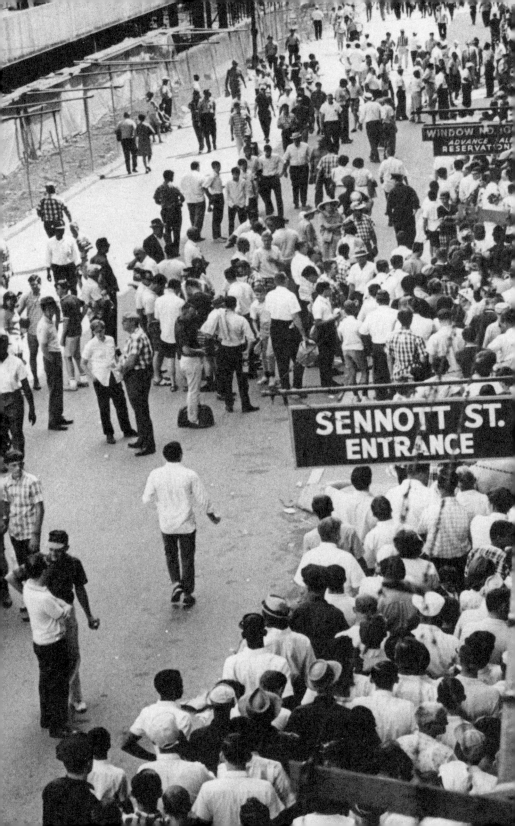

P RP
1 2 3 4 5 6 7 8 9 10
PHIL.
ST.LOU.
ATLAN.
S. FRAN.
CINCI.
HOUST.
NEXT GAME
HERE
PITTSBURGH

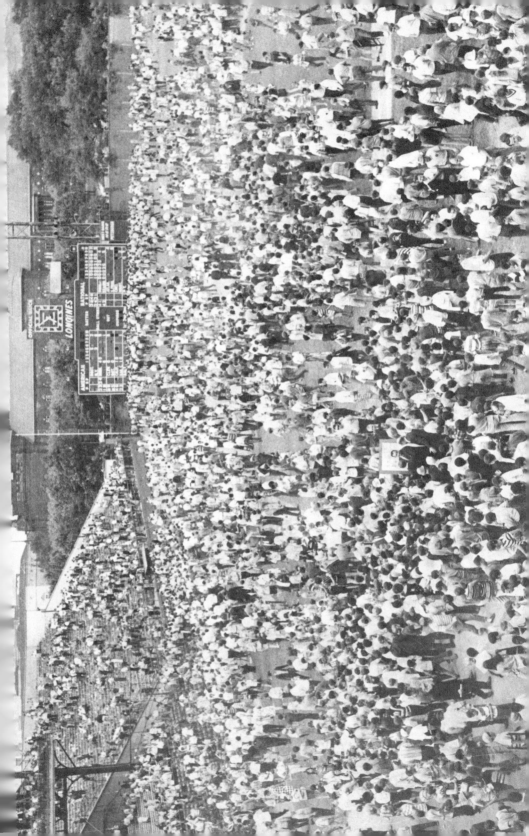

Ronnie Kline
The Callery Pa. Hummer

"In Puerto Rico, they loved the ground Clemente walked on."

Ronnie Kline recalls Roberto Clemente as a close friend when they were teammates on the Pirates. They were teammates in two different periods, across many summers and one memorable winter. Kline first came up to the Pirates as a hard throwing right-handed pitcher for the 1952 season, returned on a full-time basis in 1955 — Clemente's rookie season — and stayed till 1959. He missed being part of the Pirates' 1960 championship team, but was brought back for 1968 and 1969.

He said there was a big difference between the Clemente he found the first time around and the second time around. "He had grown up and matured," recalled Kline. "And most of the older players on that '60 team were gone when I came back, and Clemente was more of a veteran and team leader by this time. He had established himself as the star of the team, and one of the best in baseball. He was more confident and was in the prime of his career."

I asked Kline about his personal relationship with Clemente.

"We were great friends," he said. "I always hung out in right field before the game. I used to roll the ball to him out there, anything to look busy. I tried to hide out there. After the years went by, I just enjoyed Clemente's company.

"Bobby Bragan was the manager, and it was in 1956 or 1957, and we were in Chicago. Clemente was having a party there and he asked everyone on the club to come to his party. Whoever wanted to come was welcome. I went with Bob Skinner and Johnny Powers. Now Powers was from Alabama, and he didn't care much for blacks. He used to say, 'Everytime you see one you ought to shoot 'em.' Yet he went to the party. But we were the only white players who went to Clemente's party."

When Kline told this story it struck me that there had to be so many ballplayers back then who shared Powers' racist views, and why it had to be so difficult for black athletes at the time. And you wonder whether any true progress has been made in that regard.

Kline was sitting across from me in a booth of a Butler restaurant, an old-fashioned local landmark called The Hot Dog Shoppe. He was sitting next to Jim Lokhaiser, who hosts a Saturday morning sports talk show on Butler's WISR Radio, and is a long-time friend of Kline. Back when Lokhaiser was a full-time sportscaster at WISR, he accompanied Kline on travels to spring training in the early '60s. He even caught him in warm-up sessions on occasion, in emergencies, and still has the scars on his hands and shins to prove it.

Kline comes from nearby Callery, Pa., a small railroad town of a couple hundred people, and as a fireballing pitcher he was branded "The

Callery, Pa. Hummer" by Bob Prince, the Pittsburgh Pirates broadcaster. Callery is located in Butler County.

Kline would be 62 in three months, but he still had a crewcut, with a dent of sorts in the brown hair that was going gray in the front. There was still a gleam in his green eyes, and he smiled through every story. He had taken a break from deer hunting in the woods in East Brady, north of Butler, to join us. Kline said that he and ElRoy Face used to have a hunting camp up in Potter County. He and Face had roomed together on the road with the Pirates for a few years. In addition to hunting, Kline also likes to play golf, and never misses a Pirates' alumni golf outing. Kline was in an expansive mood, in good humor, sipped on steaming hot coffee, and shared some good stories.

"I thought I had the most grandchildren — six — of all my former teammates, but then I learned from Bobby Del Greco that he's got 12 grandchildren," said Kline, cracking up at his own lines. "I lost that one big."

He looked a lot better than he had when I last saw him a year earlier at a special luncheon hosted by the Pirates at the Allegheny Club where he'd sat with former teammates Bill Virdon, Dick Groat and Bob Friend. That was before he quit drinking. In between, he discovered he had diabetes and had to change his diet and some of his personal habits.

At our meeting in Butler, I asked Kline if he recalled inviting Clemente to come to any parties, or any players inviting Clemente to do anything, attend a movie, have a meal at a restaurant, come to their home.

Kline said, "I don't think he would have went. He was a loner."

Kline said he learned a lot about Latin American ballplayers and Clemente when he went to play winter ball in the Dominican Republic. He spent the winters of 1955 and 1956 pitching for Santiago. "I played in 1969 for Jim Fregosi in Ponce. Clemente was playing for San Juan," Kline said. As an aside, Kline claimed to have set a record for most wins by an American pitcher in the winter league with a 16-4 mark.

"He was a changed ballplayer when he was back home among Latin Americans," claimed Kline. "He was much looser down there than he was here. It seemed like nothing bothered him there. The fans loved him there. In Puerto Rico, they loved the ground Clemente walked on. No matter where he went, the crowds swarmed around him, and hollered out to him. I think they would have put you in jail if you bad-mouthed Roberto Clemente. The Pirates wanted him to rest, but he played so much because the fans demanded it. They chanted for him all the time. He was a national hero in Puerto Rico.

"When he was killed in that airplane crash, the Pirates called me and invited me to travel to Puerto Rico on a chartered airplane to attend the funeral services for Clemente. I was glad they asked me. We were good friends."

"My dog's the only Black Velvet in my life now."

Ronnie Kline is a recovering alcoholic. After a health scare, he had quit drinking cold turkey about six months before our meeting. At that time, former teammates would tell you at the mention of Kline's name, "You know he's been off the sauce for six months." It sounded like Kline had been a hard-drinking individual all his adult life, but Dick Groat insists that wasn't so. "I remember he didn't drink at all when he first joined the team," said Groat.

Like Groat, Kline didn't drink or smoke when he first joined the Pirates. That had a great appeal to the Pirates general manager back then, Branch Rickey, who was a bit of a Baptist in his approach to such things. "I didn't start smoking until I started playing big-league ball," says Groat. "All the guys were smoking. There was lots of idle time."

It's ironical that Kline's strength as a fire-balling pitcher was his pinpoint control. He was having a good time away from the mound. Nobody enjoyed the baseball life any more than Ronnie Kline.

During our breakfast meeting in Butler, Kline left his black labrador in the cab of his 1987 Chevy Suburban pick-up truck. His dog's name is Black Velvet, which was Kline's favorite brand of whiskey. "My dog's the only Black Velvet in my life now," Kline claimed.

Kline had quit smoking cigarettes just as abruptly, and on his own, six years earlier, when doctors were concerned about his health. "The doctors said I couldn't quit smoking on my own, and they said I couldn't quit drinking on my own. I used to smoke four or four-and-a-half packs of cigarettes a day. Kool filters, for the most part.

"I quit in 1988. The only reason I know that is because I remember that Art Rooney died while I was in the hospital. They said I had a heart attack. But that was a bunch of crap. But it was a scare."

Though he has quit smoking and drinking, he still drops in on his friends at bars around town. His son-in-law, Ed Kosich, owns John's Bar & Grill. He also frequents the Grouse House, the Hungarian Club and the VFW. Kline is kidded about going on the wagon, but he has managed to avoid the temptation to indulge in drinking booze again.

For many years, Kline operated a bar in Callery. It was called The Bullpen. He opened it in 1969, and operated it on and off until 1989. His buddy Face, a carpenter, did all the interior woodwork when it was first opened. Kline sold his saloon three times. He kept taking it back before he finally got rid of it for good.

He spent 20 years in professional baseball, 17 in the big leagues. He put in two years of military service one year after joining the Pirates. He was traded on December 21, 1959 to St. Louis for Gino Cimoli and Tom Cheney and missed out on the Pirates winning the World Series in 1960. In addition to pitching for the Pirates, he also worked for the Cardinals, Angels, Tigers, Senators and Twins before returning to Pittsburgh. In 1968, in his comeback as a 36-year-old relief pitcher with the Pirates, he won ten in a row, and was 12-5 for the season. After departing the Pirates a second time, he put in brief stints with the Giants,

Red Sox and Braves before ending his pro career in 1970. He and Face finished up playing for Chuck Tanner in Hawaii in 1970. "We were roomies, if you can picture us in the Hawaiian Islands," said Kline. "We were invited back, but we decided to call it quits."

Kline let that story sit awhile, before adding. "I'd do it all over again, and I'd do it the same way."

"Did you miss it?
Not much there, huh?"
— Kline on Callery

I have always been fascinated by people's hometowns, and how they might have fashioned them. Callery, Pa. seemed particularly cold at 6:12 a.m. on a mid-December day in 1993. It had snowed the night before, and the snow was blowing across the roads as I came into Callery. It was dark and cold and I thought I was back in Alaska in the U.S. Army. That's how cold Callery looked in the pre-dawn hour. Callery is a little community about 40 miles north of Pittsburgh, about five miles south of Butler, where I was headed this Saturday morning.

I was scheduled to meet with Kline for a breakfast interview at 9:30 a.m. in Butler, following an hour-and-a-half radio talk show appearance with Jim Lokhaiser, Bucky Parisi and Bud Daum at WISR Radio. But I wanted to check out Callery beforehand, just to see what it was like, to find out why Kline always came back to Callery after each baseball season, and why he remains there today. He grew up on Main Street, and played baseball halfway around the world, but he always returned home. Callery is two miles off Rt. 68 which runs through Evans City. General George Washington went through there once, according to a road sign.

"Did you miss it?" Kline inquired, when I told him later that I had looked in on his hometown on the way to Butler earlier in the morning. "Not much there, huh?"

So why stay?

"It's where I was born at," Kline said when I asked him why he continued to live in Callery. "If I started out in Cincinnati, or someplace like that, instead of Pittsburgh in the big leagues, maybe I would have moved. I always liked it there. Everybody is friendly and it's just a nice little town. Probably be buried there. My family is there. My Mom and Dad are there."

He refers to Henry Rea as Dad, even though he is, in truth, his stepfather ("Only Dad I've ever known," says Kline). Henry was 82, and had worked 40 years at Armco Steel in Butler. Ronnie's mother, Fern, was 80, and she had worked at Austin Bleach in Mars.

When we spoke, Kline had been married to Dorothy Wilson for 41 years. "She's from Mars — the planet!" quipped Kline, causing Lokhaiser to laugh aloud at a line he had, no doubt, heard before. "You know," added Kline, "when the Russian astronauts came to Pittsburgh they came out to Mars to have their picture taken."

210

Ronnie Kline

Ronnie Kline's best friend on Pirates was ElRoy Face.

The main industry that dominates the landscape in Callery is a chemical plant for Mine Safety Appliances Company and at the other end of town there's Herr-Voss, engineers and builders of sheet, plate and coil processing systems. "Mine Safety moved its headquarters office to Cranberry a few years back," said Kline. "The whole works used to be in Callery."

At that early hour, I also observed workmen on a well-lit dock loading trucks at Marburger Farm Dairy, a throwback to another era in that it's a family dairy farm that still delivers milk to homes.

When I was driving through Callery that morning the first street I came upon was called Kline Avenue. It's named after you know who. It's the first street off the Mars-Evans City Road.

I drove across some railroad tracks and wondered what trains had traversed the community during its heyday.

"The B&O Rail Road," said Kline, when I inquired later on. "My grandad, J. W. Kline, was an engineer for 50 years and 12 days. My two uncles worked for the railroad. My Uncle Ross was a conductor for 49 years, and my Uncle Leroy was a conductor for 47 years."

This information meant that Kline and I were kinfolk, in a way. My mother's father, Grandpap Richard Burns, had been a conductor for the B&O, and became the yardmaster in the Glenwood Yards of Pittsburgh. He moved his family, shortly after my mother had graduated from high school, from Bridgeport, Ohio to the Glenwood section of Pittsburgh. That's where I spent my entire youth.

"When I was 15," continued Kline, "before I could even get a driver's license for a car, I used to hitch-hike to Mars, and I'd run the train to Callery and Evans City and to Zelienople. I'd take over the controls of the train and go a few stops as the engineer. Then I'd go back home. I'd probably be running an engine today if I hadn't played ball."

Kline became a pitcher who gained people's attention when he was in high school. "I didn't start pitching till I was 15," he said. "I had a 17-1 or 18-1 record in the Eagle County League, a sandlot league. I played baseball and football at Evans City High School. I was an end and kicker. The school is not there anymore. Now the kids there go to Seneca Valley."

For the record, Kline studied vocational agriculture while attending Evans City High School.

"A big league scout named Homer Blackburn told me not to play football my senior year," continued Kline. "He said, 'All you can do is kick.' He said the Red Sox would sign me. A fellow named Bill Hulton ran the Butler Cubs, a semi-pro football team, and he also did some birddogging for the Pirates. Bill made me a proposal. He said, 'If I get you a tryout with the Pirates and, if you don't make it, will you play for the Cubs?'

"I was 18 when I went for my tryout at Forbes Field. There must have been a hundred prospects there. I was the first pitcher to take the mound. I struck out the first five batters, and the next one grounded out. They put a guy on first, and I had to hold him on. I had never pitched from a stretch. But I picked him off."

At Hulton's urging, Kline was signed by the Pirates shortly after graduating from high school in 1950. He started his career in professional baseball in Bartlesville, Oklahoma, then New Orleans, Louisiana, and Burlington, North Carolina. He came up to the Pirates in 1952.

He was a big, brown-haired right-hander who could throw with genuine heat on the ball. During the off-season, he always came home. He once was a car salesman in Butler, along with Groat and Jerry Lynch, and later was a co-owner of an automobile dealership in Harmony.

Kline came back from two years in the Army in time to join the rookie Clemente at training camp in 1955.

"He thought he had a gun like Mays," said Kline of Clemente. "But Mays taught him something about being too sure of yourself because you have a strong arm. Mays hit a single out to right one day, and the minute Clemente turned to throw, Mays pulled a trick. He rounded first base too far deliberately, and Clemente threw to first, and Mays kept going to second base and got there safely. Clemente learned a lesson about throwing behind the runner that day. But I also saw Clemente throw out runners at first base who thought they had singles on hard-hit balls to right field.

"He was bad at first. We're playing in Chicago, and Clemente got thrown out of the game. He got a $50 fine from the league office for the eviction. It was an automatic fine. Clemente just tore up the letter from the league office. A week later, he got another and this time the fine was up to $100. He tore that up, too. Now, before a game the umpire says Clemente can't play on instructions from the league office until he paid his fine. Bob Rice, the team's traveling secretary, sent the money in to take care of the fine so Clemente could pay. Clemente kept saying, 'No entiendo.' He said, 'No can read.'

"I remember another day when Clemente got fined. We all felt sorry for him. We were getting beat 3-1 by the Cubs at Forbes Field. There was a screen built around the lightstand alongside the scoreboard in left field. Clemente hit a shot to left field. Instead of the ball bouncing back straight off that screen around the lightstand, the ball ricocheted off the screen and went along the track by the wall out toward the deepest part of center field.

"Clemente kept running. Murtaugh was the third base coach and he put up his hands for Clemente to stop at third base. Clemente kept on going. If Ernie Banks doesn't drop the relay throw, Clemente is an easy out at the plate. But Clemente ended up with an inside-the-park home run.

"Bobby Bragan came up to Clemente in the clubhouse and held up his two hands, and asked him, 'What does this mean?' Clemente just shrugged him off. So Bragan puts up one hand and says, 'That's $25.' Then he holds up the other hand in the same motion Murtaugh did to try to hold up Clemente at third. And that's another $25. Have it in my office in the morning.' Clemente never missed a stop sign after that."

What else did Kline recall about Clemente?

"When we were on the road, the only time you'd see him eat in the same place we did was at breakfast in the hotel coffee shop. He always wanted to go to Latin places.

"I think he was a great guy. He had to be No. 1. I played with the best of them, from Musial to Mays, and I was with Yastrzemski, Clemente, Stargell, Frank Howard and Aaron. I missed Ted Williams, but I faced Williams in spring training. Groat bet me $100 I couldn't strike him out. I walked out there and threw the first pitch for a strike. The second pitch he fouled it off. Ron Brand was the catcher and he gave me the signals. I waved him off a few times, and then I threw what I thought was a strike. I knew I had the plate by an inch, but Williams just looked at it. The ump called it a ball. On the next pitch, Williams hit one that bounced off Dale Long's chest. Williams said to Virdon, 'That Kline really surprised me. He throws pretty hard.' They say he never forgot what a pitcher threw him. When a new pitcher would take the mound that Williams didn't know, he would check with others in the dugout and ask them, 'What's his best pitch?' He'd ask everyone."

Some other Kline contributions:

- "Clemente wouldn't wear his 1960 World Series ring because Groat won the MVP award. Some guys held that against Clemente."
- "Clemente always looked after the Latin ballplayers. He took good care of them. He'd get them a place to stay in Pittsburgh. We got along so good together; I'd go over to his locker and have a good time with him."
- "Maz wasn't a Clemente man, but they were always together, so it was tough to figure out. Maz says he wasn't a Clemente man, but they seemed to get along so well."
- "At one time we had on the Pirates what were called 'the seven greatest arms in baseball.' Remember Ron Necciai. He struck out all 27 batters in a minor league game, a record that still stands. Well, the next night, another young Pirates prospect named Bill Bell had 24 strikeouts for the Bristol, Virginia farm team; he was later killed in an auto accident in Florida."
- "When Bobby Bragan became the manager of the Pirates in 1956, he told us, 'None of you guys will get me fired.' The following year, he said, 'You younger guys are going to be in the World Series in a few years.' He knew we had some talent."
- "Face is more critical than some of the old ballplayers about certain things. It's too bad that he and Maz are not in the Hall of Fame. They both belong. They put Joe Morgan in as a second baseman. What the hell did he do?"

Kline captured the hell-bent attitude of Don Hoak with this story:

"You couldn't keep Hoak out of the lineup. He got hit on the elbow one day by Turk Farrell of the Phillies. It really hurt him. The next

214

day Murtaugh tells Hoak, 'I scratched you; you can't play today?' Hoak glared at Murtaugh and said, 'Are my shoes on?' And Murtaugh said, 'Yes.' And Hoak said, 'Are they slip-ons?' And Murtaugh said, 'No.' And Murtaugh's smiling now, and Hoak is still hot. 'Are they slippers?' Hoak asked him. 'No,' said Murtaugh, going along with the game. And Hoak said, 'Did I have to tie them?' Murtaugh said, 'Yes.' Finally, Hoak said, 'OK, I'm playing.' It was a memorable exchange.

"Today, you can do anything you want to do. The players decide when and where they're going to play. When I was playing, when you were sick, you had to go to the ballpark. You had to see Dr. Finegold. He'd decide whether or not you were able to play. A lot of times, you're hurting and nobody believes you. I hurt my right shoulder once, and I was going to pitch sidearm. Something popped and my shoulder felt OK after that. But even the doctors would accuse you of faking it, if you said it hurt too much to pitch.

"Once, I had a cyst on my tailbone. I went to see Doc Finegold. His nurse was Pat Koval, who married Bob Friend. I go in there and lay down on a slab. Doc Finegold gives me a shot of cortisone and one of novocain. I'm laying there and Doc says, 'I had to go a lot deeper than I expected. You look pretty good, but I should have done this in the hospital.' But we're in an office in the Jenkins Arcade, and we should be at Divine Providence. Doc Finegold says, 'Pat, give him a shot of whiskey to get the color back in his face.' Then he's having a problem stopping the bleeding. So he has Pat get me a box of Kotex. He says to me, 'You'll have to wear this for six weeks.' So I went around for a few weeks with Kotex strapped to my lower back."

Kline, explaining how he infuriated Joe L. Brown, and prompted him to trade him to the St. Louis Cardinals:

"They skipped me in the pitching rotation, and I was really upset about it. Bob Prince approached me and said, 'Hummer, you want to go on the radio?' I got on the radio. I can still see me talking into the mike, like it was happening right now. 'Are you having a problem with the manager?' Prince asks me. I said, 'No, I'm just sick of this. I want traded.' It turns out that Jack Hernon's wife was listening to the game, and she tells her husband what I said. So Hernon, who was the beat writer for the *Post-Gazette*, comes to me and tells me what his wife said she heard me say. 'Can I print it?' Jack asks me. Can you imagine a reporter doing that today? I can't imagine dealing with the media today. I can see some broad coming up to me and saying, 'How did you hold the ball when you gave up that home run?' I told Jack, 'Yeah, you can use it.' And that got me traded to St. Louis."

Don Hoak

215

"Clemente was always concerned about his countrymen."

In discussing the death of Clemente in the airplane crash off the coast of Puerto Rico on New Year's Eve, 1972, Kline recalled how Manny Sanguillen wanted to get to the airport and talk Clemente out of making the trip to take supplies to earthquake victims in Nicaragua. Sanguillen didn't think it was safe.

"Manny couldn't find his car keys," said Kline, "or he'd have probably been down there with the sharks, too. I think Clemente would have talked Sanguillen into going with him. Sangy got there late and missed the flight. Clemente was always concerned about his countrymen, so none of us were surprised to learn how he died, even though his death was a shocker to everyone."

Jim O'Brien

Ronnie Kline called his pet black labrador "Black Velvet" after his one-time favorite drink.

Clemente during his playing days with Santurce club in Puerto Rico.

Pittsburgh Pirates

Pittsburgh Pirates

Galbreath gives plaque to Clemente after he
ected his 3,000th hit at Three Rivers Stadium at
of 1972 season.

Pittsburgh Pirates

irates' Latin-American contingent in 1970 consisted of, left to right, Jose Pagan, Clemente,
rlando Pena and Manny Sanguillen.

Thank You, Roberto
A Christmas Story

". . . the moment of joy he
had given to our son."
— Ross and Lucetta Prestia

Lucetta Prestia works at the Upper St. Clair Library in my community. There was an exhibit there in the fall of 1993 featuring photographs, notepads, layouts and materials used in our book, MAZ And The '60 Bucs. She approached this author one afternoon, and told us a heart-warming story involving her late son, Ross, and Roberto Clemente. I asked her to send me a letter detailing the day they met at Children's Hospital. She and her husband Ross collaborated on this reflection:

Dear Jim:
. . . as per the request you made of Lucetta of a very special visit by a very special man. It happened many years ago.

". . . what good men do is oft'n interred with their bones." We cannot recall the origin of these words or if they are verbatim, but they continue to remind us of our gratitude for a very special visit by a very special man.

From time to time, we observed super stars making constant, albeit tearful visits to young patients at Children's Hospital in Pittsburgh. They always seem to have come at a perfect time — a child having a particularly difficult time, or a family in desperate need — never announced or expected, and always deeply appreciated.

We think of one occasion during the Christmas Season of 1969 while our son, Ross, lay in a terminal condition at Children's Hospital. (My wife and I were taking turns with the children, one at the hospital and one with two other children at home.)

I entered the room at Children's Hospital with a smile and a "Hey, what's up?" The 16-year-old former Teener League baseball player was smiling. He pulled one hand, clutching something, from under the sheets and, holding it high above his head, shouted, "A baseball . . . a major league baseball!!! An autographed major league baseball from Roberto Clemente!!! He just left, Dad. He must be in the next room!!!"

I did not feel it as important to go "next door" as it was to remain with our son to share his tremendous joy over the great visit and gift he had just received from The Great Roberto Clemente.

During days of such anguish it seemed impossible to continue doing the right things at the right time. Particularly things like "thank you" notes. Maybe we'll have time to do it next week, but the pile of neglected "thank you" notes went, regrettably, unwritten. Time passed so quickly. The situation deteriorated by the day — until, finally, it was no longer possible to send the almost forgotten overdue notes . . . and . . . within a few years, The Great One had also passed away and still we had not let him know how grateful we were for the moment of joy he had given to our son.

One may brood long and hard over an act of neglect, but surely Mr. Clemente would not have expected a "thank you" note, just as he would not have expected "thank you" notes from those he was intent on helping as he perished in that fatal airplane crash during "another mission of mercy" on December 31, 1972.

May this story be a way for us to feel assured that the good works of Mr. Clemente will not have been interred with his bones. Thank you, Mr. Clemente, for the thrill you provided during your baseball days in Pittsburgh and for the good deeds performed behind the scenes, off the field, and at Children's Hospital.

Children's Hospital

Pirates broadcaster Bob Prince introduces Clemente to some of the patients he frequently visited at Children's Hospital.

219

Jack Hetherington hosts Dick Groat at his bar-restaurant across from Edgewood Town Centre.

Bill Hillgrove and Groat are a familiar tandem on Pitt basketball broadcasts on WTAℰ Radio.

Dick Groat
Still a basketball player at heart
"He is loyal to a fault."
— Jack Hetherington

I t was not quite New Year's Eve. It was just after noon on Friday, December 31, 1993, and Dick Groat looked at home, sitting in the last booth of the dining room at Hetherington's, a restaurant-bar on South Braddock Avenue on the border of Swissvale and Edgewood. It's just off the Parkway East, a few miles from the Squirrel Hill Tunnels.

It was a white Christmas, and snow and slush were still everywhere on a bitter cold day, when the wind chill factor made it feel like it was about five to ten degrees below zero. So Groat and I were glad to be indoors in a warm refuge.

Hetherington's used to be the Sportsmen's Bar when the Union Switch & Signal was bustling across the street. But that business, like too many industrial plants in the valleys about Pittsburgh, had closed years ago, and its headquarters had been converted into an office building. Behind it loomed the Edgewood Towne Centre shopping mall, built only a few years earlier. Union Switch & Signal had relocated its offices in the North Hills.

Hetherington's was as modern as the mall, and had been refurbished to meet the needs of a changing neighborhood. It was no longer a shot-and-beer joint for men to belly up to the bar, but more of a family affair since it reopened in 1987.

The balding Groat was wearing a ballcap, and a black jersey with a red-stitched Champion Lakes Golf Club logo on the left breast, but he removed his cap when he sat down at a table. He bristled when he spotted some young men at a nearby table who kept their caps on, something routine at restaurants these days. "My dad would have knocked my cap off if he saw me sitting in a restaurant like that," said Groat. "There are no rules or manners anymore."

Richard Morrow Groat grew up in Swissvale, and starred in sports for the high school team there, and now lives in Edgewood half the year, and at his Champion Lakes Golf Course in Ligonier the rest of the time. He works for WTAE Radio, in Wilkinsburg, just east off the next exit on the Parkway, as a color commentator for Pitt basketball broadcasts.

Jack Hetherington, the owner, and his wife, Dolores, were on duty behind the bar. It was an attractive place, nicely appointed, with a bright interior that looked new. "We're more of a restaurant these days, more food than liquor," said Jack Hetherington. Groat and I both had omelettes for lunch, and lots of coffee. As usual, Groat smoked a lot of cigarettes, Marlboro Lights, and ground them out in an ashtray as we talked. He always leaves behind a burial mound of butts wherever he travels.

I wondered why he continued to smoke so much, when his wife and one of his brothers had both died in recent years of lung cancer. When he knew about the emphysema problems of former teammate Harvey Haddix. Our meeting took place less than a month before Haddix died. Groat blows off those kinds of questions. He shrugs his shoulders.

It was the anniversary of Roberto Clemente's death in an air crash on New Year's Eve, 1972, and seemed an appropriate time to get Groat to talk about his one-time teammate whom he always refers to as Bobby Clemente. Groat had been hosting a party at his golf course when he learned of Clemente's death on New Year's Eve, 1972. Then, too, the holiday season is a reflective time, and this was a particularly poignant time for Groat. It had been a grim year, one that had been understandably difficult for him to bear.

During the previous seven months, Groat had two brothers and a sister die in different months. They had simply grown old, into their mid and late '70s, and gotten ill. A week earlier, on Christmas Eve, he had driven his car back to his boyhood home, about six blocks or a mile and a half from Hetherington's, and had described the experience as "devastating." Said Groat: "I don't know why I did it; they say you can't go home again. Maybe I shouldn't have."

Groat's father was 87 when he died, and his mother 92. They came to Swissvale from Kane in 1916 and remained in the house at the corner of Hampton and Graff in a section of Swissvale known as The Hill. "My father was in the real estate business in Braddock for 60 years," said Groat. "They stayed in that home until they died."

Long-time friends often stop in Hetherington's. Groat is an old-fashioned guy with old-fashioned values, and at Hetherington's he feels comfortable. He marked his 63rd birthday there in November.

There was a sign on the bar promoting a New Year's Eve special: a filet mignon with a baked potato, vegetables, salad and roll for $12.95. Those are not New York or Chicago prices, or even Downtown Pittsburgh, for that matter.

"His loyalty is his greatest virtue," said Jack Hetherington later in the day, when Groat was getting ready to go home, and was out of earshot. "He's loyal to a fault. He believes if you were raised here that this is where you should live and spend your money. He likes to patronize local businesses."

"None of us was as gifted as Bobby was."

Dick Groat was named the National League's Most Valuable Player in 1960, the year the Pirates won the pennant and beat the mighty New York Yankees in the World Series. Groat was the shortstop and captain of the team. He also won the National League's batting crown that season with a .325 batting average.

Clemente felt that he deserved the award, and was incensed when he not only failed to win it, but finished eighth in the balloting among the baseball writers who covered the beat. That was a joke, for sure.

Clemente never wore his 1960 World Series ring as a personal protest, preferring instead to wear his All-Star Game ring. Groat had a high regard for Clemente, and thought he was one of the greatest baseball players in history. To this day, however, Groat feels he needn't apologize for winning that award.

"No doubt about it, Bobby had the greatest God-given talent I ever saw," said Groat. "Bobby was a complete player. What he didn't understand was the fact that the Most Valuable Player award is not necessarily for the greatest talent. A lot of other things go into it. He was certainly the greatest talent on that team, and you can be both the outstanding player and the MVP. None of us was as gifted as Bobby was.

"Everybody tries to make a big deal about us, but it was never any problem between us. We never had a cross word. I wasn't even conscious that he resented me winning it so greatly until deep into the 1961 season."

Groat must have wondered what was going on, however, when he and Clemente were among the Pirates presented with special awards at the outset of the 1961 season, and Clemente kicked over Groat's award as it stood on the sideline. Was it an accident? Groat still doesn't know.

I have heard Groat speak at several public forums, and he always speaks positively about Clemente. There are things Groat may grumble about in the company of close friends, but he's always a street-smart politician in front of a microphone.

"In 1971, he proved what we all said that he had so much talent," said Groat. "He didn't prove that until the 1971 World Series. But that's what we thought he was capable of doing right along.

"There was nothing on the baseball diamond that he couldn't do if he wanted to. He could have adapted his hitting style if he wanted to be more of a home run hitter, but George Sisler (Hall of Famer who was the Pirates' hitting instructor) wanted him to spray the ball around, and be a high percentage hitter.

"As a fielder, I never saw anyone play balls off the right field wall the way Bobby did. And I remember going to Forbes Field as a kid, when it was Paul Waner out there. It was spooky, how Bobby knew how to play that wall.

"I used to love to watch Bobby make the turn at second base. He could really pick them up and put them down. He didn't really run; it was more of a gallop. It was fun to watch him. I can see him sliding into third base. That's the way I picture him. He was truly, in all ways, one of the greatest who ever played the game. There wasn't anything he couldn't do.

"If he hadn't been killed, I could see him playing another five years. Bobby was always in great shape. He worked at it year round. He had a great body, and that was evident from the first day I ever saw him at Fort Myers training camp. He was a marvelous talent."

Over lunch, Groat admitted that he was not a close friend of Clemente, and that he wasn't always sure where Clemente was coming from — at first, there were language difficulties, cultural differences — and, like many of his teammates, he sometimes questioned Clemente's approach to the game. Groat and Mazeroski used to get upset at some Pirates who portrayed themselves as "close friends" of Clemente when they really weren't.

"Bobby and I got along fine, but I can't say he was one of my closest friends," said Groat. "He wasn't friendly with me like a Bob Skinner, a Bill Virdon, a Harvey Haddix, a Bill Mazeroski, a Bob Friend. I was definitely closer to those guys.

"He never hit a cutoff man with a throw from the outfield," continued Groat. "His arm was so strong, he would throw the ball to third base or home plate on one bounce, or sometimes on a line shot.

"He almost threw me out one night in St. Louis after I had singled solidly to right field. He almost got me at first. His throw got by the first baseman, otherwise he would have thrown me out. I knew I couldn't run, but that would have been humiliating to be thrown out from right field on what is supposed to be a single."

Groat wondered why Clemente took himself out of the lineup from time to time, say the second game of a doubleheader. Clemente claimed he was tired, or sick, or hurting, and other Pirates prided themselves on sticking in there no matter their personal ailments. Pirates from that era love to tell stories citing the courage of Hoak, Haddix, Mazeroski, Burgess, Skinner, Virdon, Groat, et al. Haddix, for instance, was sick the night he pitched the 12 perfect innings before losing a heartbreaker in Milwaukee in 1959. "This proves," said Haddix at the time, "if you forget the aches and pains and the discomforts, you can compete." That was the motto for most of the Pirates. It's why they had a hard time dealing with Clemente's chronic complaints. Groat also wondered why Clemente seldom threw the ball from the outfield to him, the cutoff man, or why Clemente wasn't more effective at bat when runners were in scoring position. Right or wrong, fair or not fair, these were some impressions that Clemente's co-workers had of him. Groat and Clemente were constructed differently, and they were different in their approach, that's all, so Groat didn't understand why Clemente did some of the things that he did. The feeling must have been mutual.

"He came from Puerto Rico, and he did not speak English very well for quite awhile after he joined our team," said Groat, doing his best to discuss Clemente in a more positive light.

"I'm telling you he had a body like a God. He could have hit home runs if he wanted. But he realized it was better for the team to hit for the high average. He could bounce back from a disappointing day. He could go 0-for-4 against Bob Gibson, and go out and get four hits the next day against someone else.

"Now if you ask me which ballplayer I'd pick first in that same era, I'd go with Henry Aaron, and I'd take Mickey Mantle. Aaron could hurt you so many ways, and he had the consistent power. Mantle played when he couldn't walk. Clemente was one of the all-time great players, but I'd take those guys over him."

What about Willie Mays? Many of Groat's teammates thought Mays was the outstanding player of that time. "I played with Mays in San Francisco, and I didn't care for what he was all about," said Groat.

224

Clemente compares notes with Pirates' captain Dick Groat below, and they are flanked above by Smoky Burgess and Bill Virdon during their days at Forbes Field.

My sentiments exactly.

Mays was one of the most disappointing players I ever met in the major leagues. He was a whiner, and often nasty with newsmen. He learned that from two of his managers, Herman Franks and Leo Durocher, two demigods.

I mentioned to Groat that Bob Friend had said he doesn't remember seeing much of Clemente whenever the Pirates were on the road, except at the ballpark.

"You'd see him at a pre-game meal when we were on the road, having breakfast at the hotel, and that was about it," said Groat. "He roomed with Roman Mejias, and I guess they went places together. Everybody had a roommate back then. Guys were always with their roomies. You don't have that today. I don't know how I would have handled being by myself. Skinner and I were inseparable in St. Louis. I roomed with Ralph Kiner my first year and, when I came back from the military service, I roomed with Billy Virdon from 1956 to 1962."

Since I had written my first book on the 1960 Pirates, I heard from several sources that Virdon was the toughest guy on that team, though his appearance wouldn't suggest as much. "Oh, you didn't want to rile up Virdon," said Groat, grinning at the thought. "He didn't talk the tough guy act like Hoak did, and he didn't look for fights like Don Leppert — he'd fight at the drop of a hat — but you didn't want to fool with Billy. He had that don't-mess-with-me look in his eyes. And he was strong."

What impressed Groat the most about Clemente, the man? "Bobby clearly was a good person," answered Groat. "What he did to help those people in Nicaragua was typical of Bobby. Down deep, he was a very good person. He wanted to help people. He never felt he got his just due from the news media, and he was always trying to prove himself.

"But he was kinda bashful, at first, and didn't like to talk too much. Later, he'd give the newsguys a rough time a lot, hollering at them as soon as they identified themselves or started to ask him questions. It took him a long time to get the language down where he felt confident to be interviewed.

"When Bobby wanted to be, he could be most entertaining on the bus. Every so often, he'd get all wound up and he'd be entertaining everyone on the bus. Most of the people, though, don't know *that* Bobby Clemente existed."

I asked Groat if Clemente wasn't included in so many activities among the Pirates players because of racial prejudice. "I don't think it was; it was never a big deal with me," said Groat. "I can say that throughout my entire career, wherever I played.

"In St. Louis, I treasured my friendships with players like Bob Gibson, Curt Flood, Lou Brock and Bill White. We're still good friends, and see each other when we're in the same cities at the same time. With the Phillies, I was close friends, and still am, with Richie Allen and Tony Taylor."

Groat wanted to make a few more points.

"Whenever I speak, I never fail to thank the owners who gave me the opportunity to play in the big leagues, John Galbreath, August Busch, Bob Carpenter and Horace Stoneham. I always thank the news media around the country — they treated me extremely well, especially here in Pittsburgh. I especially thank the fans from western Pennsylvania. And I enjoyed the players I played with, wherever I was playing."

Groat still drinks Budweiser because of his feelings about Busch, who owned the brewery as well as the ballclub.

More than anything, Groat was grateful for the opportunity to play in Pittsburgh right out of college — a rare transition back then — and he remembers where he came from.

"Jack Hetherington has been a friend of mine for a long time," he said as we sat in his friend's restaurant. "We grew up together. He was a traveling salesman and we used to have lunch together in St. Louis. His brothers owned this place when it was called the Sportsmen's Bar. It was a shot and a beer place back then, right across the street from Union Switch & Signal, where they specialized in railroad equipment. They used to employ 6,500 there. During World War II, they used to make .45 automatic pistols there. This was the closest bar to the company back then.

"When I was in school, I used to walk by this place every day on the way to and from school. Now they all go to school by bus. I remember how cold it was at this time of year walking home from basketball practice at night."

Groat spent a lot more time at basketball practice than at baseball practice in those days.

"I wasn't a great baseball player. I knew there was no better basketball player in the world than I was. That's how I felt anyhow. I put in ten to fifteen times as many hours on a basketball court than I did on a baseball field. I started playing basketball when I was 5. My brothers put a basket out in the yard, against the wall outside the kitchen in our house, and it was exactly ten feet tall. I got my first basketball in 1935. It was given to me by Pete Noon, the captain of the Pitt basketball team, and it was the ball that was used when they beat Temple. Pete was engaged to my sister Elsie at the time, and that's one of the reasons he gave me the ball.

"I was a better basketball player than I was a baseball player. What goes around comes around. I'm into my 15th year as the analyst to Bill Hillgrove on Pitt basketball on WTAE Radio. I'm back doing what I really love, being around college basketball. They're on the longest break now for the holidays that I can ever remember, and I miss going over to the Field House to watch practice and talk to the kids and the coaches about what's going on with the team.

"Whenever I speak, I always say, 'You're looking at the luckiest man in the whole world. I've spent my entire life doing what I enjoy doing, and I ended up back with my first love.' "

The past year had been a difficult one for Groat. In fact, the past few years had been a challenge to him. "This year I buried two brothers and a sister," said Groat, shaking his head at the memory. Three years earlier, he lost his wife Barbara. She died after a long bout with cancer. He has a memorial to Barbara on the first hole of his Champion Lakes Golf Course in Ligonier.

"The two brothers and sister who died all graduated, ironically, from Pitt in the same year. It was 1939, the same year that Marshall Goldberg (the All-America running back of the famous "Dream Backfield") was graduated from Pitt. My oldest brother Charles went to two different prep schools over two years, and my brother Martin went to prep school for a year, and my sister Elsie went to Allegheny College for a year before she transferred to Pitt. They ended up in the same graduating class. My sister Mary Margaret, who is closest to me in age, went to Carnegie Tech. She's the only one I have left now.

"I was the youngest of five. My brother Marty, who was 19 years older than me, died in June. Charley died in August, and Elsie in November. Elsie was 11 years older than me and just about raised me. My parents were old by the time I was in school, so Elsie looked after me a lot. Earlier in that difficult year, Groat had to put Elsie in a nursing care facility because she had Alzheimer's disease.

"We were a close family. In my senior year at Duke, in 1952, when we were 24-6, out of the 30 games I'll bet that my mother and father and two sisters probably saw 12 to 15 games, and that was before we had all these interstate highways. I had a great family. I was here on Christmas Eve, and I wished Jack a Merry Christmas. He closed at four o'clock on Christmas Eve. This is a place where guys from my era will stop here, so I've always been comfortable here. My children and grandchilden were all in for the holidays, and we were going out to dinner together that night. I don't know why, but I drove over to my old neighborhood. I wanted to see how the old house looked. I was just so devastated. It just looked awful to me. My mother always kept the house so neat, and it didn't look so good to me. Our house was always decorated with lights at Christmas. There were no lights. Nothing. Absolutely nothing. I don't even know if anyone is living there anymore. It was completely dark. The shades were drawn. There were no signs of life."

We drove to his boyhood home. His bedroom window had been bricked in. He pointed to a wooden stairway he says wasn't there when his family lived there. He pointed to a narrow horizontal window, and said, "That's where our kitchen was. We had a hoop on the wall outside, and we rattled my mother's dishes and her nerves just about every night of the week. We loved to play basketball."

A few blocks away, we spotted a wide two-story building where Groat had gone to grade school. It's the Newmyer Elementary School. Groat glowed when he saw the playground where he had played ball as a youngster. He had popped in a tape of Les Brown & His Band of Renown music, perfect background for nostalgic thoughts.

Dick Groat

Jim O'Brien

Dick Groat goes home again, to the elementary school he attended, and the house on the corner of Graff Avenue and Hampton Street in Swissvale, and he shows where his basketball hoop once hung. His boyhood bedroom window has been bricked in, as you may note above his head as he stands on wooden stairway by the kitchen window.

Groat stood on the steps of the school and surveyed the scene. He posed for a picture, and looked like he was standing on a victory platform. There was a proud, dignified look about him. It has always been that way. Groat is of German heritage. He has sharp features, like his face was carved out of granite. His nose is a noble one. He has always carried himself a certain way. There is still some soldier in him. Sometimes there is a lot of kid in him. Like many of us over 50, he yearns for things to be the way they were when he was young.

"We used to play baseball here during lunch time. They didn't park any cars here then. It was all playground. We used to use a tennis ball. You could really make a tennis ball curve. All the kids could throw a curve. I often wondered whether that's how I became such a good breaking ball hitter. I used to rush up here after school and hope that the big kids would pick me up to play softball.

"When I was at Duke, I had a deal with the janitor that he let me stay after practice for an hour while he cleaned up. I had about 50 minutes actually all by myself. I kept shooting even after I was fatigued. I always felt that at crunch time in a big game I'd be fatigued, too, and I could still hit the jump shot."

When Groat talks about basketball, his coal-dark eyes glow, and his true grit comes across. It's easy to appreciate why he was such a great athlete. His competitive fires still burn. That's behind the glow.

"I was talking to myself all the time. I'd say stuff when I missed a shot like 'Damn, you're never going to be the College Player of the Year if you continue to miss shots.' Plus, if you missed one, you'd have to chase the ball all over the place. If you shot it right, it comes back to you. I wanted to be consistent; it ran through my mind the whole time I was at Duke."

Groat had played with Pitt basketball players during the off-season in gyms and playgrounds about the city, but he didn't go to Pitt because he wanted to go to a baseball school, and he didn't like the "continuity offense" coached by Doc Carlson in the basketball program at Pitt. He felt he would be too limited by the slow-down, systematic offensive scheme that, frankly, was out-dated even then.

Groat was a great basketball player. I remember seeing him when I was just 12 years old playing for Fort Belvoir at the Pitt Field House. Paul Arizin came to town that same season with the Quantico Marines. Military teams were quite good at the time.

After Groat showed me his boyhood home and his grammar school and playground, he drove back down Westmoreland Avenue to South Braddock Avenue. "When I was growing up here," offered Groat, "when guys graduated from high school they'd go to work in the mill at Westinghouse, or Switch & Signal, or Westinghouse Air Brake, or you'd go to college. Now what do they do? Those places are all gone. There aren't any jobs around here because the industries have all closed. All the homes are still here in my neighborhood, but the mills aren't."

Gil Lucas, the executive producer and sports director of KBL, the sports cable channel headquartered in Pittsburgh, had known Groat for 53 years when we bumped into each other at a Big East basketball contest between Pitt and Seton Hall at the Pitt Field House on Saturday afternoon, January 16, 1994.

Lucas was looking on as Groat was going over some statistics and notes with his broadcast partner Bill Hillgrove of WTAE prior to the start of the contest. Lucas used to keep assists on the statistics crew for many years at Pitt games, but had given up the assignment. He still was seated at courtside, however. He still loved basketball.

"I grew up in Swissvale, too, and went to high school with Dick," allowed Lucas. "He was a few years ahead of me. He was the star of the team; I was the manager. We'd break into the gym some nights and stay till three in the morning. I remember the police caught us once.

"When I was in the Marine Corps, stationed at Camp Lejeune, I went up to Durham, North Carolina whenever I could to see Dick when he was playing at Duke. Just to show you he didn't change much, we broke into the gym at night at Duke so he could practice his shooting. All he wanted to do was play basketball. The key to Dick Groat is his competitiveness. He always wants to win."

The New Year of 1994 didn't get off to such a great start for Groat. On the previous Saturday, January 8, Groat got the word that his good friend and former teammate Harvey Haddix had died at age 68. He died of emphysema at Community Hospital in Springfield, Ohio, according to hospital officials.

That hurt. I had last seen Haddix in October at a sports card show at Sewall Center on the campus of Robert Morris College. He had been there with former teammates Billy Mazeroski and Dick Stuart to sign autographs, as had Bobby Thomson of the New York Giants and Ronnie Francis of the Penguins, among others.

Haddix came to that event with a portable oxygen unit to assist him in his breathing. His face was beet red. He looked different than he had when I had visited him on April 13, 1993 at his home in Springfield. When I was there, however, it was apparent that he was having serious health problems. He had some kind of breathing-assistance apparatus in every room, and went down on one knee at one point to catch his breath after he had gone down some stairs with me to his gameroom to show me his baseball memorabilia.

Haddix had a heart attack in December, unknown to Groat or any of the other Pirates at the time, and had undergone an angioplasty procedure, a method of clearing blocked arteries.

"I was talking to Harvey's wife Marcia on the telephone the other day," Groat related. "I was sitting at my kitchen table and I was crying as I spoke to her. Harvey was such a super guy, such a special friend, such a great teammate. He was some competitor.

"Then I called my old roommate Bob Skinner, and spoke to him. I wanted to make sure he knew about what happened to Harvey. And I found out that he had an angioplasty, too. I think he had it on New Year's Eve."

231

"Baseball is not life itself, although the resemblance keeps coming up."

—Roger Angell
The Summer Game

Willie Stargell

Top student in Clemente's class

*"I think he walked a little
taller than most men."*
— Stargell on Clemente

When Willie Stargell speaks people listen. They have to; he has
a compelling voice. Stargell is a large man with a soft voice.
The voice belies the size of the man. It is, at once, intelligent,
sensitive, searching, reassuring, soothing, comforting, calming. Stargell is special. He'd be great at telling bedtime stories. I could listen
to him tell stories all night, and I nearly did.

Stargell was shedding light on himself and his mentor, Roberto
Clemente, the man who showed Stargell how to be a star and a leader
with the Pirates, how to win. Stargell speaks with reverence about
Roberto Clemente. The Clementes of the world only come along once
in a while, and Stargell sounds like he was blessed to know him and
to have such a model and teacher. We all need someone like that in our
lives.

"I think he walked a little taller than most men, and shined a little brighter," Stargell said of Clemente during our three hour conversation. "He had an eternal fire going on in him once he got on the field.
It certainly wore off on a lot of us."

To hear Stargell speak, and to have him provide poignant insights,
one could easily appreciate why his presence had such an impact on the
Pirates, why they called him "Pops," and why he was so outstanding
and, indeed, a great performer for 21 seasons (1962 through 1982) with
the Pirates. He helped lift the Pirates to another level, and they were
one of the most successful teams in baseball during his tenure.

If Clemente was the soul of the Pirates that won the World Series
in 1971, then Stargell was its heart. When the Pirates won the World
Series in 1979, Stargell was both the heart and soul of the team, and
the godfather of the "Fam-i-lee" concept, the boss of the Lumber Company. His No. 8 was retired with good reason. In 2,360 games he batted
.282 with 475 home runs, seven home runs in post-season play, and 1,540
RBI. The Bucs' all-time home run king, Stargell was an All-Star Game
pick seven times. In 1979, he was the National League's co-MVP and
the MVP in the playoffs and World Series. He shared Sportsman of the
Year honors and the cover of *Sports Illustrated* with the Steelers' Terry
Bradshaw and some millworkers that wonderful year when the Steelers and the Pirates won championships and Pittsburgh was heralded
as "The City of Champions."

In time, Stargell became the 17th player elected to the Baseball
Hall of Fame in his first year of eligibility, being inducted in 1988.

In the mind's eye, it's easy to see Stargell swinging his bat as he waited for the right pitch. He was a lefty all the way. He'd rock back and forth, and swing that heavy bat in a circular motion before, in his own words, "launching myself" into the ball. He was one of the top sluggers in the game, and an inspirational force for his teammates. He was a big guy, 6-3, 190 or so pounds during his playing days, and a fearsome sight swinging that bat in a windmill manner.

It's not, however, his hefty statistics or motivational mien that make Stargell such a special fellow. It's his depth; he has the wisdom of a wise old owl. Stargell has substance and compassion. More than anyone else perhaps, he was the best of the former Pirates at explaining Clemente, both the ballplayer and the man.

"If you listened carefully and watched the way he played the game," said Stargell, "it was easy to understand and appreciate Roberto Clemente."

It was January 3, 1994, and it was snowing hard in Pittsburgh. Before it was over, a foot-and-a-half of snow would bury the 'Burgh. "I miss that stuff," said Stargell, and the smile came over the telephone long distance from his home in Wilmington, North Carolina, a port on the Atlantic Ocean. Willie's last words when we finally said goodbye were, "Stay warm." I stayed warm with his words, the Stargell stories, his unique phrasings.

For openers, I wanted to know what was going on in his life. Stargell was married for a second time the year before, and would be marking his first wedding anniversary on January 16. His wife, Margaret, is the director of two government agencies in Wilmington. Her sister, Frances, is an anchorwoman on local TV, and her oldest sister, Catherine, is on city council and is the mayor pro tem, and owns her own shipping company. So Stargell is well connected in Wilmington.

Willie's first wife, Dolores, still lives in Pittsburgh. They have four children: Wendy, Precious, Wilver Jr., and Kelli.

Stargell went to work for the Atlanta Braves in 1986 when he went there as a coach on Chuck Tanner's staff. He has remained on the staff, first as a hitting instructor and he now serves as a special assistant to Chuck Lamar, director of scouting and player development.

Stargell stopped at mid-sentence at several junctures to cough, and clear his throat, blaming it on allergies. It was like static on a radio show.

"There were a lot of people who helped me, but he gave me direction."
— Stargell on Clemente

I asked Stargell if he ever thought about how difficult it must have been for Clemente to come to Pittsburgh in 1955, a black Puerto Rican who had great difficulty in speaking English, and communicating his thoughts to most everyone. It was an ordeal just to order a meal in a restaurant.

"The only way I can respond to that," said Stargell, "is what it was like for me when I went to play winter ball in 1963 or 1964 in the Dominican Republic. I had no real knowledge of Spanish, not to mention the customs and traditions and how they looked at things and did things. I was entirely at their mercy."

Stargell was the first of Clemente's former teammates to understand that it was more than just a language barrier that kept Clemente and his teammates from understanding one another better. There was a cultural moat as well that separated them. They came from different environments and the expectations were different.

"I had to adapt," said Stargell of his off-season sojourn to the Dominican Republic. "The language problem alone was enough of a problem. I remember one time, shortly after I got there, when I was dropped off by a cabbie. I couldn't tell him when to come back and pick me up. I had to get down on the ground and smooth out some sand and draw a clock in the sand to show him when to pick me up.

"They did a lot of things differently than we do. When you grow up a certain way it's hard to adjust, but I had to accept the old adage that when in Rome do as the Romans do. Being an American, I know that Americans usually expect everyone else to adjust to us. That's why I tip my hat off to Roberto and any of the Latins or anyone from a foreign country who comes here to play sports. We have a lot of kids in our organization who come from Spanish-speaking countries, and they are often confused by it all.

"From noon till 2 o'clock in the afternoon, for instance, when I was in the Dominican Republic, they have their biggest meal of the day, something we don't do. That's their custom. That's the way they are used to living. What we do in that respect probably seems strange to them.

"One of the things that Roberto was constantly confused about was the black-white business because, as he would say, in Puerto Rico everybody is a Puerto Rican, no matter what color you are. Economics distinguished the different classes of people, but not the color.

"When I first met Clemente in 1962, we were staying at a black family's home at Fort Myers, Florida, during spring training. All of the blacks had to stay there; we were not permitted to stay in the same hotel as the white players. That was in 1962! We'd be out on the porch at night, or in the living room, or in one of the bedrooms, lying across the beds, and we'd start talking about our situation.

"This frustrated and confused him. He'd say, 'We're supposed to do the same things as everyone else at practice, but after practice we have to go our separate ways. Why?' He didn't grow up that way. He had to deal with all that and still perform. And he'd already been a star in a World Series.

"He tried to figure out what it was going to take to better things. He felt that if no one felt he was their equal, that if he played hard and consistently enough, they'd say, 'Hey, he's like everybody else.' So he was driven to succeed to prove to people that he was as good as anybody.

"He knew what the word hypochondriac meant. He saw it printed a few times in stories about him."

For the record, the definition of the word hypochondriac, according to *Webster's Collegiate Dictionary*, is "someone who suffers extreme depression of mind or spirits often centered on imaginary ailments."

"If someone asked him how he felt," continued Stargell, "he'd tell them that his back was bothering him. He was always honest that way. That was another problem he had: he was always honest when he talked to reporters. If he was hurting, he'd say so. If he was upset about something, he'd speak his mind. Too often, it came back to hurt him. He'd see what he said in print and it would come out in a derogatory way."

There were times Clemente said he couldn't play because of the aches and pains he suffered. Some questioned his courage. It brings to mind something the Steelers' Joe Greene once said in defense of a sidelined teammate who was under similar scrutiny: "No man knows another man's pain."

Wilver Dornel Stargell was born on March 6, 1940 in Earlsboro, Oklahoma, and raised in Alameda, California where he won eight varsity letters as an all-around athlete. His first stops in pro baseball, back in 1959 and 1960, were Roswell, New Mexico, in the Sophomore League, and Grand Forks, North Dakota, in the Northern League. I asked Stargell how he felt about staying in a rooming house for blacks when he joined the Pirates in spring training at Fort Myers in 1962.

"It was very nice, mind you," said Stargell. "The black family we stayed with were great people. They fed us very good meals, and created a home atmosphere for us. Mr. Earl. I'll never forget the man's name. He and his wife were some very, very nice people.

"To me, it was probably the most exciting time of my life. So I wasn't dwelling on where we were staying, or the segregation situation. I was around guys who played in the majors. I was in awe of guys like Roberto. Whatever he did, I emulated. He took baseball and himself very seriously once he stepped on the field, and so did I.

"There were a lot of people who helped me, but he gave me direction. He helped me with so many things, not baseball-oriented. When we traveled to spring training in those early days, they'd give the black guys a car. When the team bus would stop for a meal, we wouldn't be allowed to eat with the rest of the team. We'd have to drive down to the black community and eat at a restaurant there. We'd do that, too, in big cities like Miami and Tampa and St. Petersburg. If we stayed for the weekend, they'd make arrangements for us to stay in a different hotel or a rooming house, or with a black family that housed players.

"We moved from Fort Myers to Bradenton in 1969, and sometime before we moved we were all able to stay in the same place. It was called the Edisonian Hotel. I'm not exactly sure of the year we first stayed in the same place. Back then, it was a big thing."

I mentioned to Stargell that I had been talking to Dick Groat a few days earlier, and that Groat talked about how close roommates were to each other in those days, and how he learned what to do as a big leaguer when he stayed with the team's star Ralph Kiner when he first came out of college to play for the Pirates. Today, ballplayers want to have their own rooms, indeed, their own suites, and Groat believes they are missing something.

"I had a guy do that for me when I was in Triple A at Columbus before I joined the Pirates full time in 1962," recalled Stargell. "His name was Riverboat Smith, and he was a little left-handed pitcher. He'd take me out to dinner and he'd tell me to always keep my napkin on my left leg. I was eating with my little nephew the other day, and I told him to always keep his napkin on his left leg, and it made me think about Riverboat Smith."

"I was caught off guard that
so many people believed the
story. Anybody who knew me
should have known better."
— Willie Stargell

Something made Stargell start thinking about the media, too, and he showed a real understanding for what goes on there. He has some ideas about how the media and the ballplayers might have a better understanding of each other's roles — a meeting and exchange of information during pre-season camp — but it makes so much sense that no one would ever take him up on his suggestion. He espoused several interesting theories on that subject, but it was mostly intramural stuff that I won't go into here. "But I knew who I could be comfortable with," said Stargell. "I knew who I could trust. It's a two-way deal."

But he wanted to offer his side of the story on two sore subjects that still nagged at him.

"I wrote a book, and I said some things about Dave Parker that I thought were glorifying Dave," said Stargell. "But somebody pulled something out of it — a line or two — that made it look like I was just critical of Dave. And, for a short period, Dave was real upset with me. I spoke to Dave about it and urged him to read the entire book before he made a judgment. He did, and he told me there was no problem.

"I'm not sure things will ever be the same again for me in Pittsburgh because of all the stuff that was written and communicated on the radio and TV about something that happened after it was announced that I would be inducted into the Baseball Hall of Fame.

"I was coaching for the Atlanta Braves that summer (1988). The Pirates wanted to stage a promotion in which I would be honored at Three Rivers Stadium when the Braves came in for a series. The word got out that I wanted big money and a car and fur coat, and that I wouldn't participate in the promotion because the Pirates wouldn't go

Stargell with Art Rooney

Stargell gets hug from Bill Mazeroski in '71 World Series celebration.

Stargell congratulates Clemente after home run.

along with my demands, that I wanted more than they were willing to pay. I couldn't believe what was going on. Then I was called and asked to tell my side of the story to the newspapers or on the radio sports talk shows. I had no comment. I refused to fight it.

"I felt that anybody who knew me would know better. They wanted to have a day for me, but I wasn't really interested. I told them they already had two special days where I'd brought in my family and that was enough. I said 'Just wait till the Braves come to town, and I'll come out of the dugout and tip my hat to the crowd. That'll be fine.'

"Some people in the Pirates' organization weren't satisfied with that. I think they'd already lined up the promotion, before they even discussed it with me, and they didn't want to cancel their plans. There was some miscommunication about the whole thing. I told Carl Barger that if somebody had talked to me in advance there wouldn't have been any problem. They wanted me to come to Pittsburgh and take off my Braves uniform and put on a Pirates uniform. They wanted to set up a stage on the field, and they wanted me to go up and down the baselines and sign autographs for the fans. And then I'd change uniforms and go to work for the Braves when the game began. I thought it would be a slap in the face to the Braves, and to Ted Turner, my employer, to do something like that. I wasn't comfortable with that.

"Someone in the Pirates organization called me back and asked, 'What would it take to get you to come and do this?' He asked me if I wanted a car. I said I already had three cars. They asked me if they could give me a mink coat. I already had two mink coats, and since I was living in Atlanta I was already trying to get rid of my mink coats. You hardly need them in Atlanta. If you wear a mink coat in Atlanta it's just showcasing. If you do it in Pittsburgh it's to keep warm. I said I didn't need anything. They asked me if they changed the gifts to cash would that entice me to do what they wanted me to do. I said we could give it to my favorite charity. I'd done things like that a lot. But there was a breakdown on that, too. The next thing I knew I heard that I had asked the Pirates for too much, and they weren't willing to go along with it, so they had to cancel the event. I came off as an ingrate.

"I was caught off guard that so many people believed the story. Anybody who knew me should have known better. That was not my style. My father had passed at that point. He'd been there the other two times for the ceremonies to honor me. There was no way I was going to drag my mother out of California for another day. She was feeling poorly about my dad passing, to begin with. Being there without him would have been a sad event for her. But the Pirates were pushing me to do it even though it was against my own personal wishes. They were taking the 'j' out of joy. What was I going to do with another day in my honor? The other two days were great, but enough was enough. I felt strongly about this. I told them, 'I understand you people have put this in place, but I don't want to do it again.' I refused to go through all that they wanted me to do.

"People I knew who were offended by the stories wanted me to raise hell about the stories that were circulating that made me look like a

240

money-grubbing, greedy person. I just felt it would take away from a very special year of going into the Hall of Fame, so I kept quiet. But now I want people in Pittsburgh to know the real story, and to appreciate perhaps where I was coming from. They should know better than to think I'd do something like that. Back then, I just felt I didn't have to explain myself. People should have known it was not my style."

Speaking of style, I asked Stargell to get back to Clemente, and the kind of contributions he made to influence Stargell.

"I learned how to play the game from him," he said, "and it was kinda like he passed a baton or torch to me, like how to win. There are certain things you must do to win. It's a big thing. Guys come in every year who have talent. But it's more than just talent. It's not something that's easy to define, or to find.

"But we did it. We knew how to win. First of all, he'd teach us and show us how to do little things, like to be aggressive going into the corners after a ball. In order to do that, he'd take me out in the field, and show me the mechanics. He'd walk through the motions, and talk about the right steps and when to start bending, the positioning, how to maintain your balance, all that stuff. There was always a backup system, too, depending on what the baserunners did. And he'd talk about how to catch a fly ball and how to throw the ball. It's what I teach young kids today. I'd challenge anyone to go against his theory. Dave Parker was very accurate, and I was very accurate. Clemente taught us how to do it right. The Pirates now have a guy who's as good at it, whether he's at first base or in the outfield, and that's Brian Hunter. I worked with him, and I told him what Clemente told me. It still works, it still applies. Wait till you see his hands at first base. He's very intelligent, very aggressive, and he wants to play."

Stargell said there were others who influenced him as well as a young Pirate.

"The Pirates won the World Series in 1960, two years before I came up. You are talking about guys I used to just gawk at. I was in the same clubhouse as guys I had admired so much. There were guys who really impressed me, like Smoky Burgess. Dick Stuart with his flamboyant ways, the astonishing hands of Maz, the smart and solid way that Dick Groat played shortstop, the military personality of Don Hoak, and the gem of a manager in Danny Murtaugh. Guys like Ducky Schofield, who could fill in everywhere, and all the pitchers, Bob Friend, Vernon Law, ElRoy Face, Harvey Haddix, Vinegar Bend Mizell, Joe Gibbon, guys like that.

"It was a real treat to be with them. I was proud to be in the Pirates organization. I was desperate to be like them. They were definitely an inspiring force in my life. They let me look up to them when I did come up, and not one of them treated me anything less than I could have dreamed about."

In the gameroom of his home in Wilmington, Stargell said he had a framed photograph showing him shaking hands with Clemente after

241

"I hit a home run," and another showing him standing in the dugout with Manny Mota, Matty Alou and Roberto Clemente.

Was Clemente his mentor? "It's not that he had a special role in that respect," said Stargell. "He was a giver. He wanted to help where there was help needed. And he was easy to approach, easy to relate with. I could certainly feel what he was relating to."

What did you learn from Clemente about pride?

"That if you work hard and learn your skills you will have something to be proud of," said Stargell. "When called upon to produce, you wouldn't have to worry, because you would know that you'd give it your best effort. And, if for some reason it didn't work out, well then you have to learn to tip your hat to the opposition.

"He was very proud of where he came from, and felt that he was representing all Puerto Ricans. He often referred to his people in public forums. That's why his people loved him so much."

I asked Stargell why he thought Clemente had his critics, that some felt he was a hypochondriac, a malingerer, and someone who didn't have the best attitude about doing what was best for the team.

"It was a lack of understanding, more than anything else," said Stargell, still talking in even, carefully-measured terms, and never showing any evidence of irritation. "It had nothing to do with his ability. When people don't understand something, they come up with their own theories. They reach their own conclusions and they say things, but that doesn't necessarily mean it's true. People form their own opinions.

"Branch Rickey always knew he had something special in Clemente. He knew that Clemente was as special as Jackie Robinson. The Dodgers tried to hide Clemente in Montreal. It was never a case of him going through the motions. He told me he couldn't understand why he'd go four-for-four one day and the next day he'd be benched. The Dodgers didn't want to show him to the scouts; they knew they would lose him if he created too much interest. Rickey kept in touch with people in the Dodgers' organization, and when he had the opportunity he got Roberto in the player draft."

As good as Stargell was, he thinks Clemente was in a class all by himself in Pirates' history. "I run into people who had a chance to see him play," said Stargell, "and they come up to me and say they love the Pirates. Then they'll inevitably say something like, 'No offense, but Clemente was my favorite player on the Pirates.' I say, 'No reason to apologize. He was that to me, too.' They don't make any bones about where their allegiance lies. No matter how great they felt someone else was, it always comes back to Clemente when they're picking a favorite.

"Every time I've had to speak at some public assembly, usually when I'm finalizing, I always like to open it up for a question-and-answer period. I can't think of one time that someone didn't ask me about

242

Clemente entertains Matty Alou, Manny Mota and Willie Stargell.

Pirates in dugout are Jose Pagan, Clemente, Stargell, Johnny Pesky, Donn Clendenon and Jim Pagliaroni.

Roberto. 'What was he like?' Or, 'What was it like to play with Roberto?' It always makes me feel good to talk about him.

"I honestly feel that it wasn't until 1971 that people really got a chance to see the real Roberto Clemente. We, in Pittsburgh, saw him perform before that, but I'm talking about the whole audience of people. In the World Series, he was on international TV, and he never was more productive."

When did Stargell realize that Clemente considered him to be something special, too?

"He was impressed with the way I attacked a ball," said Stargell. "He created a scenario where we competed against each other, so to speak. He told me, 'Here's what you have to do to create a lot of runs. I'll be on base, and you have to drive me home.'

"So when a Brian Hunter asks what does Willie Stargell like offensively, he'll say, 'RBIs.' A lot of guys go for the high batting average. If a guy concentrates on RBIs, he'll be more selective about what pitches he goes after. The more runs you drive in the more chances your team will have to win. Clemente used to say to me, 'I insist you bring me in. I'll see how many times I can get on base and you drive me in.' We really had it going in that respect in 1971.

"I hurt my knee in Houston that year, in the first part of August. I had 30 home runs and 80 RBIs at the All-Star break. It was the knee I needed to push off of, and I had to put my leg in a locked position and I couldn't launch myself into the ball as I normally did. If it hadn't happened, I thought I could have hit 50 plus home runs that year. I finished with 48 home runs and 125 RBIs, and with a bad leg.

"Clemente's hitting style was different from mine. He had his own style. Everyone has their own style. We tell guys, 'Get to know yourself. Find your own style.' You have to keep working at it. No matter what your profession, you have to find what it's going to take to satisfy yourself. Clemente did it his way, it was an unorthodox way. He defied the rules, the traditional ways. A lot of people don't realize what a heavy bat he used. He used a U1 or G105, and the ball used to just jump off his bat.

"It was a special time for me, those eight years I was around him. I learned so much. He wasn't a coach. He could not just talk about it, he could go out and do it. He told me I had so much ability. He called me 'Willito.' He said to me, 'If you don't get hurt, you'll be in the Hall of Fame eventually.' I told him I just wanted to be consistent. And he'd say, 'If you're hitting and you are consistent, you can achieve great things as a baseball player.' He pushed me to get the most out of my ability.

"He had a tremendous amount of maturity. After he died, what was real strange, overnight I was asked to be the team captain. Murtaugh told me he wanted me to be the team captain. I told him I had to think about it. Then I asked him, 'Do I have to try and be Clemente, and be a rah, rah leader? If I'm going to be the team captain, I have to be who I am.' And Murtaugh told me, 'You play just like Clemente did, in your own way. You lead by example. Plus, as captain, you get

244

a chance to take the lineup card to the umpire and hear some sick jokes and tell some sick jokes of your own.' Murtaugh always liked to make you laugh no matter what he was talking to you about."

Where was Willie Stargell when he learned that Roberto Clemente was killed in an airplane crash?

"I was having a New Year's Eve party at our house in Pittsburgh, out in Penn Hills, and I got a telephone call from an unknown person. I was downstairs in the game room and I went upstairs to take the call. I was told it was an emergency call. The voice said, 'Did you hear what happened to Roberto?' I said, 'What did you hear?'

"The man said, 'It's coming over the radio from Puerto Rico that Clemente was killed.' I said, 'Wait a minute. That's a sick joke.' I hung up and called some friends of Clemente I knew in Puerto Rico. They said, 'Yeah, he's missing. His plane went down, and they're searching and trying to find him.' As I was talking, it was funny in a way, but everyone started walking by me and leaving my house. I hadn't said anything to anybody. It was something they sensed. Then I went numb for a long time.

"I am glad they are having a statue in his honor, and that they are showing the kids how Clemente played the game, with such grace. He was like poetry in motion. It will be a legend living on.

"His whole thing was trying to help. He was putting together a Sports City for young people in Puerto Rico when he died. He got it started, but never had a chance to complete it. This renewal of interest in Clemente and what he was all about is good. It could help some kids. I know he'd like that an awful lot. After so many years, it brings a very special man back into our lives. Let that memory, that river, continue to flow. I'm all for it."

"When you look at baseball, it's about life."

When I probed Stargell to find out why he thought baseball was different from other sports, he said, "It brought more to a family than a game per se. When you look at baseball, it's about life. And Pittsburgh has a special history of its own. There were a lot of firsts in baseball, back at Forbes Field and at Three Rivers Stadium. The first night game in World Series history, for instance, was played at Three Rivers. Forbes Field stood for so many years, and what's left of the wall is like a religious shrine to some people.

"I was talking to a guy recently who said he was at Forbes Field and he was fortunate enough to see Babe Ruth hit three home runs, and one that went over the roof in right field, right before Ruth retired. When you talk about somebody seeing something special in baseball, that has to rate high among the magic moments.

245

"I remember when people would put up a grill in the left field bleachers at Forbes Field, and they'd grill hot dogs. It smelled so good. And I'd wish somebody would hit a foul ball so I could go over there and beg for a hot dog.

"I remember how they'd open the gates in the seventh inning and let fans, especially students, come in free. They'd get in and have a chance to see ElRoy Face pitch, and he nearly went undefeated over a two-year period (1958-59). You were seeing one of the great forkball relief pitchers in the game. You were seeing history.

"I was in the Pirates' organization in 1960, in the minor leagues, and I had just finished up playing in the Northern League, and I had to report to Angel Island outside of San Francisco for two weeks of military reserve duty, and the other soldiers were treating me like I was one of the players on the Pirates. I had never met Groat and Clemente and those guys at that point, but I was a big deal because, to them, I was already a Pirate."

Stargell played pitch-and-catch with Danny Marino in early days

If Clemente cared about kids, so did Stargell. Here's an offbeat story to show that Stargell has always had a sincere interest in young people. When Stargell first joined the Pirates in the early '60s, he rented an apartment in a house on Frazier Street, in South Oakland, about a mile from Forbes Field, overlooking the J&L Steel Mill on Second Avenue.

Danny Marino, the great quarterback of the Miami Dolphins, once told me that he had played catch with Stargell on a regular basis back then. Marino's grandmother lived next door to the home where Stargell was staying.

"I didn't know that it was him until I heard him tell that story one night at a sports banquet in Erie," said Stargell. "When he said that, I thought, 'I'll be darned. I remember doing that.' I just never realized that that kid was Danny Marino. The family next door was so nice to us, and we used to lean over the fence to talk to this one couple.

"This kid would come down to see his grandparents, the couple next door, and he'd bring a ball and a glove and he'd ask me to catch with him. There were a couple of weekends when I wasn't up to it, but I couldn't say no to him. I didn't want to disappoint him. You know how a kid can have a certain gleam in his eye. He never wanted to quit. Little did I know that this was a kid who would be setting all kinds of passing records in the National Football League."

246

Remember Roberto
Memorable days at Forbes Field

"I'll never forget his eyes."
—Tommy Adams

Ken Ruffner
Psychologist
Lancaster, Pa.

"In 1960 I was 10 years old and it was the first year I was interested in baseball. I lived in Indiana, Pa. then and every game we went to was a major event, planned a month in advance. I went to my first game that year and it was the game in which Dick Groat was hit on the wrist by Lew Burdette of the Braves. I remember that so well because you could actually HEAR it hit him. And then, of course, Dick Schofield came in and got three hits. Believe it or not, my father was at the game the year before when Dick Stuart hit his 457-foot plus home run. I also got Roberto Clemente's autograph in 1963 on Team Photo Night. The Pirates were doing terribly that year and they played the Houston Colt 45s that night; I got rookie Rusty Staub's autograph prior to the game. The Pirates were losing by a run with two outs in the bottom of the ninth. Clemente hit a ground single to right and Jerry Lynch, who started in left field that night, then homered over the screen in right to win the game. Afterwards, I encountered Clemente in the stands as he was heading home. He was dressed in a green three-piece suit. I asked him for his autograph, which he gave me. I said 'nice hit' to him, but he never said a word; he just moved on. My dad and I were just about the only two people in the stands at that point. Somebody had told me which exit gate Clemente usually used and my dad let me wait around and, surely enough, Clemente did finally appear. I still have that autograph — in pencil — and it is a prized possession. I loved Roberto Clemente."

Marc Bobish
Valrico, Florida

"Roberto is loved, admired and the Latins have him as a hero. I collect football cards of the Steelers and the players who came from Western Pa. and Roberto always comes up in conversation and in cards at the shows. His rookie card in excellent shape will command $2,000. This book in conjunction with the All-Star Game in '94 and the unveiling of his statue ought to be an instant winner."

Tony Despotakis
Vandergrift

"I went to only one game at Forbes Field. I was ten years old at the time, and I took an official National League baseball with me. After the game, my dad said, 'Tony, let's go get Roberto Clemente's autograph.' Someone told us, a friend of my father, I think, that Clemente came out of a different exit than the other players. Sure enough, he appeared at the door. Clemente looked at me and said, 'Hi, little boy.' And I said, 'Mr. Clemente, would you please sign my ball?' He smiled and said, 'Sure.' I had met my god. I have a plaque made up of all his cards, and a poster. He's still my all-time favorite."

Tommy Adams
Butler

"I was 11 at the time, and living in Hazelwood, a few miles from Forbes Field. I had been fishing with a friend at Panther Hollow in Schenley Park. We hid our rods up near Phipps Conservatory and went to the game. We got into the bleachers. I knew most of the guys because they were pals of my grandfather, Red Adams, who was a policeman in Oakland. Some of them knew my dad, Billy 'Ace' Adams, who was quite an athlete. Clemente had been suspended for three games for 'chesting' an umpire on a disputed call at first base. He was in a sulk. We bumped into him outside Forbes Field and he was carrying a manila envelope. He showed us a picture of the play. He said, 'This is why I'm not playing today.' It showed him crossing the bag, and the ball wasn't in the glove yet of the pitcher who was covering the base. Then Clemente said to us, 'You boys look hungry. Come with me.' We went to the White Tower at a corner a block from the ballpark. He bought us hamburgers and sat in there with us for an hour. I'll never forget his eyes. We didn't get his autograph. We never thought about it."

Robert Shoup
Butler

"Maz and Clemente were my two favorites. I'd go early to watch them in the warm-ups. I always sat out in right field so I could be close to those two. I had so much respect for Clemente. I was one of the men who cried the day I heard he died. I turned on the radio to WISR in Butler and heard the bad news on New Year's Day, 1973. I was 26 years old when he died."

Lillian Tate
Mt. Lebanon

"A Roberto Clemente book could become a movie! We need some real heroes in the sports world."

Ike Bennett
Blairsville

"I remember going to Forbes Field with the Cub Scouts, the Boy Scouts, Little League from 1959 through 1964. It was always a big deal, making the trip in from Blairsville. I'd always end up in the seats in right field. If we weren't seated there, I'd wander out there myself. Clemente was like a magnet. I was drawn to him."

Jack Yurko
Greensburg

"I was ten years old, and I was waiting after a game at Forbes Field, and I got Roberto Clemente to sign a ball. I still have it. His signature is faded. Yeah, we played catch with it. I had another from Johnny Antonelli, and we played ball with that one, too. Same with Robin Roberts. You run out of balls and you take it out. I have the Clemente baseball in a box now. I wish now that I had never played with any of those balls. Clemente signed it 'Bob' then, and I'll never forget it."

Bill Crooks
Vandergrift

"I always tried to get number 21. But so did everyone else. I was in Little League, Pony League and American Legion, and I got his number once."

George Hoffman
Prospect

"To me he was a good player, but I admired him even more because he was able to do what he did in spite of all the quiet pressure that was put on him. He could stand up to it. I'm from Brooklyn originally, and I have always been a Dodger fan. He should have been a Dodger."

Clemente slides into second base at Forbes Field.

*"Baseball is a game
to be savored,
not gulped."*

—Bill Veeck

Bill Mazeroski

Clemente's teammate for 17 seasons

"He's just so damn real."
—Steve Blass

The rolling hills that surround the home of Milene and Bill Mazeroski were snow-covered. The scene looked like a Christmas card. They live near the wonderfully-named Walton Tea Room Road, just off Route 30 in Greensburg, about 30 miles east of Pittsburgh. The narrow winding road that leads to their ranch home had been bulldozed to the bone, thankfully, and the bright afternoon sun dried most of the surface except where the snow drifted on the curves. The snow was white-white and blinding for blue eyes.

This was the day after the coldest day in recorded history for Pittsburgh and its environs in western Pennsylvania, when the temperature dropped to a dangerous 22 degrees below zero. Mr. Eisaman, as everyone addresses the grizzled farmer who has a spread next to the Mazeroskis' 20 acres, was walking around a dark truck in front of a barn, readying to take some fresh hay and silage to his cows and some cornfeed to his chickens. It was warming up — it was about 4 degrees — but the day would be another demanding one, especially for farmers and anyone who had to work outdoors.

It was January 20, 1994, in the midst of a week-long Arctic-like cold spell that gripped Pittsburgh. The city had been renamed Iceburgh in a banner headline in the local daily newspaper because of a record stretch of below zero temperatures. The scotch pines that lined the driveway to the Mazeroski home were heavy with snow, and the boughs were bent low, forming a forest green and white tunnel effect as I approached their front door. There was just enough room for my car. "Watch out for the ice on that step," warned Mazeroski as he cracked the ice-lined door.

When I mentioned the tunnel to him, Mazeroski smiled and said, "It's low enough that it scrapes the snow off the top of my van, so I don't mind."

Mazeroski has a subtle sense of humor. There isn't much he minds. He doesn't demand much from anybody or anything. He accepts life as it comes. Which is why you will never hear Mazeroski moaning about not having been inducted into the Baseball Hall of Fame by now. To him, such an honor was not a birthright. He just rolls along, like the beautiful Laurel Highlands where good friends like Arnold Palmer and Dick Groat have homes and golf courses. Latrobe and Ligonier, where the Mellons have their country estates and horse farms, where they make Rolling Rock beer, where the Steelers have their summer training camp, are the next major roadstops east on Route 30. Maz remains a big sports fan, watching all manner of sports activity on TV; he's an avid golfer, a hunter and fisherman, an ambitious diner and there is

Bill Mazeroski tells stories at Pirates Alumni gathering in 1993.

David Arrigo/Pittsburgh Pirates

Carnegie Library of Pittsburgh

Famous moment: Maz hits home run to win 1960 World Series.

everything in this locale that he requires to sustain and entertain himself and his family.

Maz was 57 at the time of our visit, and would be 58 by the time another World Series would be played.

Bill had been to Bradenton, Florida, only the week before, serving as one of the coaches at the Pirates' second annual Camp Bradenton Fantasy Training Camp, where middle-aged Walter Mittys go to play baseball with Pirates of the past. It's an expensive vacation, but there are lots of repeaters in the ranks, and most of those in attendance think it's the greatest of getaways.

Maz was involved in a memorable exchange at the Pirates' Fantasy Camp. A fellow named Jim Fitzgerald hit a home run over the fence, and everyone went crazy. Maz told Fitzgerald, "Do you want a tip on how to live off a home run for the next 30 years?"

Fitzgerald will be telling people that story forever.

"It's always a lot of fun to get together with old teammates," said Mazeroski, "and we just have a good time with the guys. You watch them all play one day and then you draft teams. I just put myself on their level. I was just like them. You go to the bar and buy them a beer and they buy you a beer. I was just one of the guys, the way I've always been." To which his wife Milene added, "Just yourself."

Asked where he thought that quality in him came from, Maz shrugged, thought a few seconds, and, finally, said, "My mother was like that. She'd rather hurt herself than hurt anybody else. She never said anything bad about anybody. Just good stuff. And she was very religious."

Bill's dad lost part of his foot at age 18 in a coal-mining accident just before he was about to report to the Cleveland Indians' training camp. That was the end of his career as a ballplayer and as a coal miner. He worked after that for the B.F. Goodrich Company in Akron. His name was Louis. He died in 1959, the year before Bill hit his famous home run in the 1960 World Series.

Kathy Guy, director of promotions for the Pirates, serves as coordinator for the Camp Bradenton Fantasy Camp, and she said the cost of $2,995 included airfare, hotel accommodations, meals, complete uniform, some incidentals and perks. For a week, an accountant or attorney or teacher can put on a Pirates uniform and spikes and play ball with Bill Mazeroski, Steve Blass, Bob Veale, Dave Cash, Nellie Briles, Milt May, Dave Giusti, ElRoy Face, Bill Virdon, Kent Tekulve and present-day Pirates like Lloyd McClendon, Jay Bell and manager Jim Leyland. Others who made appearances at the camp included Bob Robertson, Steve Nicosia, Omar Moreno, Bruce Kison, Jim Morrison, Frank Thomas and Grant Jackson. Mazeroski had never spent a complete week at the camp, so his presence was a real bonus for everybody. Mazeroski was one of five participants at the camp who wore No. 9. There were seven wearing No. 21 — Clemente's old number. Both numbers have been retired by the Pirates.

"One guy was wearing No. 52," said Mazeroski. "I told him, 'You'll never get to Pittsburgh with that number.' Down there, they get any number they want to wear. One guy got beeped while he was at bat, and called time out while he answered his call."

Maz still marvels at how many people want to talk to him about his home run and the 1960 Bucs.

"It was their childhood, and growing up," he said, "and they remember it a lot. They love to talk about it."

To which Milene interjected, "Not that we dwell on it."

While he hit the ball for infield practice and such, Mazeroski did not go out and field the ball. "No fielding," he said, smiling at the thought. "I don't trust my hands anymore. I got through all those bad fields, like Forbes Field, with my teeth intact. I don't want to lose them now."

There is a **NO SMOKING** sign on the front of the mantel in the Mazeroskis' home. "I was sitting on a stool between Tekulve and Face in the clubhouse in Bradenton, and I couldn't stay there because they both like to smoke. I can't stand that anymore," he said.

Mazeroski doesn't miss baseball the way a Frank Thomas does. Thomas was back in Florida a week later, playing 17 innings at an All-Stars Fantasy Camp in St. Petersburg. "He loves it; he'll play baseball till he drops," said his wife Dolores. ("I hit it pretty good, too," offered Frank).

What a contrast — going from temperatures in the 60s and 70s in Florida to the sub-zero climes of Pennsylvania, which the ailing Governor Robert Casey had declared an "emergency disaster area." There were earthquakes in southern California and, mind-blowing enough, in Reading, Pennsylvania, so Mother Nature was giving people nightmares on both ends of the country.

If Charley Dressen did, indeed, once say, "I should have stood in bed," certainly Mazeroski might have shared his sentiments, only the bed would be in Bradenton. Or Greensburg.

"Geez, now I know why I don't miss being in baseball anymore," Maz reflected. "Getting up at 7 in the morning, a doubleheader every day, standing there watching those games. Being the manager, you want everyone to do well. They don't, so you're frustrated. For a week, though, it's great."

And that's how everyone felt who met Mazeroski at Camp Bradenton Fantasy Camp.

"Maz was the most popular by far," reported Steve Blass when he came back from Bradenton, also the site of the Pirates' regular spring training camp. "He's just so damn real. People have some apprehension about approaching someone of his stature, but once they say 'hello,' he lets them know he's as regular as anyone they've ever known. He's comfortable with normal people, because that's how he sees himself. Bill doesn't look in the mirror and see a legendary figure in baseball. We had about 66 guys there, and he was on the same wave length as every one of them."

Mazeroski shrugged off the remark when I related to him that Blass had told me he was "the most popular" of the Pirates at the Fantasy Camp. "That's something I didn't know," he said. "No one told me that."

257

Milene pointed out a plaque on the mantel where many of Maz's trophies and awards are on display. There, right between two of the eight Gold Gloves he won as the best second baseman during his distinguished 17-year career with the Pirates, was a plaque hailing him as "Rookie Coach of the Year" for the Fantasy Camp. His players had these plaques made up for Mazeroski and Briles. "I thought that was so cute," said Milene.

"Nellie and I coached a team that went 6-2 and had the best record," said Mazeroski. "We didn't have the best team, but we stayed the healthiest. That's the key. We had one guy snap his Achilles heel right at the outset; otherwise we stayed healthy."

Mazeroski's remark sounded like he could have been talking about the 1960 Pirates as well. They certainly were not the best team in baseball that year, but they stayed relatively healthy, refused to give up all summer long, and triumphed over the heavily-favored Yankees to win the World Series on Mazeroski's bottom-of-the-ninth inning leadoff home run that immortalized his name in a sport he dreamed of playing as a kid growing up in the backwoods of Ohio.

"This is city compared to where Bill lived as a kid," mentioned Milene. "There wasn't another family within a mile of their place. They were really isolated."

Maybe that's why Mazeroski has never been comfortable in crowds. "I stay away from places where there are lots of people when possible," said Mazeroski. "I don't like crowds."

But people love him just the same. "I was hitting a guy ground balls at Bradenton," he said, under urging to relate some stories about his experience at the Fantasy Camp. "Afterward, he tells me 'that was the biggest thrill of my life.' And I said, 'Me hitting you ground balls?' And he said, 'Yeah, you're the best there ever was.' So I guess people do enjoy mixing with players like myself."

Maz has a hard time appreciating the public's fascination with him. Before you see any of the paintings of him in a Pirates' uniform, or any of the bats and gloves and balls that memorialize Mazeroski's career with the Pirates, you see family photos. In fact, the first thing you see upon entering the Mazeroski home is a portrait done on a sand surface of their dog, Muttley, whom they had for 12 years. Milene had it done by a woman at an arts festival in Greensburg.

Muttley seemed happy to be in the house, and was particularly pleased when Maz patted him on the head, and stroked his mane, while Maz rocked back and forth in his favorite rocking chair. Hearing it creaking, Milene admonished her husband, "You have to oil that rocking chair, Stush."

Perfect. That line sums up the sort of people that are the Mazeroskis. The name is William Stanley Mazeroski. It's Polish, as a plaque from the National Polish Alliance attests. "Stush" was also a nickname for one of his contemporaries, Stanley "Stan the Man" Musial, a Hall of Famer with the St. Louis Cardinals, always popular in Pittsburgh because he was from nearby Donora in the Mon Valley. "I'm just kidding him when I call him Stush," Milene said, almost apologetically.

260

Milene had put together two montages of photos from Bill's family, showing him as a young child with his sister, Mary Lou, two years older, and their mother and father. "Wasn't he the cutest thing?" said Milene. "I just love those pictures."

"He rebelled a little bit."

Bill Mazeroski and Roberto Clemente were teammates on the Pirates for 17 years. "I think we're the answer to a trivia question," said Mazeroski. "We may have been teammates in the big leagues longer than any other two guys."

Mazeroski made the Pirates roster in 1956, which was Clemente's second campaign in Pittsburgh. The 1972 season was the final one for both players.

"I liked Clemente; he was not a bad person," said Mazeroski. "I knew he could play, no question about that. He was a very moody person when he first came up. I think it was caused by his not understanding the language, and he couldn't handle Murtaugh yelling at him. He was confused, out of his own country, and he rebelled a little bit. I think that's the way most of the '60 players understood him.

"Clemente was a heckuva guy. I liked him. I played all those years with him."

Mazeroski was most comfortable in his rocking chair when we first sat down. He kicked off his shoes, and rocked back and forth. He wore a comfortable-looking burgundy and dark blue slipover jersey, light blue denim slacks and black socks, and a satisfied grin for the most part. When I kept coming at him with one question after another about Clemente, however, the rocking chair became a dentist's chair. Maz is not a story-teller, and I was prying for personal stories, the kind that would provide insight into Clemente.

"I don't think Clemente was a great Murtaugh fan," offered Mazeroski. "Murtaugh was always all over him. Clemente didn't know how to take him.

"The best way I could explain Clemente is when he got hollered at he'd go into a shell, and he didn't play or work as hard for awhile after that. He'd be stewing. The more confidence he gained the more comfortable he became. He learned the system; he got to know our ways. He became the best I ever played with."

I asked Mazeroski if it were true that Murtaugh would single him out and get on Bill in front of the rest of the team. "Yes, he knew I could take it, that's why," said Mazeroski. "But that also grows old."

Mazeroski must have wondered what sort of stories, or information, I was after. You might have thought I was speaking in Spanish. Clemente was not a complex subject as far as Mazeroski was concerned. He was a marvelously gifted teammate, a good man, somebody he basically admired, except for one thing. . .

"The only thing I'd fault Clemente on is that he'd take days off if he wasn't feeling so hot, or if he were tired. He only worried about his hitting, but he could have made a difference defensively, if he was out in right field. What hurt was that he could do things when he was hurt that most of us couldn't do when we were healthy.

"I'd have hit much higher, if I'd taken a couple of days off to regain my strength when I was on an 0-for-30 hitting streak. But I didn't do it. The pitchers wanted me in there; they felt I could help them win with my glove. Clemente could have done the same with his glove, with his arm."

I mentioned that several of his teammates from those early Pirates teams didn't want to sit out any games if they could help it for fear that somebody else might come in and take away their jobs. They knew too well the story of how Wally Pipp took a day off as the first baseman of the Yankees and never got his job back once Lou Gehrig got out there. Gehrig went on to set a major league record for consecutive games played.

"We had Ducky Schofield there most of the time," said Maz, "and he was anxious to play. He was hoping somebody would take a day off in the infield. I wasn't looking to giving anybody an opening."

Clemente may have figured he was so good there was no one who could truly threaten his standing as a starter. Mazeroski remembers how he got better.

"Clemente really came into his own when Harry Walker became the manager," Mazeroski said.

Clemente, indeed, won the MVP in 1966, when he had career highs of 29 home runs and 109 RBI, playing for Walker.

"Walker praised Clemente to the hilt, and made him feel like the greatest player in the game," said Mazeroski. "Roberto became a leader. He would tell young players what was expected of them. He'd help players who were down. They all looked up to him.

"After the 1964 or 1965 season, he became the team leader."

Yet Mazeroski was the team captain for a ten-year period. Mazeroski didn't make as much noise as Clemente. "I'm not sure what leadership means," said Mazeroski. "I think you have to instill confidence in your players, and I could do that. I'd go talk to a guy when he was down."

I asked Mazeroski why none of the veteran players played that same role with the rookie Clemente. "There was nobody who spoke his language, there was nobody to help him out," he said. "There were no older Latins on the team; just all white guys."

Who looked after Mazeroski when he first came up?

"Guys like Bob Skinner and Jerry Lynch and Bobby Del Greco were especially friendly. I had played winter ball with them before I came up to the Pirates. They took me under their wings when I came to the big leagues."

"The only thing we didn't do was go out to dinner together."
— Mazeroski on Clemente

I had heard from other Pirates that Clemente kept his own schedule on the road. "I never saw him after the ballpark, home or away," said Mazeroski. "I never saw him drink, I never saw him smoke or chew. He was a clean-living individual, from where I was sitting. He kept himself in great shape. He had all the physical tools."

What about Clemente's arm?

"There was no need for me to go out toward right field on most balls hit out there. I went to second most of the time, and let Groat back me up. That's not the way you're taught to play, but we did that a lot. Maybe you'd go out toward right field in some of the bigger parks. In the short ballparks, he could throw it in without any help from a cutoff man.

"It was a great arm. He gave me some shin bruises. He threw it hard; it wasn't light. He threw a heavy ball. He could get the ball on one hop off the concrete wall. Without him out there, usually you could count it as a double. But if he got it off the wall on one or two hops it wasn't an automatic double. You had to earn it."

Mazeroski was portrayed by some of his teammates as not being enamored with Clemente earlier in their careers. "I wasn't an anti-Clemente man," said Maz, sharply. "His only fault was he didn't play every day. All those years we were together, it's tough to pick out certain things . . . But I was a Clemente man.

"He was a good man; he was a religious person. He talked a lot about that sports city he wanted to put together in Puerto Rico. Sometimes he called me 'Polacko.' You know, because I'm Polish. We,always talked. I agitated him. We respected each other.

"There was never a war between Clemente and me. There was never a disagreement. We played ball together. Bob Friend's locker was next to his, and I was next to Bob. So I was always close to Clemente in the clubhouse.

"We lockered almost side by side. There were no arguments. No fights. No nothing. The only thing we didn't do was go out to dinner together. We did everything else you do together as a team.

"Near the end of my career, I was getting heavy, and it was hurting my play. Clemente wanted me to come down to Puerto Rico with him in the winter. He told me he'd get me in shape. He said I could play a few more years if I'd go with him during the off-season. See, he was concerned about me.

"There's not too much you can say bad about Clemente. He was a great player. I was just happy to be there to watch him.

"He changed a game. In almost every game, a runner doesn't go from first to third on a single to right field because he was out there. That makes a big difference in a lot of games.

"When I saw him at first (in the mid-50s) he wasn't a great hitter yet. His body hadn't really filled out or matured. But if you saw him throw a baseball it was plain to see he was something special.

"I probably played with him as long as anybody. I used to laugh when anybody would ask him how he was doing. Cause if somebody asked him they'd better have some time to listen. Something was always wrong.

"Clemente hit a lot of fly balls at Forbes Field that would have gone out in Atlanta. I saw him hit many as far as Willie Stargell. He didn't have as many home runs as Aaron or Mays, but they played in parks better suited for home run hitters. Roberto realized Forbes Field was built for line drive hitters, and he styled his game for it.

"He hit to right field more than anything. And he hit to right field as hard as left-handers. He had great power. He flashed it at times.

"What he did in 1971 was open people's eyes. People who'd never seen him play before, or maybe a game here and there, found out what he was all about. The way he hit and played the outfield in that Series made you know what you missed, not seeing him play every day. Because he was something special.

"Like all the other greats, he could reach another level in something like the playoffs or World Series, or when we were playing in New York in front of his friends, or in Chicago and Los Angeles. The bigger the city the bigger his performance."

Their son, David, 23, had a bachelor's degree from Grove City College and had been graduated with a master's degree in Management Information Systems from Pitt in November of 1993, and was working for Deloitte & Touche, a national accounting firm with offices at PPG Plaza in Downtown Pittsburgh. David was commuting to work from his home in Greensburg. Their other son, Darren, 31, continued as the head coach of the baseball team at Gulf Coast Community College in Panama City, Florida. He has a bachelor's degree from Northeast Louisiana and a masters degree in physical education from Western Kentucky University. When I remarked that it was quite an achievement that both of their boys had attained master's degrees, Milene dismissed my praise. "Oh, it's not such a big thing," she said. Then again, she and her husband sometimes sound like they feel the same way about the home run he hit to win the World Series in 1960.

Despite his heroics and his Gold Glove fielding ability, the most money Mazeroski ever made in a single season with the Pirates, he says, was about $50,000.

During my visit to the Mazeroskis' home the year before, I had surprised Bill when I told him he was a rich man. "How can you say that?" he asked me. That's when I told him that he was still married to Milene, the young woman from Braddock he had first met when she was working as a secretary in the office of Rex Bowen, the director of scouting for the Pirates. They had two sons who were doing well, and making something of themselves. He had a mortgage-free home where

l Mazeroski slides home under tag by Reds' Hall of Fame catcher Johnny Bench.

ızeroski and Clemente chat with Hall of Famer Pie Traynor and his wife Eve at Three ₁vers Stadium opening ceremonies.

he was comfortable living, regular income sources, plus a solid baseball pension. This time around, I asked him, "Well, do you now agree with my assessment that you are a rich man?" He looked across the room at Milene, smiled, kept rocking in his rocking chair, and offered, "What more could you want, right?"

At that instant, the telephone rang in the next room and Milene went to answer it. She came back and reported to Bill that a friend of his had called to see if he would be interested in going ice fishing the following week at Deep Creek Lake.

We laughed at that. Earlier in our conversation, I had told him I was taking advantage of the bad weather to visit him because I figured he'd be at home. I didn't think he'd be out playing golf, hunting or fishing. "Unless you went ice-fishing," I had said.

And now the call to go ice-fishing.

"You'd need a gas drill to get through the ice today," said Mazeroski. "The ice is probably 15 or 18 inches thick. When it's below zero the ice freezes up again as soon as you finish drilling the hole. So it would be a waste of time to go out with the weather the way it is now. But I do enjoy ice-fishing when the conditions are right."

I asked him if he was looking forward to the summer of '94 when Pittsburgh would be host to both the Major League Baseball All-Star Game, but also the U.S. Men's Open Golf Tournament at the Oakmont Country Club. "I won't go to the Open," he said. "It's too crowded. I don't go where there's a bunch of people. I stay away from the crowds."

But he had agreed with his good friend and former teammate Nellie Briles, who worked in corporate sales for the Pirates and was the chairman of the Pittsburgh Pirates Alumni Association, that he would participate in some programs to promote the All-Star Game and the "Statue for Roberto" events.

It had been Briles, who also lives in Greensburg, who had picked him up and driven him to the airport to participate in the Pirates Camp Bradenton Fantasy program.

Just prior to leaving, Mazeroski had heard that Harvey Haddix had died, at age 68, of emphysema at a hospital near his home in Springfield, Ohio. It was sobering stuff. Pat Friend, Bob Friend's wife, and Sally O'Leary of the Pirates' publicity staff, were among those who called Bill and Milene to tell them the news of Haddix's death.

"That 1960 season was probably the biggest year of my life," said Mazeroski. "To see my teammates die one by one is kinda sad."

After I left Mazeroski's home, I traveled to the Sheraton Inn in Greensburg to participate in a Bucco Bash, a midwinter night's promotion sponsored by the Pirates and Latrobe's WCNS Radio. Most events of this nature had been cancelled because of the extreme cold, but several hundred Hot Stove League fans turned out to meet Pirates' Kevin Young, Al Martin, Steve Cooke and Brian Hunter, Lanny Frattare, "The Voice of the Pirates," and the Pirate Parrot. A dozen card dealers were set up in the middle of the main ballroom, a TV monitor played a videotape of a recently-released story about Roberto Clemente, and an auction was conducted of Pirates memorabilia by Frattare.

I was there to sign copies of my book, *MAZ And The '60 Bucs*. Many fans asked me if Mazeroski was coming. "I'd love to have him sign my book," one customer after another would say. Several who had already read the book told me that reading it brought back their youth. "This book is about my life," said one enthusiastic fan.

The vibes were great whenever I told anyone that I was working on a book about Roberto Clemente. His popularity today still stuns me.

John Deegan, a school teacher and baseball card dealer from nearby Latrobe, told me of the popularity of Clemente across the nation at baseball collectible shows. "He is second only to Mickey Mantle in popularity, and there seems to be a rise in interest in anything about him," said the senior Deegan. "Everybody's looking for stuff about Clemente."

I wondered why Mazeroski hadn't remained in a Pirates uniform. There were many coaches and managers older than him who were still at it. After he retired as an active ballplayer, Mazeroski was going to serve as a coach on his friend and former roommate Bill Virdon's staff in 1973. The following season, he wasn't sure whether he wanted to continue coaching. "I felt they weren't paying me enough to go through all you go through as a coach," said Mazeroski. "You're at the park before the ballplayers and you're there after they're gone. You've got 25 guys to take care of, not just yourself. And I was the third base coach, and the fans would get on you if they thought you made a bad decision regarding base-running. It just wasn't worth it. I decided I needed another $10,000 to make it worth my while, with all the traveling and stuff. I was making about $20,000 and I wanted $30,000. I went to Joe L. Brown. He said, 'No way, Maz.' Joe said he'd go for $25,000, but I held out for $30,000. And I quit. About four or five years ago, at one of the Old-Timers Games, Joe got me in a corner and apologized for the way he handled that. But I was prepared for life after baseball. I went back to baseball in 1979-80 as a coach with the Seattle Mariners for a reason. It made me eligible for all the raises in the pension plan for a ten-year period right up till 1990. Lou Gorman, who's now an executive with the Boston Red Sox, was in charge in Seattle back then. He wanted me to work with their second baseman, Julio Cruz." To which Milene added, "And he turned out OK. Bill helped him quite a bit."

Mazeroski owns Bill Mazeroski's Golf Course, a nine-hole golf course in Rayland, Ohio, and Bill's Bar, a restaurant and bar in Yorkville, Ohio, which is managed by his friend and partner Bill DelVecchio, a certified public accountant. Mazeroski lends his name to a national baseball magazine for Peterson Publishing. He got lucky with some selective stock buying, notably as an early investor in Mylan Labs — one of Bob Prince's picks that actually panned out — and he has his baseball pension. He makes an occasional promotional appearance for a payday, and participates in a lot of fund-raising golf outings. "Bill doesn't know how to say 'no' to too many people," says Milene.

267

The cold weather and the ice on the windows and doors of his home reminded Mazeroski of similar days in his youth living in the backwoods of Ohio. Most of the schools in western Pennsylvania were closed during the worst days of the 1994 winter, but that wasn't the case when Billy was a kid. "The school bus stopped about a mile from my home," he recalled. "I had to cross the same creek three times on the way to catching my bus. The creek never froze over completely; it would get mushy sometimes. Your shoes would sink into it. And it was too wide to jump. So I'd get my feet wet and I had colds every winter. But I didn't miss school."

Clemente and Mazeroski pose at Forbes Field in 1960.

Malcolm W. Emmons

Ron Swoboda
Still An Amazin' Met

"He was in a different zone."

Ron Swoboda was one of the unlikely heroes for the New York Mets in their 1969 World Series triumph in five games with the Baltimore Orioles. He was one of Casey Stengel's favorites with the Amazin' Mets, and may have best typified the team's playing personnel. He played right field and made some sensational catches in the World Series. He was a favorite with the fans, despite his Metsian misadventures at the plate and in the field. They once put out a banner that read: SWOBODA IS STRONGER THAN DIRT. He was also a favorite with sportswriters because he was comfortable with them, often joined them for a drink, and was a refreshing young man who could tell a good story. "This is the first time," said Swoboda after the Series. "Nothing can ever be as sweet again." I bumped into Swoboda in the press box at Three Rivers Stadium prior to a Steelers game with the New Orleans Saints in October of 1993. He was there as a sportscaster for WVUE-TV in New Orleans.

Roberto Clemente was the first big-name guy I ever saw up close back in 1964 when I first came to spring training with the Mets. I was an absolute rookie; I had just been signed that same year. He was the first superstar I ever saw. I was barely 20 years old. They kept us around; Stengel kept us around. Yes, Roberto Clemente. I remember seeing him . . . Roberto Clemente. The first time he went up to the plate, I was stunned. Someone threw him a breaking pitch. He took a godawful swing and fell down. 'Wait a minute,' I said to myself. 'That wasn't so elegant.'

"I walked by Clemente a few times in the clubhouse at Forbes Field. A lot of their guys would talk to you when you went through. Stargell and Veale would be talking trash. Veale would say he was going to dirty you up. Clemente seemed distant. He always seemed to feel like he wasn't getting proper attention. Out on the field, I never saw anybody do anything like him. I never saw a guy his size — he wasn't that big — use a bat as big as his. It was a 36 ounce model. He stood eight miles from home plate. You'd see him and you'd say, 'How the hell can you hit like that?' He had all this movement, and he stood as far back as you could. How can he hit a pitch away?

"I saw him hit line drives off the brick wall at Forbes Field. One of them was the hardest ball I ever saw hit. I saw Willie Stargell and Willie McCovey and Dick Allen hit some long balls against us, up and out, but Clemente's was different. I just never saw a ball hit so hard.

"He threw me out one time that I'll never forget. I was on second base when somebody hit a line drive down the right field line into the corner. There were two outs and I was running. Clemente races over

270

and takes this shot off the wall. When I rounded third, Clemente had his back to the plate. He turns and throws this seed to Jerry May, a big catcher they had in those days. I had no chance. I couldn't slide and I couldn't run over May. I just sort of flopped backward and May dug his knee and catcher's gear into me, and tore my ass up good. Nobody else makes that play. It was totally unreal. I could throw the ball pretty good myself when I was young, but he was in a different zone.

"Other times, he'd come out of the dugout limping, and then hit a topper into the ground, and he'd run like a scalded skunk to first. He'd pull off a scam."

New York Mets

Willie Mays checks out Mets phenom Ron Swoboda.

271

Steve Blass
Always good for a laugh

"Roberto Clemente was never one of the boys.
That wasn't necessarily a negative thing."

It's a photograph that Pittsburgh Pirates' fans won't soon forget. Steve Blass is leaping so high as he comes rushing off the mound, and Manny Sanguillen, all smiles, is running toward him from home plate, eager to embrace him. The date of the photograph is October 17, 1971; the place is Memorial Stadium in Baltimore.

Blass had just fired a four-hit, 2-1 victory over the Baltimore Orioles in the seventh and final game of the World Series. It was a photograph that was on display for many years afterward in the office of Pirates General Manager Joe L. Brown at Three Rivers Stadium, as well as thousands of bars and taverns throughout Pittsburgh and western Pennsylvania.

Another photograph shows Blass leaping into the arms of first baseman Bob Robertson, who beat Sanguillen to Blass. The scene is one of the most vivid memories for many Pirates' fans, perhaps second only to Bill Mazeroski circling the bases on the home run that won the 1960 World Series.

"The win was the culmination of a stirring uphill fight by the Pirates, who had fallen into difficulties by losing the first two games to the Orioles," wrote Roger Angell in the *New Yorker*. "Blass had begun their comeback with a wonderfully-pitched three-hit, 5-1 victory in the third game.

"It was an outstanding Series, made memorable above all by the play of Roberto Clemente, who batted .414 over the seven games and fielded his position with extraordinary zeal," continued Angell in an essay that was later reprinted in a book, *Five Seasons: A Baseball Companion*, published by Simon & Schuster. Clemente was awarded the sports car as the most valuable player of the Series, but Steve Blass was not far out of the running for the prize. After the last game, Baltimore manager Earl Weaver said, 'Clemente was great, all right, but if it hadn't been for Mr. Blass, we might be popping corks right now.' "

Of that famous photo of Blass leaping into the air as Sanguillen is going out to embrace him, Angell wrote in the June, 1975 *New Yorker*: "I am not a Pittsburgher, but looking at this photograph never fails to give me pleasure, not just because of its aesthetic qualities but because its high-bounding happiness so perfectly brings back that eventful World Series and that particular gray autumn afternoon in Baltimore and the wonderful and inexpungible expression of joy that remained on Steve Blass's face after the game ended."

Blass went the distance twice in the 1971 World Series, limiting the Orioles to one run in each outing. Clemente missed a bunt sign in

One of the magic moments in Pittsburgh sports history: Manny Sanguillen and Steve Blass leap for joy above, and Bob Robertson throws up arms in triumph below, after Pirates beat the Baltimore Orioles, 2-1, to win seventh game of 1971 World Series.

the third game and hit a three-run homer that sealed the victory for Blass and the Bucs. "I was sitting next to Murtaugh in the dugout," recalls Blass, "and I said, 'If you fine him, I'll pay it.' "

In the second game that Blass won, Clemente came through with a solo home run that was the only score for seven innings. The Pirates scored again in the eighth, but so did the Orioles before Blass shut them out for good.

Blass went bad, mysteriously, during the 1973 season, and one of the theories advanced about his sudden inability to get the ball over the plate, or to pitch successfully, was that he was seriously affected by the death of Clemente. Blass never pitched well in the majors after Clemente's death. He had his best season in 1972 with a 19-8 record, had an earned-run average of 2.48 — sixth best in the National League — and was selected to the All-Star team. A year later, his record was 3-9. He pitched one game in 1974, and lasted five innings. He gave up five hits, seven walks. He threw 100 pitches in three and two-thirds innings. In his final inning, Blass walked five runs home before Danny Murtaugh finally came with the hook. And that was it for Blass in the big leagues. Neither of his managers, Murtaugh and Billy Virdon, could explain what happened to Blass. Neither could Blass. Some suggested it was more of a psychological problem than a physical problem.

"Baseball has always owned me."

Blass lives in a medium-sized brick home on a hillside in Upper St. Clair, about 12 miles southeast of Three Rivers Stadium, in the same neighborhood as his long-time friend, former pitcher Dave Giusti.

Blass lives less than a mile from my home. I see him at the Upper St. Clair High School football games, the post office, riding in an open convertible in the annual Community Day Parade, at restaurant-bars, at sports banquets, and in the press box at Three Rivers Stadium where he has been on the Pirates' network broadcast team since 1986.

He remains one of the most popular of the Pirates, past or present. He has always been an engaging guy, down-to-earth and droll, good company for all. One of the qualities he appreciated about Bob Prince, in particular, was "he was equally at ease in a boardroom or a barroom." A native of Falls Village, Connecticut, he signed his first professional contract with the Pirates in June of 1960. He spent ten seasons (1964-1974) with the Pirates, compiling a record of 103-76 in 282 games.

He was a member of the 1972 National League All-Star team. Blass won 78 games in a five-year period between 1968 and 1972. He retired after the 1974 season, and remained in Pittsburgh, first as a traveling sales representative for Josten's, a national jewelry firm that makes, among other things, World Series rings and high school graduation rings, then with Frank B. Fuhrer Wholesale Co., a master distributor for Budweiser beer located on Pittsburgh's South Side. Blass thought he was out of baseball for good. "I always felt secure," said Karen Blass, "because I knew Steve wasn't afraid to work, and that he'd always have

274

a job." In 1982, Blass was back in baseball, as he teamed up with Bob Prince on Pirates cable telecasts and was retained as a member of the crew the following year when the cable rights were taken over by Home Sports Entertainment (HSE). He was back in the ballpark, back among the Pirates and the fans, and he couldn't have been happier.

Steve is a survivor. The Pirates had purged their broadcasting team soon after the 1993 season and had cut former Pirates pitcher Jim Rooker and Kent Derdivanis from the crew, and kept Lanny Frattare and Blass.

Blass was happy that he would remain active in baseball. At the time of my visit, he was looking forward to going to Bradenton, Florida the following week to work at the Camp Bradenton Fantasy Camp. He was especially pleased because he heard that Mazeroski would be among those in attendance to instruct the middle-aged male fans who would plunk down a few thousand dollars to participate in a make-believe baseball training camp with Pirates from the past.

"I'm happiest when I'm with people I know enjoy the game," observed Blass. "It doesn't matter how good or how bad some of these guys are on a baseball field. As long as they love baseball."

Blass would be back in his old element, and would enjoy it as much as any of the Walter Mittys who would attend the Fantasy Camp. He would be in a Pirates uniform again, throwing a baseball, pitching, teaching, talking baseball, having a few beers with the boys, staying up late, being a ballplayer again — even if just for a week.

"They may not have been the most talented group," Blass would later report, "but they were the strongest group at the bar. They told great stories."

I asked Blass if he ever considered, during his days as a big league pitcher, whether he was holding the baseball or whether the baseball was holding him.

"Baseball has had a hold on me since I was six years old," said Blass, harkening back to days when he tossed a tennis ball off a barn back in Falls Village with an interesting angled roof and played a game of baseball he made up. "It's diminished somewhat, but not a helluva lot. The thing I feel best about when I think about my days in baseball is that it was always fun. It's never been a tedious thing. Even in the toughest times, even when I couldn't figure out why I couldn't pitch effectively anymore, during my biggest personal tests, I always loved the atmosphere and the people I was around in baseball. Baseball's been everything to me. I love the game. I love the life. Baseball has always owned me."

When I visited him, he insisted that the nightmare of those final two disturbing seasons with the Pirates — "just walking out to the mound scared me to death," he once said — was finally behind him, and nagged him no more.

"I was always the class clown."

Blass was beaming as he shared stories about Roberto Clemente, Bill Mazeroski, Willie Stargell, Bob Prince as well as those of his wife and kids, as he sat in his spacious family room on January 6, 1994. Blass has a boyish, devilish look about him, and an enthusiasm and spirit about what he says that makes you smile. He makes you feel at home, and it's easy to be comfortable in his company.

Blass had cleared the driveway of snow earlier in the day. Pittsburgh had been buried in a foot-and-a-half of snow that week. "I'll be looking out for you," said Blass after I called to say I was on my way, "but you shouldn't have any problems."

Blass bought this home in 1972, and he and Karen were hosting a New Year's Eve party for neighbors, including Ginny and Dave Giusti, that same year when they learned that Clemente had been in an airplane crash off the coast of his native Puerto Rico. They didn't know, at first, that the Pirates leader had been killed that night.

The room has lots of pictures and plaques and bats and balls on display, along with family portraits and pictures. Steve and Karen had been married 30 years. Their two boys, David, 29, and Christopher, 27, live in Connecticut and Georgia, respectively, these days, but pictures of both at different stages in their lives are all about the room, and in photo albums I was shown with great pride.

That famous photo of Blass leaping high in the air, with Sanguillen, all smiles, charging at him, after Blass had gotten the final out against the Baltimore Orioles in the 7th game of the 1971 World Series was reproduced on a large, handsome plaque Blass said he had bought from Nellie King. Blass got Merv Rettenmund to ground out to end the game.

It was among many memorable scenes from Blass's baseball days that decorated the room, a hallway and Steve's office upstairs. "Karen calls this 'Steve's Shrine,' " said Blass, as he pointed to a corner of the family room. The room was full of memories, good and bad.

There is a plaque representing the J. Roy Stockton Award for Outstanding Baseball Achievement, a Dapper Dan Award for meritorious service to Pittsburgh, a shiny metal bat with the engraved signatures of the National League All-Stars of 1972, a 1971 Pittsburgh Pirates World Champions bat, a signed photograph of President Nixon, and a framed, decorated proclamation announcing Steve Blass Day in Falls Village.

"With Steve, everything is right out in the open," said the former Karen Lamb. "Every accomplishment, every stage of the game — you have no idea how much he loved it, how he enjoyed the game."

Blass pointed out one particular enlarged photo from 1971 that stands alone on one area of the wall as "my favorite." It showed Steve in his Pirates uniform, standing next to Karen, looking lovely in a straw hat, with their sons standing in front of them in Pirates uniforms. "It was for a Father-Son Game," said Steve, "and I got their pants mixed up. Look how tight David's are, and how loose Chris's are. He has baggy pants like Emmett Kelly." It, too, is a great picture.

276

ve and Karen Blass enjoy a day at the
ch with their boys, Chris, 2, and
ty, 4, during spring training.

Blass is swarmed over by joyful teammates
after beating Orioles, 2-1, in final game of
1971 World Series.

Nellie Briles pours bucket of water on Blass in clubhouse celebration in Baltimore.

There is a lot of Emmett Kelly, the famous sad-faced baggy-pants clown, in Steve Blass, I thought. He has always been after a laugh. He has always been a source of great fun. Even when he was hurting on the inside, Blass has been able to get others to smile and laugh.

Blass and I were both 51 when I interviewed him. He was about five months older, but I could relate well to a fellow class clown. I understood where he was coming from, and what was behind his behavior. "Yeah, I was always the class clown," Blass conceded.

Of all the Pirates' broadcasters in recent years, Blass has been the best at telling stories, at identifying the amusing side of sports, of being able to relate anecdotes. He learned the importance of such at the side of Prince, whom he greatly admired. He has several autographed photos of Prince as well as Clemente covering the walls in his second-floor office. Blass discovered long ago that it's as helpful to have a sense of humor as it is to have a fastball and curveball and slider in your pitching repertoire. He takes his job seriously, but not himself and is quick to poke fun at himself on the air.

Sparky Anderson, who managed the Cincinnati Reds and Detroit Tigers, once said, "A player can't go wrong if he remembers where he came from." Blass can't forget. He has a sign MAIN STREET hanging over a doorway which comes from his hometown of Falls Village. He remembers in his youth mowing the lawn outside the Town Hall on the village green.

His hometown was once described by Roger Kahn, in an *Esquire* essay, as "a green, picture-postcard town, set in Connecticut's Berkshires above the Housatonic River."

Kahn, who covered the great Brooklyn Dodgers teams of Robinson, Reese and Snider, and wrote of them in that wonderful book *Boys of Summer*, visited with Blass at his last spring training camp in Bradenton, Florida.

"This is the telling season for Steve Blass, whose geniality has survived harsh pressure," wrote Kahn. "In a press box or out, one has to root a bit. He's thirty-two, which is too young to have your dreams behind you, like an old man in Florida, sunning himself on a rickety chair with nothing on earth to do but wait for the laundromat dryer to stop spinning."

A small plaque on the wall of the family room has the words of the eulogy delivered by Blass at the memorial service for Clemente on January 4, 1973 at the San Fernando Catholic Church in Clemente's hometown of Carolina, Puerto Rico. Blass said it was adapted from a tribute that had been offered to eulogize the late Lou Gehrig of the New York Yankees. The Pirates publicity director back then, Bill Guilfoile, now the vice-president of the Baseball Hall of Fame, had previously worked for the Yankees, and got approval for its use and some revisions to make it appropriate for the Clemente service.

It reads:

"We've been to the wars together
We took our foes as they came;
And always you were the leader,
And ever you played the game.

Idol of cheering millions;
Records are yours by sheaves
Iron of frame they hailed you;
Decked you with laurel leaves.

But higher than we hold you;
We who have known you best,
Knowing the way you came through
Every human test.

Let this be a silent token
Of lasting friendships gleam.
And all that we've left unspoken —
Your friends on the Pirate team.

There is a framed photograph with a personal message to Steve from President Nixon. There is a framed issue of *Sports Illustrated*, the July 3, 1972 edition, with Steve as the cover boy. There are polished bats, autographed balls, prints and photos. One large print over the fireplace was given to Blass by Christopher Passodelis of Christopher's Restaurant atop Mt. Washington. "Chris called me and told me he was redoing the cocktail lounge area, and wanted to know if I wanted this," said Blass. "It's something I really treasure."

Blass also presented photographs that showed President Nixon talking to him and Dave Giusti, and Dan Galbreath, the former Pirates executive and son of the team's longtime owner, John Galbreath, the real estate mogul from Columbus, Ohio. They went to the White House a few days after the death of Clemente to get Nixon's support for a sports city in San Juan, Puerto Rico, which had been Clemente's pet project.

"We didn't know a word of Spanish and it was wild."

"I had some idea of what it must have been like for Clemente when he came to Pittsburgh from Puerto Rico," said Blass. "Back in 1963, I played winter ball for Santiago in the Dominican Republic. Santiago wasn't a resort town, it was in the interior. I got married to Karen on October 5, 1963, and we were in the Dominican Republic as newly-weds five days later, and we didn't know a word of Spanish, and it was wild. I went there because they were paying me $1,350 a month, with no taxes. This was two years after the death of their dictator Trujillo, and the country was still in an uproar. Karen would come to the ballpark at night and they'd check everyone for weapons. They had soldiers with guns standing at each end of the dugouts. Willie Stargell was there with me. I was playing for the Cibaenas Eagles.

"We were both there when President Kennedy was assassinated. That was a strange feeling — being out of your country when your leader is assassinated. You felt lost, so far from home.

"I wasn't a hero down there, but I was pretty popular. I came home the first of December because of some personal matters, and then I went back. No Americans ever did that; once they went home they never came back. But that was an important period for me. I developed a slider down there, and that was the year before I made it with the Pirates.

"It gave me some kind of sense for what a Latin would experience in coming to this country. I didn't give it much thought at the time, but it served as some kind of understanding of what you ought to do to help someone in that situation, not that it makes you perfect."

Blass often tells a story at banquets about how smart he felt about being signed by the Pirates in June of 1960 when they ended up winning the World Series a few months later. "I signed my first contract for $250 a month, and played in the minors for a few months upon graduation from high school. Then I went to work that fall as a carpenter's helper back home in Falls Village, Connecticut. I was 18 at the time and I won $18 in a pool for the seventh game of the 1960 World Series, and that was big money for me back then.

"In 1961, I went to Jacksonville. Stargell was with the team then. The white players were staying in one hotel and the black players had other housing accommodations. The bus would pick us up and then go over to the colored section of town and pick up the black guys.

"Clemente was living the same way at the Pirates training camp in the early '60s. While Clemente was sleeping in black hotels, we were practicing signing autographs. At that time in our lives, big league baseball was still just a dream. We were doing autographs with the idea that some day somebody might ask us for them. Clemente had already been a star on the 1960 World Series championship team. We, who hadn't even made it yet, had unrestricted freedom. Nobody was saying 'no' to us.

"I wonder how many people on the Pirates approached Clemente or any of the black players, and discussed this situation with them. When I was having all my problems, people like Stargell would always acknowledge what I was going through. With all the guy had on his mind, I was pleased that he hadn't forgotten me.

"Joe Brown and Danny Murtaugh were awful good to me. Murtaugh was such a psychologist. He was back managing one more time, and he'd say things so that I wouldn't feel so bad. He told me my timing was perfect, that things were awful at the time with the team, and that I wasn't missing anything. He'd say, 'You got out just in time.'

"It was tough for me. Back in 1973 and 1974, our kids were 9 and 7 and they were in first and third grade at Eisenhower Grade School. Kids can be difficult, and often cruel, and the boys were razzed because of my well-publicized problems as a pitcher."

Blass showed me a caricature of Bob Prince on the wall of his office, and pointed out a message Prince had penned on it: "Dear Steve, We've been through a lot together. But you helped me to ride out the storms." Blass smiled. "See, Bob had a way of turning things around to put a positive spin on it," he said. "He was the one who helped me, not the other way around. But I was surrounded by boosters in those days; I don't think the environment is that way these days."

There was a color photograph showing Prince, wearing bright madras slacks and Blass in a baseball uniform, with a patch on his shoulder in Clemente's memory. Next to that was a framed box score of the last game Prince worked when he was doing Pirates games on a regular basis. Prince signed it for Blass.

"Don't make excuses.
It's what you do,
not why you didn't."

Blass felt people didn't understand Clemente. "I guess I wish I appreciated him as much when he was alive as I have since he's been dead," said Blass.

"You're so close to somebody when you're around them all the time. But playing the game of baseball is so consuming. I didn't have a chance to step back and appreciate the gifts I was given by being around some special people like Clemente.

"For me, one of the things that was important was to finally get his acceptance. When I first came to the ballclub, I said very little to him. I didn't think I was qualified to say much. Winning Maz's approval was important to me, too. And you remember significant instances where you felt like you finally did."

Both acceptances came soon after the 7th game of the 1971 World Series in which Blass was the winning pitcher.

"Maz never talked philosophy, and I had roomed with him for parts of a couple of years, but he seldom had much to say. But I learned a lot from him. He gave me a philosophy which I adopted in my own words: 'Don't make excuses. It's what you do, not why you didn't.' It was a great lesson.

"Maz came up to me in the clubhouse after the seventh game, and he said, 'I judge pitchers by how they pitch when they have a one-run lead. You're a great pitcher. You didn't have a ten-run lead. You didn't have any room. You're a great pitcher. When you're sitting on a one-run lead, that's big-time.' That was a big thing coming from Maz. I'd been with the club for seven years, and I knew I was all right with him, but that kinda certified it.

"The acceptance by Clemente came a little later that same day. We were at the airport, getting ready to board an airplane after that last game. Clemente and his wife Vera had gotten on the plane ahead of us, and they went to the back of the plane and sat down. Karen was with me and we were among the last ones to get on the plane, and we sat up front. Before the plane took off, Clemente came up, and stood in the aisle. He had this little bit of a grin. He said, 'Blass, come here. Get out in the aisle. Let me embrace you.' I got up and moved toward him, and he put his arms around me, and gave me a great big hug. And that was it. That's all he said."

"Like we were the soldiers and he was the general."

I asked Blass if he had heard the complaints from Pirates who preceded him about Clemente scratching himself from the lineup from time to time because of one reason or another, often not apparent to be serious enough to sideline anyone, as the other players saw it.

"In my mind, I was associated with Clemente for nine years, and it was all my dream. I heard about some of the accusations regarding Clemente in the early years, but I didn't see that. He had a reputation for being a loner and staying aloof from the rest of the team. The bunch we had — in the late '60s and early '70s — you had to join in, and have some fun in the clubhouse.

"Our guys drew Clemente into the clubhouse shenanigans. When I first got there, he was very aloof, very much to himself. Like we were employees and he was management, or we were the soldiers and he was the general.

"Giusti was one of the guys who really got after him. So did Juan Pizarro. He'd tease Clemente unmercifully. Giusti would scream at Clemente, and get him involved.

"Clemente was never one of the boys."

Blass let that sit for a minute, then added, "But that wasn't necessarily a negative thing. We were the Dead End Kids, and he was a notch, or several notches, above that. He always had that aura of dignity. A presence. You know, in sports there is always a certain locker room atmosphere, locker room talk. He didn't take part in a lot of it."

Clemente was more comfortable and seemed to relax more when he was with two members of the club's support staff, trainer Tony Bartirome and clubhouse attendant John 'Hully' Hallahan.

"Clemente truly loved Tony and Hully a lot. Hully was part Russian, I think, and he'd run off all these Russian phrases to stir up things. Whatever he was saying, it seemed to get a good rise out of Roberto on a regular basis.

"Tony was always giving Roberto a rubdown before every game. It was a pre-game ritual. He'd work out all the kinks in Clemente's neck and shoulders. Sometimes I'd crawl under the training table, and do a bit like I was a voice in the distance giving them instructions. There was a popular TV show at the time called 'Mission Impossible.' It starred Peter Graves, Martin Landau, Greg Morris and Barbara Bain, and

I took my cue from that show. I'd say, 'Good morning, Mr. Clemente, this is your neck. Your assignment today is to get three doubles off Jack Billingham. As usual, we will disavow any knowledge of this conversation. And, Tony, get thees son-of-a-beetch outta here!' And Clemente would go crazy."

Blass had other memories of Clemente. He remembers coming into the clubhouse once (in 1967) at Forbes Field and seeing Clemente standing in front of a mirror and mouthing words to teammate Manny Jimenez, trying to teach him how to speak English. "He sounded like Tonto in the Lone Ranger," recalled Blass. He remembers Clemente offering clinics on how to play golf, though he seldom played himself. He remembers how when he and Giusti used to play poker on the airplane with Clemente and Sanguillen that Clemente would replay every hand to show Sanguillen how the game was properly played. "Every so often, you got rare glimpses of Clemente like that," said Blass.

"We were in a fog."

"We were hosting a New Year's Eve party. It was strictly a neighborhood party. We got a call around 4 a.m. when the party was still going strong. I don't know if it was Joe Brown or Bill Guilfoile who called. They said they'd gotten a report that an airplane had gone down and Clemente was on it. The party, as the result of it all, broke up.

"The Giustis were staying over at our house that night. But no one could sleep. I met Dave in the corridor out there, and we decided that since we couldn't sleep anyhow that we should go over to Joe Brown's house. He lived on Crestview Manor in Mt. Lebanon.

"We went there, and we couldn't get much information there, either, at that point. We went over to Stargell's house on the east side of town (in Penn Hills). We didn't know what else to do. I don't remember much else about that day, sequence-wise. We were in a fog.

"The Pirates chartered a plane for us to attend a funeral service in Puerto Rico. I remember going in to the Pirates office and calling ballplayers to see who'd go down there, and making arrangements for the trip. For some reason, I remember Joey Diven being on the plane.

"Dan Galbreath called in and said he was going to the White House to see President Nixon, and the subject matter was Sports City in Puerto Rico. He said he'd be stopping in Pittsburgh, and he said, 'I'd like you guys to go with me.' So Giusti and I got on his private airplane. We spent 23 minutes in the Oval Office. I remember that because President Nixon's press secretary told us he had allotted nine minutes to our visit, but that President Nixon was enjoying himself, talking to baseball people."

"Wherever I went in western Pennsylvania, I was always asked about Roberto Clemente."

Blass put two bottles of Budweiser on the table, and we each had a beer during our conversation. Blass is loyal. He worked for several years for Pittsburgh sports promoter Frank Fuhrer of the Frank B. Fuhrer Wholesale Co., Pittsburgh's master distributor for Budweiser.

"I went to work there in 1983," said Blass. "I did community relations work for him, and called on distributors and bars and restaurants. I did of lot of work with the first Family House Invitational, begging corporations to spend $400 to play in a charity golf tournament. And look how big that's gotten, which is a real tribute to Frank and his people.

"I'll bet I hosted about 400 'Bud Nights' at bars and restaurants around western Pennsylvania. I'd carry my 16 mm projector with me and show films of the Pirates and Steelers, and promote Budweiser in between. I must have done 50 of them in Homestead, and I did them in Glassport, West Mifflin, Hazelwood, McKeesport, McKees Rocks, and it was great. I've met so many fans that way, and I've heard so many good stories, some of which I've been able to use on the air.

"That's one of the ways I learned my way around this state. Karen and I lived in a lot of places in our days with the Pirates. We lived in Penn Hills, Swissvale, Forest Hills, Monroeville, Gibsonia — that was a real commute — and in Green Tree. We were in Green Tree in 1971 when we won the World Series."

Only the night before, Blass had traveled to Youngstown, Ohio on a night when most Pittsburghers were wary of venturing out to the local super market because of the treacherous roads in the wake of a major snowstorm. He had gone there as part of the Pirates Caravan, accompanied by pitchers Steve Cooke and Denny Neagle, and admitted the attendance by Pirates fans was cut down by the bad weather. Before the holidays, he'd gone with Lanny Frattare on Caravan appearances in Washington and Weirton.

"I don't think there's anyplace I haven't been around here," said Blass. "When I worked for Josten's, I was responsible for 55 high schools and my area was northeast, east and west of Pittsburgh. I did that for eight years, from 1975 when I was first out of baseball until 1983. I'd leave here at 5:30 in the morning in order to get to Oil City for the first period to show them rings. Sometimes you'd drive that in bad weather only to find out when you got there that the school had been closed.

"Wherever I went in western Pennsylvania, however, I was always asked about Roberto Clemente. People would ask me, 'What was Clemente really like? How good was Clemente?' "

That morning, as I was preparing to visit Blass, I had a thought that Blass would have a lot of Clemente memorabilia in his home. I just guessed that he would, and that he'd be showing me a record about him. Call it E.S.P., but no sooner had Blass ushered me into his upstairs office than he was handing me a 45 rpm record called "The Ballad of Roberto Clemente." It was sung by Paul New, with Pepi Lattanzi providing a

284

trumpet solo. He showed me Clemente photos and a Clemente medallion with the words "You shared your joy with the less than joyful lot." He showed me some pictures of Clemente that he thought he had Clemente sign, but wasn't sure the signatures were the genuine article, or if they were stamped. I told him they looked like the real thing to me.

As I stood in the doorway, about to depart the Blass home, Steve and Karen accompanied me. Blass went for one more laugh before I left. He told me a story about how nervous he was before he pitched in that seventh game of the 1971 World Series. "Roger Angell wrote about that Series, and he came here a few years later when I was going through my difficulties to do a story on me," said Blass. "Roger remembered how much of a kick he got out of seeing me fooling around in the batting cage before that final game, mimicking Clemente. I was in there, twisting my neck and doing all the stuff Clemente was famous for. Roger liked that. I said, 'What did you want me to do? Think about what I was facing, and admit how I really felt, and stand there wetting my pants?'"

Steve Blass looks for signal before scoreboard at Forbes Field.

Opinions Of His Peers
Cheers for Clemente

*"Close to being the most
perfect ballplayer. . ."*
— Red Schoendienst

Henry Aaron, Milwaukee and Atlanta Braves

"I knew Clemente, I guess, about as well as you could know a person who was on another club. He always thought of others and had a lot of compassion for them, especially for Puerto Ricans and his Latin friends. He was concerned about them . . . he wanted so much for them. And they looked up to him. He made it easier for them as ballplayers in this country because he cared so much for their interests. It was great for him, too, to take time out and do a thing like taking those supplies to Nicaragua. It showed the kind of person he was."

Sandy Koufax, Brooklyn and Los Angeles Dodgers

"How do you pitch to him? Roll the ball."

Pete Rose, Cincinnati Reds

"I'd say he's the best hitter I've ever seen since I've been in the big leagues."

Tom Seaver, New York Mets

"The very special thing about Roberto physically was his hands. So very powerful. He stood there, far away from the plate with that great big long bat, and with those strong hands he controlled it like crazy, hitting pitches on the other side of the plate. There was one area out there at the knees off the outside corner. If you hit that spot with a pitch, he'd look and walk away. If you missed, he'd hit the ball very hard."

Dick Williams, manager, Oakland A's

"Roberto Clemente was the greatest ballplayer I have ever watched. He could do it all."

Willie Montanez, Philadelphia Phillies

Montanez was 15 when he first met Roberto Clemente. Like every other ballplayer from Puerto Rico, Montanez idolized Clemente. Montanez was at the San Juan airport, less than a mile from where Clemente died in an airplane crash.

"I ran to the area where the plane went down. I ran there hoping to see Roberto. And when it hit me what really happened, I think I was the saddest I have ever been. He came to see me when I first started getting attention from the scouts. He came to our home and knocked on the door. He came to tell me about baseball, he came to tell me like it was. I was going to listen to him, no matter what he say. When he left, he gave me a baseball with his autograph on it. I still have that ball in my trophy room where it is my most cherished possession. I was looking at it again this morning and I am still thinking that he is alive."

Brooks Robinson, Baltimore Orioles

"If you talked to ten players they would all say he was the best in the game and I have to go along with them, just on what he's done. In ability, he was the best all-around player in the league last year (1971). He was the man."

Red Schoendienst, St. Louis Cardinals

"Clemente was close to being the most perfect ballplayer of all time."

Nellie Briles
Remembers "The Roberto Play"

"I know what Roberto can do."
— Bill Mazeroski

Nellie Briles, a former Pirates pitcher who has worked in the team's marketing and sales department, done color work on baseball broadcasts, and heads the Pirates alumni, is one of the more popular figures in the Pirates front office.

His air-blown white hair and Tim Conway comedic style still attracts autograph-seekers wherever he travels in his efforts to promote and market the Pirates, and, most of all, to sell tickets. "He's an absolute prince," said one fan.

No serious Pirates fan will ever forget how Briles came to Pittsburgh from the St. Louis Cardinals in 1971 and played a major part in the Pirates winning the World Series. He was hurting and unable to pitch in the playoffs that year, but he came on to pitch the fifth game of the Series against the Baltimore Orioles. He threw a two-hit shutout to beat Baltimore 4-0 as the Pirates took a 3-2 lead in the Series.

Briles was one of those former ballplayers telling war stories about Clemente at the Piratefest.

"I joined the Pirates in 1971, and knew about Bill Mazeroski and Roberto Clemente as special players who played the game of baseball at the highest level possible both physically and mentally. One game in particular at Three Rivers Stadium illustrates how well these two Pirate all-time greats played together," said Briles.

"In 1971, Maz was in his next to last season as a player and was not playing regularly. However, at this game the regular second baseman Dave Cash was away from the Pirates, serving a two-week summer stint for Uncle Sam, and Maz was playing every day.

"I came into this game against the Giants in the last inning with two outs and the tying run on second and the winning run on first.

"Willie McCovey, a notorious left-handed pull hitter is at bat. I'm in the stretch and I look back to check the runner at second base. I see that Mazeroski is positioned directly behind the bag. There's a big hole between first and second. Normally, we put on a shift the other way to counter McCovey. I motioned to Mazeroski to move to his normal position. He nods and moves over a few steps. I check back again and he's gone back behind the bag. I holler, 'Hey, Maz, this is McCovey! Let's play him the way we discussed him at the meeting. Move over!'

"He hollers back. 'This is the Roberto play. Trust us. Roberto will tell you about it after the game.' I didn't know what they were up to, and I didn't like it one bit, but I said, 'OK.'

"And I throw the ball and, sure enough, McCovey hits a liner right through the hole between first and second. I run in behind home plate to back up the catcher. I'm upset. I'm running with my head down. All

I can think of is that Maz should have been playing McCovey to pull the ball and, if he had, this ball that was hit would have been the final out and we would win the game. I forget who was on second, but I was sure he was going to score, and then Willie Mays was at first and I was worried that he would come in with the winning run. He was one of the best baserunners in the game. All of a sudden I hear the crowd roaring. And the ball comes in from Clemente on the fly and Sanguillen makes the tag and the runner is out and we've won the game. Everyone is congratulating one another, and I'm still miffed.

"We go into the clubhouse and I'm really upset; I'm hot. Maz and Clemente are waiting for me at my dressing stall. They're laughing. Maz smiles and calms me down. Roberto asked me how I liked 'the play.' I told him I didn't see it. 'What was it?'

"Clemente, in his Puerto Rican accent, explained the game situation to me by asking a series of questions. He said, 'If the hitter hits the ball to centerfield, can most centerfielders throw out a runner at home? Can Maz make the play on a ground ball up the middle?' I said, 'As well as anyone.' He said, 'Can the great Roberto throw out a runner at any base?' I said, 'Better than anyone!'

"Roberto then explained 'the play.' He said, 'Maz plays the hitter, whether he is a pull hitter or not, up the middle to take away the ground ball base hit because the centerfielder probably would not throw out the runner, who was on second base, at home. If the ball is hit to the right side and is hit sharply enough, 'the great Roberto' will have a chance to throw out the runner at home, and I have done it many times. You make the percentages work for you!' Then he asked, 'How did we make out?' I said, 'Great, you guys can do whatever you want to do from now on.'"

Maz said, 'Nellie, I know our players. If that ball goes through the middle it goes to Oliver in center, and Al's arm isn't that strong. He's not going to get the runner at the plate. I know what Roberto can do. We've played together a long time, and we know each other. We thought we knew what we were doing. How'd we do, anyhow?' And I said, 'You'll never hear from me again.' And I walked away."

Billboard at West End circle hails Roberto Clemente.

Nellie Briles (signature)

Nellie Briles lets loose his signature delivery.

Love Letters

"Clemente was beyond belief."

Dennis J. Broderick, Cincinnati, Ohio

"I was born in Pittsburgh, and my childhood in the '50s and '60s while living in Upper St. Clair coincided with Roberto Clemente's career with the Pirates.

"With the Steelers largely mired in mediocrity during those decades, baseball was my passion as a boy, the Pittsburgh Pirates were the object of my constant devotion and Roberto Clemente was the subject of my absolute adulation.

"'Dog' Skinner, 'Quail' Virdon, 'Deacon' Law, 'Tiger' Hoak, 'Baron of the Bullpen' Face, 'Vinegar Bend' Mizell and the other Pirates were all hardworking, admirable fellows. They were all familiar types, all believable. But Clemente, to me, was beyond belief, beyond anything familiar, too good to be true. He stood apart from the rest, in his prodigious talent, dignity and deportment.

"There was a singular quality about Roberto Clemente that captivated me in my youth. I remember still the easy nonchalance of his playing catch with other Pirates before a game would begin, his trot, with head tilted slightly upwards, as he would take right field, the grace of his basket catches, his explosion in running down a ball and throwing it to the cutoff man in the infield, his bullet, line-drive throws from the outfield, his slashing swings at the plate, the fury of his base running and the dramatic flair of his base sliding.

"Hitting, running, catching, throwing. Roberto Clemente was the most complete and best baseball player I have ever seen. He was not undeniably the best hitter, runner and outfielder in baseball history, but he was undeniably one of the very best.

"For me, the defining moment in Clemente's career occurred in an unremarkable inning in an ordinary game that I attended at Forbes Field in the early '60s. With the Pirates in the field, no one on base and Clemente playing deep in right field, a batter hit a medium-speed grounder for a single between the first and second basemen. Clemente charged the ball as the batter took off for first. Within a few feet of reaching the ball in mid-right field, as the batter was rounding first, Clemente's feet gave out from underneath him and the ball rolled into his glove as he slid on both knees toward it. The batter, taking a big turn around first and seeing Clemente slip and fall before he got to the ball, raced for second base.

"As anyone who knows anything about baseball knows, Clemente was possessed with one of the greatest arms in baseball. The batter was uninformed, foolish, or both. From his knees, from medium depth right field, Clemente threw a fast ball strike to the shortstop covering second base. The runner was out by a mile. The crowd at Forbes Field gasped in disbelief at what they had just seen Clemente do.

"Did you ever try throwing anything any distance at any speed with any accuracy from your knees? It was the greatest baseball play I have ever seen.

"In the springs and summers of my youth, Roberto Clemente was a towering figure, filling Forbes Field and my daydreams with splendor and wonder. He remains, for me, the standard against which all baseball players are measured."

Pat Perri, Anaheim, California

"I just finished reading your book, *MAZ And The '60 Bucs — When Pittsburgh And Its Pirates Went All The Way*, and I thoroughly enjoyed it. I grew up near Pittsburgh, in Baden, Pa., listening to Bob Prince, Jim Woods and Nellie King and I love my Pirates. Your book brought back many nostalgic memories of my childhood, which was a kinder, gentler, more friendly and happy period.

"I was only three years old when Maz hit his home run on October 13, 1960, so I don't remember it, but I have heard thousands of 'Where were you?' stories. My mom was pregnant with my little brother, who was born on that day. My mother went into labor and had to page her doctor who had gone to the seventh game of the World Series.

"I have a copy of Chuck Thompson's broadcast of that seventh game, which I listen to over and over again. My girl friend always asks me, 'Why do you keep listening to that tape when you already know the outcome?' No matter how many times I listen to it, I still get goose bumps and I bite my nails until Maz hits his homer. I guess you have to be a Pirates' fan to really understand. It was truly one of baseball's all-time great games.

"I went to the University of Pittsburgh and was graduated in April, 1979, with a B.S. degree in chemical engineering. During my four years there, I lived on 246 South Bouquet Street. I always wondered what it would have been like going to Pitt if the Pirates were still playing in Oakland. Reading your book, I was able to do that, if only vicariously. I have the same picture that you took for your back cover hanging in my office at work.

"I really do miss Forbes Field. I don't think people realized how great a park it was until it was gone. I have been living in California ever since and can't get enough of my sports teams. One evening last year, Ross Porter, the host of 'Dodger Talk,' had a discussion on the 1960 Pittsburgh Pirates. I was surprised, and at the same time delighted, at how the knowledgeable baseball fans held that team in such esteem.

"I started an autograph collection many years ago of the 1960 Pirates. I lack only two players from that team — Roberto Clemente and Don Hoak."

Malcolm W. Emmons

Andy Ondrey, Eatontown, New Jersey

"I enjoyed reading *MAZ And The '60 Bucs*. It brought back many happy memories. My Aunt Franny enjoyed seeing photos of Bill and Milene Mazeroski and reading about them. She went to Braddock High School with Milene.

"I think it would be fantastic if you wrote a book about Roberto Clemente. Roberto was one of my all-time favorites. Don't forget to write a version in Spanish, too.

"I once met Roberto Clemente in the late '60s at Shea Stadium in Queens, New York. My friend, Bruce Dal Canton, who pitched for the Pirates, arranged for me, my co-worker and his wife to go to a Pirates vs. Mets night game. After the game, we all went under the stands to the visitors' clubhouse. We met Bruce and he introduced us to Roberto Clemente and other Pirate players. We had a great time!"

Dennis Lebec, Huntington, West Virginia

"I was born at St. John's Hospital on Pittsburgh's North Side in 1950. I grew up in McKees Rocks, and my parents, my brother and other relatives still are scattered around the Pittsburgh area. I'm 43 years old and in my second year of teaching mass media at Marshall University.

"My father first took me to Forbes Field in 1959 to watch the Pirates. He himself played minor league baseball in the Boston Braves organization in the 1940s. He also played much sandlot baseball in the Pittsburgh area, and even pitched batting practice for a time with the Pirates. All of this qualified him for a background extra role in the movie, 'Angels In The Outfield.'

"I'll always remember going to Forbes Field and sneaking down into the box seats during late innings. It was magical, to see my heroes so close from behind their dugout. And what a great ballpark it was — the 'real' grass, that scoreboard, the screen in right, the batting cage, etc.

"There are few days in my life that are as vivid as October 13, 1960. It was one week after my tenth birthday. On the negative side, I can never forget November 22, 1963 when President Kennedy was assassinated. Or May 4, 1970, when four college students were shot and killed by Ohio National Guardsmen at Kent State University, where I was a sophomore majoring in broadcasting at the time.

"Maz's homer, however, caused nothing but pure joy, at least in Pittsburgh. And it was the first time *my* team had ever won a championship of any kind.

"As a lifelong fan of Pittsburgh sports teams, I have been fortunate, as you well know, to have savored the triumphs of the Pirates, along with the dominance of the 1970s Steelers, and the nearly unexpected surge to greatness by the Penguins several years ago. Even considering Joe Carter's heroics for Toronto in the 1993 World Series, how could anything be more dramatic (and sudden) than Maz's home run to whip the Yankees?

294

"Just for the record, on Thursday afternoon, October 13, 1960, I ran home from parochial school (where we listened to Game 7 on the P.A. system until the top of the ninth inning) to see the Yankees make their final out after tying the game.

"For a fleeting instant, I had a thought how nice it would be if my favorite Pirate, Bill Mazeroski, could become a World Series hero.

"As he strolled to the plate to face Ralph Terry, little did I know, at the age of ten, that dreams sometimes come true."

James J. White, Princeton, Illinois

"One of the things I remember as an attendee at the 1960 World Series — I was then a freshman at the University of Iowa — was the final time the 'great Mickey Mantle' got a single to right field and Mick rounded first and Roberto fired a 'rope' to first and nearly picked Mick off. I could see the smile on Mickey's face all the way up in the upper deck on the first base side. He had seen the great arm.

"Another thing I remember is the sky diver who was going to 'crash the game,' but who ended up crashing into a building behind home plate (outside the ballpark).

"Bob Oldis, one of the Pirates' back-up catchers on that 1960 team, was my brother-in-law. I was with him then (the good times) and when he was sent down to Columbus the next year (the bad times), and I was in his home the mornings his two sons died of muscular dystrophy. I was with him when he played for the great Denver Bear teams (when John Blanchard was the second string catcher behind Bob).

"Your book brought back a lot of great memories, the clubhouse, the boxes of sawdust, the practical jokes pulled on clubhouse 'boys' and each other.

"My son Mike White is getting his MBA from Carnegie Mellon and lives in Pittsburgh. He gave me your book for Christmas."

Pittsburgh Pirates

Sky diver misses mark at Forbes Field in 1960 World Series.

Pirates lineup in 1963, from left to right, Ducky Schofield, Bill Virdon, Roberto Clemente, Willie Stargell, Smoky Burgess, Donn Clendenon,

Bob Veale
A Big Man From Birmingham

"He was a good teammate."
— On Clemente

His dark eyes grew more luminous behind his eyeglasses, and the grin grew larger on his face. Bob Veale was positively salivating as he remembered the menu offerings by Miss Ann and Mr. Earl (or Early) at the boarding house where the black members of the Pirates were put up at Fort Myers, Florida during spring training in 1962.

"It was a big house with a big yard," related Veale. "There were fruit trees: oranges and grapefruit. So we always had fresh fruit. It really wasn't such a bad place."

Roberto Clemente, Willie Stargell, Donn Clendenon, Elmo Plaskett, Alvin O'Neal McBean, Diomedes Olivo, Jose Martinez and Earl Francis shared the same experience with Veale.

"Miss Ann would always put together a feast befitting a king," recalled Veale. "Lots of steaks, two and three inches thick, seemed like they were four or five pounds apiece. She'd have them on a big rack. Rare and medium rare. She'd have onions all over them. Candy yams. Corn on the cob. Fried corn and okra. Hush puppies. Corn bread. Corn sticks. Turnip greens. Mustard greens. Potato salad. Salad. There'd be a big tray with iced tea on it. Enough for everyone and more where that came from."

Veale paused between each offering. He seemed to savor each one of them.

"All she'd say is 'Don't leave nothing on your plate. Eat it and don't waste it.' She meant that, too. Every day was a different meal. Fried pork chops. Fried chicken."

"We ate better than anybody. That lady could cook up steaks bigger than steers," said Veale.

Mr. Earl's Place, as the black ballplayers called it, was a retreat of sorts. Stargell remembers they were treated well and taken care of to the hilt. The dining experience there was a lot better than what Veale and the other black ballplayers experienced when they were on the road during the spring training session.

"Sometimes we had to eat in the backyard behind the restaurant where the white ballplayers were eating," said Veale. "We'd get off the bus, and go our separate ways."

The situation remained the same until civil rights legislation was, at last, enforced in the Deep South, and, concurrently, when the Pirates moved from the Bradford Hotel to the Edisonian Hotel in 1964 and everybody on the ballclub slept and ate under one roof. Up until then, the black ballplayers had not been able to bring their families with them to spring training. They were not permitted to walk the streets at night, according to Jack Berger, the Pirates publicity director back then.

There were places they couldn't go. The Pirates would play in an annual member-guest golf tournament at the local country club, for example, and the blacks were excluded. Clendenon complained about that, and bugged Berger enough that Jack finally managed to talk the president of the country club into letting Clendenon play in that golf outing, much to the chagrin of many of the hardline club members.

"It had been a bad situation for our black players, no doubt about it," recalls Berger, now living in retirement in the Squirrel Hill section of Pittsburgh. "I told our guys, 'We don't make the local rules. That's the way it is.' We weren't strong enough to make changes. We weren't there to make changes. We were guests in the community. I remember we sometimes passed food out the back door of restaurants to the black players, unless they were able to find a decent black restaurant somewhere. It was not a nice thing at all. It was nasty."

Veale would agree. "I remember a place called Strickland's Restaurant," said Veale. "Never forget it. We'd go out there in the backyard which looked like a giant chicken coop. Clemente wouldn't even eat there. He'd say something in Spanish. You knew he was upset. He'd say something that had 'racista' in it. I learned that word real fast. He'd say they didn't have that kind of racist stuff at home in Puerto Rico. He wasn't used to it."

"A stranger to me is only
a friend I haven't met yet."
— Old Saying

Bob Veale came from Birmingham, Alabama, and he was used to it. He didn't like it. But he was used to it. "It was just part of the social structure," he says now. "It got you pissed off, though."

When Veale signed an information sheet for the Pirates publicity office back in September of 1962, he listed his ancestry as "Negroid." It was a sign of the times.

He listed his greatest baseball achievement as an amateur as striking out 22 batters in a nine inning game, and coming back with two days rest to strike out 12 men in 4 2/3 innings. He had done a military service stint in the U.S. Marines prior to joining the Pirates.

Baseball, he said, was his escape from the "poverty" of Birmingham. But baseball was not necessarily that much different from Birmingham. Certainly Fort Myers, Florida was no different. "There wasn't no beach for us, there wasn't no restaurant," recalled Veale. "We couldn't play golf at the local courses, like the other guys did. To me, as a ballplayer, it meant you was good, but you wasn't good enough."

Robert Andrew Veale Jr. was a big, bad hard-throwing left-handed pitcher for the Pirates from 1962 to 1972, and was traded that last season to the Boston Red Sox where he spent nearly three seasons, his career coming to a close in 1974.

Bill Virdon was the manager when Veale was dispatched to Boston. "I knew Bill had to make a change; I told him not to worry," said Veale. "I knew it was nothing personal. I always got along great with Virdon. He was a no-nonsense person. Even though I was the first player he had to release, I thought he was always fair with me."

During the summers of 1965 and 1966, Veale was named to the National League All-Star teams. He was that good.

During his playing days, Veale always had a vexed look, a frown on his brow, a stern, steely-eyed countenance. He was an intimidating force. If the baleful visage didn't get you, certainly the 6-6, 215 pound to 240 pound frame loomed large on the hill, and then there was that blazing fastball. In 1964, he led the majors when he struck out 250 batters in 279 2/3rd innings and, in 1965, he struck out 276 batters in 266 innings — a club record for left-handed pitchers. He is the only Pirates pitcher to strike out over 200 batters in a season, and he did it four times. He still holds the club record for the most strikeouts in a game — 16 against Philadelphia on June 1, 1965.

Veale once told Pittsburgh sportswriter Ron Cook, "I never had my fastball clocked, but I imagine it had to be in the high 90s. Me and Sandy Koufax and Bob Gibson probably threw the hardest at that time. Jim Maloney also could bring it, but he couldn't sustain it. Then came Nolan Ryan."

Veale was 18-12 in 1964, 17-12 in 1965, 16-12 in 1966, 16-8 in 1967. In short, he was the Pirates' best pitcher during that period. Only Bob Friend before him was more reliable in being out there when it was his turn. Veale set a club record for southpaws with 38 starts in 1964. Veale also holds club season records for walks (124) and most wild pitches (18) by a lefty.

He was a wild thing before the movies made that an oft-repeated expession. He led the major leagues in walks four times. One night he was pitching to Lou Brock of the Cardinals when one of the lenses in Veale's glasses fell out. He was unable to fix them, so he tossed the glasses toward the Bucs' dugout and was going to pitch without them. "Brock refused to get back in the batter's box," said Veale. "He said it just wasn't safe. I had to fix my glasses before the game continued."

When I told Veale the impression I had of him back then, of something of an angry young man, reproachful, he smiled and said, "I went to Boston after I left here, and Dick O'Connor was in charge up there. He said, 'Every time I'd see you, the way you'd look would intimidate me. You looked like you just looked through people.'

"That was all an act, the way you saw me on the ballfield. I'd pop my eyes out a little. That was only my competitive spirit. You had to have a trigger, you had to be ready to fight. The pitcher is usually the first one involved in a fight. I've always been endowed with strength. I was ready to fight."

Veale, at age 58, was still an imposing figure. But the frown was gone, giving way to a more mellowed look, and an easy smile. Veale invites company these days with his easy-does-it manner. He'd tip his brand new black Pirates ballcap back, and start talking, making himself comfortable in anybody's company. He'd become a bit of a philosopher. He took my notepad from me during our interview and wrote in a message he said would serve everyone in good stead. It read: "A stranger to me is only a friend I haven't met yet."

Veale was retired and living for the most part off his baseball pension. He said he did a little carpentry work, roofing and some odd jobs to keep busy. He took part in any baseball activities when invited to participate.

He had been a minor league pitching instructor for the Atlanta Braves for eight years and the New York Yankees for one. He left baseball in 1985 to attend to an ungodly series of personal tragedies. Back in 1987, Reggie Jackson mentioned Veale in a *Sports Illustrated* story as one of the "many qualified (black) people who vanished from baseball." This was in an article blasting Major League baseball for not providing more managing, coaching and front-office opportunities for black ballplayers.

Veale and his wife Eredean lived on Bush Boulevard in Birmingham. When I asked him how long they had been married, Bob said, "Too long." Surely, it was a stock answer. They had a daughter, Felicia, who was a teacher in Cleveland.

Nobody enjoyed the 1994 Piratefest any more than Veale. He was among a dozen Pirates of the past who joined an equal number of present-day Pirates in signing autographs for the fans. Most of the players only signed autographs during their appointed hours, and that was it. When their hour-long stint was completed, they were gone. For good. Veale visited with the people who were operating the various booths in what amounts to an amusement park for baseball fans, young and old. Veale was visible most of the day, here and there, signing autographs for anyone who asked. When he walked around the exhibit halls of the Expo Mart, he looked like a kid at his first carnival.

Occasionally, he'd stop at the batting cage, where fans were invited to test their pitching speed. Bob would hurl the ball right-handed, just for the helluva it, and talk to anyone who passed by. "The guy wasn't doing any business," explained Veale, "so I thought I'd drum up some business for the guy. People pass by with a fistful of dollars; I wanted that guy to get his share of that. I wanted to put him to work."

Veale visited with former teammates such as ElRoy Face, Bob Friend, Al Oliver, Steve Blass, Dave Giusti and Dock Ellis, and introduced himself to young players like Tim Wakefield and Randy Tomlin. "They don't know me from Adam," he'd say of the present-day pitchers. The pitcher he was most pleased to see was Vernon Law. "He grabbed me," said Veale. "He's a real guy, a man of faith and so forth. He's never shown me anything but good feelings. He's a preacher, you know. I still call him Deacon."

He chatted with the kids, teased their parents, and had fun with everybody. "To see a smile on anyone's face, you know he's absent of stress," said Veale. "Stress is bad for everybody. It'll kill you."

Bob Veale visits with his father in 1967.

At 1991 Old Timers Game

Imposing figure on mound

Veale and Vern Law loosen up.

Dock Ellis could learn a lot from Veale. When I spotted Ellis, I was reluctant, at first, to approach him for an interview. He'd had a stormy career as a pitcher with the Pirates in the '60s and '70s, and I had never interviewed him, but he'd always come off in what I read about him as a bit of a jerk. He was always so confrontational, always looking for an argument. I noticed how nice he seemed when speaking to several youngsters, and signing autographs for them at the Piratefest. He couldn't be all bad, I figured.

As soon as I asked Ellis to comment on Clemente, he started spouting off. He flared up the way Clemente used to do when approached by sportswriters. "I don't give away my thoughts about Clemente, or anything else," Ellis snarled. "The only one who knows how I feel about Clemente is my son."

"I'm getting out of here," said Veale, retreating. "I'll let you contend with Dock."

That was a cue for Ellis to espouse on some of his vitriolic views.

"If you read the early stories about Clemente," said Ellis, "you'd see why he didn't care for sportswriters, either. You'll see. Just read them."

I have and I would bet that Ellis has not. Like Clemente and a lot of other ballplayers often did, Ellis was going by what others had told him. Clemente never had a critical press in Pittsburgh. Some writers may not have fully appreciated him or understood him as well as he would have liked, and maybe some of the sportswriters weren't sensitive enough about his situation, but they did not hold him up to ridicule, either. Not intentionally, anyhow.

"Dock is still Dock," said Veale later, when I asked him to explain Ellis. "Down deep, he's harmless. There's an old saying: 'Words don't care whose mouth they come out of.' Dock lets them run. He's always been that way. He don't like to talk about things that touch home."

As a younger sportswriter, I would have been willing to have a verbal sparring session with Ellis. The idea of a debate with him held no appeal to me, especially with my wife Kathie at my side. Ellis didn't have an Afro anymore, and he wouldn't need to wear curlers in the clubhouse — a habit which caused a celebrated flareup between him and Bill Virdon, his manager — because he was now shaving his head clean. He also wore a small gold loop earring, reading glasses and a small beard. He still had a chip on his shoulder.

Ellis looked different, but he still came off as a petulant brat. Too bad. There's a saying that some guys never learn how to say hello until it's time to say goodbye. Ellis just doesn't get it, that's all.

Former Pirates pitchers Dock Ellis, above, and Bob Veale, below, sign autographs at 1994 Piratefest. Note Veale's 1971 World Series ring.

"Fill it up with oil and check the gas."
— Veale on Studebaker

Veale provided quite a contrast to Ellis. A fan goes by and hollers out, "Bob, I enjoyed watching you pitch." And Veale would respond, "I enjoyed trying to pitch." And they'd both smile.

"I'm always trying to do something to make somebody smile," Veale said. "I sign autographs and try my best to please people. You have to say hello. A smile brings a positive response. A frown brings a 'no' reaction."

He felt that Clemente was like that, too, even if Roberto was often openly critical of the media. Veale recalled that Clemente matured quite a bit during the decade they were teammates. "I liked having him on my team," said Veale. "I wanted him on my side."

But Veale used to frown when he was a ballplayer for the Pirates. Did he forget? "That was only in competition," he said. "That was like my buddy Mean Joe Greene. When the pain left he became Nice Joe Greene. I knew most of those guys — Terry Bradshaw and Greene — and was a fan of the Steelers before they started winning Super Bowls."

He said Stargell was influenced a lot more by Clemente. "Stargell had his head screwed on pretty straight to start with," he offered. "He was quite aware of what Clemente stood for, and his relationship to the black players on the ballclub. When you play with a player like Clemente, everyone tries to live up to the standard he establishes.

"Clemente picked his spots when he wanted to talk. Usually, when the team seemed to be down, he'd get going. He was real funny with his accent and all. He was a pretty astute individual. He could turn an individual inside out. It was the way he was saying it, he'd make you die laughing.

"There was a serious side to him. During a game, he'd build you up, try to instill confidence in you. He'd say, 'Stay close, I'll get you a run or two.' He was always talking about the team. Sometimes he'd get a rubdown and he'd want you to come in the training room and keep him company so he could keep on talking.

"He called me 'Poodney,' and he called Willie Stargell 'Woodney.' We both came up together, and he named us at the same time.

"Stargell and I came up the same year. We drove up from Columbus, Georgia. We rode in a Studebaker, a real clunker. We'd stop at a gas station on the way north and say, 'Fill it up with oil and check the gas.' This was at the end of the '62 season.

"Stargell hadn't been out of high school long, and was much younger than me. I was 24 or 25, and thought I had the kind of record — 11-1 or 11-2 — where I should have been called up from Columbus a lot sooner. I couldn't understand why they kept me in the minors so long.

"It took me awhile to get comfortable in the clubhouse. Clemente was standoffish with everybody. He would talk to me and ask me questions. But we weren't close friends or pals, or anything like that.

304

He was a curious type guy. But he was a real spark plug for our team, and he was great in the '71 World Series."

It was interesting to hear Veale reveal that he thought Clemente kept to himself. Before I talked to Veale, I had wrongly wondered if that was just the opinion of white players. Veale said he wasn't too aggressive in social situations himself early in his career with the Pirates. "I was real quiet," he said, "and I didn't have too much to say to anybody."

"I grew up with baseball."

Veale revealed some interesting stories about growing up in Birmingham and his introduction to baseball through his father.

"Birmingham was fine," said Veale. "It was the people in Birmingham who were the problem. There were some fine people there, but there were people who didn't care much for blacks. It was the social structure. But it's always been a big baseball town. They've always had national amateur baseball tournaments there. They're making a movie there about Ty Cobb, and he was from Georgia.

"I grew up with baseball. I was tall as a kid. When I was a junior in high school, though, I weighed only 140 pounds. I was real agile, mobile and hostile (That's a battlecry made popular by Jake Gaithers, the legendary head football coach at Florida A&M.). I was real boisterous.

"Willie Mays was from the Fairfield section of Birmingham. His dad played for my dad on the TCI team, that's Tennessee Coal & Iron. His dad was called "Cat" and he was faster than Willie. He played the outfield and the infield. I saw him play. He was with the Black Barons. The other team in Birmingham was called the White Barons. That's how they designated the two. They both played at Rickwood Ballpark. I was a batboy for the Black Barons for several years. I started helping out on my dad's team when I was seven or eight. Later on, I played the outfield and first base, before I became a pitcher. Coming up, I had my heroes. I jumped on the bandwagon for Jackie Robinson and Roy Campanella. I cheered for those guys and wanted to be like them. I liked Preacher Roe."

Coincidentally enough, some fans at the Piratefest were seen wearing expensive jackets that had Black Barons on the back of them as well as the Pittsburgh Crawfords. Those were teams in the so-called Negro Leagues. It's considered chic to wear such jackets these days. Veale's father, Robert Sr., had played baseball for the storied Homestead Grays. He had played baseball with and against Josh Gibson and Satchel Paige.

As bad as conditions were for black ballplayers at Fort Myers, Veale thought it was a significant improvement over what he experienced as a ballplayer in Jacksonville.

"The ballfield there was in a cow pasture," he said. "We were housed in quonset huts, like a military camp, and when it rained it was like being in a swamp. That was a hellhole. Things would float into the tents. Baby alligators and water moccasins would come in with the water. Scary stuff."

Veale said that baseball helped all his brothers and sisters get educated. He was the second of 14 children, and all of them went to college. Bob went to St. Benedict's (now Benedictine) College in Atchison, Kansas, a school with less than a thousand students, on a basketball scholarship. He won three varsity letters and captained the team in his senior season. He said he ended up lacking about six hours of credits to get a college degree. When he got to the big leagues, Veale sent money home to help his brothers and sisters with their school tuition.

His education continues.

"I heard Louis Farrakhan speak," said Veale. "I wouldn't go for what he was saying. He was preaching hate. To me, he sounds like Hitler."

"As a race, we have a chance."

Veale talked about a difficult year he'd had in his life. It was during a six-month span in 1985. It sounded a lot like the kind of year his former teammate Dick Groat had gone through in 1993. A series of deaths in the family and some personal setbacks tested him to his very soul.

Back in 1985, Bob lost his mother, a brother to throat cancer, a first cousin and a favorite uncle. If that wasn't bad enough, he also lost his job as a pitching coach in the Yankees' organization, and he lost his home in Birmingham. No wonder Veale likes to avoid stressful situations.

Burglars stole many of his baseball mementos and valuables, including his 1971 World Series ring. They also burned his home to the ground. They have never been caught.

Bob had to start from scratch to build a new house and look after some other personal needs. He never could afford to replace the ring, which meant a great deal to him. He had always worn his World Series ring with great pride.

In January of 1993, Veale was one of the instructors at the Pirates' Camp Bradenton Fantasy Camp and one night he talked to a few of the campers about that difficult experience in his life.

The campers, about 50 in number, led by Mike and Jim O'Brien of San Francisco — no relation to this author — donated money to replace the World Series ring, and had it created by Josten's.

In late July of 1993, the campers held a reunion at Three Rivers Stadium and Veale was invited to join them. They presented Veale with his World Series ring. Veale had tears in his eyes, and then everybody had tears in their eyes. There weren't many dry eyes that day.

"I never had anyone do anything like that for me," said Veale, showing me his shiny new ring. "People who didn't hardly know me . . . It was heart-warming. Your cup runneth over when something like that happens in your life. It's better than winning the World Series.

It makes you think there's a chance for things to get better. It tells me one thing: as a race, we have a chance."

Lest anyone think that Veale had a live and let live outlook when he was pitching for the Pirates, consider this story where Veale voiced his displeasure with a situation he felt unfair. "I got into it once with Bob Rice, our traveling secretary, when we were out in California," said Veale. "He put Al Oliver in a room with me at the last minute. They brought in this little cot for Al to sleep on. I told Rice, 'Get somebody to bring a real bed up here for Al. He has to play.' He couldn't have slept on that little cot and then gone out and played baseball.

"Al was unhappy enough in those days. When he came up, there wasn't any place for him to play. He was an outfielder and a first baseman, and we had Stargell in left field, Virdon in center field and Clemente in right field and Clendenon at first base. Later, we had Bob Robertson. Al was always saying, 'Just give me a place to play.' One thing he could do was swing that bat and he could catch. He wasn't short in no department. He had outstanding confidence. He was like Clemente in that respect."

Jim O'Brien

Eredean and Bob Veale were shining couple at Piratefest.

Vernon Law
Still The Deacon

Vern Law (signature)

"I think of his wife and family. I know how much they miss him."

That little wave. That's the first thing I noticed as Vernon Law sat across a table from me and talked about Roberto Clemente. There's a natural wave in Law's gray-blond hair, and it's always added to his distinctive and handsome appearance. Some people would kill to have a natural wave like Law in their hair.

Law was wearing a gray glen-plaid suit and a sharp colorful contemporary tie. He looked downright natty, dignified, as always. He stood out, at 6-2, 200 or so pounds, from the crowd, most of whom were wearing the most casual of attire: sweatsuits, jackets and jeans, baseball caps, everything with sports logos front and back, slacks, sneakers.

Law was seated across from the entrance of the Tribute to Roberto photo and memorabilia exhibit which was the main attraction at the 1994 Piratefest at the Expo Mart in Monroeville on the last weekend of January. Super Bowl Weekend.

Class act. Vernon Sanders Law has lived up to that reputation for a long time. Former Pirates general manager Joe L. Brown once alluded to Law as "the nicest man I ever met." John Galbreath, who owned the Pirates back then, said of Law: "He never gave anyone a bit of trouble."

I saw Law looking for and embracing several ex-teammates who were also in attendance, and chatting with them to catch up on their lives. He teased them if they were dressed too casually. "I was especially close with my roommate Smoky Burgess, but they're all my friends," said Law. He was six weeks away from his 63rd birthday, a grandfather now, some lines across his brow, but personable and eager to share his thoughts about Clemente.

In some respects, they had little in common, coming from completely different cultures and backgrounds. In other respects, they had much in common. Law was born in Meridian, Idaho and bred in Boise, Idaho, which is a long way from Carolina, Puerto Rico. Law has been a deacon and elder in the Mormon faith. He was nicknamed "The Deacon." His religion and his family were always paramount in his mind, just like Clemente.

One of the first things that always comes to my mind when I look at Law is that his wife's name also starts with the letter V — it's VaNita — and they have six children whose names all begin with the letter V, one girl and five boys, including Vance Law, who had a solid major league career as an infielder and put in a stint with the Pirates in the early '80s. And that he was the winning pitcher in two of the games won by the Pirates in the 1960 World Series, and that he started and nearly

Vernon Law checks out "Tribute to Roberto" exhibit.

came away the winner in the seventh game against the mighty New York Yankees.

The Pirates had a two-run lead in the fifth inning when Law struck out Mickey Mantle, Roger Maris and Yogi Berra in order. Law was pulled for a relief pitcher in the sixth inning. He remembers his reaction to Bill Mazeroski's game-winning home run.

"I remember jumping off the bench and running out toward home plate with my teammates as Maz rounded the bases. When he got to third, the stadium went crazy, and we all just disappeared into a sea of people."

For his efforts, Law won the National League's Cy Young Award that season. Clemente was a big contributor to that championship season, and was a candidate for MVP honors.

When asked to consider Clemente, a teammate during 13 of Law's 16 seasons as a valuable right-handed pitcher with the Pirates, Law said, "I think of his wife and family; that's the first thought I have. I hope all is well with them. I know how much they miss him.

"It's too bad that people have these things happen to them, and that they have to go through life without their partner. I think Vera has handled it well. But I'm sure it's been a hard road.

"Then, of course, I think of him as a ballplayer, and what a complete athlete he was, and what a wonderful person he was. He had a great smile most of the time. He was a real inspiration to our ballclub. We knew we could count on him.

"You think of him making outstanding catches in right field, and throwing those strikes to the bases. He was not a showboat; he was not a selfish person. There's so much of that today, and I'm not thrilled about it. There's a difference between having flair, and taking it too far.

"We knew when we had Roberto on our ballclub we knew we had a chance to win. He certainly helped me on so many occasions with his glove or bat, or both. I've been through the exhibit here, and it's obvious how Roberto had a lot of friends. I had my picture taken with Roberto on more than one occasion, and I'd like to think we were friends. We got along well.

"Even so, he dedicated himself to his family. Roberto was a private person, and I suppose people would say that about me, too."

"I was very naive back in those days."

Law had grown up in a nearly white-only environment out in Idaho. Law lives in Utah today where blacks are more of a minority than anywhere else in the country. He had no experience with blacks before he became a pitcher for the Pirates in 1950. When he rejoined the Pirates in 1954, after serving two years in the military service, Law had his first black teammate in Curt Roberts, a second baseman for the Bucs.

310

"Being from where I grew up out west, I wasn't too familiar with prejudice when I came to the Pirates," allowed Law. "I hated to see the way the black ballplayers were treated. They were part of our ballclub, yet they were not always treated right, especially in the South. I remember they couldn't stay with us or eat with us. That was not right. I'm glad that's all come and gone and is done with.

"They have their own rich heritage, and they deserve to be treated like everyone else.

"It wasn't until I got into baseball that I was witness to this stuff. To me, at first, they were probably a curiosity. But it didn't take me long to learn to like them. When I first saw them staying in other places, and eating in other places, I thought it was something they chose to do. I was very naive back in those days."

Law was the best-known Mormon in baseball and carried a notebook with him that served as a guide. In this notebook, Law had a page titled, "Words To Live By." He tried to follow the quotations he had saved.

The quotations included:

"I have never met a man who is not my superior at something. A good timber never grows with ease: it needs a strong wind and storms to give it strength. A discouraged man is not a strong man. Don't be satisfied with mediocrity. Will Rogers once said, 'We're all ignorant, only we're ignorant about different things.' There is nothing wrong with youth. Actually only ten percent of the youth are bad and these ten percent get all the publicity."

Law was also guided by a set of rules for his way of life. They are: "I will never uphold my opinion to the extent of angering another. I will never forget that I am one of God's marked men. I will always remember that I am made of the same stuff as the worst sinner, and without God's help I would be worse than he. I will always have a happy smile for everyone, especially those who like me least."

He was genuine about this. Though he never saw himself in this light, Law was a cut above most athletes.

"It was a privilege to play with Roberto Clemente."

The images from the "Tribute to Roberto" exhibit brought back many memories for Law and all the visitors.

"Sure, it brought back memories," said Law. "I can remember the games. I can remember the situations in which those pictures were taken. Roberto had a great career. He is one of the few people I can say I was fortunate to play with.

"I was sorry my son Vance never had a chance to really know him. He had a Roberto Clemente bat, but somewhere along the line it got lost. None of us knew what was going to happen with that sort of memorabilia. There was no market for that stuff back then.

311

J. Honus Wagner

"I could have had Honus Wagner's autograph on anything I wanted to. When I first played for the Pirates, Honus Wagner would sit on the bench with us. He was a coach emeritus, or something like that. He'd go into the clubhouse and have a few Iron City beers from time to time. Pie Traynor was there, too. We had two Hall of Famers with us every day."

Ralph Kiner, who became a Hall of Famer himself, had told me that having Wagner and Traynor around the team all the time was like a real-life version of the movie *Field of Dreams.*

"My career spans the best years of baseball," said Law. "The people we had around us, the excitement at the ballpark. It was a privilege to play with Roberto Clemente. Religion and family. Anyone who shares a common belief, naturally there's a bond. That certainly was the case with Roberto."

Pittsburgh Pirat

Key contributors to 1960 championship effort were, left to right, ElRoy Face, Bill Mazerosk Vernon Law and Roberto Clemente.

Manny Sanguillen
Still Searching, Still Smiling

*"I feel like the spirit of him
will always be in right field.
To me he is still the great one."*
— Sanguillen on Clemente

Manny Sanguillen tells many stories about Roberto Clemente, his close friend and fellow Latin American. Sanguillen, who grew up in Colon, Panama, had similar problems to Clemente when he came up to the Pirates in 1967 — fitting in, figuring out the language, figuring out pitchers, ordering dinner at a restaurant, pleasing the manager, proving himself — so they shared more than a common background. They formed a deep bond.

Baseball experts said Sanguillen was second only to Hall of Famer Johnny Bench as catchers on the major league baseball scene in the early '70s. He was that good, cat-quick, an instinctive hitter who swung at every pitch, or so it seemed, a spontaneous, ever-smiling character, a clubhouse hit, and Clemente was his mentor. Like Clemente, he had a strange gait when he ran, and he ran the bases with abandon, sometimes in a foolhardy manner early in his career. "Crazylegs," that's what his teammates called him, much to his chagrin.

Sanguillen wanted to share a story about the time he shared a cab with Clemente on their way to Baltimore's Memorial Stadium for the seventh game of the 1971 World Series — a personal showcase for Clemente's considerable skills.

"We're going to the ballfield and the taxi driver wants to talk," said Sanguillen. "There had been a controversy in the papers between Frank Robinson and Clemente. They were knocking each other. The cabbie had been reading the paper when we got in to go to the ballfield.

"The cabbie says, 'Hey, where you guys from?'

"And I tell him we're from Pittsburgh. He checks us out in the rearview mirror and he says, 'You the Pittsburgh Pirates?' We nodded. 'You know this guy Roberto Clemente?' And I say, 'Yeah.' And the cabbie says, 'Oh, man, Frank Robinson, he said that Roberto Clemente is no good. He said Roberto Clemente should sit down and watch him play, so he can see the best rightfielder in baseball.'

"And now Clemente is kicking me, and smiling, and telling me to keep the cabbie going. And the cabbie keeps talking about this controversy, and what Robinson said, and Clemente is grinning so wide. When we get to the stadium, Clemente tells me, 'Let me pay.' He pulls out a $100 bill and he signs his name to it, and he gives it to the cabbie.

"The cabbie looks at the bill and he screams, 'You Roberto Clemente!!!' This cab driver is going wild.

"Clemente tells the cabbie, 'I like you. Because you motivate me. You just made me feel better.'

"The cab driver says, 'I want to go to the game.'

"Clemente gives him four tickets.

"Later on, during batting practice, we see the cab driver up there in the stands, waving to us. We wave back.

"Then Clemente comes to me, and he says, 'Manny, you're the only Latin catcher who's ever caught the seventh game of a World Series. You have to show me how good you are.

"And I said to him, 'What are you going to do today?' He said, 'The first pitch, Mike Cuellar is going to knock me down. The second pitch, I'm going to hit the ball to left-center.' That's exactly what he did. Only he hit it out of the ballfield. For a home run. Every time I see Mike Cuellar, I remind him of that time.

"One week after the World Series, I heard from the cab driver in Baltimore. I had given him my address, and he wrote me a letter. He said he bet the $100 that Clemente gave him, and some of his own, on the seventh game. He said he won $3,000. He said he didn't have to drive a cab for awhile. He said he was going to rest the whole month with his family.

"We saw him again when we got to spring training. He said he spent $500 to see us again. Now that's a good story about Roberto Clemente. That's the kind of guy Clemente is."

Sanguillen grinned, satisfied with himself.

I had been cautioned by Kathy Guy of the Pirates' marketing office not to bring up Roberto Clemente's name when I interviewed Sanguillen. She had been handling the Pirates alumni at their autograph booth at the Piratefest, and she escorted Sanguillen when he came to talk with me. She told me earlier that Sanguillen had said he didn't like to talk about Clemente any more. It saddened him.

So I didn't. But Sanguillen didn't go very long before he brought up the subject. Then he told this wonderful story. And he smiled. Sanguillen is always going to be associated with the ghost of Roberto Clemente. It is his legacy, like it or not. And what's not to like?

"For me, I am the best."
— Roberto Clemente

After the seventh game of the 1971 World Series, Sanguillen was among those amused by the antics of Roberto Clemente, as he proclaimed that maybe now he would get his due and proper recognition as a great baseball player.

One of the comments Clemente made was misinterpreted by the media and baseball fans. That was nothing new. He said, "For me, I am the best." Some people thought that he was bragging, but that expression is an old Spanish saying that means, "I did the best I am capable of doing." And he had!

314

Manny Sanguillen
was all smiles
at 1994 Piratefest.

Jim O'Brien

PIRATES

Clemente was saying stuff like, "I have peace of mind now. Now everyone knows the way Roberto Clemente plays."

Sanguillen was standing nearby, and he turned to newsmen and said, "Everything he is saying is true, you know. He is a great one, maybe the greatest. It is strange that he has to remind people . . . everyone should know it and feel it."

"I knew he was going to be a living legend."
— Sanguillen
on Clemente

Manuel de Jesus Sanguillen was squatting in a catcher's position, something you figured he would never do voluntarily the rest of his life, especially with aching knees. He'd gotten down to check out some baseball caps in a Pirate Clubhouse Store, an outfit and gift shop with Pirates' paraphernalia, that was set up at the Piratefest at the Expo Mart in Monroeville in late January, 1994. Sanguillen has always enjoyed shopping. He still has a quick trigger on his wallet.

Sanguillen was seven weeks away from his 50th birthday. His dark hair was thinner, but his signature smile was as wide as ever. He remained almost a caricature of himself.

Notice that when Sanguillen speaks about Clemente he speaks in the present tense. "He's still here," insists Sanguillen. Sometimes Clemente's widow, Vera Clemente, talks that way, too. So do Clemente's most fervent fans, of which Sanguillen is still at the head of the class.

Sanguillen was one of the Spanish-speaking ballplayers who was influenced and inspired by Clemente. As a child, Sanguillen said he was torn between soccer and baseball.

"I thought about it . . . if I try soccer, maybe I can be a Pele. If I try baseball, maybe I'll be a Clemente."

Sanguillen was happy to see the "Tribute to Roberto" exhibit at the Piratefest, and he was looking forward to the unveiling of a statue of Roberto Clemente come July and the 1994 All-Star Baseball Game at Three Rivers Stadium.

"I'm proud to see him honored this way," Sanguillen said, and then added something contrary to the truth. "I knew he was going to be a living legend."

Sanguillen went on. "He gave his whole life to the city of Pittsburgh, to Puerto Rico and to his family. He always wanted to be the best that he could be, and he wanted us all to do the same.

"It's a great feeling to see this. It reminds me of all the time we put in at the hotels on the road, and on the planes, and at the ballparks. I came in from a rough town, and he helped me find my way in baseball."

Baseball was not Sanguillen's first choice when he was growing up in Colon. He played soccer and basketball and even boxed before he was coaxed into trying baseball. "Oh, I hear about Roberto Clemente

316

as a big star," he said. "Everybody knows about Roberto. But I don't think about baseball. I wanted to be a professor in school and teach when I grew up." He put in two years at the University of Panama.

Sanguillen spent 13 years in the big leagues, from 1967 to 1980, and all but the 1977 season were spent with the Pirates. He was traded away and spent that one summer with the Oakland A's, before Joe L. Brown brought him back to Pittsburgh.

He had a .296 career batting average, and was picked for three All-Star Games. He was at his best from 1969 to 1971, batting .303, .325, and .319 during that span. In 1971, that World Series season, Sanguillen drove in a career-high 81 runs, and a personal-best 26 doubles. "He was a slashing line-drive hitter," wrote Bob Smizik in *The Pittsburgh Pirates — An Illustrated History*, "who never met a pitch he didn't like."

Sanguillen didn't start playing baseball in Panama until he was 19, and a year later he turned pro. He was eager to make up for lost time.

Neither baseball nor the English language came easy for Sanguillen. "Everywhere I went, people helped me," Sanguillen once told Charley Feeney of the *Pittsburgh Post-Gazette*. "Way back, I didn't understand a lot of things about catching. I don't know all the rules. I do the best I can.

"When I first came to Pittsburgh, Manny Mota helped me understand English. Danny Murtaugh helped me in the minor leagues. He used to come watch me play. Johnny Pesky helped me at Columbus. So many people helped me. I can never forget them. Matty Alou . . . Willie Stargell . . . Roberto Clemente . . . Joe Brown . . . everybody. I never forget them."

Clemente cautioned those who mistook Sanguillen's constant smile for the mask of a clown.

"Don't let Sanguillen's smile fool you," Clemente once remarked. "He takes this game seriously. Smiling doesn't always tell everything. Some guys can smile all season and never help a club. Sanguillen has made himself the best catcher in baseball. He has done it by hard work."

Steve Blass remembered that Sanguillen was good behind the plate, too, working with pitchers.

"He's deceptive," said Blass, "in that he puts more into catching than people realize. You tend to think of him as a hitter who can throw well. But he can spot my weaknesses before I can. I pitch from a three-quarter delivery. If I drop below that, I'm in trouble. Manny notices any little change.

"In the seventh game of the (1971) World Series, my slider wasn't working at first. But Manny didn't give up on it. You can't do that with a pitch. It started coming around in the fourth inning and he called for it 80 per cent of the time the rest of the way. The Orioles had seen how bad it was earlier and were surprised."

Hall of Famer Pie Traynor said of Sanguillen in the summer of 1970: "He can't miss being the greatest catcher in Pirate history." And, indeed, he developed into same. He and Traynor are both members of the Pirates' all-time team.

But such skills and sagacity were behind him now, as we spoke in January of 1994. Only his enthusiasm and smile stayed with him. He was living in Boca Raton, Florida with his second wife, Rhonda, who was from Pittsburgh. He had two children from a previous marriage to Kathy Swauger, who had grown up in McKeesport. Manny Jr. was 21 and had been signed as a catcher by the Kansas City Royals, and Sarah was 16 and was a junior in high school.

When I asked Sanguillen about his son's baseball skills, he said, "He has the talent to make it. He's a good ballplayer. He has my body, everything."

When I asked Sanguillen what he was doing these days, he answered, "I'm working and representing baseball players. I am very close to Orlando Merced."

Merced, of course, is one of the Pirates present-day stars who grew up in Clemente's neighborhood in San Juan and idolized the Pirates' star.

When I asked Sanguillen how things were going, he said, "No complaints. I thank God I'm in good shape."

In his last business venture in Pittsburgh, back in the early '80s, Sanguillen went bankrupt trying to sell sportswear at an upscale shop at Station Square on the city's South Side.

"I go to Bible school and I pray in his memory," said Sanguillen. "I used to be serious when I first came up. I didn't laugh, because I wasn't sure of myself. He made me laugh. When I signed to play ball, I was just 20. I was confused, and he came to my rescue."

"I was blessed to be touched by The Great One."
— Manny Sanguillen

Sanguillen tried to explain himself. "I try to be friendly with everybody," he said. Seeing all the photos of Clemente displayed at Piratefest caused him mixed emotions. "I think it hurt my heart, and it make me happy, too. I am often asked to talk about Roberto Clemente.

"I talk to any people, American and Spanish, any color. Guys come in from college who are doing papers on Clemente, and they want to talk with me. I'm always friendly about that; I was blessed to be touched by The Great One.

"One year at a pro golf tournament in Boca Raton, Chi Chi Rodriguez, who was a big fan of Clemente and also a Panamanian, bring me into the clubhouse. I met Jack Nicklaus, Arnold Palmer and Lee Trevino. They were playing in the International. Nicklaus kept asking me questions about Clemente; he wanted to know about The Great One. Everybody wants me to tell them stories about Clemente."

He remembers Clemente telling him of his dreams, of developing a sports center for youth in Puerto Rico. "I used to go to his home in Puerto Rico, and I have continued to do this since his death," said Sanguillen. "I go to the Ciudad Deportiva, and I work with the kids.

Manny Sanguillen was a great catcher and an ambassador of good will, often visiting patients at Children's Hospital and participating in many community outreach efforts by the Pirates.

Clemente always asked me, 'How can I get to the youth?' Here was somebody who was a warm person; he wanted to spend time with every young person in Puerto Rico and help them grow.

"If you do good for others, something good is going to come to you. That's what Roberto Clemente did for the Pittsburgh Pirates. He planted good seed. Everything that came from it was something marvelous. To him, it was important the kind of life you lead.

"Clemente . . . I don't think he's dead. He's like my dad. My dad, Iagilio, worked for the government as an electrician. He was my hero. He passed away when he was 90. I pray for both of them every day. I pray for Clemente family, my family. Clemente still moves people like this."

Clemente opened his heart and his home to a young Panamanian ballplayer. They understood each other in many ways. "Roberto used to take Manny under his wing," said Pittsburgh postal worker Phil Dorsey, Clemente's constant travel companion. So Clemente was all for it when Sanguillen decided to play winter ball with the San Juan Senators in the winter of 1972.

Sanguillen went there to learn how to play right field. The Pirates wanted to have a replacement ready as Clemente was cutting down on the number of games he was playing, and they were also eager to create more playing opportunities for Milt May as a catcher.

It was only natural that Clemente asked Sanguillen to accompany him on his mercy mission to Managua, Nicaragua after the devastating earthquake destroyed the city on December 23, 1972.

Clemente was originally scheduled to fly out of San Juan on December 30, determined to deliver the first-aid supplies, and to make sure they got into the proper hands.

Sanguillen played ball that afternoon and rushed out of the clubhouse to catch up with Clemente. But his car blew up on him. He had to get his car fixed. Manny was very upset that he missed the flight.

Then he learned that Clemente's departure was put off to the next day. This time Sanguillen thought he was ready for a New Year's Eve departure from San Juan International Airport. He was all set to go when he couldn't find his car keys.

Manny and his wife searched everywhere for his keys, but they could not find them. It was seven o'clock, too late to get to the airport, when Manny finally found his keys, high on a shelf in their apartment.

Manny thanked God — he has always been a devout Christian — for keeping him from boarding the fatal flight.

"You just can't keep
an honest man down."
— Willie Stargell

Sanguillen was regarded as a giving man, much in the same spirit as Clemente. He was happiest when he was helping other people. Sanguillen couldn't sit still. He was always in motion.

One of his biggest fans was, understandably enough, Willie Stargell.

"Do you notice Sangy before games?" said Stargell, after Sanguillen became a backup performer for the Pirates, and had been relegated by Chuck Tanner in 1979 to warming up pitchers in the bullpen. "He works like he's going to play. He never bitches. He never complains. You know, no matter what, you just can't keep an honest man down."

Tanner called Sanguillen in out of the bullpen at Baltimore's Memorial Stadium on October 11, 1979. He called him in to pinch-hit in the ninth inning with runners on first and second and two outs. The score was tied 2-2. And this was the second game of the World Series. The Pirates had lost the first game.

"I got an eerie feeling when I saw him come in," said Stargell. "It was a warm feeling. I knew right then I didn't have anything to worry about."

It was the second World Series for Sanguillen. He shared the glory with Roberto Clemente in that first one, in 1971, when the Pirates beat the same Orioles in Baltimore in seven games. Clemente hit .414 in that Series; Sanguillen got 11 hits himself and batted .379.

This was the next time around, and Clemente was missing. It was eight years later. Clemente was dead, and Sanguillen was slowly dying on the Bucs' bench. He was 35 and his best years were definitely behind him. Sanguillen was determined to get a hit. He had so many people he wanted to get a hit for — his wife, his teammates, his friends in Pittsburgh and, most of all, the man he called his big brother. And, sure enough, Sanguillen drilled a game-winning single to right field.

"I carry the memory of Roberto Clemente in my heart," said Sanguillen after the game. "I hope we play the whole Series for Roberto. I dedicate my winning hit to Roberto. I thank God and give the ball to No. 21.

"I work for the Lord," continued Sanguillen. "I pray before every game. I pray none of us get hurt. I pray that we win this one for Roberto."

After Clemente's death, his place in right field was taken, theatrically enough, by Sanguillen.

"We miss Clemente so much," Sanguillen said at the time, "and I don't try to say I'm going to do what he used to do. I'm just going to try and do the best I can."

It was an overwhelming challenge. Comparisions to Clemente would be inevitable. If Sanguillen failed to catch a certain ball, somebody would surely cry out in complaint, "Clemente would have had it!"

321

There was even criticism on the Pirates' bench. "Sanguillen in right field was a joke," pitcher Jim Rooker remarked. "There was no question about it. The guys would laugh about it. You'd watch Sangy in right field, and you knew it wasn't going to last."

Sanguillen couldn't fill the void, and neither did others who gained the assignment, namely Richie Zisk, Gene Clines or Vic Davalillo. It wasn't until the Pirates called up a 6-5 giant of a man from Charleston called Dave Parker that they had someone who could, in time, play the position with distinction. Parker wasn't appreciated either, and parted Pittsburgh on a negative note, but he was quite a gifted ballplayer, and certainly one of the Pirates' all-time best performers.

Sanguillen never said he could replace Clemente. It was particularly difficult for him because no one revered Clemente more than he did. He had been close to Clemente, a man who most Pirates found it difficult to get close to.

Sanguillen felt the loss of his friend, and discussed it with sportswriter Bob Smizik.

"I really feel bad," he told Smizik, who worked the Pirates' beat for *The Pittsburgh Press*. "I feel like Clemente to me was like a brother. I'm still looking for him and I miss him. I don't want to talk too much about him. You know how much fun we had together . . . how much I used to kid around with him and him with me.

"Remember last year in Washington (an exhibition game with Baltimore) when I won the home run contest. He said before I won that I was going to make the club look bad because I'm no home run hitter. After I win and we got to St. Louis he wanted to go to the ball park at four o'clock in the morning and have a contest with me."

Despite the positive relationship, or maybe because of it, Sanguillen still felt strange in right field.

"I don't take Clemente's place," he said. "He is still right field. I feel like I don't belong to right field. I feel like the spirit of him will always be in right field.

"God take him and I am going to do my best because he is gone. Anyway, how you find a player to replace Roberto and who can do the things Roberto did, day in and day out, for 18 years?"

"I'm still looking for him, and I miss him."
— Sanguillen on Clemente

When Sanguillen spoke of still looking for Clemente, it brought to mind how Sanguillen was among those who searched in vain for Clemente after the airplane crash on New Year's Eve, 1972. Sanguillen would have been on the flight if he hadn't misplaced his car keys. He was late in getting to the San Juan International Airport.

Sources at the San Juan airport said the four-engine DC-7 plunged into the ocean as it was making its takeoff. The improperly loaded plane was owned by a San Juan air-cargo operator who had drawn criticism for his operation from aviation officials in the past.

Six foot waves hampered the search in waters 1 1/2 miles north of the airport. The U. S. Coast Guard said a suitcase and some wreckage were found. Then the pilot was found. His name was Jerry Hill. Sanguillen swam in the waters with Navy divers, and rode in boats with the Coast Guard, but had no success.

New Year's Day is a religious holiday in Puerto Rico and at Catholic masses throughout the island prayers for Clemente were hastily inserted in the services. Puerto Rican radio stations cancelled all regular broadcasts.

Several days later, other members of the Pirates organization came to Puerto Rico to pay tribute to their lost colleague. But Sanguillen did not attend the funeral service in Carolina. He was manning a dredging boat off Piñones Beach. Thousands watched from the beach, and they saw Sanguillen, bare-chested, and in soaked shorts, trying to be of help. He was still searching for his friend. He was bone-tired, but he was still hopeful.

nny Sanguillen wears No. 21 patch in honor of the late Roberto Clemente as he looks his pitch.

Remember Roberto

"My sister saw his plane go down."
— Ed Walters

Arthur J. Rooney Jr.
Vice-President, Pittsburgh Steelers

"I remember that Jack Butler and I and our wives, Kathleen and Bernie, went on a vacation to Puerto Rico. We hailed a cab at the airport to take us to our hotel. The cabbie didn't speak very good English. But, with a real accent, he asked, 'Where you from?' We said, 'Pittsburgh.' He turned the car around, without a word, and headed in the opposite direction. I thought he was taking us for a ride, to take us for some more money, you know. He finally pulls up and stops at a beach. He starts shouting 'Roberto! Roberto! Roberto!' And that's when we realized that this was where Clemente's plane had crashed, and where he was killed. It was very touching. I wasn't a baseball fan like my dad, and never met Clemente. Jack and I were football guys. But we were moved by this. And we soon learned that Clemente was treated like a god in Puerto Rico."

Ed Walters
Ben Avon

"My mother is Puerto Rican and I was born there, and we traveled throughout Latin America, and we came back there when I was in seventh grade and stayed through my college days. We lived in Hato Rey, a suburb of San Juan. My name there was Ed Walters Perez. That was my mother's name. Clemente was known there as Roberto Clemente Walker. In other words, son of Clemente and born of Walker. My sister Janet was 12 years old and she was going to sleep over at a friend's house in Isla Verde, by the beach near the airport in San Juan. It was late in the evening and they were out on the balcony. They heard an airplane take off, and then there was a strange, rumbling sound in the sky. They looked up and they saw some bright light; it might have been fire. My sister saw his plane go down. It wasn't until later that they learned an airplane had crashed into the water with Clemente aboard. There was a state of shock for everyone in Puerto Rico. There were a number of baseball players from Puerto Rico — Orlando Cepeda lived up the street from our family — but Clemente was by far the most popular. Baseball was one of my loves, and what happened hurt us all deeply."

324

Clemente's youngest child, Roberto Enrique, has cushy seat at second base.

Dolores Drabek Viverette
Churchill

"You can tell by my maiden name that I took the loss to Atlanta in the seventh game of the (1992) National League playoffs real bad. I've al ways been a big baseball fan. I grew up in Monessen and used to come in and see the Pirates play at Forbes Field. In 1972, I was 19 and a stu dent at the Washington (Pa.) Hospital School of Nursing, and I took the bus in from there with some other students and saw 28 Pirates game at Three Rivers Stadium that year. I used to sit on the third base line I liked that view. We had box seats; if I was going to come that far wanted good seats. I was home in Monessen for the holidays. On New Year's Day I was watching the TV when I heard the news that Roberto Clemente was killed. It was a very empty feeling. At first, there was disbelief. When you're young, even when you're in nursing school and working in a hospital, you think of people like him as being immortal I was at Three Rivers that season when they had a Father-Son Game and I remember seeing Roberto with his kids and wife. They were so young. His death was a true tragedy. I was only ten when Presiden Kennedy was killed, and it wasn't as personal as this. I had put togethe scrapbooks on the World Series in '71 and '79, and I decided to put one together on all the stories about Clemente's death. I clipped out storie from the *Monessen Valley Independent, The Press* and *Post-Gazette* and *Sports Illustrated.* I had some autographed pictures of him. He was one of my favorite Pirates. I have to get that scrapbook out and look at it.'

Jim Clister
Mt. Lebanon

"We've been taking a youth baseball team to Puerto Rico for the las four or five years. In fact, we're about one hour away from our first prac tice (on February 6, 1994) to get ready for this year's trip. We're taking 15 year olds this time. We have what is called the Jim Clister/Gilber Carrillo Foundation of Pittsburgh. Carrillo was my baseball coach a Arizona and he, of course, was Latin, and that's how I got intereste in this. We have about 15 kids from the South Hills, mostly from Mt Lebanon, and we pick up four to six kids on our team down in Puerto Rico when we go there. Last year, I went out to the Carolina (Clemente' hometown) Little League and picked the kids for our team at tryouts Anywhere from three to six come back with us to Pittsburgh. They stay at my house and play in a league with us and then tournaments through out the summer. Last year, one of our coaches, Frank Carey, an atto ney from Mt. Lebanon, got such a kick out of going to the Clemente home and seeing all his trophies and stuff. Mrs. Clemente is on our board an she has us out to her place every year. She is a great hostess. And w play some games at the Ciudad Deportiva. And we see the statue o Roberto. It's still a thrill."

Dottie Stegon
East Pittsburgh

"My sister Marie and I went on a trip to Philadelphia in the mid-50s to see the Pirates play the Phillies, and we were staying at the same hotel, the Warwick, when we saw Roberto Clemente coming through the lobby. He was so alone he looked like an orphan. I said to Marie, 'Let's ask him if he'd like to join us for dinner.' And she said, 'Why not? What's the difference? He's our ballplayer.' We took him to dinner at the hotel. We became good friends after that. We had our parents at the Allegheny Club at Three Rivers Stadium for their 49th anniversary. Here comes Roberto Clemente walking through and he came right over to our table, and I introduced him to our father and mother. He couldn't get over them being married 49 years, and he made a fuss over them. He said, 'People don't stay married that long anymore.' He talked to them for about five minutes. My mother said, 'I've had a good day, but this was the nicest part of the day.' That's all my parents talked about after that. The next year we sent him an invitation to come to our parents' 50th wedding anniversary. He sent the invitation back, with a short note saying he'd be unable to come, but congratulated my parents and signed it. That was special to them."

John Meiser
Pittsburgh

"I went to games with my neighbor's parents, and we'd wait and get autographs after the game. The important thing was to ask as politely as possible for autographs. In 1971, I had my picture taken with Clemente. Another time, I was waiting for Clemente at Gate C — he'd come out there to avoid the crowds. But for some reason he came out of Gate A. I ran to him and said, 'Mr. Clemente, can I have an autograph?' He said, 'My hands are full. Follow me to my car, and I'll give you an autograph.' I walked to his car — it was a pretty good walk — and he put his stuff in it, and he comes over to me and says, 'What do you want me to sign?' I give him my scorecard. He signed it. 'What else do you want?' he said. I said, 'That's it. Thank you.' He said, 'Where you headed?' I told him I was going back to Gate A where my buddy, Mark Bande, would be waiting for me. Mark was in my wedding this past year. Clemente says, 'I'll give you a ride.' He drives me round the circle under Three Rivers Stadium. He's got a big yellow Cadillac, and I'm sitting next to him in the front seat. I'm feeling like a real big shot. He drops me off just as all my friends are coming out. Mark was standing there when I got out of the Cadillac. His mouth dropped. He said, 'Like wow! How'd you get a ride?' When I got back to school, I told everybody about how I got a ride with Roberto Clemente."

Kent Tekulve

Ken Tekulve (signature)

Recalls '71 spring training camp

"I probably learned more about pitching from Clemente than I did from any pitching coaches."

Whenever Kent Tekulve talks to kids about baseball and about how to succeed in sports and one's life pursuits, he is never sure where the words are coming from, or who first offered them. They may be from his first grade teacher back home in Cincinnati, or from some ballplayer or manager he met at Geneva, New York or Salem, Virginia or Sherbrooke, Quebec or Charleston, West Virginia when he was toiling in the minor leagues, or someone he admired when he was pitching in the big leagues with the Pirates, the Phillies or the Reds.

Some of the wisdom he offers, he is certain, came from Roberto Clemente, but it may have been distilled through or mixed with the wisdom of Willie Stargell.

There are pictures and paintings and remnants of both Clemente and Stargell in the spacious baseball showcase that is the gameroom of Tekulve's home in suburban Upper St. Clair, about 12 miles south of Pittsburgh and Three Rivers Stadium.

Tekulve, a 6-4, 180 pound right-handed pitcher, had quite a baseball career for someone who hardly looks like an athlete. Two months away from his 47th birthday when I visited him in late January of 1994, he seemed as skinny as ever. He still had that toothy smile, that sparkle in his bespectacled eyes, and that easy self-deprecating conversational style that has endeared him to Pirates fans for a long time.

This was one of the greatest relief pitchers in baseball history, the long, tall, sidearming version of ElRoy Face, as fearless and competitive as they come, despite the deceiving appearance. His sidearm delivery was as different from most pitchers as Clemente's batting antics were unique, so they were kinfolk of a kind in their unorthodox styles. Face had his forkball, and Tekulve had that whip, that sidearm delivery where his knuckles nearly scraped the front of the mound on some offerings.

During his nearly 17 seasons, Tekulve established Major League records for most relief appearances (1,050) and most innings (1,436 1/3) pitched in relief. He tied major league records for most consecutive games won by a relief pitcher — three from May 6 through May 9, 1980. He established a National League record for most career games pitched (1,050) and career games finished (638). He established Pirates club record for career saves with 158. He broke records established by Face and by Hoyt Wilhelm, a Hall of Famer. Tekulve's career record was 94-90, with 184 saves.

If you don't believe this, just check out all the stuff in his gameroom that is showcased as impressively as anything that appears at the Baseball Hall of Fame in Cooperstown, New York. It's all there. As Casey Stengel would say, you can look it up.

One of the most prized items in the room doesn't really belong to Tekulve. It's a game jersey, or blouse, once worn by Roberto Clemente, a size 42 Rawlings' jersey with No. 21 on the left breast, that Tekulve took as a souvenir somewhere along the way.

Tekulve treasures that jersey, displayed under glass, and the memory of time spent with Clemente at spring training at Pirate City in Bradenton, Florida back in 1971.

Tekulve didn't make the Pirates team that spring, his third year in professional baseball, but he learned enough from Clemente to serve him in good stead throughout his career.

"That was the only year I was around him at all," said Tekulve. "I didn't get invited to spring training with the Pirates in 1972, Clemente's last season. He did things differently from most of the regulars on that team.

"Back then, most of the regular players would play two or three or four innings, then go out and do some running in the outfield. They'd go to the clubhouse from there; they'd take a shower and be out on the golf course by the time guys like me were even getting in the games. Not Clemente.

"He'd come down to the bullpen area in right field. It was a spacious area, with lots of room between the foul line and the stands at McKechnie Field (named after Bill McKechnie of Wilkinsburg, who managed the Bucs back in the '20s). The pitchers and catchers would fill the benches down there. There would be several Latin players, too, because they wanted to catch Clemente when he'd come down. So Clemente would just plop down on the grass and hold court. He loved to talk about hitting.

"He'd be sitting there, talking to all these young kids. It wasn't about mechanics, you know, like how to hold the bat, or where to stand, or stuff like that. It was more about theory, what he was trying to do as a hitter.

"It helps explain his unorthodox style. You'd never teach anyone to stand up at the plate like he did, or to hold the bat like he did, or to swing at some of the pitches he lashed at. He wanted to hit the ball with the bat going down through it. The ball would come off the bat with backspin. It will carry that way. I realized it more when I played golf because the same thing applies there. If you hit up at it you get topspin and the ball goes down.

"Most guys just want to make contact; they're happy if they can put their bat on the ball. But Clemente was more precise in what he wanted to accomplish. He wanted to keep his hands back, and hit down on the ball with that heavy bat he used. Hearing him talk, you knew he was somebody on a separate level. They say Ted Williams was like that.

Kent Tekulve throws with whip-like action in 1979.

"He'd sit there four or five innings a day, just talking about things. Like balance, things he was trying to accomplish at the plate. I probably learned more about pitching to good major league batters from Clemente than I did from any pitching coaches.

"I'd go back to my room at Pirate City and figure out how I could counteract that. How could I keep batters off balance? How could I offset the sort of things good hitters like Clemente could do? I'd go over in my mind all the things he talked about. I'd sit around my room for hours. How could I keep hitters from doing what they wanted to do? He was so detailed. He was so in tune to this. He wanted to talk to these kids. Everybody learned from him."

Tekulve thought he'd be playing with Clemente in a Pirates uniform, but it never happened. "I thought I was there to make the club," recalled Tekulve. "I was like every other starry-eyed kid. I thought I was ready for the big leagues. In truth, I was there to throw batting practice and to shag flies in the outfield. My number was 72; I should have known better."

That 1971 season was spent at Salem and Waterbury, the 1972 season at Sherbrooke and Charleston. He didn't get a call from the Pirates until late in the 1974 season, and he still spent most of the 1975 season at Charleston — he was there the year that Steve Blass went back to the minors in an unsuccessful attempt at finding himself as a pitcher. In short, Tekulve took quite a while to get to the big dance. Tekulve spent six and a half years in the minors before he made it to the big leagues for good.

He missed out on being a teammate of Clemente, on being a member of the 1971 team that won the World Series under Danny Murtaugh. But he was blessed, he believes, to come to a ballteam that was led by Willie Stargell, a Clemente disciple.

He was there to play an integral part in the Pirates winning the World Series again in 1979 under Chuck Tanner.

"That '79 team was Stargell's team," recalled Tekulve. "He was 'Pops,' and we were the 'Fam-i-lee,' and all that stuff. But all the things that Stargell showed us he learned from Clemente. Whenever I'd question Stargell about something, he'd smile and say, 'That is Roberto. You're getting it secondhand from Roberto. That's what he told me.' He was like Clemente in many ways. He didn't say much. He didn't want to say much. 'Just watch me,' that's what he was saying.

"I sat on the opposite side of the clubhouse from Stargell. Looking at him after a game, you couldn't tell if he was 4-for-4, 0-for-4, whether he struck out four times or whether he had seven RBIs. There was a consistency about his behavior. Not too high, not too low.

"We all drew from his personality. And he'd say, 'That's the way I got it from Roberto.'

"What I really got from Roberto, and from Stargell, is how analytical you have to be. What are you trying to do? That's what you have to ask yourself, whatever sport you are playing. Whatever job you're doing.

"Whenever kids talk to me, they think I'm telling them something. But it's a culmination of the experiences I've had along the way in my baseball career."

"He wasn't born. He was drawn by Norman Rockwell."
—Jim Murray

None of the ballplayers I have visited in writing about the Pirates had a gameroom as nice as Tekulve's. Everything is done in a first-class manner. Tekulve told me he converted the original garage in the house to this game room, and extended the house by building a new garage with a porch on top of it. We sat at a card table to talk, and Tekulve's head was framed by the oranges, greens and blues flashing from a jukebox behind him, and we were warmed by a blazing fireplace. It was 25 degrees outside, and there was snow on the ground, but Tekulve wore a short-sleeved jersey.

He was kidded about his summer attire by his wife, Linda, to whom he had been married for 17 years. She joined us at the table and teased her husband from time to time. They appear to get along well, and are a down-to-earth couple, even though two cleaning ladies showed up while I was there to assist with the housekeeping.

Their gameroom has a pool table, a pinball machine, a popcorn machine, a wet bar with about eight chairs at the black leather rail, an extra large TV screen, and through sliding glass doors you can see a driveway with two basketball hoops rimming it, and a large van nearly filling it.

"We moved here in late October, 1979," said Tekulve, "right after we won the World Series. I was the shortest-lived hero in World Series history. I had just come from a celebration in the city to mark our triumph, and as soon as I got home, Linda said, 'Go downstairs and pack the boxes. We're moving.' I was there in the basement packing boxes, and everything was back to normal."

Jerseys he wore with the Pirates and Phillies — No. 27 for both — and the one he wore with the Reds — No. 43 — are encased in glass with brass plates explaining their significance.

He was wearing the Phillies uniform, for instance, when he pitched in his 847th game on September 16, 1986, breaking the National League record for appearances set by ElRoy Face. He was wearing the Reds uniform when he established a Major League record for appearances with his 1,019th game, breaking the mark set by Hoyt Wilhelm.

There are Six Rolaids Relief Man plaques displayed on a pillar for the years he was the Pirates' most effective relief pitcher.

On the wall behind the bar is a plaque showing him with Willie Stargell. When Stargell left the Pirates, he gave a personalized plaque to many of his teammates, front office workers and such, showing them with Willie, and with a personal inscription with kind words handwritten by Willie.

Willie wrote the following message to Tekulve:

"Thinking back on what all we've been through, the one thing, for all it's worth, you've been just one helluva man. Glad I knew you."

Tekulve points out that he stuck "a few extra stars" around the plaque. Remember the stars Stargell passed out to the players for exceptional play, affixing them to their old-fashioned ballcaps?

"Players like Stargell helped me gain confidence," said Tekulve. "My personality kinda evolved. I was extremely withdrawn and shy, insecure about my abilities early in my career. I went through the minors like that. Willie and Blass were among those who told me when I got to the majors not to try to do anything different from what I had done in the minors. I came up thinking that everybody I was pitching to was Babe Ruth, trying to be too fine and precise with my pitches. Blass said, 'Here's my advice: If it's good enough to get you here, it's good enough to keep you here.' "

There is a large print of a painting of Stargell by LeRoy Neiman on a nearby wall.

There are bats affixed to a wall in a fan-like manner, starting with a bat from Marietta College, and there's one for each minor league and major league team that employed him.

"We were told early on to always remember where you've been, and to always remember the people you met on the way up because you'll see the same people on the way down," said Tekulve. No matter his many achievements, Tekulve has never gotten a big head. He pricks his own balloon.

In that respect, there is a framed copy of a column by Jim Murray, the marvelous sports columnist of the *Los Angeles Times* that is one of Tekulve's favorite stories. It is paired with a caricature of Tekulve that makes him more of a stick man than he really is.

Murray's tongue-in-cheek column began this way:

"The first gander you get at Kent Tekulve, the Pittsburgh Pirates pitcher, you gather he wasn't born. He was drawn by Norman Rockwell. If he didn't have an Adam's apple, he wouldn't have any profile at all. When he turns sideways, you can't see him. Whatever he eats makes lumps."

There are photos of the Tekulves with their kids, some great ones showing Tekulve playing with them at the ballpark when they, too, were wearing baseball uniforms.

At the time of my visit, the four young Tekulves were Chris, 16, Jon, 15, Beth, 12 and Brian, 9. The year before, each of them was in a different school in Upper St. Clair. Linda was involved with some responsible position with the PTA or PTSO at each of the four schools. She has often served as the secretary of such groups. Kent and his buddy, Pirates broadcaster Lanny Frattare, and Lanny's wife, Liz, often lend a hand when dirty work is involved in a behind-the-scenes capacity in school and community projects.

Tekulve had just returned from participating in a Pirates Camp Bradenton Fantasy Camp at Bradenton, Florida. He was scheduled to appear and sign autographs the coming weekend at the Piratefest — an annual weekend opportunity for Pirates past and present to mix with their fans at the Expo Mart in Monroeville, a suburb just east of Pittsburgh — and then he was returning to Florida to participate in a Fantasy Camp for the Phillies at Clearwater. "I enjoy those as much as the guys who attend them; it's a chance for me to relive my career," said Tekulve.

"I'm just doing two weeks of Fantasy Camp this year," said Tekulve. "Last year I did four straight weeks of that stuff and it was way too much. It was too long away from home, too many nights at the bar. . ."

"You don't. . .," Linda scolded him.

"That's part of what they're paying me to do," said Tekulve, worming his way out of that one. "Socializing with the troops is a big part of the Fantasy Camp experience."

Tekulve is as popular in Philadelphia as he is in Pittsburgh. He had worked the previous four years in a community relations capacity for the Pirates, making many public appearances throughout the tri-state area on their behalf, while doing part-time work as a color commentator on cable telecasts of Phillies games. He divided his time between the two cities.

His future was unclear at the time of our visit. Tekulve had turned down an offer from the Pirates to join their regular broadcast crew — teaming up with holdovers Steve Blass and Frattare, and newcomer Greg Brown, in from the Bucs' farm club at Buffalo. Tekulve simply wasn't satisfied with the financial offer made by the Pirates. He still had his job with the Phillies and was hoping to build on that.

It seemed a shame. Tekulve can tell stories, something the Pirates need in their baseball broadcasts. He's popular with the Pittsburgh crowd, and he has the kind of Nellie King charm and easy-does-it delivery that would be soothing to the ears.

Whenever the other broadcasters tired, who better to bring in to relieve them than Tekulve?

"I've been touched by the reverence with which they speak of his skills."

Tekulve completed his baseball career with the Cincinnati Reds, his boyhood team, in 1989. "That was the year all the trouble came down for Pete Rose," recalled Tekulve.

In his four-year stint representing the Pirates in a public relations capacity, Tekulve said he really came to appreciate Clemente and the impact he had on Pirates fans.

"Since I've been doing this," he said, "I've had more opportunities to be in places with older fans who saw Roberto play from the beginning of his career, to meet people who were around when he was here.

Just their reaction to him has been revealing, their stories of the way he played the game.

"I only got to see Clemente play for three or four innings a day in spring training in 1971. Like everyone else, Clemente gets better through the years. Everyone does. I've been touched by the reverence with which they speak of his skills.

"Clemente could do everything, and they respected him for that all-around game. So many players have come and gone since then, and we had some real good ones here, especially in the outfield. But he's still head and shoulders above them all.

"These older people have talked about him. It's almost like a mission. If you saw Clemente play, it's almost like a job for you to tell people what he did. Wherever I'd go, elementary school kids knew about him. They knew he was a great player. That's not true with all players of that era.

"I was recently in Phoenix and I went into a restaurant and came upon Bob Gibson and Curt Flood. When I got back here, I was talking to some kids about Bob Gibson, and one of them said, 'Who's Bob Gibson?' But that'll never happen in Pittsburgh with Roberto Clemente."

Pittsburgh Pirates

Manager Chuck Tanner congratulates Kent Tekulve.

Al Oliver
His Dad And Clemente Were His Heroes

*"I was one of the best kept
secrets in baseball."*

A l Oliver had an idea. He was at his home in Portsmouth, at the southernmost tip of Ohio, and I told him I wanted to talk to him about Roberto Clemente. That was fine with him. After all, Roberto Clemente had been one of his heroes. But before I could say anything, Oliver said, "You know, I'm looking for somebody to write a book about me. It will be called *Al Oliver: One Of America's Best-Kept Secrets.* You know, I was one of the best-kept secrets in baseball."

I assured him that any serious or not-so-serious student of baseball had surely heard of Al Oliver. Or simply "Scoop," as he was nicknamed. Or "Angry Al," as some of the fans still refer to him. He was a tremendously talented, 6-1, 210 pound ballplayer who proved to be one of the most productive performers in Pirates annals. Oliver was often a loud individual in the Pirates' clubhouse. He stood on the soapbox often and preached his message. But he was a helluva ballplayer and, once you scraped off the hard edges and knocked the chip off his broad shoulder, a helluva guy.

He was unhappy for a lot of oft-expressed reasons. At first, he had a hard time cracking the lineup. Then he was platooned, and then he was shuttled back and forth between the outfield and first base. He had spats with management. There were times, he wasn't talking to them. Being black, he said, worked against him in his bid to be somebody. It was a familiar refrain.

Like the lead character in the musical "Oliver," in his desperate search for a steady place in the Pirates' scheme of things, he was often singing the same song, "I'll do anything. . ."

When he was playing, he complained about the lack of publicity he got in the Pittsburgh papers, as well as around the country. Oliver looked like an unhappy camper. But he never stopped trying to do his best, and he became a much-respected player.

"As for hitting a baseball, I'm the best," he said, sounding a lot like you know who. "Nobody hits the ball as hard and as consistently as I do."

The years and other experiences have mellowed the man. Oliver is easy to like and, at 47 in the winter of 1994, he was good company. Oliver does deserve recognition and respect as one of the Pirates' finest. Perhaps he protested too much. One of his goals was to be a Hall of Famer, but he didn't draw enough support the first time he was on the ballot to remain eligible. In truth, Oliver was outstanding, but he was on the next level just below Hall of Fame status, just like Frank Thomas and Dick Groat, if the truth be told.

Like many of Pirates of the past, and some of the present, Oliver always felt unappreciated. From a publicity standpoint, Oliver once observed, "Playing in Pittsburgh is like being behind the Iron Curtain." Not bad, as quotes go. It was the same way with Roberto Clemente. It was the same way with Dave Parker. Bob Friend always felt that the 1960 Pirates never got their due. Groat agreed. Do you think ElRoy Face feels he got the recognition he deserved — induction into the Baseball Hall of Fame — or the money he should have made? Dick Stuart is still stewing over slights, real and imagined. Frank Thomas thought he didn't get his due in his hometown. I worked for nine years in New York, and that's where you had to be, the ballplayers felt, to get the real publicity, the big endorsements, or at least in Chicago or Los Angeles, the major markets. In truth, many ballplayers have labored in those cities, and never felt they were properly promoted, marketed or loved by the fans, either.

Oliver, for one, would have been difficult to satisfy no matter where he played. He had his fans — "The Scoop Group" — but he wanted more. His personal pride, his ego, his ravenous appetite for acceptance, were insatiable. That's not a knock at Al Oliver. Writers must have egos, too, or else they wouldn't write. They must feel their opinions are important, their words are worth reading, worthy of being set in print. There are attorneys and accountants and teachers who seek the same sort of attention and appreciation Oliver has always sought, somewhat in vain. Remember, a prophet is not always heard in his own country.

In many ways, Oliver was one of the best Pirates ever to play the game. He couldn't break into their all-time team, however, any more than he could break into their star-studded lineup when he first came up to the team late in 1968. When he came up for an honest shot in 1969, he was just one of several promising Baby Bucs, notably Bob Robertson, Manny Sanguillen and Richie Hebner. The Pirates were loaded in those days, among the best in the National League or the American League. At first, it was tough for Oliver to get the playing time he required to hone his skills, to beef up his batting average, to shoot for his goals, to shoot for the stars, to be productive in the Pirates' attack.

In time, however, he found his place, indeed, forged a place, though it was a different place from time to time, sometimes in the outfield, sometimes at first base. He was a contributor to a championship season in 1971. He had two doubles and two RBIs in that 1971 World Series. In time he was a member of the much-feared "Lumber Company." But he was gone, in 1977, to the Texas Rangers (where he became a much-feared designated hitter as well as an outfielder), and missed out being a member of the "Fam-i-lee" that won the World Series again in 1979.

He played 18 years in the big leagues, and he batted .300 or better in 11 of those seasons. Oliver played on five NL East champions in Pittsburgh before being traded to the Texas Rangers in 1977. After four seasons in Texas, he went on to play for Montreal (1982-83), San Francisco (1984), Philadelphia (1984), Los Angeles (1985) and Toronto (1985).

He won the NL batting crown with Montreal in 1982 at age 36 with a .331 mark. He also played in seven All-Star Games, was the first player to amass 200 hits and 100 RBIs in the same season in both leagues and finished his career with 2,743 hits, and a .303 lifetime batting average. However, he got little consideration when his name appeared on the Hall of Fame ballot for the first time in 1990.

"It didn't bother me at all," Oliver said, not being honest with himself or anybody else. Sure it bothered him. "I never seemed to get the acclaim that a lot of other guys did. I never understood why but there's nothing I can do. Hank Aaron didn't get his credit until he was chasing Babe Ruth's home run mark. It took death for Clemente to get credit."

Always it comes back to Clemente.

He credits Clemente for much of his success, and his growth as a human being.

"Playing with Roberto automatically made you a better player, but playing next to him took you to a higher level," said Oliver. "To have known him, you were a better person. I can only say the latter about one other person and that was my father. They both were for real.

"I wish I could have been surrounded with more of those kind of people. Outside of my parents, Roberto had the biggest impact on me. He might have been the only one in the organization who understood me. He was raised the same way. He proved you could have an ego and not be egotistical. Confident but not cocky. Humble when needed to be, but, above all, maintaining your dignity. And self-respect in spite of all the negative obstacles that were in his way.

"Pride means, among other things, that you never want to look bad. Part of confidence is never giving up. Luck means getting the ball to fall safely."

As usual, that statement tells one as much about Al Oliver as it does about Roberto Clemente.

They were a lot alike in many ways, and shared many common experiences, setbacks and successes, but they were, indeed, different as well. Clemente thought Oliver was a little crazy with his hyper ways when he first emerged on the Pirates scene. Clemente contributed to taming this wild young stallion from Portsmouth, Ohio.

"He was into human beings."
— Oliver on Clemente

I talked to Al Oliver once more at the 1994 Piratefest at the Expo Mart in Monroeville on the last weekend of January in 1994. Things were different for Al Oliver than they had been when I talked to him the year before. He had been divorced eight years earlier, and was now dating a woman he liked a great deal. He didn't know when he was moving, but he was moving. He had given up his job after three years as the start-up baseball coach at Shawnee State Junior College in Portsmouth. Somebody there, I was told by one of his friends, had given him some grief. "I don't have to coach; I have a good income for me," he said. Oliver

Al Oliver was popular at 1994 Piratefest.

had looked after his money pretty carefully during his career. He had his baseball pension, and he thought he could make some pocket money by delivering motivational speeches across the country. He had formed The Al Oliver Foundation, a charitable fund-raising organization to help others in need. Delivering speeches was second nature to Oliver, as easy as delivering extra-base hits. He still had his sweet swing, and a strong voicebox.

"I was talking with the girl I'm dating, and we watched a video about Clemente's career," he said. "We couldn't believe how it was so similar to my own story. The confidence factor. The pride. The personality part. It was unreal. We were both misunderstood. We were not always perceived as we really were.

"Color was not important to Clemente. When it came to color, he had no problem with anybody. He was into human beings. He was a private person, and he didn't go to a lot of places. We lived together in the same apartment (Chatham West) in Green Tree in 1971 and 1972. We were close, but I was not as close to him as much as, say, Sanguillen."

For some reason, I asked Oliver if he had ever met Mal Goode, the first black network news reporter, who came from Pittsburgh and had befriended Clemente and many other black ballplayers. "Sure," said Oliver. "He spoke at my going-away party. He flew in when I went to Texas. He was someone you could talk to when you had a problem."

Oliver wanted to talk about his upbringing.

"I lost my parents when I was young. So I needed somebody looking after me, when I came up to the majors. I always knew where Clemente was coming from. He had taken some shots himself and came back to always play his best. When he died, some of the same people who portrayed him as a great humanitarian had not appreciated him when he was alive. There was a lot of hypocrisy, absolutely. They didn't know him.

"You had to have a certain personality type to identify with him. Back home in Portsmouth, Ohio, people always compared me and Larry Hisle. I was cocky and Hisle was humble. We grew up together, and we made it to the major leagues at the same time, and we were always compared."

Hisle came up for a cup of coffee as an outfielder with the Philadelphia Phillies, just like Oliver did with the Pirates, in 1968. He played 14 years in the majors, also with Minnesota and Milwaukee in the American League.

"As people, we were both fine people," noted Oliver. "One outgoing. One was an introvert. We came out of the same high school in Portsmouth.

"With me, Roberto definitely had the biggest influence. When I came to the big leagues, I was ready to play. My dad had given me the basics. What Roberto did with me...he understood me. He reassured me that I was on the right plane. Coming from him, it just reinforced what I felt was right. To him, there was nothing wrong with being positive and confident. I was always that way. My parents made me feel good about myself. My attitude about myself came from home.

340

"My dad had a very difficult job. He worked in a brick factory. He developed silicosis from breathing all that dust. The years piled up on him. It was awful to see a physical specimen like him deteriorate. "He worked from 8 to 4. He took his lunch to work every day. He normally showered at the brickyard. Once in a while he just came home, and he'd still have that brick dust on him. He still had that brickyard scent about him.

"What brings it back is that the factory is torn down now. I can't help but think of him and the hard work he put in whenever I drive by that place. When I see where that factory used to be, I think about a man who gave me direction. It was part of the Harbison-Walker Refractories, which had its headquarters here in Pittsburgh. It's like when I used to pass Forbes Field, I'd have the same sort of feelings. That's where it all started for me, as a major leaguer. And now it was gone.

"My dad was an impressive-looking guy. One time he was working on the night shift. He left the house at three in the morning. Twenty minutes later, I heard the key in the door and he's coming back home. He came back into the bedroom. He said, 'Son, I don't feel well.' It scared me to death. I looked at my dad as a pillar of strength, like a rock. He never complained. So I knew he was really sick. It bothered me. In those days, people didn't like to go to a doctor unless they were sure they were dying. I took him to the doctor. It turned out he'd had a heart attack and didn't know it.

"He lost his wife, suddenly, in 1958. He came home from work one day. She hadn't been feeling well when he left to go to work. He came in and she was lying on the couch, just like she was when he left. He went over and kissed her. She was cold. She had died while he was at work.

"That had to be a major blow. I was 11 years old at the time. Ten years later, in 1968, my dad died, too. That's when I got called up to the Pirates. I was scared to death."

And that's when Clemente came into his life.

"I just thank God that I had the opportunity to play with him," observed Oliver. "I can't think of anyone who could have had an impact on Al Oliver, because very few people can move me. I had a chance to tell my dad what he meant to me, but I never had the chance to tell Roberto. But, deep down, I think he had a sense of how I felt about him.

"If I had not played with him, I don't know if I'd have had the kind of career I had. I was there during the glory days of the Pirates. I had the right attitude. He instilled in me that it's all right to be positive."

I mentioned to Oliver that when I mentioned his name to a passerby a few minutes earlier, the man responded by saying, "Angry Al." Oliver smiled about this.

"'With a bat in his hand, no man's meaner,'" said Oliver. "That's what Bill Christine wrote once. I've always remembered that. He said, 'If you were a baseball, you'd be deathly afraid of Al Oliver.'"

"He was like a father figure."
— Oliver on Clemente

I had interviewed him the year before at a sports card show at Duquesne University's A.J. Palumbo Center, and he had offered some off-the-cuff but incisive comments about Clemente.

"Clemente and I had the same kind of personalities," Oliver said. "He was like a father figure. Like my father led me as a human being, Roberto ended up leading me as a major leaguer. I never had to be told what my job was, but he was my mentor; that's what he was to me.

"I saw what happened with him, and it made it easier to accept certain things, though I never liked it. Clemente was a superstar, but it took a long time before he won national acclaim. He was upset about that, and I didn't blame him. I had the same complaint. I don't think I won enough national acclaim. I have said it before — I had the talent to be recognized as a superstar. I thought the Pirates fans, though, appreciated me not only as a player — but more important — as a man.

"To see Clemente hustle out ground balls, and the way he attacked the ball, the way he went after balls, the way he was reckless going for balls against the walls or fences . . . that's the same way I always played."

"Where were you when the Pirates won the 1960 World Series?" I asked Oliver.

"I was a ninth grader in Portsmouth, Ohio, which is about 90 miles south of Columbus. I collected baseball cards in the mid-'50s. That's when I got hooked on baseball. Of course, I was aware of Clemente. I didn't follow the Pirates as a team, but I knew about Clemente. Clemente and Dick Groat were the two Pirates I liked. Why? I don't know. With Clemente, I liked his own unique style and flair. With Groat, I think it was because he was such a great competitor, and he was smart."

Did he remember what it was like coming into the Pirates' clubhouse for the first time as a rookie?

"I didn't do a lot of talking with Clemente," he said. "but there was a mutual relationship, and a mutual respect. Roberto saw something in me early, that I didn't think anyone saw, and that was one of his qualities. He said to be proud of who you are and where you come from.

"He saw early in my career that I was being platooned. He said, 'Al, don't worry about it. One day you'll get an opportunity to play on an everyday basis, and you'll be one of the best ballplayers in the game.'"

Clemente's complimentary remarks to Oliver stuck with him.

"That couldn't have come from anybody except my father, who, unfortunately, died in 1968," observed Oliver. "I came from his funeral to the Pirates in September of that first season. He was a very religious man, and he was ready. He was Albert Oliver, and I'm Al Jr.

"The Pirates called me up from their farm team in Columbus, Ohio. It was ironic. I was not only coming from my father's funeral, but the Pirates were playing against the Cincinnati Reds, one of the teams I followed as a kid.

342

Al Oliver with Dave Giusti

"In the second game of a doubleheader, I looked at the lineup card in the dugout and saw I was playing right field. I never played right field in my life. I could run and I guess they figured I could do it. 'Let's put him out there.' Number one, I was a nervous wreck. Not only had I never played the position, but right field was Roberto Clemente's place. That was real pressure.

"Right away, Vada Pinson hit a real shot to right center field. It was a bullet. I had no idea what I was doing. I ran like crazy and stuck my glove out and somehow got it. One of the tips Billy Virdon gave me about playing the outfield was to never give up on a ball. I think about that play sometimes. I think about what might have happened to me if I had missed it. What would it have been like to break in on a negative note?

"Roberto Clemente was simply the greatest ballplayer or person I ever saw. I feel that by knowing him and by playing with him, that I was a better person and a better player. I'm glad I had the honor of playing next to him.

"Not a lot of people knew where he was coming from. I did. Every day I wake up and put this ring on, I think about him. He's responsible for it. In that 1971 World Series, he put on probably one of the best one-man shows anyone ever put on. He showed the world what he could do. We knew in Pittsburgh, but he let the world know what a unique talent he was, in every way. He was the heart and soul of the 1971 team. That was the year he showed the rest of the world what the people in Pittsburgh knew for 16 years — he was a great ballplayer. But it was more than that. I think people learned what a great person he was, the great qualities he had. He showed the character he had.

"He's the reason I have this ring and that the 23 other guys on the team have theirs. He took that club to the world title. He showed us what a true leader was.

"A lot of guys get on center stage and falter, but he put on an unbelievable performance."

Oliver looks at the 1971 World Series ring on his right hand. "It means everything to me," he said. "It's what you work all your life for. It's what you dream of getting."

The next year was Clemente's last with the Pirates, and Oliver held on to words Clemente offered him in his final season. "He told me, 'Don't worry about it. Maybe one day they will wake up to your ability like they did to mine.' That really helped me, coming from him, because I knew he went through the same thing.

"What I had always strived for was to play every day in the majors. I thought I had the talent, but I felt I could not prove it to myself or others unless I got the opportunity to play on a regular basis, rather than being platooned here and there."

Oliver was not the only ballplayer from Portsmouth who was platooned by the Pirates. Rocky Nelson, who still lives in Portsmouth with his wife Alberta, shared first base with Stuart, or Dr. Strangeglove, from 1959 to 1961. "I haven't seen Rocky for about four months," said Oliver.

Recognition came slow for Oliver, but it did come.

"The highest compliment ever paid me in baseball was when my peers in the National League voted me the best centerfielder in the National League on the 1975 *Sporting News* All-Star Team."

". . . Al Martin reminded him of a young Al Oliver."

I spotted Oliver talking with the Pirates young outfielder Al Martin in a dining area back stage at the Piratefest. Martin had hit 23 home runs in 1993, the most by any Pirates rookie since Ralph Kiner had 23 in 1946. His 64 RBIs were the most by a Pirates rookie since Al Oliver had 70 in 1969. But he also broke Kiner's record for most strikeouts by a rookie with 122. Martin was talking to Oliver about his hopes of hitting more home runs and cutting down on his strikeouts.

Oliver offered advice eagerly and it wasn't five minutes before he mentioned Roberto Clemente, and then Andre Dawson, who'd been a teammate in Montreal. Oliver was gripping an imaginary bat, showing Martin how to hold his hands back, yes, the way Clemente always did.

When I later mentioned that I saw him talking to Martin, he said, "Three weeks ago, a friend of mine from West Virginia told me that Al Martin reminded him of a young Al Oliver. When I met him today, I told him that. He said, 'I'm glad we met today. That's all I've heard, too.'

"I told him, 'I'll be checking you out now.' He needs to cut down his strikeouts. He's talking about waiting a little longer on off-speed pitches. That's what he's got to do. That's his weakness now. That happened to be my strength.

"My hands were quick; he's got to work on that. He said 'Nobody can throw a fastball by me.' I like that. That's how I felt. When he said that, he meant it, I could tell. Some people say it, but you can see he meant it."

I asked Oliver how he felt about seeing a "Tribute to Roberto" exhibit at the Piratefest.

"Thank God they haven't forgotten this man. There were a lot of us who saw him play, and some who had a chance to meet him. There were fewer who got to know him. He was the epitome of the Pittsburgh Pirates, really, hard-working, out to defy all odds. He was a teammate. I'm going to West Palm Beach from here for a Fantasy Camp. When I go to these camps, someone will always come up to me and ask me, 'Who was the best you ever played with?' And I just look at them."

Al Oliver

Other Pirates
Remembering Roberto
"He was God's gift to baseball."

ormer Pirates were asked by Sally O'Leary of the club's publicity
office to offer their reflections on Roberto Clemente for use in
the Pirates Alumni biannual newsletter, *The Black and Gold*.
They are reprinted here with permission:

Tommie Sisk, pitcher (1962-68)
"My locker was next to Bobby's for the entire six years I played with
the Pirates. I watched him and listened to him on a daily basis. He had
great pride in being Latin. He consistently brought this to people's attention. Each year he played winter ball at his home town of San Juan,
not for the money but because he felt he owed it to his town folk. One
winter I pitched for him when he managed the San Juan club. I met
his wife and children to whom he was deeply devoted. Although a national hero in Puerto Rico and this country, he never took on the air
of being a celebrity. He was always just one of the guys, yet separate.
I never saw Bobby drunk, disorderly or chasing women, as I did other
guys. I always believed he felt the obligation and responsibility of being a major league baseball player was to set an example for the public.
Don Drysdale used to deck Bobby or hit him regularly. I remember telling Don if he ever decked or hit Bobby when I was pitching I would do
the same to him. He said he would do it right back to me. I said, 'OK,
then we'll just stand out there and continue to drill each other until
one of us quits.' He never threw at Bobby when I was pitching, and
Bobby told me how much he appreciated this."

Johnny Pesky, former Red Sox star and Pirates coach (1965-67)
"Clemente to me was not only a great player, but a great human being.
He was God's gift to baseball. He was extremely good to the coaching
staff and gave us every courtesy."

Harding Peterson, catcher (1955-59), coach/manager in farm system (1960-66), farm system and scouting director (1967-1978), Pirates vice-president/general manager (1979-85).
"He was a very caring person and extremely thoughtful. He showed me
those qualities in many ways. Here's an example: One night, during
spring training (about 1969), when I was farm director, Howie Haak
and I were in our room at Pirate City. There was a knock on the door
and it was Roberto. He was dressed in a nice suit, white shirt and tie
and said he was going to dinner. The three of us chatted for awhile and
in our conversation I mentioned that my back was bothering me.

346

He said, 'Wait a minute, Pete.' He was gone for a couple of minutes and came back with a bottle of liniment and told me to lie down on my stomach. I said, 'Roberto, you are all dressed, ready to go to dinner.' He said, 'Never mind. I take care of your back.' He took off his suit coat and tie, rolled up his sleeves and massaged my back for almost ten minutes. In the process, he worked up a sweat, but he was determined to help my back. I will never forget how he was more interested in helping my back feel better than going out to dinner in a beautiful suit."

Bobby Bragan, manager (1956-57)

"Roberto Clemente was the best right fielder I saw play in the majors. Not the best hitter, but the best right fielder!"

Tom Saffell, outfielder (1949-51, 1955)

"I was on the Pirates club in 1955, which was Clemente's first year. He was such a competitor that when he struck out or popped up, he would come back to the bench, place his batting helmet on the floor and proceed to jump up and down on it until it was all in pieces. After he wrecked a few helmets, Fred Haney, our manager, started making him pay for them, and that cured him from losing his temper."

Bob Oldis, catcher (1960-61)

"Roberto had a jar of honey in his locker and would take a spoonful almost every day. It amazed me. I wish I would have at least tried it. He had all the tools in baseball and used every one of them to be the best. And he was."

Harvey Haddix, pitcher (1959-63), and pitching coach (1979-84). Haddix sent in this note before he died on January 8, 1994.

"I don't know why, but we called him Herschel. On our trips home from the west coast, he and I usually were the only ones awake. He was a very private individual, but still very friendly. We always talked about the games and our other activities on those trips from the coast. It was a good time because we would talk about all three cities out there. He was also very superstitious, and very neat personally."

Fernando Gonzalez, infielder (1972-73, 1977-78)

"I was with Roberto in his last baseball clinic in Aquadilla, Puerto Rico. He told me, 'As long as I have my baseball uniform on, I will play hard.' He always wanted to prove that the baseball players in Puerto Rico and their knowledge of the game were as good as any other part of the world. He wanted a fair opportunity for everybody."

Clem Labine, relief pitcher (1960-61)

"Roberto was probably one of the best all-around players I had the pleasure to see play. He, like all the great players, had that quality of making you sit on the edge of your seat, whether it was hitting, fielding, running or throwing the ball — a real Hall of Famer."

Dick Cole, infielder (1951, 1953-56)

"After playing two years with Roberto, my greatest feeling was 1971 during the first day of the World Series in Baltimore. I was walking Downtown and Roberto was in a limousine heading for the ballpark. He opened the window and hollered at me, 'Oye, Viejo.' I will never forget that moment."

Bruce Dal Canton, pitcher from Brownsville, Pa. (1967-70)

"I can remember a play he made in old Forbes Field with a runner at third and one out. A fly ball was hit down in the right field bullpen area, where there was a high screen to protect pitchers when they were warming up. Roberto caught the ball in the bullpen and, from home plate, you lost sight of him. The only thing you saw was a ball come out of that bullpen on a line to home plate. The runner started down the line and had to hold up or he would have been an easy out at home. Not only did he have one of the strongest arms I'd ever seen, but he was also most accurate."

George Freese, infielder from Wheeling, W.Va. (1955)

"The short time I was with Clemente in 1955 and playing against him in Puerto Rico, I once said to some players, 'I don't think he will ever be a hitting instructor' with that stance he had, and such a wild thing."

Art Swanson, pitcher (1955-57)

"The worse he felt physically the better he seemed to play. He gave it 100 per cent every day, every play. No one played the crazy right field in Pittsburgh better. I think my favorite quote from him came when Bobby Bragan asked him why he didn't find one batting stance and stick with it. Bob replied, 'Bobby, it no matter how you stand, it matter where you end up!' "

Vernon Law, pitcher (1950-51, 1954-67)

"I heard Roberto say many times after playing in a night game and then having to get to the park early for a day game, 'Me no feel good; couldn't sleep,' he'd say. It was always difficult coming from a night game to a day game. We all complained about that. I'm glad to have played and been a teammate of Roberto. He was the best in so many aspects of the game. Besides being a great ball player, he had a very infectious smile and was pleasant to be around. He enjoyed a good laugh and, at times, could be a real prankster not only in the clubhouse, but at the hotels

aded weapons were wielded in 1957 by, from left to right, Roberto Clemente, Frank
omas, Lee Walls and Bill Virdon.

Roberto Clemente compares bats with Matty Alou in late '60s.

where we stayed. As a player, he excelled. He could go from first to third as fast as any player I saw or played against, and that included some of the best — Lou Brock, Maury Wills and Willie Davis."

Carl Taylor, catcher, outfielder (1968-69, 1971)

"I never once saw him not run out a routine out, and I mean he ran hard all the way. I saw a lot of great players and he is the only one I can say that about. In the game of life, you were never too small for Roberto Clemente. You were never a rookie; you were always somebody in Clemente's eyes. Thank you, Robby, for being my friend."

Bill Virdon, outfielder (1956-65), manager (1972-73), coach (1968-71, 1986, 1992-94)

"My fondest memory was the cooperation and effort he gave in the clubhouse and on the field his last year and my first year as manager, 1972. No one could have done more to make it easy for me to take over the club."

Jerry Lynch, outfielder (1954-56, 1963-66)

"I asked Roberto his theory on hitting. He told me you should get 30 hits every 100 times at bat. I told him that's not what I meant. I said, 'What do you do about techniques with stance, plate covers, pitchers, etc.?' His answer was: 'I look at the ball and hit it.' He made it sound simple so maybe we all make it too complicated. Except maybe we didn't have his talent."

Chuck Goggin, infielder/outfielder (1972-73)

"At the end of the 1972 season, we had just clinched the National League East title and Roberto had 2,999 hits. The Mets were in town for our final homestand. Everyone was there to see Roberto get his 3,000th hit. I had the opportunity to start my first major league game and get my first major league hit in the same game that Roberto got his 3,000th. Umpire Doug Harvey stopped the game and retrieved the ball for me. After the game, Roberto and I posed for a picture with each of us holding the baseballs from my first hit and what turned out to be his last (regular season) hit. I shall cherish the moment and the photograph forever."

Jim Marshall, first baseman, outfielder (1962)

"He always kept a jar of honey in his locker. My son Blake, when having a chance to come into the clubhouse, always ran for Roberto, sitting on his knee — the two of them eating honey. Watching him hit, sometimes with both feet off the ground at contact, and having the best throwing arm in baseball are things I will remember. I also saw him hit a long home run over the scoreboard at Wrigley Field. I miss him. He was kind to all players; you didn't have to be a star."

Milt May, catcher (1970-73, 1983-84), hitting instructor (1986-1994)

"As a young player, I was in awe of Roberto Clemente's ability to hit in a seemingly unorthodox manner. As a hitting coach, I am in awe of how fundamentally sound a hitter he actually was."

Ronnie Brand, catcher (1963)

"My thoughts about Roberto are not so much about the ballplayer, but more of the man I respected as a teammate and an opponent for nine years. The quality of his play was directly indicative of his values. He gave all he had every game. He was kind and helpful to all of us younger players. He had a desire to be appreciated and drove himself to higher levels of performance than others. He recognized the need to excel in all phases of the game, and he encouraged everyone to do the same. Some others could do what he could, but nobody matched his flair. I loved watching him play because he loved playing. One real important thing, which probably cost him his life, was that if he thought he was right to do something, he did it with all he had in him regardless of the risks or what anyone else thought. He was a hero on and off the diamond. He is a hero in my memory."

Where Were You?
Looking back to Lawrenceville
"They were such happy days."

Letter from Denise Szersznski Fortunato who lives in Scott Township:

In 1960, I was a spunky little 15-year-old sophomore at the then all-girls St. Augustine Catholic High School, located at 37th and Butler Streets in Lawrenceville. Much to the exasperation of my nuns, they could never quite squelch that problem with my deportment, specifically, my inability to be quiet in class.

Therefore, I frequently found myself after school at the blackboard writing some promise 500 times that we all knew I would break the following day. On October 13, 1960, the Students With Hidden Portable Radios Team, of which I was a member, was keeping an ear to the progress of the game and an eye on the dismissal clock.

I was personally also wrestling with the dilemma of what to do about my appointment with the blackboard scheduled for after school that day. I knew Sister Francis Mary would kill me if I skipped out. I also knew I'd die if I missed the end of the game. So, since death was inevitable either way, I zoomed out the front door with the dismissal bell still ringing in my ears, vowing, like Scarlett O'Hara, to worry about it tomorrow.

Carol Verderber's house was nearby on Mintwood Street, so she and I and about four others raced over to catch the end of the game. My girlfriend, Gerry Jendrejewski from neighboring St. John's all-girl Catholic School, joined us. We got to Carol's house just in time to see Maz hit the homer and then I just remember pandemonium in that house, that block, and the entire neighborhood.

I don't recall whose idea it was, but we decided to head for Downtown Pittsburgh. In those days, it was not unheard of to walk to town from Lawrenceville, Bloomfield or Polish Hill. Personal safety wasn't a worry then, and not too many families had cars to chauffeur kids around, so we walked a lot. About seven of us started out for Downtown on that warm fall afternoon, just full of unmitigated joy. Around the old fire house at 34th and Liberty, across from Pittsburgh Brewing Company, we noticed many cars headed towards Downtown and got the idea to hitch-hike so we could get to the epicenter of the celebration quicker. I suggested that it might be better for only two of us to "thumb" while the rest of us would hide in the station and come out after we found an unsuspecting Samaritan. Well, in a very short time, doesn't this fabulous, shiny, new white convertible with red leather interior pull up. I can't remember the make, but it must have been a Cadillac or Oldsmobile. It was a block long and contained only two occupants, a fellow and his little son.

352

He asked if we wanted a ride, we said yes, signaled to the rest of the gang and piled in. I'll never forget the look on the poor guy's face as he watched his car fill up with girls all over the place, with Gerry and I perched on top of the folded-down ragtop. God bless him, he took it in stride and off we went like a homecoming queen and her court. Over the years, I've wondered about the identity of that good-hearted fellow, if he remembers us and if we did any damage to that gorgeous car. I hope he does and that we didn't.

That night in town was probably the most carefree and troublefree time I have ever experienced in a crowd of that size. We jumped from car to car and rode all over town. Everybody was a friend. We laughed, hugged, ran through confetti knee high. It was like the movies you see of when World War II ended and they danced in Times Square. I don't remember how we got back to Polish Hill where Gerry and I lived at the time. Perhaps it was another Good Samaritan, or maybe we walked.

We had no liquor or nicotine in us, but we were high on the excitement in the air of that night. I do remember that Gerry had found a "Keep Off The Grass" sign on a pole somewhere and we were walking up Brereton Avenue singing, "Keep The Gateway Clean, Keep Off The Grass," and making up the words as we went along.

A common architectural design on that street is party-wall homes fronting the road with covered walkways in between leading to courtyards and rows of homes in the back. Gerry left the sign in the walkway that night. The next day we found out her neighbor, a pretty macho guy, had come in later that night and thought he was confronting a burglar in the dark. The twang of the sign as his fist hit metal woke up quite a few people. Except Gerry and I, of course. We were deep in sleep with dreams of Maz and the '60 Bucs.

Oh yes, Sister Francis Mary. Well, she was waiting for me the next day. For some reason, she had this roll of plastic wrap in her hand and, as she gestured while making her speech about good Catholic girls, she kept bouncing it off my head. But lightly, because I know that she loved me like a daughter and only had my best interest at heart. I had to do double detention, but it was worth it all the way!

I hope you've enjoyed reading this recollection as much as I had remembering it. Times are so changed. Even the 1971 celebration in town was different. By then, I was 26 and taking my 16-year-old brother to town, hoping to recreate for him the fun I'd had eleven years earlier. It was a memorable time for him, and he recalls it fondly. But already, I could see the threads of violence creeping into our society.

Some store windows got smashed, and a cab was rocked and overturned. These acts were not done in anger, but rather in an undisciplined exuberance. By today's standards, it was fairly mild mayhem. But I remember feeling a bit sad that my brother could not experience the innocent fun I'd had. Our country likely will never see times like the '50s and '60s again. And I am glad to have been born to that time. They were such happy days.

Dr. Joseph Finegold
The team doctor

"He loved all those boys."
—Bea Finegold

D r. Joseph M. Finegold was not feeling so good. He had been in failing health for some time now. He had his good days and he had his bad days, his wife, Bea, told me whenever I called. We had to cancel several appointments at the last minute, simply because he was not up to it. I was all set several times to visit the Finegolds at their home on Aylesboro Avenue in Squirrel Hill when she told me we would have to do it some other time.

One of his neighbors, Lee Gutkind, an English professor at the University of Pittsburgh who writes wonderful books about the city's medical community and has always been a big baseball fan, told me, "I hear he's not doing that well."

Dr. Finegold was the team physician for the Pirates and the "house doctor" at the ballpark for 27 years, before retiring from the post in December of 1979, shortly after the team had won the World Series for the third time in his tenure. It seemed like a good time to get out.

When Dr. Finegold stepped aside, Pirates executive vice-president Harding Peterson said of him, "Joe Finegold is a distinguished member of the Pirate family. We're not going to miss him because he will continue to be a member of the family. We thank him for his longstanding, unselfish contributions to our organization."

I wanted to talk to Dr. Finegold about one of his most celebrated patients, Roberto Clemente.

My deadline for completing this book was closing in on me like Steelers linebacker Greg Lloyd, and Dr. Finegold was the final piece in the Clemente puzzle. I had to talk to him. Before it was too late.

Finally, after several false starts, I had an opportunity to talk to him in early March, 1994. In truth, he still was not up to it. But Bea Finegold filled in beautifully.

He had been in and out of the hospital and his doctor's office, and he was not doing well. He was 85 and had been in ill health for five or six years, according to his wife. He frequently came down with pneumonia when he was hospitalized, and he had a myriad of problems. Bea would stay in the hospital overnight with him on most occasions, and I could tell she had a great bedside manner. She loved him dearly, it was so evident by her manner and her affectionate remarks.

"He hates this; he gets so frustrated," said Bea Finegold, to whom he had been married for 47 years. She was Bea Sheffler from Vandergrift when she met him during their student days at the University of Pittsburgh. She remembers him at his best. "Mentally, he wants to do things, but, physically, he's not up to it. He was always so active. He'd be at the hospital and ballpark all day long when he was the physician

354

for the Pirates. He still gets up and says, 'What are we going to do to-day?' His mind is still good. I'm amazed at his memory. I was never good at names, but he comes up with them routinely," she said.

The Finegolds' home was not far from Schenley Park, and only a few miles from Forbes Field and the Oakland medical center, which is why they bought the home.

"He loved his work," said Bea. "He loved being a doctor; he loved all the players. He's really a good person; I have to tell you that. He's a very kind person, which is important when you're a doctor."

In my earlier interviews with Pirates of the past, I preferred to have their wives present for the interviews because they knew their husband's best stories, and often prompted them to share this tale or that tale. Plus, people like Bill Mazeroski and Sam Narron, the old bullpen coach, would ask their wives to fill in the spaces when they could not come up with a name, date or detail. None of the wives was as helpful, however, as Bea Finegold. She was always so cheerful, and kind, and apologetic when she had to cancel a meeting. I must have spoken to her on the telephone twenty times, trying to arrange an interview with her husband. She did her best. "It's just difficult," she said.

Dr. Finegold was not himself, hence Bea's observations about him. Whenever I attempted to ask him any questions about Clemente or the Pirates, Dr. Finegold would speak rasply, and then burst into tears. At times, he cried uncontrollably, and begged off, and gave way to Bea.

"He has all these wonderful memories," said Bea, "and he starts to cry. He does the same thing when we look at pictures. It hurts when someone like Harvey Haddix dies, or when he hears that one of the ball-players is in ill health, or had a heart attack or something like that.

"He was so close to all of them. It was different in those days. People didn't move around like they do now. The team was like one big family."

To him, they were all the same. I figured Clemente was notorious for complaining about his health — he had, indeed, been accused of being a hypochondriac — yet Dr. Finegold said, "He didn't come to see me any more than the other players. They were all concerned about their health."

Dr. Finegold was being loyal to Clemente because, in truth, all the players I spoke to said that Clemente was constantly seeking the attention of Dr. Finegold and the team trainers, Danny Whelan and Tony Bartirome. They said that no matter what Clemente complained about, whatever was bothering him, Dr. Finegold had the same reme-dy. "Take two aspirin, and try to get some sleep," he'd say.

Dr. Finegold forced a smile when I shared that story.

"He says that's right," said Bea.

With some prompting from Bea, Dr. Finegold did share a story about an incident that would indicate that Clemente was a constant companion of his when he was the team doctor.

"The players were always kidding; they were like a bunch of little kids," recalled Dr. Finegold, with some help from his wife. "One day they told me that Clemente wasn't feeling so good, that he was on the training table. The room was dark and they told me the lights had gone out. I could make out a figure on the table. I reached for his wrist to take his pulse. They had a life-size wax figure of Clemente under the sheets. It was cold to the touch. At first, it gave me a start when I felt for a pulse and it felt so cold. I got upset. They never let me forget that one."

Bea loved the Clementes, just like her husband. "Vera was a beautiful young woman," said Bea. "I thought Vera was a lovely woman. Roberto was always very gracious. He was very pleasant, amazingly social, though language was always a barrier. A lot of people hung around him. That fellow Phil Dorsey, the one that got into all that trouble with the post office, was always with him."

Now Clemente was dead, and so was Danny Murtaugh, most of the coaches, old friends like Lenny Levy, Frank Oceak and Bill Burwell, and players like Smoky Burgess, Don Hoak and Haddix, and earlier players like Lee Walls and Ted Kluszewski. And Dr. Finegold was all too aware that his turn was coming. And he cried.

He had devoted all of his adult life to looking after people's health, helping them as a caregiver and surgeon. He came from a family of physicians. His brothers, Abby and Aaron, were both doctors. Abby's son, Richard, is a urologist in Pittsburgh. One of the Finegolds' two sons, David, is a doctor, an endocrinologist, who does diabetes research at Children's Hospital. Their other son, Stan, is in marketing and promotions in Philadelphia. "We wanted him to be a doctor, but he had other ideas," said Bea. "I think it's a great career. I'm coming back as a doctor in my next life." Being a doctor was demanding, but it was exciting and rewarding, and being a team doctor for a baseball club like the Pirates was a special bonus.

When I think of team doctors, I always think about Dr. Allan Levy, who was the second most important doctor — giving ground to Dr. J, or Julius Erving, with the New York Nets. "I consider every operation a success," Dr. Levy once told me, "when I don't cut myself."

The Finegolds smiled at my story.

Bea said they did not know too many people at the Pirates' office these days, but mentioned Jeanie Donatelli and Sally O'Leary as longtime favorites of the Finegolds. Donatelli had been the secretary to Joe L. Brown, and was still working in the same capacity for Cam Bonifay, the current general manager of the Pirates. Donatelli was in Bradenton, Florida with the ballteam at spring training. O'Leary had been working in the Pirates' publicity office over 30 years.

"He was a typical family doctor," said O'Leary. "He was available to anybody and everybody all the time. That's what I remember best about him. You could go into his office at the Jenkins Arcade, and he would take care of you right away. He might even have you come in through the back door. He had samples there and he'd take care of you right on the spot. He was there for all the players and their families and the staff. He took care of everybody."

356

Dr. Joseph M. Finegold checks out ElRoy Face's injured hand at spring training camp.

Dr. Finegold's former nurse, Pat Koval, is kissed by Pirates manager Danny Murtaugh when she married Pirates pitcher Bob Friend in ceremonies at Verona, N.J. at end of 1957 season. Murtaugh was matchmaker in this romance.

He was more than a doctor to many of them.

Bob Friend's wife Pat was a nurse for Dr. Finegold. "What a solid guy," offered Friend when I asked him about Dr. Finegold. "Everybody leaned on that guy. He was an important cog of our team. Those kinda guys only come along once in a lifetime."

Clemente was always worried about what he was going to do after his ballplaying career was over. He was always talking about different things that interested him. "He was always concerned he would not be able to make a living," said Bea Finegold. I told Bea that Vera Clemente and Phil Dorsey had both told me that Roberto often told them he didn't expect to live long, and was always telling them to do this or do that because he wasn't going to be around much longer. "Isn't that eerie?" said Bea. "Wonder why he felt that way?"

Bea traveled with her husband most of the time when he went on road trips with the Pirates. "He preferred it that way, and Joe L. Brown was very understanding," said Bea, looking back to better days.

"We went on a trip to California, and Roberto asked my husband to go with him to a shoe store in Los Angeles," said Bea. "He saw how the ballplayers were always buying expensive shoes and boots, and he thought he might want to buy a shoe store someday and operate it.

"He had my husband try on some boots, which were in fashion at the time. Roberto bought him a pair. It was about 98 degrees in California at the time, and my husband didn't wear high boots, to begin with. When Willie Stargell saw him, he said, 'Now you're one of the brothers!' He treasured those times with the players and the way they kidded him all the time."

Sometimes this was misinterpreted, Bea pointed out. "When Les Biederman retired and went off the baseball beat, his place was taken by a fellow named Bill Christine," she related. "One day, Christine was in the clubhouse, standing behind a pillar, as my husband and Roberto were ribbing each other. Joe got the last word by saying, 'If you don't like it, you can go back to Puerto Rico!' There was a story in the next day's paper saying that Dr. Finegold and Clemente were feuding. Joe Brown told my husband not to say anything about the story, not to lend any credence to it. Joe said if we talked about it, we'd make it look like there was something to the story. My husband and Clemente couldn't have been any closer. He loved all the players. Roberto was one of his favorites. He was like a racehorse. He just required special attention."

When I suggested that Dr. Finegold was not being totally forthright with me when he would not concede that Clemente was a chronic patient. "You have to understand something about my husband," said Bea. "He loves the whole world."

Then she offered some background on her husband that I had never heard before.

"He did surgery overseas during World War II," she said. "He was wounded and received the purple heart and the bronze star. He went in behind General Patton. He was in a M.A.S.H. unit.

"At first, he was examining inductees at the draft board, and he couldn't stand sending other people's children off to the service. So he volunteered to go himself. They sent him to Massachusetts General Hospital for a crash course in amputations before they sent him overseas. He went to Africa and then he went to Italy. He participated in the assault landing at Anzio. He was in the European Theater from 1942 to 1946 and, after a short leave at home, he was scheduled to go to Japan when the war ended."

So he has battle ribbons in addition to his three World Series rings. He was looking after the Pirates when they won it all in 1960, 1971 and 1979. "Doc Finegold was known throughout baseball," said former Pirates publicist Jack Berger. "He was a beloved and respected man." There were no pictures of Doc with any of the Pirates on the walls of the Finegold home.

"I'll take the blame for that," said Bea. "I've been working (in retail sales) all these years, too, and I never got around to it. We should be a little better organized. But we're not."

Her husband should have been in better health, too, but he was not. It hurts to see people you love get old.

"When he was younger, he had such tremendous energy," said Bea. "He loved all those boys. He was there through some great years. It was a wonderful part of his life.

"He's grateful for the wonderful experiences he has had. He's led a multi-faceted life. You take it one day at a time. Each day is important to him now. He's a doctor, and he knows his situation, and he knows he's living on borrowed time."

Dr. Finegold in foreground is surrounded by his beloved friends in Pirates clubhouse following 1960 World Series victory. They were, from left to right, John Hallahan, Bill Virdon, Joey Diven, Danny Whelan, Don Hoak, Bill Mazeroski, Joe Brown and Dick Groat.

"His spirit finds
its way into the
spirit world,
lifted on the wind
above the grandeur
and beauty of the earth."
—Yellow Wolf
Kiowa Indian
1920

Susan Wagner
Clemente Statue Is Hers

*"Roberto Clemente was
like an artist's dream."*

Susan Wagner was cutting away at the soft rose-brown clay, with what looked like a surgical tool, a scalpel, changing the chin of Roberto Clemente. This was a bust of Roberto Clemente, mind you, not the statue of Roberto Clemente. This was sort of a preliminary or conceptual model for what may turn out to be the biggest and best-known project of her life. Susan Wagner is a sculptor, or a sculptress, whichever you prefer. She sculpted the statue of Roberto Clemente that was scheduled to be unveiled at ceremonies for the 1994 Baseball All-Star Game at Three Rivers Stadium.

The room was full of natural light, and it fell on the face of Roberto Clemente and Susan Wagner, as she worked away to show me how she did what she did.

"When I knew I had finally gotten his face right," she related. "I stood back and stared at him. And then I cried."

She wouldn't say anything about the statue itself. It was being cast in bronze at Tallix Moris Singer, Inc., a fine arts foundry in Beacon, New York, near Newburgh, about an hour's drive north of New York City. The Pirates had put a veil of secrecy on the project, swearing her to silence about all aspects of the statue: what it looked like, what sort of pose Clemente would be in, whether he was smiling or serious, whether he was reaching out to poke a single into right field, or whether he was making a basket catch. No one outside of the family and club administrators such as Steve Greenberg, vice-president for marketing and operations, were to see it until the official unveiling. L.D. Asterino was the architect. Roberto's sons, Roberto Jr. and Luis, liked what they saw, and gave their approval for the statue to be cast.

"I loved it," remarked Roberto Jr., after going to Beacon with his brother Luis, along with Alicia Berns, a New York-based agent who represents the Clemente estate, and her husband Norman. "I loved everything, the details. I think why she did such a wonderful job is because she wanted to do this so badly. She convinced people that she was the one to do it. We loved it."

Their mother had mixed emotions about the statue, when she first heard about the project. "What if it doesn't look like him?" Vera Clemente asked aloud. But she liked the collage, or renderings, she was shown. Susan Wagner would not say what the statue looked like. This was all secret stuff, not to be divulged even if a writer put a sculpting tool to the sculptor's throat.

"I'm not allowed to tell what it will look like," she said. "That's under wraps. They don't want it leaked."

361

I also recognized the feeling and the expression of how she felt about completing her end of the assignment. "It was exactly like having a baby," she said. "You're happy and blue at the same time. There's a sense of loss."

I did get the impression, however, from a lengthy discussion with Susan Wagner that it would, indeed, look like Roberto Clemente, and that he would have a proud look about him, and that Pittsburghers could take pride in Susan Wagner's work.

After all, she is one of us: a Pittsburgh-born and bred artist. She and her husband, Richard, reside in a turn-of-the-century house on South Aiken Avenue in a little-known East End community called Friendship, that is a piano-player's long finger of Bloomfield that stretches between Garfield and Shadyside, toward East Liberty.

Some very rich people once resided on this street, but that was a long time ago. "The man who created Kennywood Park lived just down the street; it's the house with the two cement lions out front," interjected Susan Wagner. "Phil Musick grew up in this area."

So did Bill Hillgrove, a colleague of Musick's at WTAE Radio, and "the voice of Pitt sports." Musick was working on a photo book of Roberto Clemente at this same time. As a long-time fan of his work, I was looking forward to his book as well as completing my own. Some of the homes on South Aiken Avenue have been restored and are beautiful, especially inside, and some have been allowed to deteriorate, and scar the landscape. It's a mixed bag. The Wagners have put in a lot of work on their house. It has the touch of an artist wherever one looks. Susan says she furnished it from house sales, garage sales, flea markets. It has an eclectic look about it, but the colors are mostly on the soft side, and the rooms have an inviting, comfortable look. There are extra-thick moldings everywhere, along the ceilings, at every doorway, and the floors and moldings are oak, birch, cherry, and black walnut, the kind that would cost a fortune these days. The floors are quarter-cut oak with borders of black walnut, which you don't find much anymore. Some woodwork was painted white, which was a sign of wealth in those days, says Susan Wagner. The fireplaces are all different, the stairway wide and impressive, as if Scarlett O'Hara might descend the steps at any moment. There is a jukebox in the lobby, and another one upstairs.

Some of the rooms aren't quite finished, and there's also the look one finds in apartments inhabited by graduate level college students in nearby Oakland and Shadyside. On one shelf in a third-floor office, for instance, was an empty Iron City beer can with Clemente's likeness on it. A souvenir, so to speak. Open books were scattered about the top of a desk, with a word processor at the ready.

Susan Wagner works in the third floor of this house, with lots of natural light streaming through windows, even some stained glass. There are strips of stained glass at the top of all the windows in the house.

In the corner of her work studio, there was a stand-up white and gray Westinghouse broiler, with a storage cabinet below it, that caught my eye. Susan said she used it to heat her clay. It looked exactly like

Sculptress Susan Wagner works on bust of Roberto Clemente she used to land commission to create Clemente statue at Three Rivers Stadium. Her studio is in third floor room of her home in city's Friendship section.

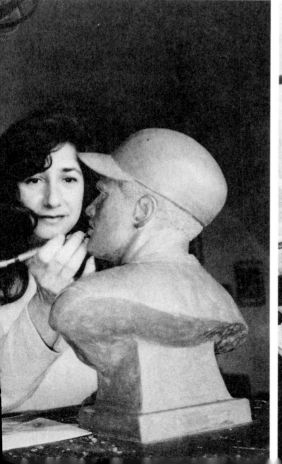

one we had alongside the stairway leading to our kitchen when I was a kid. There was a shelf on the wall above that broiler in our home that held a radio. My mother used to listen to Pirates' ballgames on that radio while she was doing her ironing. That's how I was introduced to Pirates baseball.

As a child, Susan Wagner remembers sitting out on the backyard patio with her father listening to radio broadcasts of Pirates baseball games. "I liked the sounds. That meant summer to me," said Susan Wagner.

As for the early enchantment with Clemente, she recalled, "I remember hearing about his death on the radio, and I remember my parents being sad. My mother cried."

Susan Wagner was introduced to live Bucco baseball because of the Clemente statue. She had, unbelievably enough, never been to a baseball game at Three Rivers Stadium or Forbes Field, though she was 43 years old, and had lived in several locales in Greater Pittsburgh. Her father had gone to games at Forbes Field, but has never been to Three Rivers Stadium. He scorns the place, like so many Pirate fans from his generation.

She went to see a game with some women friends in the summer of 1993, and it was both an exciting and scary experience. "My friends were so proud about me being chosen to do the statue that they told everyone around us about it," she recalled. "They said, 'Susie is doing the Clemente statue.' People were coming over, shaking my hand and asking me for my autograph. They wanted to touch me. They were talking to me about the statue, how they wanted it to look. Everyone was in love with this man. It was frightening. They were asking me how I was going to do it. By the end of the game, I was terrified. They begged me not to do a Caliguiri."

That was a critical reference to the statue of Richard Caliguiri, the former mayor of Pittsburgh who died while in office, that stands on Grant Street in front of the City-County Building. It's been called "the swamp thing" because it looks like the mayor had just emerged from a swamp. It looks like he's clothed in wet leaves or seaweed, and that something is dripping from him. It's a matter of style. Some cynics say its presence only adds to the homeless population of Downtown Pittsburgh.

She was aware of the criticism of the Caliguiri statue, as well as the popular acceptance of the statue of Steelers owner Art Rooney that was dedicated in ceremonies outside Three Rivers Stadium on October 7, 1990. The Rooneys had definite ideas about the sort of statue that would befit their father's image and his relationship with the fans. It was done by Raymond Kaskey, who had grown up in Carrick and had a degree in architecture from Carnegie Mellon University, and whose parents lived in nearby Avalon. Art Rooney would have approved. People particularly like the fact that the Rooney statue is close to the ground, and it's possible to sit on a bench beside him — yes, him, not it — or to walk up to him and hold his hand. "I really like that statue; I think it's great," said Susan Wagner. I told her I often visit that statue, and actually find myself talking to Art Rooney. It's that real. It might be the Catholic influence in my upbringing that makes it seem natural to talk to statues.

When the word got out about the planned Clemente statue, Susan Wagner said she started to get telephone calls from people who knew him, such as Sister Mary Paul, a nun who knew Roberto, and wanted to find out what Susan Wagner was doing. "Another woman called and ended up crying on the phone," said Susan Wagner. "They were very leery. This was a man they loved, and I had to do a good job."

Susan Wagner was aware that Pittsburgh provided a tough audience. Major art projects had been submarined in advance in Pittsburgh because of public criticism over planned works. The Three Rivers Art Festival is always a controversial forum. "What's it gonna look like, Susan?" became a popular refrain.

She was asked more questions along these lines when she appeared at Shaler Area Middle School just before Thanksgiving the previous year to speak to students who had a goal to raise $10,000 for the statue fund in a "Read For Roberto" program aimed at boosting book-reading among the students and doing something worthwhile in the community at the same time.

"I sculpted a baseball mitt for them," she said. "They were great kids; they were so enthusiastic. They were going to own a piece of the statue."

Roberto Clemente would be the second Pirate with a statue outside the team's home park. Back in 1955, a statue of Honus Wagner — no relation to Susan — was dedicated in Schenley Park, near the bleachers at Forbes Field and, with the Pirates, moved to Three Rivers Stadium in 1970. That, too, has always been a popular statue, though it's high up on a pedestal.

"I work through realism," said Susan Wagner. "That's my strength. I don't know how many times I did his face all over again, to make sure I was getting it right. There was a lot of pressure on me — to do it right. I talked to the girl who did the song about Roberto Clemente, and she told me she felt the same way.

"I am trying to please the people of Pittsburgh and not other artists. This is Roberto and I fell in love with him. He was a beautiful man. Roberto Clemente was like an artist's dream. I had always wanted to do him. I had even done a picture of him for *The Pitt News* during my student days. I can't let these people down, I thought. I have to make it look like Roberto.

"The creative process is so difficult to begin with. And then you have the additional burden of pleasing people."

The more thoughts and ideas that Susan Wagner and I shared with each other, the more we realized how much we had in common. I was in the home stretch of completing this book on Roberto Clemente. Things had started to happen that were unreal, people were dropping down on me out of the heavens that I had wanted to interview. The Clementes came to Pittsburgh and they were so easy to talk to, and I was so comfortable in their company. They approved of what I was doing. They were eager to help, to share stories and personal sentiments. We were all on the same page. Ballplayers appeared that I wanted to talk to, from Utah, Alabama, Florida and Ohio, coming to Pittsburgh for the Piratefest, and it was all coming together.

I, too, became more aware of the special feeling that fans had for Roberto Clemente, how they cherished his memory, how he had been a part of their lives, of growing up, and how saddened they were when they learned that he had died in an airplane crash off the coast of his native Puerto Rico on New Year's Eve, 1972. So many remembered where they were when they got the bad news. It was a benchmark in their lives.

I was away from Pittsburgh, from 1968 to 1978, working in Miami and New York, and that's another reason I didn't realize the almost religious zeal Pirates fans felt for Roberto Clemente.

I found myself praying for guidance, for direction, for the ability to do this book right, and provide Pittsburghers and Clemente's family and his fans everywhere with a book that would please them. That would do credit to Clemente's special skills and enduring spirit. That would show the specialness of the sports scene and the people of Pittsburgh.

Susan Wagner liked the fact that Clemente was a humanitarian.

"When you're in any of the arts, what you really have to do is give," she said. "When you give, that's when you are rewarded. It's serving a wonderful purpose. It's helping people."

"It's a Pittsburgh statue . . .
I have to sculpt it."
— Susan Wagner

Susan Wagner is a 1981 graduate of the University of Pittsburgh. She has a bachelor's degree in art and anthropology. Her husband Richard has an engineering degree from Pitt, plus a master's in telecommunications. He works for Westinghouse Electric Corporation, solving computer software problems. Their diplomas on the wall of Richard's office looked just like mine. They were Pitt people. Another link. She said she had done illustrations for *The Pitt News*, the student newspaper. Another link. "My dad tells me I was born at Allegheny General Hospital on the North Side," she said. "We lived in Springdale and Homewood, and I went to high school in Penn Hills. Then I had an apartment in Monroeville and then with my parents in Point Breeze. And now I'm in Friendship."

I asked Susan Wagner how she was chosen to do the statue. She said the Pirates put out a call for artists to submit their ideas for a statue of Roberto Clemente. She believes about eight or nine artists answered the call, including one from Puerto Rico and two from New York. "You had to put your idea in a three-dimensional form," she said.

I asked her how she heard about the call, and that's when I learned something that seems to have made Susan Wagner a natural choice for the assignment.

366

Some of Pittsburgh's most popular statues

Pittsburgh Steelers

Steelers owner Art Rooney

Pittsburgh Pirates

Honus Wagner at Forbes Field

Jim O'Brien

Mayor Richard Caliguiri

Jim O'Brien

Doughboy in Lawrenceville

"I was up in Cooperstown when I heard about it," she said. "I thought, 'It's a Pittsburgh statue; maybe I'll have a chance. I have to sculpt it.'"

"What were you doing in Cooperstown?" I asked.

It turned out that Susan Wagner had sculpted the official likenesses of about 50 Hall of Fame baseball players, managers and owners over a ten-year period. Anyone who has visited the National Baseball Hall of Fame and Museum in upstate New York has seen what amounts to a personal exhibition of her work.

Since 1983, this artist has completed the bas relief bronze plaques of the inductees for the Baseball Hall of Fame. She did most of these without having ever attended a major league baseball game, until the summer of 1993.

The Pirates were unaware that she had been doing these plaques for the Hall of Fame when she was the unanimous choice to do the Clemente statue. The artists were not permitted to identify themselves when they submitted their entries. She was chosen anonymously. "Some people figure I got this because I had connections," she said. "That's not so."

Matthews International Corporation, a Pittsburgh bronze foundry located on West Liberty Avenue near the suburban entrance to the Liberty Tunnels, has been producing the plaques off and on for over 30 years. The company's bronze division selected Susan Wagner to do the sculpting on a free-lance basis.

It was the turning point in her career. She had been doing sculpting work in West Virginia and Greensburg, while supporting herself as a waitress, saleswoman and word processor. She got her first job at Matthews doing memorial ledgers, or gravemarkers.

Her moonlighting sculpting work picked up to the point where in 1984 she was able to become a full-time artist.

She did the Desert Storm War Memorial now on the base of the U.S. Army 14th Quartermaster Battalion in Greensburg.

She has done all of the work for the Baseball Hall of Fame strictly from photographs. She did the same thing with the Clemente statue project, also seeking out many who knew him to make sure she captured his personality and style as well as his likeness. "I had to get to know him," she said.

She remembered a quote about Clemente that captured him well, she thought, though she wasn't sure how to pronounce the name of the man who said it, Bowie Kuhn, the former commissioner of baseball. "He had about him a touch of royalty," Kuhn had said of Clemente. That went well with what Wagner was attempting to do.

"I'm a realist artist. I try to get an exact likeness, not my interpretation of the person. I want to show the special characteristics that each individual has."

She said she previously felt the most pressure when Willie Stargell was the lone inductee to the Baseball Hall of Fame in 1988. "He was right here in Pittsburgh, and I knew I'd hear about it if I didn't do it right," she said of her plaque portrayal of the Pirates' slugger.

Joe Gabig, sales manager for the bronze division at Matthews International, said the players and their families have always been positive in their response to the plaques. "Susan is a real pro," said Gabig. "We get nothing but compliments on her work."

Bill Guilfoile, vice-president of the Hall of Fame, and a former publicist for the Pittsburgh Pirates, comes to Pittsburgh each year to check out Susan Wagner's work before they are cast in bronze.

"She's outstanding," Guilfoile says. "Whenever we want the plaques done, we ask for Susan."

Guilfoile checks them for accuracy, and she's able to make any alterations he might suggest. "They're still in clay form," she said. "I can make them (any changes) on the spot. Once we have his approval, the models are cast in bronze."

She loved the challenge and the audience. "I knew all of America would see this," she said of her Hall of Fame efforts. "The first year, they found nothing wrong with them, and we've had a wonderful relationship ever since."

There's another Pittsburgh connection at Cooperstown. When Guilfoile comes to Pittsburgh to see Susan Wagner, he also visits Geyer Printing, on the Oakland side of the Bloomfield Bridge, where the Hall of Fame's attractive annual guidebook is printed.

"I saw Clemente play."
— Jim Graham

Susan Wagner's father stopped by during my visit, entering through the back door and into the kitchen where I was enjoying a coffee Susan Wagner had offered to me. His name is Jim Graham. He spoke of his pride in what his daughter was doing. "She's done this all on her own," he said. "She's been drawing like this since she first went to grade school. She didn't get any of this talent from me or her mother."

He remembers her always drawing pictures of horses and cats. Those were her favorites. Today, she has cats named Malcolm and Kimberly, but no horse.

Her father was having some problems with a hearing aid. "I think the battery went low on me," he apologized. I had to holler when I asked him questions, and he still had difficulty hearing me. He answered questions I didn't ask.

He said that he remembers all the way back to Pie Traynor as a kid. He always liked Ralph Kiner and Vernon Law, and that he also liked Roberto Clemente. "Sure, I saw Clemente play," said Jim Graham. "I had one difference with him, however. He was a right-handed hitter, yet he was always hitting the ball into right field. He should have been hitting the ball to left field and up the middle. I've always followed the Pirates, especially when they were contenders. You have to be a contender in this town."

Susan Wagner flinched. Hearing her dad being critical of The Great Roberto Clemente and the Pirates when they're not contenders might have made her realize that criticism can come freely from Pittsburghers, no matter the subject. She can expect more of the same.

Jim Graham, who was 77, had worked as a securities broker for Mellon Bank before retiring in 1979. "Our office was at William Penn Way and Fifth Avenue when the Pirates won the World Series in 1960," he recalled. "Someone pulled the wires down on a trolley car in front of the clock at Kaufmann's Department Store. Traffic was stalled, but no one cared. It was crazy. It was some celebration. Now, to see my daughter doing this, I feel a great pride."

Jim Graham looks on with pride as his daughter, Susan Wagner, works in her studio on Clemente bust.

Jim O'Brien

Phil Dorsey
Roberto's Buddy

"Look at a picture of him.
His eyes follow you."
— Dorsey on Clemente

Phil Dorsey was Roberto Clemente's closest friend during his days in Pittsburgh. Dorsey was a postal worker at the main clearing office, first in Downtown and then the North Side. They were introduced to each other one day in 1955 at Forbes Field by Bob Friend, the Pirates pitcher. Friend and Dorsey served in the same military reserve unit. Dorsey was a first sergeant in the Army, a Korean combat veteran, a supervisor in customer service at the post office. Dorsey was a black man who even today can speak only a few words of Spanish. Dorsey and Clemente clicked, and they became constant companions.

Dorsey was a frequent visitor to the Pirates clubhouse, traveled to other cities with the team from time to time, and was always waiting for Clemente at the airport in Pittsburgh when the Pirates returned from a road trip. No matter the hour, Phil was waiting at the curb.

"He was a good guy," recalls former Pirates pitcher Dave Giusti. "He was always looking to do something for somebody. He was accepted for what he was — Clemente's valet."

Dorsey befriended Clemente when Clemente was a single man from a foreign country, lonely and confused by his surroundings and a strange language, and the demands of major league baseball. They went to movie theaters and restaurants together. Clemente was as fond of Chinese food as he was his native cuisine. They both liked to shoot pool and play cards. They would split a hundred pennies and play blackjack for hours.

They were always in some kind of competition. "And no matter what it was, Robby hated to lose," Dorsey said. "He was tough. If I would get 20, he would come up with 21. He would usually wind up with all my pennies."

"I thought they should go first class."
— Dorsey on his bosses

Dorsey looked after Clemente's every need. He was, at once, a friend, chauffeur, valet, business manager and, later on, a baby-sitter for the Pirates right fielder and his family after Roberto married Vera Christina Zabala from his hometown of Carolina, Puerto Rico and they had three sons.

Clemente was a fussy sort, a clean freak. Dorsey was disorderly in his housekeeping. In that respect, they were like Felix Unger and Oscar Madison in Neil Simon's "The Odd Couple." However, Dorsey did keep Clemente's car clean and well maintained, and would later provide similar service for Willie Stargell, Manny Sanguillen and Bill Madlock. But he did more for Clemente, and was closer to Clemente, than he was any of the other Pirates.

Philip Wellington Dorsey III, his full handle, always drove the classiest cars in Pittsburgh: a Cadillac of his own, a Cadillac of Clemente's, a Rolls Royce that belonged to Madlock. He drove his superiors at the post office from here to there in the city in those cars. Everyone was looking good. "I thought they should go first class," he said. Dorsey was making good money — between $48,000 and $50,000 a year ultimately — and had come a long way from his boyhood days in Homewood and Westinghouse High School ("I played a little bit of ball there for Pro Burton.") At the request of his bosses, he brought Clemente to the post office a few times, to meet the other workers, to sign autographs. Dorsey secured free tickets to the Pirates' games for other employees. One of my closest boyhood friends, Rick Reagan, who quarterbacked our sandlot football teams, was a co-worker. So was "Tiger Paul" Auslander, once Pitt's unofficial basketball mascot.

Dorsey walked tall through the post office. Understandably, he felt like a big man. Dorsey doesn't acknowledge it now, but he played the role as Clemente's right-hand man to the hilt.

"How do you say 'no' to your boss?"
— Phil Dorsey

That was the history of their relationship. I had seen Dorsey in Clemente's company on many occasions. It all seemed so long ago as I sat in the cluttered living room of Dorsey's home in the western end of East Liberty, bordering Garfield and Bloomfield. Clemente had died and Dorsey was serving a prison sentence. All that could go wrong in his life had gone wrong. Or so it seemed, anyhow.

This was the first weekend in February, 1994, and Dorsey had only a few weeks left to serve of his incarceration before he would again be a free man. February 17 was the big day, his last day in confinement. "I'm not going to let this break me," he said convincingly. There was nothing downbeat about Dorsey's demeanor.

Dorsey's close-cropped hair had turned white since I last saw him, as if he'd just come in out of the snow. He was wearing a white T-shirt with a Bartles & Jaymes inscription across his still sturdy chest, Army issue khaki pants — a leftover, no doubt, from his military days — and white sweat socks. He slipped on some shoes when I invited him to go out for lunch and a tour of the neighborhood.

I mentioned that I needed to stop somewhere and get some film. He called upstairs to his daughter and told her to bring me a roll of film. Just like that. I was set to shoot some more pictures.

Let's just say I was as eager to get out of his house as he was to get out of prison. The set-up could be best described as Early American clutter. It was a wall-to-wall mess. Dorsey excused the appearance of

372

Phil Dorsey seemed to always be at Roberto Clemente's side whenever he was signing autographs or meeting fans.

the house by saying, "they're painting the place," pointing to freshly-painted blue walls, but that could hardly account for the condition of the rooms I squeezed in and out of, one pile of items after another pile of items, as Dorsey insisted on showing me food supplies on the back-porch, which he had purchased sometime back at a PX in an area military facility. He said he had also been accused of trading stamps for food, and bartering with stamps for other materials.

Dorsey was home for the weekend on what is called "house arrest." He had two more weeks to serve of a 27-month sentence for crimes committed in the early '90s while working at the North Side postal office. His attorney was Larry O'Toole, who had become a judge in the Common Pleas Court. Dorsey was accused of stealing a large amount of stamps. The official charges for which he was imprisoned, according to Dorsey, were for "false statement, conversion of postal property and unlawful use of labels." He said his supervisor served an 18-month sentence for his involvement. "I just did what he told me to do," Dorsey said. "I didn't make a dime on what we did. This was when the cost of postage for a first-class letter went up from 25 to 29 cents. My boss said we were destroying stuff that could be sold to collectors. Like we had 25 cent pre-stamped envelopes celebrating the Steelers winning the Super Bowls. We were selling stamps and envelopes that were supposed to have been destroyed, but we were selling them through the post office. The government got all the money. My boss wanted to boost our business volume so it would look like he was doing a great job. We were ranked 15th and he wanted to be No. 1."

Many of these stamps and embossed pre-stamped envelopes — in the hundreds of thousands, for the record — were found in Dorsey's home by postal inspectors. "They came in here like gangbusters or something; there were 16 of them!" recalled Dorsey. "They were here only because we didn't have any place to store them at the post office." He admitted he gave some of them away to friends, but insists he did not sell them.

"If Ollie North did what he did and got off with it," Dorsey snapped, "how come they put me away?"

Many of his friends on the Pirates had been questioned by postal inspectors during the investigation. When I asked him if he hadn't felt embarrassed by what happened to him, considering his strong association with the Clemente family, he shrugged his round shoulders.

During my visit in his home, Dorsey spent most of the time declaring his innocence of any wrongdoing. To hear Dorsey, he simply followed his boss's orders — "How do you say 'no' to your boss? He's the one who promoted me," he pleaded — and was wrongly accused and convicted. It was a familiar refrain. Who knows? "I was a first sergeant in the Army. When they gave you orders, you might think it's wrong, but you do it."

Dorsey had served 18 months of his sentence in a federal prison in Big Spring, Texas, just east of Midland and Odessa, and the southeast corner of New Mexico, or a long way from East Liberty. ("I'm the first guy they ever sent from Pennsylvania to Texas. Why? Was I a danger to society?")

Big Spring is full of big, bad men. "They had murderers, kidnappers and drug peddlers there," he said. "They had guys doing 10 to 20 years for selling $20 worth of cocaine." More recently, Dorsey was in a half-way house of sorts out in New Brighton, near Beaver Falls, just west of the Pittsburgh International Airport. He signed out of the New Brighton facility, called Penn Pavilion (located, coincidentally enough, at 701 Penn Avenue) at 5 p.m. on Friday and had to be back by 5 p.m. Sunday. During the two nights he was at home, he had a 9 p.m. curfew, and had to call in, and officials would call him at home to check on his whereabouts at any time after that. "I can't go out from 9 to 6," he said.

What really bothered him, he said, was that his daughter was dismissed from her job as a custodian at the post office soon after his conviction. She remained unemployed.

The only thing that was in order in the rooms I toured was an impressive collection of stamps, neatly filed away in albums, filling several shelves. "I've been a stamp collector for a long time," Dorsey said, without a hint of a smile. Those stamps had been confiscated by postal inspectors, but returned to Dorsey when they were deemed his legitimate possession.

Phil knows stamps. He also knows his Pirates. He showed me a poster-sized version of a 20 cent stamp to pay tribute to Roberto Clemente. "I told them it should be a 21 cent stamp; it would have been more appropriate," Dorsey said, "and I told them he shouldn't be wearing a white cap. The Pirates never wore a white cap like this. But they never listened to me."

His daughter, Patti Jo, and her son, named Philip Wellington Dorsey IV, live at Dorsey's home on Broad Street, on a hillside just above the Eat'n Park Restaurant on Penn Avenue. It's less than a mile from the Bloomfield home of Susan Wagner, the sculptress of the Roberto Clemente statue whom I had visited only minutes earlier on the other side, or nicer side, of Penn Avenue. "We were the first blacks on Broad Street," Dorsey said. "My kids were going to Peabody High School. It was nice. But now these streets are dangerous. It's scary."

Dorsey's son, Philip S., has two sons and lives in New Jersey.

Dorsey's home is a block away from the Pennley Park Apartments where the Clementes and several other Latin and black ballplayers on the Pirates lived in the mid-to-late '60s. It was familiar territory. That's where my wife Kathie and I lived — for $180 a month for a two-bedroom apartment — when it was a fairly new apartment complex when we were married in the summer of 1967. We lived on the third floor in one wing, overlooking the neighborhood fire station and a playground, and the Clementes lived on the top floor of the adjoining four-story building.

Those days were coming back to me in a rush as I rode by the apartments, and Dorsey pointed out where the Clemente's apartment was located. He mentioned that Matty Alou, Juan Pizarro, Jose Pagan, Maury Wills and Alvin O'Neal McBean also lived there then. He said Manny Sanguillen and Rennie Stennett lived there later on.

"I brought them here," said Dorsey, boasting a bit. "I got them a rate here. But they had to pay for a full year's rental, even though

375

they weren't here during the off-season. And I caught them (the apartment landlord) renting one of the apartments out to someone else when one of the players wasn't here. They just put his furniture in storage downstairs and put someone else in there."

The neighborhood brought back some memories, good and bad. Broudy's Bar & Restaurant was still there on North Negley Avenue, but Dorsey said it had different owners, and wasn't the same. I had eaten hot roast beef and turkey sandwiches there, as well as draft beer in icy mugs. Sportswriter Bob Smizik was a frequent barside companion. His brother, Frank, a Pittsburgh educator, lived at Pennley Park back then, nor far from their boyhood home in Stanton Heights. There was a noisy neighbor named Bucky Gloucester who used to raise a ruckus at Broudy's on weekend nights.

I remembered another neighbor, a professional wrestler named Professor Tanaka. I remembered seeing some tenants carrying a television set through the parking lot one day and kidding them about doing second-story work. And, to my later amazement, that's exactly what they were doing. They were arrested for stealing in the building.

It was at Pennley Park that I got the telephone call telling me that my father was slipping away. He would die at Homestead Hospital before Kathie and I could get there that morning. He died from emphysema, the same as Harvey Haddix. He was 63.

Dorsey would be 68 in a month, and would be able to celebrate his birthday wherever he wished. His mother had died out in California while he was incarcerated, and he felt badly that he missed her burial. His brother took care of everything.

"He's dead," Dorsey said of Clemente. "Now it's just me and my daughter and my grandson."

He said the Clementes call from time to time, to see how he's doing. I had told Vera that Phil would be home that weekend, and she said she would call him while she was in Pittsburgh. "She's a nice, nice person," said Dorsey. "She has to be to have been Clemente's wife."

His government pension was on hold, until debts were paid to the postal system, and he said he wasn't sure of its status. "I had 38 years, 11 months and 12 days to my credit," he said. "I served over three years of active military service in Korea." When I asked him if he saw action in Korea, he said, "Yeah, sure. I stayed in the Army reserve and I went to work at the post office when I came home."

He says he was set up. He believes some workers were jealous of him at the post office and were glad to see him get in trouble. "I heard I was getting too big for a nigger," he said.

Pittsburgh Phil Dorsey

376

il Dorsey points to fourth floor apartment where Roberto Clemente and his family
ed in late '60s at Pennley Park in East Liberty, near Dorsey's home. Dorsey was on
veekend leave with two weeks remaining on 27-month sentence for crimes commit-
l while working at Pittsburgh's main post office.

Roberto Clemente

USA 20c

FIRST DAY OF ISSUE

PIRATES

CAROLINA, PR
AUG
17
1984
00690

OFFICIAL FIRST DAY COVER

PITTSBURGH PIRATES

ROBERTO CLEMENTE

FIRST DAY COVER

OUTFIELD

"Phil's not a bad guy.
But he's a thief."
— Al Covelli
Postal Inspector

A different version of this story is offered by Al Covelli, the lead postal inspector on the case. Covelli, speaking from his office at the general mail facility at California Avenue on the city's North Side, said "This was a real black mark on the post office. It made our management of such affairs look bad; that we weren't monitoring our materials better.

"I come from Clairton and I've known guys I grew up with who got into trouble with the law," said the 55-year-old Covelli. "They're not necessarily bad guys. You're from Hazelwood; you know guys like that, too. Phil's not a bad guy. But he's a thief. He wanted to be a big shot."

According to postal inspection records and public documents, Dorsey was indicted on September 11, 1991. He was charged with eight counts of converting $275,700 worth of stamps, embossed stamped envelopes and philatelic (postage) materials to his own personal use. He was charged with five more counts of reporting falsely on postal service forms. On one occasion he reported that $150,000 worth of stamp stock had been destroyed when, in truth, it had not been. He was charged with one count of unlawful use of postal labels to avoid the payment of postage.

"He was sending stamps to his family, friends and ballplayers around the country," commented Covelli, "and he wasn't even using postage to send them. He certainly had enough stamps in his possession to do that."

Dorsey pleaded guilty to stealing $275,700 worth of stamps and embossed envelopes, according to Covelli, and he was sentenced to 27 months in prison by U.S. District Judge Alan N. Block. He was fined $4,800 by Judge Block on February 7, 1992.

Dorsey had been serving as the chairman of the destruction committee after postal rates were changed, and the order had come through to destroy the stamps at the former first-class rate. This was when stamps went from 25 cents to 29 cents for a one-ounce mailing.

"We took 11 inspectors, not 16, to his house," said Covelli. "I didn't want to arrest him at the post office and embarrass him in front of his friends. Plus, we had to go to his house because that's where he stored the stamps and envelopes. I needed all 11 guys, believe me.

"We carried stuff out of that house for six hours. The daughter was running around the neighborhood, picking up stamps from the neighbors. She had postal supplies in her room as well. That's why she was dismissed. I never saw anything like it in my 22 years in the postal inspection business.

"Phil kept telling us he had the stuff at his house because there was no place to store it at the post office. He wouldn't give up on that story. We never did find any evidence that he had sold any of the stamps.

379

"When I was upstairs in his house — and what a dump it was — I saw 12 large boxes of brand-new baseballs, Pirate warm-up jackets, brand new suits from one of the most expensive men's clothing stores Downtown. They'd never been worn. Phil wore the same outfit to work every day."

Covelli said the federal government put a freeze on Dorsey's pension in order to recover what he owed them, but Covelli said Phil would keep his pension. "I hate to tell you this," he said, "but once you put in 30 years in government service and you are 55 or older, you can commit murder, rape or steal whatever you want and you still get your pension. Phil will get his pension for the rest of his life, once he settles his debts.

"It's a shame, though. He could have retired three years ago, and taken a buyout. He was making good money, about $48,000 to $50,000. His daughter was making good money, too. He was in the limelight with the baseball players. And he had everything he needed. He got greedy.

"When they unveil that statue of Roberto Clemente at the All-Star Game, I wouldn't be surprised if Phil is in the front row."

"It was the best of times."
— Phil Dorsey

When Dorsey switched subjects and spoke of Clemente, his voice softened and lost its anger. "A lot of people didn't understand him, but he was easy to get along with," said Dorsey. "What we had was special. If they had to go someplace, they'd leave their kids with me. My wife, Carole, died in 1976. She looked after them, too.

"It was the best of times. From when he got here and he started learning the words, we were tight," Dorsey said. "Some of the Latins thought they were white, but Clemente knew he was black."

When Clemente first came to Pittsburgh after spring training in 1955, he lived in an apartment at Webster Hall, a hotel on Fifth Avenue in Oakland, in between St. Paul's Cathedral and Forbes Field.

Later he moved in with Roman Mejias, a Cuban who played right field briefly before Clemente came to the Pirates. Their apartment building, unknown to them, also housed working prostitutes.

Their male customers were coming and going at all hours. "Hey, who are these guys?" Clemente kept asking his friends. "How many different guys are staying here, and what do they do? They go in and out at some weird hours. I cannot get any sleep in this place."

By 1958, Clemente was living in the home of Stanley and Mame Garland in the Schenley Heights section, just above Schenley High School. Stanley also worked at the post office and the Garlands, like the Dorseys, attended Clemente's wedding in Puerto Rico.

The Pittsburgh Courier, a national black weekly newspaper with headquarters in the Hill District, accused Clemente in an editorial of not wanting to associate with black people. Dorsey remembers how upset Clemente was by that charge.

"Look at me," Clemente would say to Dorsey, "and tell me what you see. Tell me who I am. What am I? I am Puerto Rican. What else am I? Tell me what you see. What else am I besides Puerto Rican? You can see, tell me. I do not understand what they mean when they say I do not like to be around black people. I am a black man, but I would like to be around anyone who likes me and I like them.

"He said, 'You've got to be the best you can be, whatever you are.' He told me one time, 'To be a friend, you don't lie.' We didn't talk much about baseball. We were always talking about other things. I've had a good life. Clemente and those other guys trusted me and I feel like I didn't let them down. Hey, I had a job, I was making good money, and we became good friends. It was great. The papers made me out to be a bad guy when I got into this trouble, but that's not the truth.

"Our postmaster, Ed Coll, asked me if I thought I could get Clemente to come down to the post office. And he did. Another time, I took his ring down there from the '60 World Series and showed it to everyone.

"Joe O'Toole in the Pirates front office got mad at me because he thought I had control over him. But I didn't. I just looked after him. Roberto would give me money to send his mother a mail order, and I'd take care of it. I had good reason to be at the ballpark a lot. I've worked at the ballpark in the evening and on weekends. I belonged to Union No. 508, and I sold tickets at Three Rivers.

"I've gone to spring training with the team, even after Clemente's death. I would arrange my vacation time and my military leave and go down to Florida for a few weeks of spring training. The guys wouldn't let me pay for anything. Heck, Madlock even took me to Japan when he was playing there. They'd take me on trips, and Joe Brown would OK it.

"I was at the World Series in New York and in Baltimore both times. In fact, Roberto's mother stayed at my mother's place in New York during the '60 World Series. We were all one big family.

"Roberto was just a nice guy. I didn't pick his friends. He wasn't that close with a lot of people, outside of his own family. He always said Pittsburgh was his home, too. He loved the fans and the people here."

"We were all one big family."
— Phil Dorsey

Dorsey and I had lunch at the nearby Eat'n Park. I had been there many times during the past 15 years. My mother was living in Lawrenceville, a few miles west, and we would frequently go there for lunch. So it was a familiar setting. I had sat in the same booth with my mother on many occasions.

Dorsey smiled through wide-gapped teeth as he talked of his ordeal and of Roberto Clemente. He ordered a grilled cheese sandwich and a glass of lemonade. I wondered what it felt like for him to be able to order

381

whatever he wanted to eat, instead of having it determined for him by the day's offering at wherever he was doing time.

"We take things like this for granted," he said. Commenting on his relationship with Clemente, he said, "Somebody would say to him, 'Hey, Roberto, your chauffeur's here.' And he'd say, 'He's not my chauffeur. He's my friend.' He said I should get business cards printed up, listing me as personal manager to Roberto Clemente.

"No one had more women after them than Roberto, and that includes someone like Mario Lemieux," said Dorsey, diverting to a new topic. "White, black, Latin, you name it; they all wanted Clemente's attention. They were always asking me to introduce them to him, or handing me notes to give him. He was a handsome man, and he talked with his eyes. Look at a picture of him. His eyes follow you. His eyes always look like they're telling you something.

"He'd tell them, 'I need my sleep.' When he was single, he wasn't a priest or a brother. He was human. After he got married, he'd tell the women, 'Hey, I'm married. You lost.'

"He'd share a suite with someone else on the ballclub, and I did the same thing later with Stargell or Madlock, and I'd get the waiting room in between them. They'd have me get things for them, and they'd pay me back later. I screened calls for them. I remember for the 1971 World Series, Clemente bought more tickets for people and never got paid back. He'd have cousins up from Puerto Rico, and he'd pay for them to fly back and forth.

"He cared about people. He said, 'No matter what I would have been, from a garbageman to an electrician, I'd do my best. If I was going to be a garbageman, I'd be the best garbageman.' He never thought he was the best, and it drove him to be better.

"He had a hard time sleeping. He'd say to me, 'If I could sleep like you, I'd bat .400.' He'd stay up and watch Erroll Flynn swashbuckling movies. He loved Tyrone Power, too. When he was a kid, they came and filmed a Tyrone Power movie in San Juan. It was some kind of pirate movie. He remembered that." Phil paused a moment. "Oh, we had such good times together," he added.

"When we were in Puerto Rico, he used to give me money and have me get change. And we would walk around and he would give money to the kids. He would do things like that."

Dorsey disclosed some similar stories once in an interview with sportswriter Bill Christine. There was this occasion, Dorsey said, when Clemente was approached by a poorly-dressed man who was accompanied by two children outside of Forbes Field.

"I don't want your autograph, Roberto, but I just wanted to tell you that you're a helluva ballplayer," the man said.

Clemente continued to chat with the man, and learned that he had been laid off from his job at a Pittsburgh steel mill. Roberto took the man and his children out to dinner and, according to Dorsey, the tab came to around $40.

Dorsey shows off his stamp collection and his grandson, Philip Wellington Dorsey at his home in East Liberty.

On another occasion, Clemente came out of the ballpark and spotted a girl in a wheelchair with her mother standing behind her on a street corner. He asked them what was going on, and they told him they had missed their ride to Aliquippa. It had already been a long day, but Clemente invited them to get in his car and he gave them a ride home. Dorsey drove the car.

"He had this feeling that he would not live to be very old," Dorsey said, referring to Clemente's fatalistic tendencies. "His father was still alive and in his 90s, but Robby was always talking about what had to be done after he died. He acted like everybody he knew would outlive him. He was always telling me how to help Vera, and who to call and all, when something happened to him."

"Do you miss him?" I asked.

"I missed him more the first year after his death," said Dorsey. "It changed my schedule around so much."

"Do you pray to him?"

"I don't pray to him," replied Dorsey. "I don't know where he is. He told me there were caves under the water in that area where his plane went down. He could swim; he was a good swimmer. I figured he wasn't dead. I figured he'd gone into one of those caves, and that he would come back."

Kind of the way Errol Flynn and Tyrone Power did in those movies they watched together.

"He wasn't God and he wasn't the devil," declared Dorsey. "But I'd like everybody to know that he was closer to one than the other."

After I left Dorsey at the door of his home, I drove into Shadyside to Maser Galleries to buy some enlarged framed photographs of Forbes Field. They are a popular item, along with prints and photos of Roberto Clemente at the Walnut Street art gallery. The owner, Ron Maser, was a left-handed pitcher on the baseball team at the University of Pittsburgh during my student days. He was from McKeesport and drew regular rave reviews in *The Pitt News*, mostly because his best buddy, Ted Colton, also from McKeesport, was the sports editor. Maser has been in the art business for 18 years, and has had much success with sports themes, renderings by the likes of LeRoy Neiman and Bernard Fuchs, and Pittsburgh scenes, such as those by Nat Youngblood. One of his customers when I came into the store was, ironically enough, Pirates pitcher John Candelaria. "He's a regular customer; he's bought stuff here before," said Brenda Maser, the owner's wife.

Another note of irony: as I was driving, I was listening to the news reports on the car radio. A report came in from Jackson, Mississippi that the man who killed civil rights leader Medgar Evers in 1963 had finally been convicted. Byron De La Beckwith, the bombastic racist who eluded justice for 30 years, was convicted earlier in the day of murdering Evers. He was immediately sentenced to life in prison. Evers, a Mississippi field secretary for the NAACP, was shot getting out of his car shortly after midnight on June 12, 1963, after attending a meeting to watch a televised speech on civil rights by President Kennedy.

Roberto Clemente Jr.
The Oldest Son

"Everyone told me how lucky I was.
I didn't feel lucky, I felt lonely."

The headquarters office for the Roberto Clemente Foundation may have been the most sparsely furnished office in Downtown Pittsburgh. There were two desk units, a telephone and two framed prints of Roberto Clemente on the wall. That was it. It could have passed for a sports bookmaker's digs.

This was on the fifth floor of The Bank Tower, an historic building at Fourth Avenue and Wood Street. There is a PNC Bank on the first floor, an Integra Bank across Fourth, and the Abbott Building across Wood.

From the window, one could see the PPG complex, sparkling on a snowy, sunny afternoon in February, 1994. Roberto Clemente Jr., 28 and the oldest of three sons of Vera and Roberto Clemente, was running late. He was running around town, as he had been doing every day for months, soliciting support for his mission. His father never ran with more abandon, with more hell-bent determination.

Roberto Jr. wanted to properly memorialize his father, the famous Hall of Fame outfielder for the Pittsburgh Pirates, by establishing and developing an expanded youth baseball program in the urban communities of Pittsburgh. He wanted Pittsburgh to be better represented in the national amateur baseball picture. He wanted Pittsburgh kids to pick up baseball bats to play ball, not to battle a rival gang. He wanted to do something that day so that Pittsburgh children could have better tomorrows.

His late father, like Dr. Martin Luther King, had a dream. He wanted to sponsor and build sports communities for the children of his native Puerto Rico, to lift their lives, to give them something to enjoy, to help them grow, to give them an opportunity perhaps to play big league baseball like he did. Dr. King and Roberto Clemente were both killed too early in their lives to realize their dreams, one by an assassin's bullet in Memphis, the other in an airplane crash off the coast of San Juan while on a mission of mercy to help others.

And now Roberto Clemente Jr. was, like so many well-intentioned men and women before him, attempting to carry on the torch. To keep the flame alive. It would be a tough assignment. There were many problems in Pittsburgh with the inner-city youth, a growth of ill-intentioned gangs, of gang warfare, of senseless killings, drug-related drive-by shootings, mostly blacks vs. blacks, and most of the city's playgrounds and ballfields were deserted most of the time. It seemed like every day's news carried a report of another senseless killing. Overall crime was down in the city, we were told, but homicide was considerably up.

Parents feared for their children's safety and the children, for the most part, were not that interested in sports, or playing games these days. It wasn't cool. They were home, playing computer games, watching stupid stuff on television, or hanging out on street corners. Roberto Clemente Jr. wanted to change that. He thought his father would approve. He thought his father's name could open some doors. After all, Pittsburgh was preparing to host the 1994 Baseball All-Star Game, in early July, at Three Rivers Stadium. As part of the pre-All-Star Game festivities, a statue of Roberto Clemente was going to be unveiled.

Roberto Clemente's likeness appeared on huge billboards about town, videos on his life had sold out at the Giant Eagle stores throughout the tri-state area, he was featured in TV commercials aimed at calling attention to the All-Star Game and selling season tickets for the financially-strapped Pirates. Roberto Clemente had been the focal figure at the Piratefest, a mid-winter celebration of baseball aimed at keeping the fires burning for baseball fans, and there were posters, lithographs, calendars and books coming off the printing presses celebrating Clemente's career. And there were those framed likenesses on the walls of the office at the Bank Tower, and ones on the walls at the condominium unit Roberto Jr. and his wife were sharing in Robinson Township.

Roberto Jr. was hop-scotching around the streets of Downtown Pittsburgh, visiting the new mayor, Pittsburgh native son Tom Murphy — who grew up with a proper appreciation for sports, the Pirates and Roberto Clemente — city council members, county commissioners, news media officials, potential corporate supporters for his foundation. Anybody who might help him.

He was getting help. His office, for instance, was provided rent-free by an old friend of his father, Dan Galbreath. Dan's late father John, a Columbus, Ohio-based sportsman/entrepreneur, owned the Pirates when Roberto Clemente was the star attraction. He also owned The Galbreath Company, a commercial leasing and management firm headquartered at One Mellon Bank Center. His firm was responsible for leasing space at The Bank Tower. The building was owned by Ed Ryan, the founder of Ryan Homes, once the nation's largest home builders, and listed under his Merna Corporation aegis. Ryan had earlier donated the adjoining building, a failed midtown mall called The Bank Center, to nearby Point Park College. It had been renamed the Library Center, a combination of the Carnegie Downtown and business branch with the Point Park College library.

It is an oft-underappreciated part of Pittsburgh's landscape. The Bank Tower is a beautifully-restored old building. It is a blend of the old elegance of marble and Oriental carpets and the efficiency of modern office space. An impressive entrance greets tenants and visitors with its spiral marble staircase and brass elevator doors. There is more of the same along this Fourth Avenue stretch. It was familiar territory. During my junior and senior years at Taylor Allderdice High School, I used to go in and out of the buildings in this midtown area, picking

Roberto Clemente Jr. talks about his program to promote youth baseball and education programs in Pittsburgh as Pirates president Mark Sauer looks on at City-County Building.

Roberto Jr. sizes up statue of the late Mayor Richard Caliguiri, a big fan of his father.

up copy for the real estate section of the classified ads for *The Pittsburgh Press*. I was a copy boy, and I was picking up copy for the Sunday paper.

I was daydreaming, thinking back to those days, when Roberto Clemente Jr. came into the office. He is 5-10, about 200 pounds, a little over his playing weight, a little more than his father in his prime, and a cheerful fellow. He always dresses well, just like his dad. The pastel colors he favors are more Miami and Puerto Rico than Monroeville and Pittsburgh, but he has quickly recaptured an old home in Pittsburgh, a city his father and family came to love, where he spent much of his youth, especially his summers.

Suddenly, the room did not seem so empty anymore. Like his father, Roberto Jr. can light up a room. A woman named Vivian Lavery gave him a handful of messages on pink note papers. Ms. Lavery is a secretary/receptionist whose services he shares with other fifth floor tenants. In recent weeks, she had been handling lots of calls for Roberto Clemente Jr.

Pittsburgh was caught up in an early frenzy for the All-Star Game, eager to recapture the beauty and excitement the city knew when Roberto Clemente was playing right field for the Pirates, first at Forbes Field and then at Three Rivers, and leading them to two World Series titles, eager to recapture the glory days when the Pirates, Steelers and Pitt football team ruled the world, eager to again be considered The City of Champions. Eager to clean up its image. Again.

Roberto Clemente Jr. had to work hard to line up the sort of support he needed to make the Roberto Clemente Foundation a lasting memorial — not a one-summer deal — to make a significant difference in the inner-city children's lives. It was a wondrous task.

He had allies. In his company, I had met Richard B. Kantrowitz, a CPA who was serving as treasurer for the Clemente Foundation. Kantrowitz's parents, Pearl and Henry Kantrowitz from Squirrel Hill, were friends of the Clemente family and had often visited them in Puerto Rico. Richard's face was a familiar one; we had gone to Allderdice High School and the University of Pittsburgh in the same class. He was on the business staff of *The Pitt News* when I was the sports editor of the student newspaper. He would be my ally, too, assuring the Clemente family that I could be trusted. There was Jana Halloran Phillips, an attorney for the law firm of Kirkpatrick & Lockhart at the Oliver Building, which represented the Clemente family. There was Alicia Berns, a New York-based agent who along with her husband, Norman, represented the Clemente's commercial interests through their Pro Star Management firm. They were talking about opening an office in Pittsburgh. Luis Clemente, the brother of Roberto Jr., was planning to relocate from Miami to Pittsburgh, and expand some family business interests, and to help with the Foundation. Others were lining up to be on the Clemente team. Civic officials found it appealing to their personal interests, their intentions to improve conditions in the city, to do something positive.

Richard Kantrowitz was out of Pitt a few years back in 1966, and was an avid baseball fan. His mother Pearl developed a new-found interest in baseball because of her son's fervor for the sport. She asked a friend with Pirates connections to invite Roberto Clemente for dinner at her home in Squirrel Hill, and he came. Clemente was single at the time.

"He got comfortable in our home in a hurry," recalls Kantrowitz. "He kicked his shoes off, and had a wonderful time. He came back the next year for dinner, and the next year, only this time he was married, and he brought Vera with him. She spoke English, but she was reluctant to speak the language because she wasn't sure of herself. My mother took her under her wings, took her shopping, and showed her around town, and they became good friends. When the boys came along, we even baby-sat for them.

"We visited the Clementes in Puerto Rico. We had a nice relationship with them. When Roberto came in to town to get this Foundation going, he called on me for help. There is still a respect for my family. When he ran into some early obstacles, he said, 'Nothing's getting in my way; I'm going to do this.' I never saw anybody in my life so dedicated to doing something.

"I never saw one person walk into a room and get the response he gets. He's not a star in his own right, yet people look at him, and swarm around him, as if he's his father. When you stand around him in a room for awhile, you think you're with his father. He doesn't have as thick an accent as his father had, but his mannerisms and presence are similar to the father. It's uncanny."

Roberto Jr. had already been active in baseball's RBI program (Reviving Baseball in the Inner Cities) in Puerto Rico. Now he wanted to do something in Pittsburgh. His Roberto Clemente Foundation, a non-profit organization, was designed to aid the needy in areas of education and athletics.

He tried to play baseball, and showed considerable talent at one point, but like the sons of so many famous athletes and performers, he found the challenge more than he could handle. He had a bad back, just like his father, and he gave up the ghost in 1991 after a short go at minor league baseball in the Phillies organization. His father's other love was children, so Roberto Jr. gravitated naturally toward the children of his country.

"I love working with kids," Roberto Jr. says. "It's something you can't put a price on, if you have patience and see them come out with self-esteem and self-respect. So it's something that I really enjoy doing."

He and his brothers, Luis, 27, and Enrique, 24, continued to spend their summers in Pittsburgh, at a home their mother Vera owned in Green Tree, so Pittsburgh became their second home. "I love the city and I love the people, just as my dad did," remarked Roberto Jr.

"Being a part of the RBI program in Puerto Rico, I saw the benefits. When I went to St. Louis for the RBI World Series this summer (1993), I realized Pittsburgh didn't have a team there, that it didn't have such a program."

He decided he would do something about that. The motives were clear to young Clemente. "Because I believe that with all the problems with society, it's the kind of program each major city needs," he said.

The New York Times devoted a lengthy article to Roberto Jr. and his mission in mid-January, 1994. He told writer Claire Smith, "Not having my father since I was seven years old and having the name that I carried has been very difficult sometimes. I guess I grew up very quickly and matured at an early age compared with other youngsters.

"We want to really make a point to the kids that they need to stay in school. So we're going to do an education-through-sports program.

"We're going to try to guide them with tutoring, with after-school programs, help them out with their homework. And, at the same time, we'll try to keep them out of trouble, and off the streets, guide them through and find out their abilities in sports, and try to get some scholarships for college.

"I am trying not only to literally start the Roberto Clemente Foundation, but to unify all foundations and entities that are working for the same goals here in Pittsburgh. To try and make it as a whole family. Because there are people here who are trying to do well, but doors are not opening for them. If I could help, I will try for them as well."

The interview took place in early January. His father's death had occurred on New Year's Eve, 1972. "This time of year is difficult for me, for the whole family," he said. "But I guess what you learn from this is that if you do good in life you will be rewarded. And I believe that even though my father disappeared 21 years ago, people still respect the kind of man he was. That is still very uplifting for me. So trying to do good in the community is something that makes me feel good."

One of my early mentors at Pitt was Hall of Fame basketball coach Doc Carlson, who was in charge of the student health service when I was a student in the early '60s. He spoke about "blessed boomerangs" — how if you tossed out good things then good things would come back to you.

"I know what it is like
to grow up without a father."
— Roberto Jr.

I had an opportunity to talk with Roberto Clemente Jr. on several occasions early in 1994, several times with his family at the Piratefest, over a drink at the Radisson Hotel in Monroeville, at his condominium in Robinson Township, at his Downtown office, at the City-County Building, and over the telephone several times. He was always easy to talk to, and his dedication and determination appeared quite genuine.

He was introduced wherever he went, and people warmed to him quickly. He attended the Dapper Dan Sports Banquet at the Downton Hilton, where his father had been honored on so many occasions, and where the Pirates' Jay Bell was being honored as the Pittsburgh Sportsman of the Year. Roberto Jr. sat at a table hosted by Bob O'Connor, a city councilman from Greenfield, a friend of mine owing to our similar roots and long-time interest in Pitt athletics. I had worked with O'Connor when he was the vice-president for Pappan Restaurants and area Roy Rogers Restaurants. "He got a nice hand when he was introduced, and people are drawn to him," reported O'Connor the day after at a Pitt basketball game. "We went out together afterward, too, and he handles himself well."

Everyone was eager to shake his hand. Some asked for his autograph. It had been that way at the Piratefest. The Clementes had loaned the Pirates much memorabilia from their father's career: photos, uniforms, plaques, trophies, all sorts of souvenirs from his Hall of Fame career. It was used in a "Tribute to Roberto" exhibit at the Expo Mart in Monroeville.

"It makes me feel good to see this," Roberto Jr. said when we sat down, just the two of us, to reflect on what was going on around him. "I grew up without a father. I know what it is like to grow up without a father. I had no one to talk to me. No father image. No person there to let me know what is going on. What to expect about life.

"There was a man named Victor Henriquez. I call him my uncle. His wife grew up with my father; they were like sister and brother. He took the time to take me to the ballpark, and to events, and he talked to me.

"Otherwise, no one was talking to me. No one was asking me, 'How are you doing?' I felt really lonely. When I was growing up, everyone would say 'You're so lucky to have a father so famous like Roberto Clemente.' I'd say, 'Why?' I didn't feel lucky; I felt lonely.

"So, as an adult, when I started working with kids, I found out that I wanted to do this. Maybe it's in the genes. It seems natural for me to do it. This was his mission in life; now it's my mission."

I asked him how he felt about the warm way he and his family had been received by the fans at the Piratefest.

"It really feels good, to see the response of the people," he said. "Little kids were telling me, 'He's still my hero.' They never saw him play, yet they are so interested in him. Talking about him, or sharing stories like that, was something my family enjoys doing. Plus, we love to see Pittsburgh.

"There's a difference between the way my father is viewed here and in Puerto Rico. He is loved here in Pittsburgh very differently than he is loved in Puerto Rico. He was a poor kid from Carolina who made it to the big leagues with baseball. Every time he'd go back, he'd go back to his people. He was one of them. He'd see a volleyball game and he'd take off his jacket, loosen his tie, and he'd join in the fun. He was a Puerto Rican, one of the guys.

"There was a different kind of respect for him in Pittsburgh. He did not grow up here. He was not a Pittsburgher (or "Pittsburgh guy" as Art Rooney would say). Here, he was a Pirate. He played in Pittsburgh. Here, he was a Pittsburgh Pirate. They've had statues of him for a long time in Puerto Rico, and now, at last, they will have one of him here in Pittsburgh. We are so proud.

"In respect to my coming to Pittsburgh, something that happened last summer convinced me to move to Pittsburgh. I went to St. Louis for the RBI program. We had set up such a program for the kids at our Sports City in San Juan. We got teams in Puerto Rico to come. But there was no team from Pittsburgh. Something about that bothered me. I knew what a great baseball town Pittsburgh was when my father played here.

"My family has been on its own for quite awhile. My dad would tell my mom, 'I want you to learn what I do,' like household things, buying stuff and business. 'I need you to know this. Because I'm not going to live long.' My mom say, 'No, Roberto, don't talk that way.' She never sat down to find what he was doing. So we needed help to get our affairs in order.

"Right after the accident, there were so many people in our house for a month. It had been the same way in December, as it always was during the holidays. So many people in the house. They had to close off the street there were so many people coming to our house, so many people who wanted to see what was going on. That lasted for two weeks. After that, the house was empty. Deserted. We were by ourselves, and, in a way, we still are."

I asked Roberto Jr. why his mother, who was such an attractive woman, had never remarried.

"We did talk about that years later," he said. "In her mind, she still loves my dad. She fell in love once and that was it. She has never looked at another man as a man. I often compare her to a saint. She is a saint!

"She took my father's dream, and started up a project of that nature, with Sports City. Now I am starting up a project here in Pittsburgh. I need some help to do this. We are working for what he believed in. He cared about children."

"If my father hadn't been a ballplayer, I believe I'd have been a ballplayer."
— Roberto Jr.

I asked him if he had mixed emotions when he toured the photo and memorabilia exhibit dedicated to his father. Did it kick up bad feelings, too?

"It always hurts," he admitted. "I'm so used to pain. It is painful. Sometimes more. Other times, when holidays come. Those days for me are very painful. I truly miss him."

Had it been a treat to visit with some of the players who had been teammates of his father?

"I had very little time to speak to Vernon Law, for instance. We kinda missed everyone. It was good to see Manny Sanguillen and Al Oliver. I always wanted to be a catcher, like Manny. I always wanted to hit left-handed. They loved my father. Willie Stargell feels that way,

Author Jim O'Brien teams up with Roberto Clemente Jr.

Vera Clemente is flanked by her sons, Roberto Jr. and Luis, as they check out displays at 1994 Piratefest "Tribute To Roberto."

too. When I was playing around as a kid, I'd be Willie Stargell, twirling my bat like he did. We enjoyed seeing his former teammates talk about him in the tape that was done about his life. I have to shake Joe Brown's hand for what he said. 'If you don't want to hear the truth, don't ask him how he feels.' My dad was always honest with reporters, and often it came back to haunt him. He'd say, 'My back is hurting, my shoulder is hurting.' He didn't hide what was on his mind. But that's all behind us now."

How did his mother feel about the resurgence of interest in her husband in Pittsburgh?

"She's happy and overwhelmed," he replied. "She's happy this has happened this year. She's happy her husband and our father is going to be remembered this way.

"The name I carry now is going to help a lot of people. We have to work together to get something accomplished in my father's memory here in Pittsburgh. I was born in Puerto Rico, in Santurce, in 1965, five minutes before my dad's birthday (August 18). Now that I'm back in Pittsburgh, I feel like I have been born again.

"People here have been telling me my dad was the best guy in the world, the greatest Pirate ever. Most of the comments have been similar: that this statue was long overdue. It makes me feel very good. They say, 'Thank you for being here.' Over three hundred people say the same thing: it's long overdue."

Roberto Jr. once played for the Little Pirates in Pittsburgh. Frank Thomas coached him at one point, and thought he had much ability. I asked Roberto Jr. how he dealt with the fact that he didn't realize his dream to become a big league baseball player.

"I have mixed emotions," he said. "At times, I feel fortunate that it didn't work out as I wanted it. I look at it in different perspectives. It hurts, because I love the game. I really love it. If my father hadn't been a ballplayer, I truly believe I'd have been a ballplayer. It was too much to follow him.

"I let it bother me, at first. It really bothered me. The pressure. I was putting pressure on myself, without knowing it. It really hurt me. You're constantly reminded of the father you miss. There were comments and criticism that I was no Roberto Clemente; that really rubs it in. It really hurt, like there was some weakness in you. When I was a kid, I kept to myself. The other kids thought I was stuck up. But I was hurting. As a minor league ballplayer, I couldn't be myself. It would have been hard living with that comparison.

"My brothers don't like baseball. They'll walk out of the room if a baseball game is on TV. My little brother, Ricky, he suffers the most. Everyone has suffered in their own way. He was three years old when the accident happened. He didn't even remember him. He had no idea what he was all about. He grows up with this image, just pictures and clips. He never felt that warmth, the touch of the father. To see a picture, but not to know what it was like to be touched, to be hugged, he is the one who has the most difficulty."

Why didn't Ricky come with your family this weekend?

Roberto Clemente plays with first-born son, Roberto Jr., at family's living room at Pennley Park Apartments in East Liberty.

"He hates flying," said Roberto Jr. "He hates only one thing and that is flying. He loves Pittsburgh, but the fear of flying is still very strong in him. He can't stand it. On a couple of the trips he made with us, we had to give him a tranquilizer, just to get him on the plane. He gets really bad."

It is ironic that one of the playmates of the Clemente children, Orlando Merced, who lived across the street from their home in Rio Piedras, became a big league ballplayer and plays right field for the Pittsburgh Pirates. Orlando is living his friend's boyhood dream as well as his own.

Roberto Jr. may have been uncomfortable with that thought. He shifted subjects, and spoke of what a thrill it was for young players from Puerto Rico to board an airplane the previous summer and fly to St. Louis to play in an RBI tournament.

"You'd see all these kids from different places, away from home for the first time in many cases," related Roberto Jr. "It was the first time they would be staying in a hotel, and it culminated when they played baseball in Busch Stadium. And I looked around, and I say, 'Where's Pittsburgh?' I find out they don't have a program. I love the city. I love to help the kids here.

"There was this peace march in Manchester, on the North Side, and I walked with this woman. She told me the story of losing her son in a shooting. I could see the hurt in her eyes. There are many mothers in this city who want something better for their children.

"I called Dan Galbreath and I told him I needed some office space, and he came through for me. And now we're in business."

"We're happy to have Roberto Clemente Jr. here."
— Mayor Tom Murphy

This was the City-County Building at three o'clock on a Thursday afternoon, February 10, 1994. Roberto Clemente Jr. took his seat on a stage, sitting to the right of Mark Sauer, the president of the Pittsburgh Pirates. This was at a press conference called by Mayor Tom Murphy to announce details of a "Look At Us Now" region-wide campaign to showcase the city in celebration of Major League Baseball's All-Star Game, which would be played at Three Rivers Stadium on July 12.

Mayor Murphy was on the dais, along with a former mayor, Pete Flaherty, now one of the three Allegheny County Commissioners, Jim Ferlo, the president of City Council, and Susan Anton, who was appearing at the Benedum Center with the Radio City Music Hall Rockettes, and who threw out the first pitch of the press conference to the Pirate Parrot.

Roberto Clemente Jr. had arrived, at last, I thought. This was official. His Roberto Clemente Foundation was going to get official certification from the city fathers. The stamp of approval. They would help him in his efforts.

I arrived at the press conference early, before the principals arrived, and the first person I recognized was Baldy Regan, a former City Council member once known as "The Mayor of the North Side," a good friend of Mayor Murphy, and someone I had known since I was 14 years old and he was working at Joe Goetz's sporting goods store in Downtown Pittsburgh. Baldy Regan was a good friend of the Rooneys and he has always been involved, in one way or another, with sandlot and amateur sports in Pittsburgh. He had been named to be the director for the B.I.G. League.

I talked with him and with Bob O'Connor of City Council, and then Ray Werner, of Werner Chepelsky & Partners, Inc., a creative ad agency in the city's Strip District, who had come up with the slogan "Look At Us Now" for the campaign.

TV cameras and lights were set up, causing those on the stage to squint. The bright lights caused young Clemente to get a little nervous when he spoke of his mission in Pittsburgh.

"Our goal is to create a youth baseball program that will provide quality athletic and educational opportunities in Pittsburgh neighborhoods," he said in prepared remarks when his turn came at the podium. "One very important part of Pittsburgh B.I.G. League is our RBI program. And in this instance, RBI stands for Reviving Baseball in the Inner-City.

"We've already reviewed the participation of city neighborhoods and have set a meeting with neighborhood organizers to discuss our plans for starting the program in Pittsburgh this year."

One of his goals was to increase the numbers of youth, ages 5 to 18, who have an opportunity to play baseball and to strengthen existing youth baseball programs.

"Our goal," continued Clemente Jr., "is to create a youth baseball program that will provide quality athletic and educational opportunities in Pittsburgh neighborhoods. Quite simply, our goal is to make sure that every child will have the opportunity to play baseball.

"RBI is a program, not a baseball league. And the very important difference between the two is that we've developed a program with an educational structure to make the kids more college-ready. We see baseball as the hook, but the education is the key.

"Pittsburgh is going through some changes, and it's a difficult time in many respects. Pittsburgh is a place where my family and I grew up. My father loved the city. We want to give something back to Pittsburgh. I want things to get better, and I hope Pittsburgh is in a World Series again soon."

Organizers outlined plans for the RBI program, which initially would involve youth 13 to 15 years old, to expand in 1995. The Pittsburgh B.I.G. League program would be a cooperative effort among the Pirates, the City of Pittsburgh and the Roberto Clemente Foundation.

The Pirates were to provide clinics headed by their coaches and players, the use of Three Rivers Stadium for tournament games, Pirate game tickets, tickets for the '94 All-Star Game workout, Pirate scouts and fund-raising opportunities. Funding for specific programs was to come through the Roberto Clemente Foundation.

Mayor Murphy said, "Speaking to my generation, imagine what it would have been like to have played ball as a youngster in Forbes Field. Imagine what it would be like for kids today to play at Three Rivers Stadium. That's one of the opportunities this program will provide. It's an exciting alliance. We're happy to have Roberto Clemente Jr. here to work with us on this program."

Ferlo concluded by saying, "On behalf of my colleagues on Pittsburgh City Council, I want to commend Roberto Clemente Jr. for his commitment to the young people of Pittsburgh. We are honored to have him involved in an issue that is a critical priority for Mayor Murphy and the future of the City of Pittsburgh."

Jim O'Brien

The Clementes were an expectant family at the outset of 1994. Vera Clemente, center, was looking forward to being a grandmother again as the wives of two of her sons were pregnant. Roberto Jr., left, and wife Zulma joined with Luis and wife Olga Beatriz.

REMEMBER ROBERTO

Other Views

"Besides scrupulous accuracy,
a mark of a good reporter
is the ability to put
the reader on the scene,
which demands a visual and
auditory memory for details.
The superior reporter
enables the reader
to know the subject
of the piece personally,
maybe even to think as
the subject thinks and
feel as the subject feels."
—Red Smith

The Pittsburgh press box
Views from daily visitors

"He wasn't a saint."
—Phil Musick

Al Abrams, Pittsburgh Post-Gazette

"We were in Cooperstown, New York, a few years ago. Baseball's Hall of Fame Museum was full of visitors on a sunny morning. Among them were Pirates and Tigers players in baseball uniforms, sans spikes. They were to meet in an exhibition an hour later. Roberto Clemente had a small camera whirring every few minutes. He was taking pictures of displays featuring yesterday's superstars . . . Honus Wagner, Ty Cobb, Christy Mathewson, Tris Speaker, Grover Alexander . . . to name a few. A Pittsburgher said to Roberto, 'This is where you belong. Some day they will be taking pictures of your shrine here.' And Roberto replied 'Thank you. I guess a fellow like me has to die to get voted in by the writers.' "

Bill Guilfoile, Vice-President,
National Baseball Hall of Fame and Museum, Inc.
Pirates Public Relations Director, 1970-78

"I received a phone call from Byron Yake, sports editor of the Associated Press in Pittsburgh about 3 a.m. on New Year's Day, 1973. He relayed the devastating news that Clemente was aboard a plane that had crashed taking off from Puerto Rico bound for Nicaragua with relief supplies. Naturally, my first call was to Pirates GM Joe L. Brown. Apparently, when we finished our conversation, Joe did not hang up his phone and I was unable to get an outside line. Realizing that there were many media people to be called, I ransacked my wife Loretta's purse and our children's piggy banks for all the change I could accumulate. I then proceeded to a public phone booth outside a Bethel Park Li'l General Store. From this site I proceeded to call Charley Feeney, Bob Smizik and other media from Pittsburgh and the surrounding area. It was, indeed, a sad occasion."

Phil Musick, The Pittsburgh Press

"And when I heard he was dead, I wished that sometime I had told him I thought he was a hell of a guy. Because he was, and now it's too late to tell him there were things he did on a ballfield that made me wish I was Shakespeare. Roberto Clemente — and roll those r's and forget Bob or Bobby or Rob because he was Roberto — has virtues today he didn't own last week. And every time he's eulogized by people who didn't know him, I want to shout, No . . . no . . . he wasn't like that. He wasn't a saint. He was intemperate and headstrong and prouder than a lion.

and often his enemies, real or imagined, weren't worth the passion he invested in them. Once in a while he would turn away from a kid seeking an autograph, berate an honest reporter, and it made you want to shake him and say, 'No, man, that's not you.' . . . The corrosive dominant pride, tormenting him and flailing him in the headlong pursuit of excellence; the native intelligence at terrible odds with a foreign tongue he battled but never mastered, a softly sardonic wit; a warmth that rarely broke through the facade he painfully constructed because he was a private man."

Bob Prince, KDKA Radio

"I remember so vividly that when he did not win the MVP Award in 1960 he would not wear his World Series ring. He felt he had been terribly overlooked and was very upset about it. He would not wear that ring. He wore instead the All-Star ring because that was the ring that said to him he was the greatest player in the game today."

Les Biederman, Pittsburgh Press

"I knew Roberto Clemente as a Pirate rookie in 1955, a 19-year-old Latin who spoke little if any English but with a tremendous amount of natural baseball ability. I watched him grow into the superstar he was, the best ballplayer I ever saw and I saw him in every game he played from 1955 through 1968. He could do it all and do it all better and more often than anybody else."

Charley Feeney, Pittsburgh Post-Gazette

"In the baseball clubhouse, Roberto Clemente was a man of many moods. He could remain silent for hours. He could shout louder than anybody else. He could curse with the best of them. He could tell jokes. He could laugh. At home with his wife, Vera, and his three sons, Roberto says he was different. 'I never use bad language at home,' he said. 'When I'm home, I enjoy the company of my wife and my children. They are special to me.' Roberto Clemente was special to every Pirate fan. He probably was the greatest player ever to wear a Pirate uniform. Babe Ruth had his critics. And Roberto Clemente, a true super star, had his critics, too. It hurt him when he felt he did not receive the credit he deserved as a great ball player."

Bob Smizik, The Pittsburgh Press

"It was August of 1972. The Pirates were in San Diego. Roberto Clemente, thirty-eight, had just returned to the lineup after missing a large portion of the summer with an inflamed Achilles tendon. Because of that and other injuries, he was to play only 102 games that season. The Pirates were a powerful team, and by the standings, at least, they had not missed Clemente. They had, in fact, lengthened their lead in his absence. If the intensely proud Clemente was bothered by that fact, he never let on. Some of his teammates were certain he was. Most

401

of his teammates were already on the field involved in pregame practice. A reporter had engaged Clemente in a bit of idle talk. Clemente, as he was known to do on occasion, went on at some length with the reporter. He spoke of the disappointment of missing so many games, and then said something shocking. As though to discount the shortened season he was going through, he said, 'But I am going to play five more years.' It was a revelation. Most figured Clemente had one, maybe two years left. Clemente thought he had five. As it turned out, cruelly, he had no more seasons in the sun. But what about those five more years? Would they have been a possibility?"

Edwin Morgan, The Pittsburgh Press photographer

Ed Morgan was in San Juan, Puerto Rico in mid-December, 1972, to shoot photographs of Clemente and his family, and is thought to be the last Pittsburgh news person to see him.

"It was a warm and sunny day in San Juan, capital of Puerto Rico. A pleasant breeze fanned the countryside as my wife and I and another couple arrived at the home of Roberto Clemente in the oldest city under the American flag. It was December 15 and the Clementes were getting ready for Christmas. Roberto went into his garage and emerged with a monkey on a leash and put it into the cage. This brought squeals of glee from his three children who were running around wearing Pirate hats. He engaged in some small talk with me. In the ten years I covered Clemente as a news photographer for *The Press*, I never knew him to indulge in small talk. It was all business. A little later in the afternoon, as Roberto was pulling away in his car, I shouted that I would see him at spring training in Florida. Little did I realize it would be the last time I'd ever see Roberto Clemente."

Sally O'Leary, Pirates publicity staff

"I have two memories that reveal Roberto Clemente's considerate nature. In the late '60s, my brother Bob wanted to get Roberto's autograph for my mother, who was a big baseball fan. I watched him go down to the railing during batting practice, where it was easy to get the players' attention at Forbes Field. Roberto came over and I saw him talking to Bob. Roberto was gesturing the way he could, waving his hands. Bob had him sign a scorecard. Then Roberto disappeared for awhile and he came back to Bob at the railing a little later. I learned that he said to Bob, 'Why didn't Sally give you a photograph of me to sign?' Roberto had gone back to his locker in the clubhouse and brought Bob a photo of himself which he autographed 'To Grandma O'Leary, Best Wishes, Roberto Clemente.' I thought that was pretty special for him to do that. We still have that photo. On another occasion, the last day at Forbes Field, Roberto gave signed baseballs with the day's date and special inscriptions to several people, and he signed one with a personal message to me."

402

Jack Berger, Pirates Publicity Director (1954-1970)

His father was Jack Berger, a popular sports cartoonist at The Pittsburgh Press *for 42 years until his death in 1962. His mother, Marie McCabe, came from Tecumseh Street in Hazelwood. She lived next door to Pete Dimperio, who became famous as the football coach at Westinghouse High School, and across the street from my cousins, the Everett Burns family.*

"My mother was terribly hard of hearing, and she never went to a ballgame in her life. She and my dad were visiting me at spring training camp in Fort Myers in the mid-50s. A young player was coming into camp and his name was Roberto Clemente Walker and I was told by Joe Brown to pick him up at the airport. I asked my mother if she wanted to go out with me, just to keep me company. He'd just come from reserve duty with the U.S. Marines. Soon after he got in the car, he said, 'I no like to fly. I hate to fly.' Somehow my mother managed to hear that, and she had heard me talk about what we did travelwise, and so forth, and she said to him, 'You'll have to learn to like to fly. The team flies all the time. You'll have to learn to live with it.'"

Sportswriters talk baseball at dining table of press room at Forbes Field.

Myron Cope

One of Pittsburgh's natural resources

"He walked naked to the world."
— Cope on Clemente

*Myron Cope celebrated his 25th anniversary as an on-the-air personality at WTAE Radio in 1993. Cope started out providing early morning commentaries on sports, and became the color commentator to Jack Fleming's play-by-play call of the Pittsburgh Steelers, and also became the host of the most popular sports talk show in town. Cope created "The Terrible Towel" and stirred up much enthusiasm for the Steelers at Three Rivers Stadium, and was in the midst of all the madness when Pittsburgh was celebrated as "The City of Champions." He remains one of Pittsburgh's natural resources, one of its rare treasures. He grew up in Squirrel Hill — worked as a vendor at Forbes Field in his youth (if you can imagine him hawking hot dogs for Myron O'Brisky) — and was graduated from Taylor Allderdice High School and the University of Pittsburgh. I first met him when I was 14 and had just become the sports editor of the **Hazelwood Envoy**, a bi-weekly in my hometown. He once gave me this bit of advice: "Sit down at the typewriter and start writing. Just get started. That's how you write." Here is the commentary he delivered on January 2, 1973:*

T
he death of Roberto Clemente touched Pittsburghers deeply, and at the risk of oversimplification, we'd guess it touched them for at least two good reasons. One was that Clemente died while on a humanitarian mission, and the other was that he was simply so *human*, which is to say, so vulnerable to the smoldering fuses that ignite human emotions. The sophistication, the cool, the cynicism of so many athletes was beyond his grasp. He walked naked to the world, a man who could not contain his feelings.

Truthfully — yes, let's not be maudlin about this — truthfully, he often exasperated this reporter, for he had a hair-trigger temper that frequently led him to launch into clubhouse tirades against slights that seemed more imagined than real, more flimsy than substantive. He took pride in his talent, so he cried out for national recognition, but six years ago, when we wrote a lengthy article for *Sports Illustrated* that acclaimed him as a *great* talent, he took bitter exception to the article because it dared to discuss his propensity for aches and pains. Lightweights of the airwaves — television sportscasters who have never done a day's honest research in their lives — are now glibly vilifying working journalists as no-goods who branded a genius a hypochondriac. But we recall speaking to a Puerto Rican physician named Roberto Busó, Clemente's personal physician, and he calmly explained that the simple truth of the matter was that Roberto Clemente had a low threshold of pain. No

404

disgrace there, but as Dr. Busó put it, and we quote, "If his back hurts, he worries, and then it becomes a vicious cycle, leading to more things."

And, we say, why wouldn't it, for Clemente was an emotional man, and that was his beauty. It drove him not only to physical anguish but also to nearly incredible performances on the field as well as to the good work he was engaged in at his death. Often, although not so much in his maturing years, he seemed almost paranoid in his complaints against this or that, but when he said he loved mankind you had to believe him, because even the heat of his most bitter outburst almost always blew over, and where he had been loud, he would suddenly become reasonable and even eloquent. A man to confuse you? Yes, absolutely, but only because man's full range of passions ran strong in him. Cunning he was not. Honest he was. And the proof is that he was no *honorary* chairman of that relief committee for Nicaragua — he was no figurehead chairman in name only; he was not merely a celebrity lending his prestige but not his heart or his labor to a cause. *Honorary* chairmen do not disappear into the Atlantic in the performance of duty.

ESPN's Dick Schaap, left, and Nellie King were among Myron Cope's many colleagues who turned out for his 25th anniversary party at WTAE's studios.

405

Bow-tied Branch Rickey sits with sportswriters at Forbes Field, left to right, Chilly Doyle, Les Biederman and Jack Hernon.

Charley Feeney of Post-Gazette

Roy McHugh of Pittsburgh Press

Luke Quay of McKeesport Daily News

Luke Quay
An All-Star Official Scorer
"The world lost a dedicated humanitarian."

Donald "Luke" Quay was an ardent sports fan, but baseball was surely his first love. He joined The Daily News *in McKeesport as a staff writer in 1942. He became sports editor in 1958. He resided in White Oak and he died in McKeesport Hospital in early July, 1976. Luke listed among his accomplishments being the official scorer for National League playoff games involving the Pirates and the 1974 All-Star Game which was played at Three Rivers Stadium. He made a scoring decision that delayed Roberto Clemente's 3,000th hit, and drew the scorn of an irate Clemente in the clubhouse afterward. Clemente got his 3,000th hit the following day. "Deep down," Clemente conceded, "I think I would rather have a clean double to left center." It was the last regular season hit of Clemente's career. Though he was often critical of official scorers, Clemente liked Luke Quay. The feeling was mutual, as revealed in this column written by Quay the day after Clemente's death in an air crash. It is reprinted here with permission of* The Daily News.

W E'VE lost a good friend," Tony Bartirome said yesterday. But the Pirates trainer sort of simplified things in talking about the sudden death of Roberto Clemente in the crash of a plane carrying supplies to earthquake victims in Nicaragua.

Those of us fortunate enough to have been close to Roberto are heartsick over his death. But the whole world is a lot poorer place today because of his passing. A great human being is gone forever and we can ill afford to lose men of his caliber.

"The reason I called is because the first thing I thought about was the baseball he gave you late last season," Bartimore said. Tony was referring to the ball the umpire presented to Clemente on Friday night, September 29, when it was thought for a moment The Great One had collected his 3,000th hit on a high chopper over the mound which was bobbled by second baseman Ken Boswell of the New York Mets.

The official scorer had ruled it an error, but there was a mixup in the computer room and it wasn't flashed on the scoreboard until after the game had been stopped and the ball given to Clemente. The crowd was starting to rise to give him a standing ovation before the error sign went up and Clemente, naturally, was disappointed with the ruling.

He was quite upset after the game and made his feelings known. But it wasn't long before Roberto was insisting that he didn't want his 3,000th hit to be a questionable one. And the next day, he lined a double into the left-centerfield pocket to reach the milestone. Nobody realized it at the time, but it was the last regular season hit of his career.

It was the kind of sudden outburst of anger that was typical of Clemente. He had a fiery temperament and often flew off the handle.

407

But he never held a grudge and was the most loved and respected player on the club. Roberto was the counselor and advisor of everybody connected with the team.

Only a man like Clemente would have given the ball that he honestly believed should have been his 3,000th hit to the official scorer who ruled it an error. And he could even see some humor in the situation by writing a personal message on the ball that will always be a cherished souvenir. *(It was on display at '94 Piratefest.)*

"It was a Hit," Roberto wrote and continued. "No, it was an error. No, it was superman Luke Quay. To my friend Luke with Best Wishes — Roberto Clemente."

Clemente cared about people and he cared about their feelings. He would never knowingly hurt anybody and was proud of his close relationship with Pirate fans. But more than anything else, he dedicated his life to helping his people in Puerto Rico.

His baseball career was nearly over and there even was a possibility the 38-year-old outfielder wouldn't have been back next season. There were so many things Clemente wanted to do and he was anxious to get started on other things besides baseball.

"I want to open a string of clinics all over Puerto Rico for the old people without any money," reported Clemente, who had great faith in chiropractors. "I have this chiropractor friend here in Pittsburgh who is going to move to Puerto Rico and I'm going to work with him in the clinics. I don't think I'll be able to do that and still play baseball."

And Roberto had a lot of other plans. He wanted to go into the big equipment business and provide bulldozers, tractors, graders and other earth-moving machines for small Puerto Rico towns which couldn't afford to buy their own. And he figured he would have to be on the scene and not in the United States playing baseball to make the program work.

Clemente also believed young Puerto Rican players never got what they were worth when they signed baseball contracts. So, someday, he wanted to arrange personal service contracts with all the young prospects in the country and see to it that they got top dollar when they were ready for organized baseball.

These are only some of the things that he'll never be able to do. He went to his death trying to be of service to his fellow man. The Pirates lost one of the greatest baseball players of all time. But the world lost a dedicated humanitarian. And many of us lost a friend that we really loved.

My 11-year-old son knew Roberto and was one of his worshipping young fans. For awhile, he kept hoping that a miracle would happen and Clemente would be found unharmed.

But when it became apparent his idol was dead, Gibby went to his room early yesterday morning and cried his eyes out under the large charcoal drawing of Clemente that was given to him several years ago by Roberto. He also cried himself to sleep last night after getting up to watch the television tribute to the Pirate star. And his father felt like doing the same thing.

Pat Livingston
A Clemente fan come-lately
"He played baseball with a royal flair."

*Pat Livingston started writing sports for **The Pittsburgh Press** in 1949. He had a law degree from Duquesne University, and an undergraduate degree from St. Francis of Loretto. He had been an officer and a frogman in the U.S. Navy, defusing underwater mines so our submarines could pass safely through enemy waters. He may have been the first scout in pro football, checking out college talent for Dr. Jock Sutherland when he was coaching the Steelers. Livingston covered the Steelers for over 35 years, and was inducted into the media section of the Pro Football Hall of Fame in 1979. He was the sports editor of **The Press** from 1972 to 1983 when he retired. He was my boss when I covered the Steelers for **The Press** from 1979 to 1983. He still holds out for Franco Harris's "Immaculate Reception" as the most magic moment in Pittsburgh sports history — over Bill Mazeroski's home run that won the 1960 World Series — but says "that's purely personal; I know most sports fans here would feel differently." Pat has always had personal opinions, and was never reluctant to share them. Here is the column he wrote for the January 2, 1973 issue of **The Press**, which is reprinted here with his permission.*

It's just as well the Steelers didn't beat the Miami Dolphins on Sunday. In the light of the developments that night in the skies above Puerto Rico, nobody would have cherished the memories of the city's football celebration.

I didn't know Roberto Clemente well. Until last spring, I scarcely knew him at all, but in the Pirates' brief — but happy — pennant race last summer, Roberto Clemente made a deep and lasting impression on me.

And what impressed me most were not the fabulous talents of this black-skinned athlete, but the spiritual leadership he exerted on his team, the fierce pride which burned within him, the solemn dignity which marked his aloof manner. If there is such a thing as charisma, believe me, Roberto Clemente had it.

I saw him first almost 20 years ago, a firm-muscled youngster on an outfield platform at Forbes Field, where the Pirates were introducing a new team, player by player, to a curious group of fans who came out for the ceremony. Clemente stood out among those uniformed athletes, a lithe, hard-muscled boy whose eyes never wavered as he surveyed the throng of strangers beneath him.

"There's something regal about that kid," I thought as I watched him.

The passing years confirmed that first fitful impression of the young Puerto Rican. He played baseball with a royal flair befitting a prince of the game but, more important, he conducted himself off the field in a manner that brought pride to the Pirates, to the city and to the game he played with such abandon and zeal.

Roberto Clemente was not an easy man for a stranger to know, particularly if that stranger happened to be a sports writer. For weeks, there was a defensive quality to his answers as he replied nervously to my questions, but as the pennant race heated up, I thought I detected a softening of the protective, insulating shell he had built around himself.

By October, unapproachable Roberto was one of my favorite Pirates. For many of the same reasons, I think, he was one of the Pirates' favorites as well.

"I won't miss him so much as a ball player — but as a man," said Bill Mazeroski, a teammate of 17 years, when he learned of the death of Roberto Clemente.

Clemente was much easier to talk to when the subject involved others — his family, or the people of Puerto Rico, the great loves of his brief life. I've had friends who had visited Clemente at his island home and every one of them spoke glowingly of the personable, hospitable nature of the Pirate star in his familiar Caribbean environment.

"I spent three or four days in Puerto Rico," said a writer friend (Myron Cope) who had gone there to do a story on Roberto, "and the way he insisted on driving me wherever I wanted to go was embarrassing. I had the uneasy feeling I was imposing on him, that I was being driven around the island by a $100,000-a-year chauffeur."

You didn't see much of Clemente on Pirate trips. Around the hotel lobbies, he was practically invisible and I suppose that was the way it had to be. No matter where he showed up, people pressed in on him with autograph books and pens, mobs of them, so I suspect Clemente's favorite place was the refuge of his room.

On the subject of his children — his three sons — and the children of Puerto Rico, Clemente was extremely eloquent. One of his missions in life, he felt, was to do things, not only for his sons, but for their island playmates as well. "They are the important people, the children," said Clemente. "When one is as fortunate as I have been, there is always a debt to the children."

That, obviously, was the attitude that triggered Roberto Clemente, a deeply religious man, to undertake the mission of mercy which led to his tragic death Sunday night. His humane concern for his fellow man, the earthquake victims of Nicaragua, was such a cause as would compel him to leave his beloved family on a holiday eve.

The city of Pittsburgh, as well as the Pirates, lost a great ballplayer in Roberto Clemente. Unfortunately, they have lost something of greater value, something all of us can ill afford to lose — a decent, considerate upstanding man.

Requiescat in pace, Roberto.

Roy McHugh
A respected wordsmith

*"Over and over, the sportswriters
gave Clemente his due."*

*Roy McHugh, the sports editor and later a general columnist of **The Pittsburgh Press**, set high standards for everyone who worked with him or
for him. I recall that I once asked him to read a manuscript of mine about
Henry Aaron, whom I had interviewed in Atlanta for a cover story for
SPORT magazine. I asked McHugh to go over it before I submitted it
to the editors in New York. "Show me Aaron in a scene," McHugh scolded
me. "You're quoting everyone else about him, but I don't have any feeling that you were there interviewing him. Show him as you saw him.
Put him in a place." In short, set the stage, just like you do when you're
writing a play. Then let the dialogue follow. I have never forgotten
McHugh's admonition. It has helped me in writing all my stories, all
my books. When McHugh told me that MAZ was "a good book," and
spoke of some scene-setting he particularly liked, I beamed. I told him
of his influence on my work. His approval meant a lot to me. It always
has. He wrote this tribute to Clemente the day after Clemente's death.*

Something about Roberto Clemente, and it was not just his skills
as a baseball player, attracted total strangers in a deeply personal
manner, and the circumstances of his death confirmed what they
felt instinctively, for Clemente died helping strangers.

He died a hero's death, really. There are baseball players of a special kind who make an imprint on their times, and Clemente may have
been among them. Baseball, as we are told, is losing its relevance, it
no longer had a place in the national mystique, but it does keep producing symbols.

Babe Ruth was identified with a particular flamboyant decade, the
twenties; Lou Gehrig with the stark pioneer virtues, unflinching en-
durance and stoicism; Jackie Robinson with great social changes in this
country, with a new way of looking at black men. In Puerto Rico, Roberto
Clemente was a symbol, a symbol of territorial pride, and in Pittsburgh
he symbolized, as Pie Traynor and Honus Wagner before him had done,
the ties between a home-town baseball team and its public.

When a symbol passes from existence, it leaves a disturbing void.
It takes a piece out of those who remain. It causes a sort of general
melancholy.

So Babe Ruth, wasted with cancer, was led before 60,000 well-
meaning viewers in Yankee Stadium to croak a few words into a microphone. In much the same setting a dozen years earlier, Lou Gehrig, dying of a spinal-cord disease, had said in a choked voice that he was

the luckiest man on the face of the earth. Jackie Robinson's woes — blindness, diabetes, a failing heart, the loss of a son in an automobile accident — were doleful harbingers of death. Clemente went suddenly, in the full flush of the acclaim he knew he deserved.

He was not a falsely humble man. He wanted to be recognized and he wanted to be appreciated. But his reputation grew slowly, and the reason, he often said, was sports writers.

When he would tell them, "My bad shoulder feels good, but my good shoulder feels bad," they took it as humor. They portrayed him as a comic figure, it seemed to Clemente. Always he spoke of his injuries. To write about them, he thought, was to accuse him of hypochondria; not to write about them was to doubt that they were genuine.

The sports writers should say that, though he was hurt, he still played. The problem was that even when he felt bad, he looked good, a man with no physical flaws, symmetrical in features and build.

Only the fans, Clemente believed, realized his true worth. It was not quite an accurate appraisal. Over and over, the sports writers gave Clemente his due — there was no better right fielder, no one in the game with as powerful and accurate an arm, no one who hit more consistently, no one who tried harder, running out every ground ball, diving and skidding after every catchable fly.

Through every passing season, Clemente persuaded more skeptics, not all of them sports writers. Hitting home runs did not interest him, he would say — he was a line-drive hitter, a right-handed batter who flung himself at the ball and propelled it to right field — but he would hit tremendous home runs now and then just to show he could do it. And when eventually Clemente had knocked in more runs than anyone else who ever played for the Pirates, there were no more complaints that he left too many runners on base.

The 1971 World Series established for all to behold that he did not have a weakness as a baseball player. He came out of it a certified marvel, his abilities undiminished after 17 years in the major leagues.

"I now have peace of mind," he said. As he aged, he lost his capacity for outrage. He no longer flared up at the reporters who offended him, his humor became deliberate and subtle. "Oh, I am perfect," he would say when they asked him with mock solemnity how he was feeling. "If I say I am not perfect, you will not write it anyway."

He would talk with reporters endlessly and seriously. "I do not hate any human being," he said more than once, and it was probably nothing less than the truth.

On July 25, 1970, the Pirates scheduled a ceremony to honor Clemente before a night game at Three Rivers Stadium. From Puerto Rico, his admirers had come in planeloads. They were wearing pavas, the headdress of the native farm workers, hats that resemble boats with a cargo of loose straw. Clemente's parents were there, his father, who was 90 then, a wisp of a man, and his stout, dignified mother. So were his dark-eyed wife and their three small children.

Clemente stood beside them with his head bared, and then the Pirates' other Latin-American players walked up to him one by one and saluted him, bending slightly forward, not quite touching his cheek. Clemente began to blink. When he tried to speak into a microphone, he had to stop for a minute, bowing his head and brushing at his eyes.

"I don't know if I cried," he said after the game, "but I am not afraid to cry. A man never cries from pain or disappointment, but we are a sentimental people. I don't have words to say how I felt when I stepped on that field."

ler Press editor John Troan, at left, chats with Roy McHugh and Nellie King at lunch-
at Three Rivers Stadium to induct new members into Pirates' Media Wall of Fame.
brams and Les Biederman were inducted posthumously in 1993 ceremonies.

Samuel Hazo
A poet who loved the Pirates
"It was a sad day."

Samuel Hazo is the author of 14 books of poetry, four novels, a play and a book of essays and memoirs called The Pittsburgh That Stays Within You. *Hazo writes: "Often as I walk or drive through the city and observe how the new has replaced the old, I find myself wondering if I can remember what had been there." In his book, he paints a poetic picture of his beloved hometown and its treasures. "I am never totally happy when I am away from Pittsburgh for a protracted period of time." He is a professor of English at Duquesne University and the Director and President of the International Poetry Forum. He lives in the suburb of Upper St. Clair. He still has a baseball signed by Roberto Clemente on the occasion of his son's third birthday. He recalls the reaction in Mexico, which he was visiting, when the news came out that Clemente had been lost in an air crash. "His disappearance took everything else off the front page of the newspapers in Mexico," said Hazo. "It's a Catholic country, of course, and it's considered very important to have a body to properly anoint and bury. So it was doubly difficult for the people there to deal with his death. That was a sad day." Hazo's reflections are reprinted here with his permission.*

At the onset I must confess to a visceral and incurable allegiance to the Pirates — the allegiance of the lover, fraught with everything from disgust to ecstasy but always there. It was there during the Kiner and Hank Greenberg years, the era of Branch Rickey and Joe L. Brown, the Pirates-Yankees World Series of 1960 so deliciously keened over by James Reston in a *New York Times* editorial entitled "O Cruel and Fateful Acts of Piracy," the Baltimore series of 1971 and then Baltimore Segundo in 1979, the death of Roberto Clemente, the drug trials, the slow-rebuilding under Syd Thrift, Larry Doughty and Mark Sauer, the steadiness of Jim Leyland.

Clemente deserves special mention. Memories rise up and lap and overlap — the matador stance at the plate and in the field, the special hauteur that only the Latin Americans can muster, the public face and demeanor that (for me) seemed reminiscent of a similar decorum in Joe DiMaggio both on and off the field, the constant concern, as was the case with DiMaggio, to be sartorially flawless. Watching Clemente play right field in Forbes Field and later on at Three Rivers Stadium was as electric as watching him bat. Clemente hit off his front or left foot breaking the basic rule that a batter's power came when he anchored his strength on his back foot. Instructors simply said that Clemente was an exception, and, judging from the results and taking due notice of his 3,000 hits, they all agreed that it was wise to have left his stance to its unorthodoxy. As a fielder, Clemente did not merely play right field he owned, he diagrammed, he wrote the book on right field. Whether he was playing the bounces when the ball ricocheted off the treacherous angles of the right field corner of Forbes Field (Pete Reiser of the old Brookyn Dodgers once knocked himself out by slamming into one of the abutments there) or, on occasion, when he actually threw out from the deepest part of right-center field a runner attempting to score from third after the catch, Clemente fielded and threw like a master. His unorthodoxy frequently included throwing behind the runner as he rounded first or second (a no-no for most other fielders), but many was the baserunner who saw that Clemente's throw actually beat him to the base that he had rashly passed and tried too late to re-touch.

Clemente's death was a genuine period of mourning in Pittsburgh. He had just assumed the mantle of a superstar after an outstanding season and post-season. Having felt that he had been underestimated and under-praised (he was correct) for years, he nonetheless did not batten on the publicity when he returned to Puerto Rico. Instead he used his fame to focus attention on earthquake victims in Nicaragua. He even rented a plane and stored it with supplies and promised that he would personally deliver them to the Nicaraguans. He appeared on television nightly, exhorting his fellow islanders to join him in the effort. Finally, he boarded the improperly loaded plane and headed for Managua. After take-off, the load shifted. The pilot attempted to return to San Juan but never made it. When it was announced that Clemente had perished in the crash, Willie Stargell and other teammates wept openly. Manny Sanguillen even volunteered to dive and retrieve Clemente's body. I followed the Latino developments closely because I happened to be in Mexico at the time. His death was like the death of a great matador; it cast a pall over the country. Three days after the crash one newspaper headline, with a certain reverence, read simply: *No se encontró* . . . He has not been found.

Vera and Roberto Clemente show off son Roberto Jr. Art in background was Roberto's handiwork.

Charley Feeney
They called him "Pally"

"Clemente was nice to my nieces."

Charley Feeney covered the Pittsburgh Pirates from 1966 to 1986. He came to Pittsburgh from New York where he had worked for the Journal American. *He talked funny, and he talked fast, like he was always five minutes from deadline. He still talks that way. He talks in a clipped manner, with nonessential words missing, like the old Western Union wires. He gets in your face, or under your chin when he talks. Talking to Feeney is like fighting with a fast and furious bantamweight boxer. He never comes up for air, and he punches in the clenches. He runs the back of his hand across his mouth as he talks, as if he'd cut his lip. He was everyone's pal, so they called him 'Pally.' He knew his baseball, and he still does. He and his wife Bea share an apartment one floor below ElRoy Face in an apartment complex in North Versailles, just east of Pittsburgh on Route 30. It's the only place they have ever lived since they came to Pittsburgh. I remember talking to him in a press box at Al Lang Field in St Petersburg in the spring of 1972. I was covering the Mets for* The New York Post, *and they were about to play an exhibition with the Pirates. Feeney was always kind to younger writers, and tried to help them. Feeney pointed out a large young man running in the outfield, and suggested I keep an eye on this Pirates prospect. His name was Dave Parker. I remember Parker hit a deep drive over the head of Mets' centerfielder Tommy Agee that afternoon and raced to third with a triple. Impressive stuff. Parker spent that season in the minor leagues, but he joined the Pirates for good the next year and went on to become one of their all-time best ballplayers. Feeney winters in Bradenton, Florida, the site of the Pirates training camp. After a lifetime as a newspaperman, he doesn't even have a typewriter or word processor now. I couldn't imagine a writer without a word processor or something like it these days. But he was kind enough to send me some thoughts about Clemente he had printed by hand.*

During the 1967 season, the producers of the movie, "The Odd Couple," contacted Roberto Clemente about grounding into triple play for a segment they planned on using in the movie. Clemente reportedly agrees to do it. It's going to be done in New York where they are filming the movie about a sloppy sportswriter and his neatnik buddy who share an apartment.

Prior to going to New York, the Pirates play in St. Louis. Lee Biederman of *The Press* makes a remark to Clemente in the visiting clubhouse at Busch Stadium.

Biederman: "Roberto, if you hit into a triple play in a movie, will be featured in Puerto Rico. It will say, 'The Odd Couple starring Roberto Clemente.' You will be the star. Do you really want to hit into a triple play?"

Clemente makes no comment.

A day later in St. Louis, Bob Prince makes a similar remark to Clemente.

Clemente makes no comment.

Then I made the same type of comment to Clemente.

Again, Clemente makes no comment.

Next, the scene is Shea Stadium in New York. It's a day game and Clemente and a few other Pirates arrive around 10:30 a.m., before the team bus gets there.

Officials of movie production and Mets p.r. man Harold Weissman approach Clemente in visitors clubhouse. As they near Clemente, who is at his locker, he says, "I won't hit into a triple play for anybody!"

Weissman and others in movie plead. Clemente says, "I won't hit into a triple play for anybody!"

Weissman hears from Clemente teammates that Pittsburgh media bugged Clemente about looking bad to his people back in Puerto Rico.

Weissman first blames Prince. Next he blames me. Weissman never suspected Biederman, who made the first comment to Clemente. After more pleading with Clemente, Weissman and the movie people give up.

Somebody mentions Bill Mazeroski as a replacement. Maz agrees for $600, or something like that.

The scene: Maz at bat, Pirates runners on first and second, none out. Maz is supposed to hit a grounder to third. He fouls off the first pitch. He hits the second near the third base bag for the start of a triple play. It took two takes and that was it!

Here's something else that happened that same day:

Harry Walker, the Pirates manager, makes up lineup cards. One has Gene Alley batting sixth and Jose Pagan batting seventh. It is posted on scoreboard. Another card, given to Mets and the umpire, has Pagan sixth and Alley seventh.

First time they bat, nothing happens. Next time, Pagan hits three-run double. Sheriff Robinson, Mets coach, points out discrepancy to umpires. Result: Pagan is declared out for batting out of order. Pirates lose three runs, lose game. Less than a month later, Walker loses his job.

Here's a personal story: My two nieces, Noreen (age 11 at the time), and Laura (8) Cronin are visiting Pittsburgh from Glendale, Queens. They meet Clemente at Forbes Field. He talks briefly with them.

A few weeks later, while driving my nieces to New York, our car, with my wife Bea driving, goes out of control on the Pennsylvania Turnpike near the Bedford exit. Nobody seriously hurt. Our car was totaled.

Clemente heard about the accident. A few weeks later, when Pirates were in New York to play the Mets, I told Clemente during batting practice that the two young girls were in the stands. He took a couple swings and stopped when he saw the girls standing in the first row behind the screen behind home plate. He went over to them. "Are you all right?" Clemente asked them. "Did you see a doctor?"

417

The girls, as young as they were, were awed that Clemente showed such concern for their welfare.

They are both married with children, and they have often related the Clemente story to their friends.

In May, 1966, I was hired by Al Abrams to cover baseball for the *Pittsburgh Post-Gazette*. The *New York Journal-American* had folded and Abrams hired me after many of my friends, Jimmy Cannon, Pat Lynch and Art Rooney, had gone to bat for me. Before I joined the *P-G*, Cannon told me, "You are going to a town where the best player in baseball is, but nobody knows it."

In September, 1966, the Pirates were playing in LA, and were involved in a three-team race with the Dodgers and Giants. Cannon was in LA, and asked me to help him set up an interview with Clemente. Clemente was polite, but said he didn't want to talk to a New York writer. No reason.

Pirates officials did nothing to change Clemente's mind, even though Cannon's opinion of Clemente's greatness was known. Cannon wrote a column, a nationally-syndicated column, mind you, praising Clemente with no quotes from Clemente. And Clemente often complained that writers ignored him. . .

"If I didn't see it, I wouldn't believe it."

There's another story, about The Throw, which happened in the late '60s at Forbes Field. Clemente made the most remarkable throw I ever saw . . . and he got an error on the play!

The Bucs were playing the Cardinals, it was one of the middle innings and the Cards had runners on first and third. I don't recall the runner on third, but Orlando Cepeda was on first. I believe Tim McCarver singled to right, and the runner on third scores. Cepeda is about to stop at second, but the ball rolls through Clemente's legs, and Cepeda takes third (reason for the error being charged to Clemente). The ball rolled to the warning track in right (not close to the foul line), and Clemente picks up the ball with his back to the plate. He whirls and throws a no-bounce strike to Milt May at home plate and Cepeda is out trying to score.

After the play, I looked around the press box to find the oldest baseball observer there. Leo Ward, the traveling secretary of the Cards, had been watching baseball since the teens. His quote: "If I didn't see it, I wouldn't believe it."

Arthur Daley
A Samaritan on a relief plane
"In Tribute to Roberto Clemente"

My first assignment in baseball at The New York Post *was to write a sidebar, or secondary feature, on a game between the New York Yankees and the Baltimore Orioles at Yankee Stadium. I don't recall the score or any details of the game, but I remember I was seated between two of the greatest sports columnists in the country, Arthur Daley of* The New York Times *and Red Smith of* The New York Herald-Tribune. *Both went on to win the Pulitzer Prize for their efforts. Milton Gross of* The New York Post *was nearby, as was Jimmy Cannon, who was writing a nationally-syndicated column. These were the giants of the game. They were all mentors. For a 29-year-old sportswriter, it was the big time. I felt like a rookie might if he got to play next to Joe DiMaggio or Mickey Mantle in the Yankees outfield. Daley was a dignified gentleman, yet he was always approachable and had a quick smile. When he died, on the way to work just before he was to retire, Daley had worked 47 years with* The Times, *written 20 million words, 11,000 columns (Sports of The Times), usually 800 words in length. This one, about Roberto Clemente, is reprinted here with permission from* The New York Times, *copyright 1973.*

One of the first news bulletins of the year hit with a sickening jolt. In the emotionless language of radio bulletins, announcements were made early yesterday that a plane on a mercy mission to stricken Nicaragua went crashing into the Caribbean and that Roberto Clemente, one of the Samaritans aboard the relief plane, presumably crashed to his death with it.

This is shocking news, distressing news. During his 18 years with the Pittsburgh Pirates the gifted Roberto had gained recognition as a man of towering dignity, highly esteemed not only as a person but as a ballplayer. He was a genuine superstar and few of his contemporaries could surpass him in skill. Roberto was the complete ballplayer. He did everything extraordinarily well. He could run, throw, field, hit and hit with power. These are the five ingredients on which players are rated and the Pirate outfielder ranked at or near the top in each.

He won four batting championships and one Most Valuable Player award. He had 13 years of over .300 and he still hit .312 last season when he supposedly was easing into the twilight of his career. Twilight? Roberto just didn't seem to acknowledge it. At the somewhat advanced age of 37 in 1971, he batted .414 in the World Series with at least one hit in each of the seven games, thereby duplicating a feat he had performed 11 years earlier in another Series against the Yankees.

If there was smoldering resentment within Roberto that he never got the acclaim he deserved, he was entitled to such an attitude. Willie

Mays was given instant acclaim when he first arrived on the scene and was endowed with superstardom almost immediately. But Willie the Wonder had the advantage of starting with the New York Giants and that put him in a matchless showcase. Roberto never had one in Pittsburgh.

When Giant writers in those early days would rattle off a list of Willie's impossible catches, Pirate writers would dutifully recite impossible catches that Roberto made, all of equal value. But only Willie's stuck in memory.

Many of Mays's throws also became engraved enduringly in consciousness, but Roberto had a better and more accurate arm, one that never seemed to diminish in strength. He once made a throw home from the iron gate at right-center field in old Forbes Field. It reached the catcher on the fly. The distance was 460 feet. Such was his reputation that he scared runners, causing many to hold up rather than risk being shot down by his gunner's arm.

Once he threw out a runner on a bunt, a rather fancy play for any outfielder to make. Bill Mazeroski, a teammate, attests to it and he is a man of great probity. It was a freak play, of course. It would have to be. The Pirate strategy with runners on first and second with none out was to have the third baseman race in for a bunt, while the shortstop covered third. Outfielders instinctively played shallow. But this particular batter mangled his bunt, tapping the ball on the fly to the vacated shortstop spot. Baserunners hesitated and held up. Roberto came tearing in from the outfield, made a quick pickup and forced a runner at third.

Originally signed by the Brooklyn Dodgers, he may have been victimized by a quota system that some said was in effect in those unenlightened days. The Pirates drafted him from the Dodger farm system and thus did his advancement toward stardom begin. Perhaps it would have been swifter and more noticeable in Brooklyn. Who knows? Also unknown is whether this would have made him a different kind of ballplayer.

Ebbets Field was a neat little playpen with all fences within easy reach of the Dodger clout of that era. But Roberto landed instead in Forbes Field, most spacious ball park in the majors. Smart man that he was, he shunned the home run which might have tempted him in Brooklyn.

He became a line-drive hitter, spraying them in all directions, but his favorite target was the opposite field, right field. Awesome was his accumulation of hits over the years and last year he achieved a goal that only 10 ballplayers in all recorded history ever reached. A few days before the end of the season, Roberto lashed a double off the wall on one hop and the scoreboard became alive with the number, 3,000. He had just made his 3,000th hit.

"Roberto is the greatest ballplayer I ever saw," often said his former manager, Danny Murtaugh. It is not too extravagant an estimate. Roberto was a great one in so many ways. He even went out with a flourish typical of the man, seeking to extend a helping hand to those in need.

Pittsburgh Pirates

World Champion
Pittsburgh
Pirates
1972 Official Score
THREE RIVERS STADIUM

Game program from September 30, 1972 when Roberto Clemente doubled in the fourth i
Mets' Jon Matlack for his 3,000th regular season hit. This program, belonging to Stanley G
chairman of Geyer Printing, was personally autographed by Clemente under the boxsc

Iron City Beer

Rita - Stanley - Richard - Bernie
SEPT 30, 1972   ATTENDANCE 13,117

AZEROSKLIN 5TH

PITTSBURGH PIRATES	1	2	3	4	5	6	7	8	9	10	AB 11	R 12	H 13	RBI	PO	A	E
Goggin 2B	H		H		K		4-3										
Bennett CF	4-63		6-4		4-3		9										
Davillo, / Clemente RF	K			300	41		K										
Galzell 1B		5-3		8		W		H°									
Zisk LF		W		W		W		6-3									
Sanguillen C		W		H		E°		2									
Pagan 3B		4-63		K		6											
Fernandez SS times in CF			K	H		8											
Ellis P			K	3		7											
Johnson in 7TH																	
TOTALS R / H	0 1	0 0	0 0	3 3	0 0	3 0	0 0	0 1									

Double + Left Center

21

Rege Cordic
Like loafing with great ole' pals

"It was probably my favorite time period."

Rege Cordic grew up in the Scotch Bottom section of Hazelwood, below Second Avenue in between Hazelwood and Greenfield, and became the most popular wake-up deejay KDKA or Pittsburgh ever knew during a 13-year-run (1954-1966) with Cordic & Co.

What a great book! As you might recall, my sister sent me an autographed copy of *Maz And The '60 Bucs*. Not only did I deeply appreciate your "Pittsburgh Guy" reference in your personal inscription, but I loved the subject matter.

As I think of it, it was probably my favorite time period filled with wonders like Forbes Field, Pittsburgh Railways and the Glory Years of KDKA Radio. And then the Pirates!!! Who could ask for anything more?

You captured it all so wonderfully — it was like reliving it again. Like sitting and "loafing" with great ole pals — Murtaugh, Prince & Nellie, Skinner, Face, my radio-buddy Groat, Virdon and Vern Law, just a few — and, of course, Clemente.

Your treatise on Joey Diven did it, however. Tears of laughter halted my first reading so often — I gave up and came back later when I was in a more serious mood. Like Joe Brown once told me, "In Oakland on Saturday nite, you could set your watch by the start of this week's Joey Diven fight!"

Congratulations again — you caught the joy, the sadness and the reality of a magic time for many — all my friends are together again. Hope to meet you one day — I owe you a drink!

Rege Cordic

Artwork on opposite page done by Rege Cordic depicts J&L's South Side Works in 1940.

Gene Carney
View From Right Field

"He could have made it on character."

Gene Carney, who goes by the handle of "Two Finger Carney," lives in Utica, New York, where he writes and publishes a newsletter for base ball fans called Notes From The Shadows of Cooperstown. *Carney grew up in Pittsburgh as a fervent fan of the Pirates. The following is an ex cerpt from the manuscript for his yet-to-be-published book,* Dear Patrick Hot Stove Deliveries From A Father To A Son, *and is reprinted here with Carney's permission.*

Out in the right field stands, you could keep a close eye on Roberto Clemente, the superstar right fielder, who made basket catches (no one else did, except Willie Mays) and mastered the caroms of liners off the wall. Sometimes he'd disappear from the sight of those in the upper deck, if he backed up close to the wall for a deep fly. Then the rest of the crowd would let you know if he got it or not.

Kids flowed to those right field seats *before* games, to watch Clemente rehearse basket-catches and practice laser-throws to the plate (That's what I call them today — back then, outfielders were "rifle armed.") He'd drift back to the warning track — that grassless arc run ning pole-to-pole in the outfield which let fielders know that they were nearing the edge of their safe world and nearing a collision — then snag the ball and let it fly. Those rockets no doubt were also closely observed by opposing players, and kept many runners from even *thinking* about taking an extra base, or trying to score on a hit to Roberto. And if a batter took his time getting out of the batter's box on a hit to right, Clemente would try to nail him *at first*. "Arriba" was both his nick name and a personalized cheer for the stylish play of this wonderful proud Puerto Rican.

Like kids everywhere in any era, the kids in right field pleaded for baseballs, and Clemente often obliged, lobbing them over the screen or into the upper deck. They weren't autographed — in writing — but they sure had Roberto's mark on them. I never got close to one, but ev ery kid felt special when No. 21 smiled, then went back to his work.

Clemente's death, like his life, was stunning. For Pittsburghers it was also a death in the family.

Just as four months before, when my father died, my first reac tion was to write. This time, for the first time in my life, I sent a letter to a newspaper, to Al Abrams, the sports editor of the *Pittsburgh Post Gazette*, even though I was living in Cleveland. Apparently, it was not published, as thousands of others also wrote. Mine was not a brief let ter, but a dense two-pager (single-spaced), about a person of whom I was very proud, who had dignified my city and my game. My letter praised

Clemente as a saint, to those for whom baseball was like a religion. To my family.

I have a carbon copy (no Xerox available to me then) of my letter, and I am surprised when I read it today, to see that even then I saw a kind of growing gap between the players and the fans. There had been none between Clemente and his fans in Pittsburgh: he stood tall, not for commercials, or for some fashionable position, but for clear human values, for what we called "virtues" — which are the opposites of "vices." Roberto had not been faultless — no one is. But his good deeds shone.

In his final at-bat during the 1972 regular season schedule, Clemente had gotten his 3,000th hit. His credentials for the Hall of Fame were impeccable. Soon after his death, he was elevated to the Hall in a special election. He had the stats, but he could have made it on character.

View from upper deck in right field at Forbes Field

Murray Chass
From baseball fan to baseball writer
"Clemente was an exception."

*Murray Chass marked his 25th year as a sports writer at **The New York Times** in the summer of 1994. He grew up in the Squirrel Hill section of Pittsburgh, and was graduated from Taylor Allderdice High School (1956) and the University of Pittsburgh (1960). He was the sports editor of **The Pitt News** and upon graduation, he worked at the Pittsburgh bureau of the Associated Press. He helped me early in my career. He urged Ted Colton, who succeeded him as the sports editor at Pitt, to name me to the post as Colton was about to graduate, even though I was just finishing my first year at school. His essay on Roberto Clemente is reprinted with permission from a book called **Cult Baseball Players**, edited by Danny Peary and published in 1990 by Simon & Schuster. It is reprinted here with Peary's permission.*

The baseball rests on a shelf in the family room of my home, encased in a plastic holder to keep the name from fading. It is one of three baseballs that reside there, the only balls I have had autographed since I transformed myself too many years ago from baseball fan to baseball writer.

The other two balls have a unique standing in my newspaper career. They are signed by Hank Aaron and Darnell Coles, and they are there because they represent the two times I have been hit by batted balls while sitting in a press box covering a game (When I asked Coles for his signature on his foul ball, I don't think he understood what I was talking about when I told him about the Hank Aaron baseball.)

The third ball did not hit me. I don't even recall where I picked it up. Nor do I remember when I asked for the autograph. Actually, as my children know all too well, I have a policy against asking players for autographs. But every policy has an exception, and it was a rare exception when I asked Roberto Clemente to sign this particular baseball.

"Best wishes, Roberto Clemente," it says, sitting on my shelf.

The autograph was an exception because Clemente was an exception.

As a boy growing up in Pittsburgh, I was as avid a Pirates fan as old Forbes Field ever held. In my earliest years as a fan, several seasons before Clemente arrived, the players I rooted for the hardest were not of Clemente's stature. But then, the Pirates did not have many players of that stature. Ralph Kiner was there at the time, hitting home run after home run, but he was not my hero. My heroes were Ted Beard and Tom Saffell, two outfielders about whom no one has written books, chapters or even paragraphs.

When Clemente joined the Pirates in 1955, I was finishing my junior year in high school. For five years, I watched him, enjoyed him, rooted for him as a fan. Then, I began watching Clemente professionally. I could still enjoy the way he played, but I could no longer root for him. My new status forced me to adopt a different perspective and a different approach to this player who could be so easy for a fan to adore but so difficult for a writer to cover.

There was the summer, for example, when the Pirates were in New York (where I had moved in pursuit of my career) and I went to Shea Stadium to do a story on him. I did not expect him to remember me from my Pittsburgh days so I introduced myself.

As soon as he heard that I was a New York writer, he made it clear he would not speak to me. He did not care for baseball writers generally, but at this time he specifically wanted nothing to do with the New York variety of baseball writers. It seems that one New York writer had written a piece about his celebrated physical ailments, a subject that wasn't his favorite, and had mocked him by suggesting that he was a hypochondriac and had been treated by a witch doctor in Puerto Rico. For this, he was angry with New York writers.

Faced with a non-interview, I was tempted to say to him, "How can you do this? I'm from Pittsburgh and I used to root for you." When I related this story years later to a friend of Clemente's, he told me that that approach would have probably enabled me to salvage the interview. But, I told myself at the time (and would reiterate today), that was not the professional thing to do.

A few years later, I approached Clemente in another clubhouse, this one in Baltimore, and this time he talked freely — to me and dozens of other writers. The Pirates had just won the 1971 World Series, and Clemente was the hero, the player who batted .414, compiled a .759 slugging percentage, and made possibly the best throw in a World Series that didn't get the runner.

All of this and more accomplished by a man who a year and half earlier had said that the 1970 season "could be my last year."

Had Clemente quit after the 1970 season, he would not have become the eleventh player in major league history to amass 3,000 hits in his career, and he would never have attained the fame and appreciation that truly belonged to him.

As absurd as it seemed then and still seems now, Clemente did not become a nationally recognized superstar until the 1971 World Series. It mattered not that he had played for seventeen years, won four batting championships, eleven Gold Gloves and one Most Valuable Player award, played in twelve All-Star games and batted .300 twelve times, including eleven times in a twelve-year span (he would, in 1972, make that thirteen times and twelve in thirteen years). Fans throughout the country inexplicably remained ignorant of just how great a player he was until he showed them in seven televised games in October 1971.

Fans in Pittsburgh did not need those games to show them how great Clemente was. They had known for years. His teammates and opponents did not need those games. They had known, too.

429

"People in Pittsburgh and people who had to deal with him on the field knew," says Willie Stargell, Clemente's teammate and fellow Hall of Fame member. "He commanded their respect. That was the peace of mind that really made him feel good. He knew in due time that people would put him up there with the best players who ever played in the National League. He knew he didn't have to take a backseat to anybody. You talk about Aaron, Mays, Clemente. They're all right there."

Stargell would get no argument from Al Campanis, who as a Brooklyn Dodgers' scout discovered Clemente in 1953 in a tryout camp in the town of Santurce in Puerto Rico.

"He was rare," Campanis says. "He was the best natural athlete I had seen. He could run so well, he could field, he could throw, he could hit. When you see a star, you tingle all over."

Clemente, no overwhelming physical presence but a rock hard 5'11" and 185 pounds, sent chills up and down tingling spines with his flamboyant style of play. He executed his inside-outside swing with flair, seemingly snatching the baseball out of the catcher's glove and lining it to right field. He ran the bases with flash, his strong legs churning like pistons and his arms pumping in unison. He chased fly balls in the outfield with abandon, sliding across the grass to catch the ball or catching it on the run and throwing it to third or home, where the runner always knew he would be in jeopardy.

His actions were not the work of a player who used his ailments to excuse himself from the lineup. He is No. 1 in Pirates' history in games played, just as he is No. 1 in times at bat, hits, and total bases. He is third in runs scored, runs batted in, doubles, triples, and home runs.

"Most of the time," says Bill Virdon, a former Pittsburgh center fielder, addressing Clemente's alleged hypochondria, "if we felt he was hurt, he was going to have a good game. That's kind of the way it turned out."

A play he made in the second game of the 1971 World Series epitomized Clemente's dazzling defensive ability. He raced toward the right field line for a fly ball hit by Frank Robinson, wheeling around counterclockwise as he caught the ball, and whipped it to third, where Richie Hebner just missed getting the sliding Merv Rettenmund.

Virdon, who played next to Clemente and managed him, recalls another unforgettable example of the Clemente style of play.

"In a game at Forbes Field," Virdon relates, "he caught the ball over his shoulder and ran into the concrete wall in right field where the fence angled out. There were some ornaments on the fence that jutted out, and he was going headfirst into it. Somehow he threw his head back and he got cut under the chin instead of getting hit in the throat. It probably saved his life. He caught the ball and hung on to it. When I got there and turned him over, all I could see was the gash under his chin. But other than that, he didn't hurt himself."

There was, obviously, nothing subtle about Clemente's style of play on the field. Nor was there in his actions and words off the field. He was outspoken and he cared about people. The two traits often meshed.

430

"I am very outspoken," he once acknowledged. "When I hear something that is unjust to my teammates or somebody else, I'm going to say something about it."

Clemente often railed at writers for the lack of recognition he felt they accorded him. No question exists in my mind that if he had played in New York, he would have rivaled contemporaries Willie Mays and Mickey Mantle for the adulation of fans and the attention generated by newspapers, magazines and television networks.

But Clemente was as outspoken, if not more so, about the way Latins and blacks were slighted generally. He was in the advance guard of people who criticized the baseball establishment for shunning blacks for managerial jobs. He also spoke out against the reserve system that bound a player to one team until he was traded or released.

He was the first nonwhite players representative on the executive board of the players' union, and he spoke out there, too. Richard Moss, former general counsel of the union, recalls an important meeting in New York that was attended by about 125 players.

"He stood up at that meeting," Moss says, "and talked about why it's important to stick together. He hit everything on the head. He was so influential with the players. It was a very stirring talk."

Marvin Miller, who was the union's executive director, went back even further and remembered a time before Clemente became the Pirates' player representative.

"We were meeting in Mexico City and the Pirates' rep and alternate rep couldn't attend," Miller relates. "I called Roberto. I told him my concerns, that the player reps couldn't come and it was an important meeting. He said, 'You think it's important?' I said, 'Yes.' He said, 'I'll be there.' "

Miller and Moss had a special relationship with Clemente. Like me, they lived in Pittsburgh (working for the steelworkers' union) when he began playing for the Pirates and became ardent fans. The difference was that when they moved to New York, they could not only continue being fans but they could also solicit his cooperation and get it. "He was my favorite player as a fan before I got involved," Moss says, "and he was one of my favorite player reps."

So many people have fond memories of Clemente, but none have fonder ones than Stargell, who became a legend himself in Pittsburgh. Stargell talks of the effect Clemente had on his baseball career and how he touched his life in many ways. "He was like the big brother I never had," says Stargell, prefacing a story about how Clemente gave part of himself to others.

"I remember we were up in Montreal one time." Stargell relates. "Something happened to my back and I couldn't play. I was left in the clubhouse for treatment. Roberto didn't play the first game. He stayed in the clubhouse through the entire game and gave me an ice rubdown. He put this cold ice in his bare hands and would rub and apply pressure to different areas of my back. He said I would be able to play the next day based on things he had learned. It must have been about forty minutes of constant rubbing with that ice. We all know when you put ice in your hand for any period of time, you must release that ice after about five minutes at the most, but he was so into what he was doing, it didn't faze him at all. That was a lesson, too, of what winners are all about. Winners are people who give of themselves and that's what he did in so many ways. A winner to me is not just someone who has great ability. A lot of people have God-given talent, but not many people have the ability to give of themselves and do things for others, bring important issues to the table. It didn't surprise me that that would be the way he would leave this earth because he gave so much of himself."

Clemente, his 3,000th hit attained in the last week of the 1972 regular season, was killed in a plane crash on New Year's Eve that year. It wasn't just a crash of a commercial plane flying to some exotic vacation spot. Clemente, at the age of thirty-eight, father of three young sons, was killed doing something else. He was chairman of a Puerto Rican relief committee that had chartered the plane to take supplies to Nicaragua, which days before had been devastated by an earthquake. Clemente could have let others deliver the plane-load of supplies, but he personally wanted to make sure the supplies were reaching the right people.

"New Year's Eve is one of the most sacred days in Puerto Rico, where everyone spends time with their families," Stargell says. "For him to do that, it was totally out of character in terms of the tradition of his country. But he said, 'Hey, I'm very fortunate that I have my family, and I want to do something for people less fortunate.'"

In his eighteen years in Pittsburgh, Clemente excited the fans as few players had. He inspired his teammates, too. "They held a memorial service for him in Puerto Rico, and a lot of the players were there," Richard Moss recalls. "Manny Sanguillen was out in the bay diving for his body the whole time. Al Oliver didn't stop crying the two or three days they were there. Usually players don't react to other players like that."

Like everyone else, I was shocked at the news of Clemente's death. Unlike most people, though, I was a participant in the next development, albeit posthumous, in Clemente's career. The Baseball Writers Association of America, whose ten-year members vote for the Hall of Fame, decided to waive the five-year waiting period and have a special election, with Clemente's name the only one on the ballot.

As great as Clemente was and as certain a future Hall of Famer he was, I was reluctant to vote yes on this ballot because I was concerned that it might set an undesirable precedent. After debating with myself, however, I finally marked the yes box. I realized that if I didn't vote for Clemente then, I would never again have the opportunity because, as certain as his talent and his character were, so were his chances for election into the Hall of Fame on his first try.

Les Biederman with Joe L. Brown

Maury Allen with Hall of Famer Johnny Bench at New York Baseball Writers annual dinner

Maury Allen
An admirer in New York

*"We waited so long to understand
and appreciate him."*

Maury Allen was a colleague of mine during the nine years I wrote for
The New York Post. *We shared the baseball beat one year — in 1972 —
covering the New York Yankees and Mets. I went to spring training with
the Mets and he with the Yankees. At the All-Star Game break, we
switched teams for the remainder of the year. That was how the baseball
beat was handled at* The Post. *Maury Allen has had a life-long love affair with baseball. The Brooklyn Dodgers were his boyhood team. He was
usually the happiest man in the press box. Some sportswriters snickered
at his constant cheerfulness and enthusiasm, but I thought he was one
of the best on the baseball beat. He was among a group of new wave sportswriters branded "chipmunks" by the late Jimmy Cannon. Allen's enthusiasm always came across in his articles, and the nearly thirty books
he has authored. Nowadays, he writes for the* Herald-Statesman, *a daily
newspaper in Yonkers, New York. He says he attended a Fantasy Camp
a couple of years ago with many of the Dodgers of his youth and "it was
a genuine thrill." He says today's teams are operated by businessmen,
not baseball men, and something has been lost in the transition. This
article was written by Allen for the program of the 50th annual dinner
of the New York Chapter of the Baseball Writers Association of America
in January, 1973, and is reprinted here with Allen's permission. Clemente
had been honored the year before at the same event. I had a table for ten
at that banquet, mostly buddies of mine from Long Island. Clemente stole
the show with his sterling performance that night.*

Roberto Clemente leaves behind some marvelous numbers after
his name. He also leaves behind a beautiful family, his proud
people, his good works.

Less than a year ago, he graced this very dais when we honored
him for his play on the field. He called out, not for attention to his baseball skills, but for greater dignity and appreciation of his people, more
tolerance, more love and understanding.

He spoke, not of baseball games won but of battles not yet fought.
He spoke of his hopes for a sports complex in Puerto Rico for the kids
of his land, for fun and joy and life. He had been underappreciated and
overly criticized.

It took his full career to win his fight for his manliness, and all
from this country — and any other country which enjoys our national
pastime with us — owe him a debt of gratitude.

Let us not weep for this brave and good man. Let us be thankful
we finally recognized his power and glory before the final out.

He played the game with a passion and a verve we may not see again in our lifetime. He never allowed himself to be crushed or taken by the easy roads. He was a man among men.

His good friend, sportswriter Les Biederman, wrote in these pages last January, "Clemente was called to the microphone in the Pirate clubhouse after their proud victory. He asked permission to say a few words in Spanish to his mother and father in Puerto Rico. 'On this, the proudest moment of my life, I ask your blessing,' he said. How many athletes think of their parents at the moment of their greatest glory?"

The loss of Roberto Clemente is strongest for his parents, his wife, his three handsome sons, his friends, his countrymen. His loss is harder for all baseball. We waited so long to understand and appreciate him.

MAURY ALLEN'S
TOP 100 ALL-TIME
BASEBALL PLAYERS

1. Willie Mays
2. Hank Aaron
3. Babe Ruth
4. Ted Williams
5. Stan Musial
6. Joe DiMaggio
7. Ty Cobb
8. Lou Gehrig
9. Walter Johnson
10. Rogers Hornsby

11. Jackie Robinson
12. Roberto Clemente
13. Christy Mathewson
14. Tris Speaker
15. Mel Ott
16. George Sisler
17. Grover Cleveland Alexander
18. Lefty Grove
19. Bill Dickey
20. Mickey Mantle

Other Pirates in Top 100: 40. Paul Waner; 46. Ralph Kiner; 58. Maury Wills; 67. Willie Stargell; 73. Billy Herman; 75. Dave Parker; 80. Jim Bunning; 87. Pie Traynor; 92. Joe Gordon.

—From Maury Allen Baseball's 100
Galahad Books, New York City, 1981.

Stan Musial

Babe Ruth

Mickey Mantle

Dick Young
The best baseball writer

"Always ask yourself
'Is it worth it?'"

*I learned a lot from Dick Young during my nine years (1970-1979) in New York, writing sports for a rival newspaper, **The New York Post**. He was a celebrated columnist for **The Daily News**, but even more so he was heralded as the best baseball beat writer in the land.*

His silver hair was always combed just so, and he was a dapper dresser, and he walked with a cocky air about him. To some, he was downright arrogant. He had a chin that was chiseled from granite, and he almost dared some to take a swipe at that chin, a smugness, a sense of humor, and a belief that he knew what was best for everybody in baseball. Dick Young knew baseball.

I was 29 when I first arrived in The Big Apple, and Young, one of the senior citizens of sportswriters even then, took a liking to me. He offered advice freely and I soaked it up. He became one of my many mentors among the media veterans.

He said a sportswriter should wear a business suit, or at least a sports jacket and slacks when he went to the ballpark, and especially when he came into the clubhouse to interview the managers or coaches and the players. "The clubhouse is your office," he said. "You should dress for a day at the office.

"Notice how the owners dress. Notice how the ballplayers dress. If you dress like the clubhouse boy they'll treat you that way."

He cautioned me about what to write and what not to write. "Remember when you are on a team plane that you are there as their guest. The same goes for traveling on the team bus. If you overhear something on the plane or bus, it's best you keep it there.

"No matter what you write, you should always ask yourself, 'Is it worth it?' You don't want to shut off your sources. If you write something strong, or controversial, be sure to show up in the clubhouse the next day, even if it's your day off or you're on vacation. Face the music. If they've got something to say, let them say it. But let them know you are doing your job, and you're going to be back the next day. Don't let bad feelings fester. Get it out in the open as soon as possible. And stand up for yourself. Don't back down on what you write."

No one ever called Dick Young "a houseman."

On one of my first road trips with a New York sports team, I was in San Diego with the Mets. Young and I were the only sportswriters staying with the Mets at an old hotel in the middle of downtown San Diego. The rest of the writers were out at a newer, posher hotel complex in the suburbs.

Young and I were both sitting around the hotel swimming pool one day, both in swimsuits, both typing away on our portable typewriters.

The Mets made a trade that day, and he and I were the first to report it. It reinforced what Young felt about being on the road with a team, even in sunny southern California. "My newspaper did not send me out here on a vacation," he said, smartly. "I'm out here to work. That doesn't mean I can't get a tan, but it means I don't want to get burnt by any other sportswriters getting a story I miss because I'm in the wrong place at the wrong time."

Young was a conservative voice, often thought to be living in an earlier century by some of the younger sportswriters. He wasn't quick to champion blacks in sports, but when he came around to it, he did so with his usual brutish passion.

Before Young died, I had an opportunity to talk to him on the telephone one day at the offices of the Pittsburgh Steelers, and say "thank you" for all that he had taught me.

No one celebrated Roberto Clemente any more than Young did in a column written on Oct. 13, 1971. It had a Pittsburgh dateline. The 1971 World Series belonged to Clemente. As the media made much about his ability, it annoyed him. "I play thees way for seventeen years in the majorleagues," he said. "Why they just now find eet out?"

*Here's Young's column on the subject, reprinted with permission of **The Daily News**.*

The best damn ballplayer in the World Series, maybe in the whole world, is Roberto Clemente, and as far as I'm concerned, they can give him the automobile right now.

Maybe some guys hit the ball farther, and some throw it harder, and one or two run faster, although I doubt that, but nobody puts it all together like Roberto.

"He's showing the others how to play the game, isn't he?" said Lee McPhail at Press Hq., where lots of people, in lots of little groups, were talking up the Roberto Clemente-for-the-automobile (as Series MVP) movement.

They were talking not only of how well Clemente plays the game, but how hard he plays it. Mainly how hard. In this day of the primadonna athlete, the guy who isn't in the mood to run out a ground ball, or chase a fly, Roberto Clemente gives dignity to the word hustler.

The true test of the baseball hustler is what he does when his team is losing. In the first two games, when the Orioles were beating the brains out of the Pirates, you would hear baseball people saying, "How about that Clemente!" and there was a professional admiration which those in the game like to believe is their exclusive property.

"Greatest throw I ever saw by an outfielder," said Andy Etchebarren after Game 2. He meant the play by Roberto Clemente in the middle of the game. The strangest part was that the throw didn't get anybody; didn't mean a thing. It came in the midst of a six-run Baltimore inning, at a time when a player on the losing team might be expected to start going through the motions.

437

Clemente raced to the right line, caught Frank Robinson's fly on the glove side, did a complete spinning turn and fired a strike to third, where the runner was sliding in on a tag-up advance. The runner was Merv Rettenmund, a quickie.

"You'd have had him, if it weren't Rettenmund," a praising newsman said afterward.

"Eef I have my good arm thee ball gets there a leetle quicker than he gets there," said Clemente.

Roberto has been playing with a sore shoulder since late July. It is one of the inside jokes of baseball that Roberto Clemente always is playing with some ache or pain, and the more he hurts the more dangerous he becomes. Somebody once said that three years after he is dead, Roberto will lead the National League in hitting.

"They laugh at me, but I heet thee ball," says Roberto, pointing to his teammates.

There is very little humor in Roberto Clemente, and none at all where baseball is involved. It is his life, his escape. It has given the little boy from Carolina, Puerto Rico, with the running nose and the kickout knee in his pants, a chance to become rich, to live in a large and elegant home he has had built in Rio Piedras, and you do not laugh at such things.

"When we have a meeting een thee clubhouse, when Harry Walker ees thee manager," says Roberto, "thee writers say that Clemente he ees taking the team away from Walker. Thee press crucify me, but they do not know what ees all about. I tell thee players, either you play baseball, or you don't play baseball. Eet ees not too much that you geev one hunert percent. That ees thee on'y theen that make me mad, when a player don't ron."

In Game 3, Roberto Clemente hit a ground ball to the right side first time up. It was stamped DP. The Orioles got one. In the seventh, Clemente led off with a bouncer back to the box. Mike Cuellar knocked it down, picked it up, was aghast to see the batter streaking down the line, hurried his throw, high, and Clemente was safe. The next batter walked on four pitches, the next batter hit the ball out of the park. Mike Cuellar's composure was shattered. The game was over.

"It all began with Clemente hustling to first," said Cardinals star Joe Torre. "He knows only one way to play this game."

He knows, too, that he must take care of himself or he will squander the gifts he has been given, as do so many. "I weel go home after the Worl Series," he says; "an' rest my shoul'er for a leetle while, then I weel exercise to make eet strong, an next year I come back, an' hope eet weel be the way eet should be. I have eet always een my head to take good care of my body. Some players go home an' start drinkin' and eatin' peanuts and come to camp weeth beeg bellies."

Roberto Clemente is a 37-year-old roadrunner. He has spent 18 summers of those years playing baseball for the Pittsburgh Pirates. He has batted over .300 thirteen times, and for the last three seasons, in his decrepitude, he has hit .345 . . . .352 . . . .341.

But everybody has numbers. Don't mind the numbers. Just watch how Roberto Clemente runs 90 feet the next time he hits the ball back to the pitcher and ask yourself if you work at your job that way. Every time I see Roberto Clemente play ball, I think of the times I've heard about how "they" dog it, and I want to vomit.

New York Mets

Casey Stengel and Roberto are all smiles at Shea Stadium.

More On MAZ And The '60 Bucs
Reviews And Reflections

*"The most beloved sports team
in Pittsburgh history."*

Dave Ailes, sports editor, Pittsburgh Tribune-Review

The 1960 Pirates captured the heart of the city and the attention of a nation at a time when baseball was still a fun game — unfrittered by salary negotiations, free agents, signing bonuses and drug problems.

Maybe it was the fact that no pro team in Pittsburgh had won a championship of anything for 33 long-suffering seasons. Maybe it was because the 1959 Pirates finished fourth, just two games over .500 and the 1960 Pirates were expected to slide down the National League scale. As always.

For these reasons, and a couple of dozen others, the '60 Pirates became the most beloved, most talked about, most written about and, arguably, the most remembered sports team in Pittsburgh's history.

"Destiny's Darlings." That's the tag attached to the Pirates when, at 3:36 p.m. on October 13, Bill Mazeroski sent a 1-0 pitch from Ralph Terry on a journey that turned a city upside-down.

The details of that season and the men who shaped it, are the centerposts of a 512-page, attractive and interesting book, *MAZ And The '60 Bucs*. It's the fifth and bourbon-smooth best, in a Pittsburgh Proud series of books by Jim O'Brien, a free-lance writer and native son.

During exhaustive reviews and interviews about Pittsburgh baseball, the author came across countless facts that have slipped through the cracks in the intervening 30 some years.

Mostly, though, you'll take a ride with O'Brien through the improbable 1960 season — capped, of course, by a homer that is etched in the minds of Pittsburgh baseball fans as much as the moment they learned of JFK's assassination. Dozens told O'Brien precisely what they were doing when Maz began running the bases.

The book is a well-researched, fascinating look at a team that stands alone in Pittsburgh baseball folklore. It's available at all district book stores. If you don't buy it, O'Brien's liable to come down your chimney with it on Christmas morning. He seldom takes no for an answer. Either way, I recommend it. Unequivocally.

Alan Robinson, Associated Press writer

O'Brien, who previously wrote two books on the Steelers, has turned a detective's eye for detail to an appealing team that understandably seems to grow in popularity and status as the years go by.

O'Brien chronicles not only the Pirates' unexpected drive to the National League pennant, but also their near-miraculous resiliency in defeating the New York Yankees in a World Series that still defies description more than 30 years later.

The Pirates were outscored in the series 55-27 and withstood losses of 16-3, 12-0 and 10-0 — the worst in the history of ANY World Series team — before winning an excruciatingly tense 10-9 victory in the best Game 7 ever played.

O'Brien disdains the normal April-to-October chronology approach and devotes individual chapters not only to the stars — Mazeroski, Haddix and Hal W. Smith — but also to a diverse group that include Forbes Field's ushers and Sam Narron, a long-forgotten coach.

One of the best chapters is on Haddix, who once pitched the best game in major-league history but had a hard time climbing the stairs of his home due to emphysema (and died from it nine months after the interview).

Andrew Wilson, Allegheny Business News

The book contains the reflections of most of Maz's Pirates teammates from the 1960 squad and subsequent years, several New York Yankees including Mickey Mantle, Whitey Ford and Yogi Berra, and the memories of sportswriters, ushers, Oakland residents, other sports stars and countless Pittsburghers who either saw the game in person or remember what they were doing when Maz brought down the town.

This book, like the first two books on the Steelers in his "Pittsburgh Proud" series, *Doing It Right* and *Whatever It Takes*, was printed at Geyer Printing in Oakland. The type-setting was done at Cold-Comp on Penn Avenue Downtown. O'Brien takes great pride in having his books done right here in Pittsburgh. His first two books have virtually sold out, and his new book is selling well.

MAZ And The '60 Bucs is more than a sports book. It is a book of memories. Memories of Forbes Field, the '60 Bucs, Maz, Clemente, the University of Pittsburgh, and Oakland in the 1960s fill each page. While some of these memories belong to Mr. O'Brien and the former players he interviewed, many of the memories belong to ordinary Pittsburghers who were invited to share their memories of 1960. Including the memories of ordinary people in his book is a stroke of genius.

For Pittsburghers, Maz's home run is part of the collective consciousness. O'Brien is optimistic about his self-publishing efforts. And like Maz in the 1960 Series, he's looking to hit a home run.

Doug Huff, sports editor, The Wheeling-Intelligencer

Nobody has a passion for a community or its sports teams any more than Pittsburgh-area journalist Jim O'Brien. The real appeal of O'Brien's well-researched books is the personal touch. Pittsburgh Pirates fans should not leave home without it. That would be a copy of *MAZ And The '60 Bucs*, the newest book in the "Pittsburgh Proud" series by O'Brien. It should be included in the personal library of all those tri-state fans who follow the Bucs.

Gene Carney, Notes From The Shadows Of Cooperstown newsletter

The book is hard-core nostalgia, if you happened to be a Buc fan in 1960. You are dazzled that you knew these players so well, from pre-game and post-game radio & TV interviews, from columns in the three or four newspapers of the day, from being physically close to them, at and around Forbes Field.

Reading *MAZ* was like attending a family reunion. A lot of retelling of stories, most of them wonderfully familiar, but still funny or sad. And there were some I never heard before, or long forgot.

MAZ is a feel-good book. I felt good that so many of the players from that team have kept in touch, have made the reunions, have succeeded in some other career. And that their memories of 1960 are so much like my own. If ever a team busted their butts for a city, this was it. I know that sounds corny, maybe delusional to some. But that's the way it was.

Les Harvath, baseball coach, sportswriter Jeannette Spirit

Through O'Brien's eyes and by virtue of his pen and down home writing style, *MAZ And The '60 Bucs*, relives not just the momentous occasion, but that memorable year as well. Pittsburgh personalities Bob Prince, Dick Groat and the great Roberto Clemente receive their due, as O'Brien adeptly provides in-depth personality profiles of the sports figures who made Pittsburgh their home. He has also authored two books on the Steelers with a genuine style becoming familiar throughout the area. Included in *MAZ* are the unique insights on sports personalities, fascinating profiles, and man-on-the-street interviews with people who have been witness to Pittsburgh sports history.

Jim Lokhaiser, WISR Radio, Butler, Pa.

I was working full-time at WISR Radio when I went to Fort Myers to cover the Pirates in 1961. At that time, Fort Myers was a small town with little to do after dark. The facilities at the ballpark were bad. The locker room was smaller than the one we have at Pullman Park in Butler. The thing I remember most about the clubhouse was the toilet facilities. There was a total of one toilet for both the players and any media people. Standing in line was the order of the day.

Since we had to find a room at a motel in the city it was a must to have a rental car or find a ride to the park each day. I did rent a car and was put in charge of getting Pie Traynor to and from the park each day. After a couple of days, he talked me into driving him to the dog track each night.

Most conversation in the winter of 1961 during spring training was the lack of media coverage, especially after winning a World Series. Both Pittsburgh newspapers, a couple of TV stations and two photographers were there and that was it. I was very young and new at the radio business, but Joe Brown made sure I was taken care of. Jack Berger, the public relations director, took me under his wing and made me feel at home. As a matter of fact, Jack and Nell, his wife, remain good friends today. We see each other often, mostly for dinner.

One of the most unique interviews I did at Fort Myers was with Harry "The Hat" Walker. He was Pittsburgh's batting instructor. I asked him one question about his hitting philosophy and twenty minutes later, I had to stop him to change the tape. He was a true teacher of the game. I was there when Maury Wills came into the Pittsburgh camp after being obtained in a trade. He was a true bastard.

When the Pirates moved their spring training camp to Bradenton, Florida, I was one of the first to be housed there. I roomed with a *Press* photographer named Ed Morgan. The other photographer there was Jim Klingensmith of the *Post-Gazette*. Players like Richie Hebner, Al Oliver and Bob Robertson were rookies at the time. Robertson was a third baseman until they, the coaches, saw him throw from third to first. He damn near killed four or five old people who were sitting behind first base. They moved him from third to the outfield and, finally, to first base. Another true bastard.

Enough of this. Your book sparked so many memories. I could tell you a million stories about my trips to Florida. I fished with Bob Veale, drank with Hully (equipment man John Hallahan), and got asked to leave the clubhouse by Manager Larry Shepard. Another true bastard.

Jim O'Brien

im Lokhaiser and Ronnie Kline take coffee break at The Hot Dog Shoppe in Butler.

The Readers Always Write

*"This Christmas my sister, Mary Kay Leters, presented me with your book, **MAZ And The '60 Bucs**. This is the third year in a row that my sister has given me one of your books. I really enjoyed **Doing It Right** and **Whatever It Takes**, as I had your earlier books, **Hail to Pitt** and **Pittsburgh: The Story of the City of Champions**. But this book on Maz and the Bucs is special. I was dreading the approaching moment when the book ran out of pages. That ball club has always had a very special place in my heart. It seems that every few days a memory of that club will zip through my mind. As for Maz, he has always been my favorite and I was struck by what you wrote on page 86: 'I suggested to Mazeroski that he was much richer than most of today's ballplayers, like Jose Canseco, Rickey Henderson, Bobby Bonilla, Doug Drabek and Barry Bonds, none of whom seem as contented as Mazeroski.' You are right. Part of Maz's richness rests in the fact that he has remained a very important part of people's lives years after he retired from baseball. Maz is a rich man, indeed."*

— Frank R. Nowak, Stafford, Va.

"My wife and I were in seats 24 rows back behind third base. Three rows ahead sat an individual in an open shirt with a bottle of whiskey which he kept sipping on. By the time Maz struck his mighty blow, this poor guy was in his undershirt sound asleep."

— Jack Truschel, Pittsburgh

"I enjoyed every sentence in the book. I was there during the glory days as director of the scouting program for the Pirates. The pictures and the stories brought back many super memories."

— Rex Bowen

"The times were just so much more simple and innocent. 1960 is as far away from us now as the 19th Century. The Pirates victory in 1960 is a testimonial that is still valid today — a testimonial to hard work, patience and perseverance. Most members of the team were common men with average baseball ability, but their accomplishment is legendary. I was a senior at good old McKeesport High School in the fall of 1960. I had just returned to my home room to pick up my books to go home when Maz hit the home run. I still remember the books I was carrying. When I got home, I set off firecrackers on Ohio Avenue in White Oak. I'm sure the neighbors appreciated that. I can't wait to read your next book. I don't agree with Carly Simon anymore: 'These are the good old days.' I find myself wishing a lot that it was 1960."

— Gordon W. Hill, Penn Hills, Pa.

*"Am reading **MAZ And The '60 Bucs**, and it has brought back many fond memories. I can appreciate your positive feelings for the Pittsburgh area, since I have lived my entire life here. I attended a small parochial school in Polish Hill, graduated from Central Catholic High School in '63, and Duquesne University in '67, and put in a year of graduate studies at Pitt in '68. Thanks for the memories."*

— Rich Garstka, Munhall, Pa.

"Growing up in northern Michigan, I was never a Pirates fan. My dad liked the Tigers, but I was always a Brewers and Cubs fan. However, since I've lived in Pennsylvania I have heard many folks reminisce about the magic of the '60 Pirates season. Enough so, that my curiosity got the better of me, and I started reading your book. I had a hard time putting it down! As I progressed through the book, I could almost feel the excitement Pirates fans felt 33 autumns ago! Somehow you've been able to capture that special essence that makes baseball the sport that memories are made of. If only today's players had a little more of the character of the '60 Bucs."

— Pete Frecchio, Program Director
FM-WDSN Radio, DuBois, Pa.

*"I bought **MAZ And The '60 Bucs** yesterday at South Hills Village and finished it just this minute (9:15 a.m.). You've done an absolutely outstanding job of not only re-creating and re-living that unforgettable day, but also included so many different and interesting facts and other happenings in 1960! I enjoyed your books about the Pittsburgh Steelers, but you've outdone yourself with this book."*

— Olin J. DePolo, Bethel Park, Pa.

*"This past Christmas, my parents, who still live in Pittsburgh, gave me **Whatever It Takes**. I just loved it and believe me I read it on one cold Sunday afternoon. I am a native Pittsburgher and I am still true to all the Steel City teams. One day I hope to go back and live in our beautiful city."*

— Hank Zourelias, Lynchburg, Va.

"I thoroughly enjoyed both of your books on the Pittsburgh Steelers. They brought back a lot of memories. I am a native Pittsburgher, being born and raised in Elizabeth and living five years in Upper St. Clair. Although my career and my family has taken me elsewhere, my allegiance and heart will always lie in the Steel City."

— Thomas A. Edwards, Coral Gables, Fla.

*"I just finished reading **Whatever It Takes**. Thank you for bringing back the Steelers of the '60s for me. J.R. Wilburn, Roy Jefferson, Paul Martha, WOW! I remember thinking as a 12-year-old 'the Steelers aren't that good, but Ben McGee and Dick Hoak could play for almost any team in the league.' Then to be rewarded as a loyal fan with the greatest team in the history of the game during the '70s . . . well, it can't get any better.'*
— Allan D. Weisel, Morrisville, Pa

*"I am really enjoying your book, **Whatever It Takes**. You not only have a lot of good stories to tell, but a very personal way of telling them. I can easily imagine talking with you over coffee at church. It gives me a close and memorable feeling of Pittsburgh and my many friends. I am glad you didn't leave Pittsburgh. Your true calling is there to pass on all the sports legends. I am traveling a lot more now, especially to the west coast. Bringing along your book is like bringing a special friend and enjoying the conversation."*
— Tommy Michaels, West Simsbury, Conn

"My family had always been Pirates fans. My Dad loved Rosey Rowswell and his 'Open the window, Aunt Minnie!' call. We listened to many games on the radio before TV coverage became available. On that glorious, wonderful day in 1960, I was at home, caring for my three children, the youngest born on August 1, 1960, was sick. I had the TV on, watching it on and off all afternoon. Maz's home run was unbelievable. My husband worked in Downtown and when he got home he told us about office workers shredding paper (much of which was missed the next day) and throwing it out windows, blowing horns, people hugging each other, some non-believers stunned at our Bucs! That evening, taking my son to the doctor, we picked up a sailor who was hitch-hiking. He had come through Downtown and he said everyone was crazy; it was one big block party. I will never forget that day. We the lowly Pirates had beat the mighty Yankees to become World Champions!!! Thanks for writing a book about them. They mean so much to so many people."
— Joanne Shade Phillip

"My dad Eldon played for Notre Dame and, instead of playing with the Bucs and his military service pal Don Hoak, became a Pirates scout, got married and had me — the first of ten children. We attended every Giants game when the Bucs were in Candlestick and I wore out my transistor radio and ear plug when they took on the Giants in Pittsburgh. With that plug wired down my school sweater, I listened to that seventh game of the 1960 World Series on October 13, 1960 and remember a sick feeling as my mom picked us up at school with the Pirates down by a couple of runs halfway through the game. That game and that season taught my brothers and I the importance of hanging tough — like the Pirate team. That lesson and that memory will live on forever as will the spirit

446

of Roberto Clemente, God rest his soul! My brother Mike and I went to the Pirates Fantasy Camp in Bradenton, Florida this January. We hope to attend the unveiling of the Roberto Clemente statue in July, 1994. Maybe we are cousins. . ."

— James D. O'Brien, Lake Arrowhead, Calif.

*"Thank you so much for writing **MAZ And The '60 Bucs**. I have found it to be a great book. Let's hope the book becomes a national success and maybe opens some eyes for the Hall of Fame for my father."*

— Darren Mazeroski, Baseball Coach
Gulf Coast Community College
Panama City, Florida

*"I bought your book, **MAZ And The '60 Bucs**, as a Christmas present for my brother, Bruce Wilson. We grew up in Squirrel Hill and spent many an hour listening to the Pirates broadcasts. We would take the street-car down to Forbes Field to see the games. During most of our youth the Pirates were in the cellar, so we, like other fans of the Bucs, really were thrilled in 1960 when we won the World Series. My brother was distracted during that final game because his first child, a daughter named Muffy, was born about 2:30 that afternoon. I gave him the book to bring back that good time and possibly to help him fill in the gaps of the events of that day."*

— Marilyn Wilson Bonner, Maple Glen, Pa.

*"Now that I have read your book on the 1960 Pirates — although I was not even born in 1960 — I am able to have interesting conversations with my old co-workers about the 1960 team. I find myself asking them where they were when Mazeroski's home run cleared the wall. Being 30 years old, I have little recollection of Forbes Field. However, your words and corresponding photographs were like a time machine putting me back in 1960 and being part of the Oakland and Forbes Field experience. Although I have read several books on old stadiums (**Lost Ballparks** and **Green Cathedrals**), this book revealed more about Forbes Field and how much I wished I could watch baseball there today. Although your two books on the Steelers were great, I found this to be the best. Sorry, I did not read your book on the Sports History of Pitt, because being a Penn State grad makes it forbidden reading."*

— Barry Lyons, Perryopolis, Pa.

*"Your book, **MAZ And The '60 Bucs**, is fantastic! I keep re-reading it. You also captured my youth because I could relate to so many of your own stories."*

— Bob Rulong, Mt. Pleasant, Mich.
(formerly Moundsville, West Va.)

447

Share Roberto's Dream

The Roberto Clemente Foundation is a non-profit, charitable organization established by the family of Roberto Clemente to continue his dream of providing all children with a better life through sports and education.

The Foundation will provide children in the Pittsburgh area with an opportunity to learn, enjoy and participate in sports of all kinds in order to instill in them the qualities of responsibility, character and leadership.

The Foundation also will emphasize the importance of education through supplemental tutoring and will rehabilitate local parks, playgrounds and ball-fields. If you would like to help continue Roberto's dream, please send your tax deductible contribution, payable to the "Roberto Clemente Foundation," to Roberto Clemente Foundation, Bank Tower, 307 Fourth Avenue, Suite 508, Pittsburgh PA 15222. Thank you for your support.

FROM THE PARLOR TO THE ALTAR
Romance and Marriage in the 1800s

DAILY LIFE IN AMERICA IN THE 1800s

FROM THE PARLOR TO THE ALTAR
Romance and Marriage in the 1800s

by

Zachary Chastain

Mason Crest Publishers

MASON CREST PUBLISHERS INC.
370 Reed Road
Broomall, Pennsylvania 19008
(866)MCP-BOOK (toll free)
www.masoncrest.com

First Printing
9 8 7 6 5 4 3 2 1

Library of Congress Cataloging-in-Publication Data

Chastain, Zachary.
 From the parlor to the altar : romance and marriage in the 1800s / by Zachary Chas-
tain.
    p. cm. — (Daily life in America in the 1800s)
 Includes bibliographical references and index.
 ISBN 978-1-4222-1779-5 (hardcover)   ISBN (series) 978-1-4222-1774-0
 ISBN 978-1-4222-1852-5 (pbk.)   ISBN (pbk. series) 978-1-4222-1847-1
 1. Marriage—United States—History—19th century—Juvenile literature. 2. Courtship—
United States—History—19th century—Juvenile literature. 3. United States—Social life
and customs—19th century—Juvenile literature. I. Title.
 HQ744.C48 2011
 306.810973'09034—dc22
                                      2010029720

Produced by Harding House Publishing Service, Inc.
www.hardinghousepages.com
Interior Design by MK Bassett-Harvey.
Cover design by Torque Advertising + Design.
Printed in USA by Bang Printing.

Contents

Introduction

History can too often seem a parade of distant figures whose lives have no connection to our own. It need not be this way, for if we explore the history of the games people play, the food they eat, the ways they transport themselves, how they worship and go to war—activities common to all generations—we close the gap between past and present. Since the 1960s, historians have learned vast amounts about daily life in earlier periods. This superb series brings us the fruits of that research, thereby making meaningful the lives of those who have gone before.

The authors' vivid, fascinating descriptions invite young readers to journey into a past that is simultaneously strange and familiar. The 1800s were different, but, because they experienced the beginnings of the same baffling modernity were are still dealing with today, they are also similar. This was the moment when millennia of agrarian existence gave way to a new urban, industrial era. Many of the things we take for granted, such as speed of transportation and communication, bewildered those who were the first to behold the steam train and the telegraph. Young readers will be interested to learn that growing up then was no less confusing and difficult then than it is now, that people were no more in agreement on matters of religion, marriage, and family then than they are now.

We are still working through the problems of modernity, such as environmental degradation, that people in the nineteenth century experienced for the first time. Because they met the challenges with admirable ingenuity, we can learn much from them. They left behind a treasure trove of alternative living arrangements, cultures, entertainments, technologies, even diets that are even more relevant today. Students cannot help but be intrigued, not just by the technological ingenuity of those times, but by the courage of people who forged new frontiers, experimented with ideas and social arrangements. They will be surprised by the degree to which young people were engaged in the great events of the time, and how women joined men in the great adventures of the day.

When history is viewed, as it is here, from the bottom up, it becomes clear just how much modern America owes to the genius of ordinary people, to the labor of slaves and immigrants, to women as well as men, to both young people and adults. Focused on home and family life, books in this series provide insight into how much of history is made within the intimate spaces of private life rather than in the remote precincts of public power. The 1800s were the era of the self-made man and women, but also of the self-made communities. The past offers us a plethora of heroes and heroines together with examples of extraordinary collective action from the Underground Railway to the creation of the American trade union movement. There is scarcely an immigrant or ethic organization in America today that does not trace its origins to the nineteenth century.

This series is exceptionally well illustrated. Students will be fascinated by the images of both rural and urban life; and they will be able to find people their own age in these marvelous depictions of play as well as work. History is best when it engages our imagination, draws us out of our own time into another era, allowing us to return to the present with new perspectives on ourselves. My first engagement with the history of daily life came in sixth grade when my teacher, Mrs. Polster, had us do special projects on the history of the nearby Erie Canal. For the first time, history became real to me. It has remained my passion and my compass ever since.

The value of this series is that it opens up a dialogue with a past that is by no means dead and gone but lives on in every dimension of our daily lives. When history texts focus exclusively on political events, they invariably produce a sense of distance. This series creates the opposite effect by encouraging students to see themselves in the flow of history. In revealing the degree to which people in the past made their own history, students are encouraged to imagine themselves as being history-makers in their own right. The realization that history is not something apart from ourselves, a parade that passes us by, but rather an ongoing pageant in which we are all participants, is both exhilarating and liberating, one that connects our present not just with the past but also to a future we are responsible for shaping.

—*Dr. John Gillis, Rutgers University Professor of History Emeritus*

1800 1801 1803 1804

1800 The Library of Congress is established.

1801 Thomas Jefferson is elected as the third President of the United States.

1804 Journey of Lewis and Clark— Lewis and Clark lead a team of explorers westward to the Columbia River in Oregon.

1803 Louisiana Purchase—The United States purchases land from France and begins westward exploration.

1825 1838 1839 1843

1825 The Erie Canal is completed— This allows direct transportation between the Great Lakes and the Atlantic Ocean.

1838 Trail of Tears—General Winfield Scott and 7,000 troops force Cherokees to walk from Georgia to a reservation set up for them in Oklahoma (nearly 1,000 miles). Around 4,000 Native Americans die during the journey.

1839 The first US state, Mississippi, grants women the right to hold property in their own name— with their husband's permission.

1839 The first camera is patented by Louis Daguerre.

1843 Congress passes a law giving women the legal right to make wills.

1812

1812 War of 1812—Fought between the United States and the United Kingdom.

1820

1820 Missouri Compromise—Agreement passes between pro-slavery and abolitionist groups, stating that all the Louisiana Purchase territory north of the southern boundary of Missouri (except for Missouri) will be free states, and the territory south of that line will be slave.

1823

1823 Monroe Doctrine—States that any efforts made by Europe to colonize or interfere with land owned by the United States will be viewed as aggression and require military intervention.

1824

1824 "Redwood," a novel by Catharine Sedgwick, is published, in which the Shaker community is described, including their practice of refusing marriage.

1848

1848 Seneca Falls Convention—Feminist convention held for women's suffrage and equal legal rights.

1848 The Oneida Community is founded in upstate New York by John Noyes. The new community encourages a form of group marriage called "complex marriage."

1848 Married Women's Property Act is passed by the state of New York guaranteeing that married women retain control of their property during a marriage.

1854

1854 Kansas-Nebraska Act—States that each new State entering the country will decide for themselves whether or not to allow slavery. This goes directly against the terms agreed upon in the Missouri Compromise of 1820.

1855

1855 Lucy Stone and Henry Blackwell sign a statement prior to their marriage stating that they protest laws which give the husband superiority and dominance over his wife.

1861

1861(-65) Civil War —Fought between the Union and Confederate states.

1862

1862 Emancipation Proclamation— Lincoln states that all slaves in Union states are to be freed.

1862 Homestead Act passed, promising 160 acres of free land to any U.S. citizen. To keep their land, settlers had to build homes and "improve" upon the land.

1865

1865 Thirteenth Amendment to the United States Constitution—Officially abolishes slavery across the country.

1865 President Abraham Lincoln is assassinated on April 15.

1865 Mississippi Black Code bans blacks from marrying whites, punishable by life imprisonment.

1877

1877 Great Railroad Strike— Often considered the country's first nationwide labor strike.

1878

1878 Thomas Edison patents the phonograph on February 19.

1878 Thomas Edison invents the light bulb on October 22.

1886

1880 (-1900) Almost all states increase their age of consent — the age at which a person can legally consent to sexual acts— from ten to at least sixteen.

1886

1886 The Statue of Liberty is dedicated on October 28.

1867   1869   1870   1875   1876

1867 United States purchases Alaska from Russia.

1869 Transcontinental Railroad completed on May 10.

1870 Fifteenth Amendment to the United States Constitution—Prohibits any citizen from being denied to vote based on their "race, color, or previous condition of servitude."

1870 Christmas is declared a national holiday.

1875 Page Law puts an end to immigration of Chinese women, fearing interracial marriage and that the Chinese might begin to form families in the U.S.

1876 Alexander Graham Bell invents the telephone.

of the 1800s

1890   1892   1896   1898

1890 Wounded Knee Massacre—Last battle in the American Indian Wars.

1890 The Mormon Church officially bans the practice of polygamy.

1892 Ellis Island is opened to receive immigrants coming into New York.

1896 Plessy vs. Ferguson—Supreme Court case that rules that racial segregation is legal as long as accommodations are kept equal.

1896 Henry Ford builds his first combustion-powered vehicle, which he names the Ford Quadricycle.

1898 The Spanish-American War—The United States gains control of Cuba, Puerto Rico, and the Philippines.

Part I
Changing Times

Practical Marriages

It's hard to believe, but marriage wasn't always about love. Or even about one person finding happiness with another. In fact, both ideas are relatively new to the conversation surrounding marriage. The young man standing beneath his true love's window while he strums songs on his guitar, the long romantic drive in the moonlight, candlelit dinners for two—all these were foreign to the idea of romance and marriage at the beginning of the 1800s. But they were quickly on their way. Times were changing.

In the year 1800, marriage in both Europe and the United States was largely an economic arrangement. To marry outside of one's social class was rare. Marriages took place for a variety of reasons, with love as an occasional bonus. People married for money, hoping to move up a few notches on the economic ladder, or they married for political reasons. Kings married their daughters to princes in order to grow their armies and their kingdoms. Merchants' daughters were wed to other merchants' sons to consolidate a business. Marriage itself was a business. The wealthy married one another to stay wealthy, and the poor married one another to survive.

A struggle between two cultural forces emerged in the 1800s, however. Traditional views on marriage and romance came head to head with new ideas about how men and women should behave and what they should expect from one another.

The American Dream, the Land of Opportunity

In the history of the world, the United States added a very interesting chapter when it declared and won its independence. As a new nation, the United States was founded on principles of democracy and freedom for all. Much more so than most Europeans, Americans have always felt that they can do anything and be anyone. The very creation of the new nation was an experiment, a chance to start the world over and see what happened next.

The changes of the 1800s only furthered America's image of itself as the "Land of Opportunity." The middle class grew larger. Technology and the Industrial Revolution pushed the population away from rural communities and into the city looking for jobs. Waves of immigrants landed on American shores hoping for a better life.

America in the 1800s was the perfect place for a new concept of marriage to be born. The American spirit of democ-

Factories offered new jobs to women. This led to changes in women's role within marriage.

racy encouraged people to break down economic barriers. Americans believed that even the poorest man could, with enough hard work, become a wealthy man (or at least lead a respectable life). America was the land of opportunity, and this applied to marriage as much as it did to money. If any man could move up the economic ladder, then why couldn't he marry a woman from any place on that ladder?

A bride in all her finery represented part of the American dream.

Romanticism

The Romantic Era began in Europe in the late 1700s, but carried over into the United States throughout the 1800s. Today, we connect the word "romantic" with the emotional feelings between a couple, but in the 1800s, the word referred to the idea that an individual's emotions, imagination, and intellect were as important (if not more so) than society's expectations. Romanticism was a nineteenth-century movement that encouraged rebellion against the structures of the past. According to this way of thinking, individuals should think for themselves.

Romanticism should not be confused with "romance." Romanticism was a system of ideas and a way of seeing the world; romance is love or affection between two people. The two became interwoven in the United States in the 1800s, however. The writers and artists who expressed the ideals of Romanticism encouraged young men and women to look at romance and marriage differently.

They emphasized the desires of the individual, making it more acceptable to pursue romantic love over traditional marriage for money and survival.

Expectations of Society

Pushing back against these new ideas—against individualism, the importance of personal feelings, and opportunity for everyone—were the traditions of the past. People in the 1800s didn't just suddenly throw up their hands and marry whomever they wanted; quite the opposite, actually. For the most part people continued to marry as they had always done: for money, power, safety, or convenience. Marriage, after all, had deep roots in society, and it would not be changed overnight.

Religion and Marriage

For one thing, marriage had strong connections to religion. The American population was largely Christian in the 1800s. More specifically, Americans were largely Protestant. That too would change as the 1800s wore on and immigrants brought their native religions with them. People wanted to stay together and continue their family's traditions in the new land. Catholics tried to get their children to marry other Catholics. Jews wanted their children to marry other Jews. Religion was a huge factor in a marriage. Not only did it determine whom a person could marry, but it also determined what the wedding would be like and often how the marriage would operate. Christians and Jews, for example, have different ideas about how husbands and wives should behave.

Jewish families in the 1800s in the United States tended to socialize with—and marry—other Jews.

Ethnicity and Marriage

Going hand in hand with religion was ethnicity. Marriages between two people of different nationalities or ethnic background or race became more common toward the end of the 1800s, but even then it was the exception, not the rule. You have to realize how different things were back then. Today, most Americans identify with a cultural heritage such as Italian-American, Irish-American, and German-American; "Americanness" is the common bond between all these groups, and generally the dominating part of these groups' identities. But in the 1800s, people were more likely to be first-, second-, or third-generation immigrants who identified strongly with their ethnic heritage.

Northern Europeans made up the largest part of the early American population, and they tended not to marry outside their own cultural group. A person of English descent, for example, would be very unlikely to marry an American of Italian or Spanish descent. Something we take for granted today, that someone with the last name Gonzalez might marry someone with the last name Smith, was very uncommon in the 1800s. Even if they had about the same skin color, chances are these families spoke different languages and came from very different backgrounds.

When this German family arrived in North America, they brought with them traditions from home, and found others like themselves to share those traditions with.

Marrying into the Family

In the nineteenth century, most people viewed marriage as the wedding of two families (rather than merely the wedding of two individuals, as we think of marriage today). It wasn't as simple as one man marrying one woman. This was the result of a more traditional society in which husbands and wives usually lived with one of their families (that's right, in the same house!), or at least lived in the same community. Different cultures had different rules about this. (In most Native American cultures, for instance, it was common for the man to move in with his new wife's family.)

But in America, where land was as bountiful as dreams for a better life, this too became less common. New

Families who moved west often lost their connections to their extended family back East.

The family was very important in many Native American cultures, with women playing a strong role. Europeans often did not understand or appreciate Native American society.

husbands and wives were more likely to be mobile, to move away from their families and live on their own. Pioneers often traveled thousands of miles to start entirely new lives, leaving their extended families behind forever. Remember, most American were immigrants or the children of recent immigrants to a foreign land. The drive to leave home was already inside them.

INCREDIBLE INDIVIDUAL
Jane Austen

Born in 1775 to a family in the lower ranks of the upper class, Jane Austen is remembered today as one of the most read and loved writers in the English language. Austen wrote a total of four full-length novels, all published in the early 1800s. She died in 1817, shortly after the publication of her last novel. She was young at the time of her death—only 42 years old—and she never enjoyed the fame her writing would one day bring her, both at home and abroad.

Austen's stories are usually about women, and almost always focus on their dependence on marriage to gain social standing and economic security. Many critics of Austen's day called her novels "realistic" (implying that this made them less interesting!). They are remarkable for their ability to see into the moral consequences behind society's rules and regulations. A fine example of such writing is from one of her most famous novels, "Pride and Prejudice," in which a very young woman marries a soldier. The young woman loses her public standing and is put into economic and physical danger by marrying the older man, a very real danger for young women at that time.

Although Jane Austen lived in England, where social class played a far greater role than it did in the United States, her novels reveal much about the English-speaking world's attitudes toward marriage, romance, and women's roles in the nineteenth century. She was a skilled observer, putting into words the tensions of her day. The clash of individual and society, romance and societal expectation: these were the subjects of Austen's day, and they fascinated her.

INCREDIBLE INDIVIDUAL
Catharine Sedgwick

Catharine Sedgwick was born in 1789 to a middle-class family. Her father was a lawyer and politician, and he made sure his daughter was well educated at a Boston "finishing school"— a school with the purpose of educating well-off girls just like Catharine. Soon after completing her education as a student, Catharine took charge of a school in Lenox, Massachusetts, as a teacher. Although she was a fine teacher, it soon became clear that she was most talented as a writer. She wrote short stories for periodicals that brought her money and some fame, but she poured most of her passion into her novels.

Sedgwick's stories were popular in her day. Both men and women were interested in what she had to say. Through her fictional stories she promoted what is called "republican motherhood"—the idea that children should be raised to understand and uphold the ideals of republicanism (where the government is elected by the people). Sedgwick and others saw that the role of the woman in a family was changing in the newly created United States. They argued that it was essential for a woman to be well educated in order to pass on the proper ideals to her children.

Sedgwick herself never married. Interestingly enough, her decision not to wed was based on her commitment to a higher ideal for marriage: she would not settle for anything but love. The idea that love could and should be a part of marriage was a fairly radical concept, one that would dramatically change marriage in the 1800s, and Sedgwick and her books were a part of this change. Reflecting back on her life in her diary, she wrote: "I certainly think a happy marriage the happiest condition of human life. . . . It is the high opinion of its capabilities which has perhaps kept me from adventuring in it."

SNAPSHOT FROM THE PAST

1888, Durango, Colorado

Although frontiersmen often took Native women as their wives, as regions became more "civilized"—with white women and families settling in the area—inter-marrying between whites and Natives became unacceptable.

Amos Stanton Lee was seventeen when he first saw her. He remembers it perfectly because it was on his birthday. His mother had taken down some of her strawberry preserves for his pancakes that morning, as his birthday gift. His daddy was in the barn milking, doing Amos' chores for him as a birthday gift. He told Amos he was allowed to take the cattle out alone that day, and that's what he was doing when he saw her riding horseback. She didn't have a saddle, but she was riding fast and hard.

It wasn't out of the ordinary to see Navajos riding in that part of the country, but Amos had never before seen one who was a girl his age. When she noticed him, she slowed a bit, glancing for a moment in his direction. Without thinking, he raised his hand a little in a wave. She didn't wave back, but he thought he saw her smile.

The next day Amos had to attend the wedding of one of their neighbor's daughters to a wealthy rancher from Denver. He sat unhappily in a pew near the back of the church, watching the exchange of rings. His sisters kept whispering things about how fancy the bride's dress looked, and how she was so lucky to find a rich man in these parts. Secretly, Amos hated the frills and lace things. He thought about the Navajo girl, and what he knew could never be.

Snapshot from the Past

1890, New York City

Emma Levy came to America from Poland in 1890 when she was twelve years old. She was the only child and the pride of her small family. Like many immigrants, she remembers the first time she saw the shining new Statue of Liberty with her open arms, and of course those wonderful words—"Give me your poor, your tired, your huddled masses yearning to breathe free." At that moment, packed into a tight crowd on the top deck of their boat, Emma and her family were exactly those three things: poor, tired, and huddled together.

But they adjusted quickly enough. Emma's uncle had already been living in New York City for five years when they arrived, and he loaned them enough

By the end of the nineteenth century, the Jewish community in New York City was thriving. They had brought with them from Europe their own marriage customs.

money to rent a miserable apartment in a Jewish neighborhood on the Lower East Side of Manhattan. Very quickly, Emma's father and mother made it clear that they intended to have her married as soon as possible. "Here in America, the Jews must stick together," her mother reminded her again and again. Her father made a point to take the family Uptown for temple every week, even though it meant almost an hour of walking from their home.

Her father and mother had a plan. They knew that the German Jews from Uptown were integrated into society. They had seen how these German Jews had, over time, become a part of the American life and had prospered greatly in it. They wanted their daughter to belong in this society, in Uptown Manhattan. Emma never saw her father and mother so kind, so sociable, as when they were talking with the families of eligible young men.

Emma was never sure who began the talks or how, but it finally happened: her family began the Shidduch with another family. (Shidduch was how Jews arranged marriages for their children.) Emma's parents fretted over their clothes and adjusted their furniture whenever the young man's family came to talk. Finally Emma asked her mother, "Will I ever meet the young man? What if I don't like him?"

Her mother only shook her head, smiling. "Oh Emma. We have bigger things to worry about right now."

Part II
The Growth of Romance

Dating versus Courtship

Dating didn't exist in the 1800s. There was no popcorn and a movie, no parking the car at a scenic overlook, no hamburger and a milkshake. The concept of "dating" as we know it today was only barely peeking its head around the corner when the 1800s came to a close. But another concept, called courtship, did exist.

Courtship can be defined, for our purposes, as any act that prepares for a marriage proposal. Dating is really just a complicated and more informal form of courtship. Dating involves "courting" multiple people to find a potential mate, while courtship involves only one target—and the objective is always most definitely marriage.

But dating and courtship are different in other ways as well. Perhaps the most important of them is that dating occurs outside the home, while courtship usually occurred inside it. The parlor was considered to be a safe place for a young woman to entertain a male suitor. Certain rules needed to be followed in courtship: a "gentleman" (man) would ask permission (usually of the girl's parents) to "call upon" a young lady (which meant he would come over to her house). The lady (or her parents) would either agree or politely decline. If she agreed, they would decide upon a time when the gentleman should call upon her.

By the end of the nineteenth century, bicycles were becoming more common. Bicycles gave women greater freedom to get away from the house for a little while on their own, allowing courtship to move out from under the watchful eyes of parents. Here, the young man is being struck with an arrow of love as he talks to the woman.

The Parlor

This is where the parlor comes into play. Most middle-class and upper-class families had a special room located somewhere near the front of the house. This was a fancy room with all the family' finest possessions—family photographs, paintings and portraits, musical instruments, knick-knacks, and fine furniture. It was a place for lively discussion, table games, and musical entertainment. Here is where the young man and woman would meet, usually under the watchful eyes of her mother.

Of course, this was only the basic formula. Many couples chose to break the rules, especially in America. In fact, that famous French visitor to the Americas in the 1840s, Monsieur Alexis de Tocqueville, noticed that American youths were given much more privacy than Europeans of their same age. In general, Europeans were astounded by the trust that American parents gave their children. You might not think so today—but allowing a young man and woman to talk alone in a room was a daring idea back in the 1800s!

A recreation of a typical nineteenth-century parlor at the Marshall County Historical Museum in Plymouth, Indiana.

Private versus Public

Here's where another big difference comes into play between dating and courting: one was a public activity and the other is private—and yet dating evolved because some families lacked a private place within their homes for couples to court, and so the couples resorted to seeing each other in public spaces. In fact, some historians believe the word "date" originated among the lower classes in America. Poor girls without parlors or front porches on which to entertain gentleman were sometimes forced to meet men outside their homes, at restaurants, cafes, and other places. The lack of a fancy parlor meant that these young people escaped the watchful eyes of their parents—and possibly found some privacy for themselves in the process!

Dating is an activity between two individuals, while courtship involved the whole family, even the entire community. Because courtship took place under the watchful eyes of so many people, it ensured that young men could not take advantage of young women. This prevented a woman from becoming pregnant and abandoned by a man who had changed his mind.

Going for a sedate stroll or meeting in a park or other outdoor spot was an acceptable variation of "parlor courting," so long as the location wasn't too remote or private.

Sex Is for Making Babies

This raises the question of sex between young people in the 1800s. With a few exceptions (the" free love" utopian communities being one), sex was viewed as a way to make babies, and its proper place was marriage. This was before the time of birth control or modern contraceptives, and long before the time of "sexual liberation." Sexual gratification was seen as a bonus, to be enjoyed, certainly, but not to be demanded or expected. This viewpoint may seem old fashioned to our modern perspective, but cultural structures like this actually protected young women. Being left "barefoot and pregnant" after a lover had abandoned them was a risk that was all too real for young women who dared to become sexually involved before marriage. Women had few options for supporting themselves, and childcare facilities were nonexistent, so an unmarried woman who found herself pregnant was truly "in trouble."

So, What Were American Girls Looking for in a Man?

When Alexis de Tocqueville visited the United States, he felt that American women were less impressed by gallantry than their European sisters, and in general this seems to be true. Gallantry can be loosely defined as acts of courage or bravery, fine speeches or fancy airs, to be put on in front of a woman for the purpose of winning her affections. Europeans had a long tradition of gallantry, a series of formal acts designed to win a woman's heart, such as poetry and song, or waiting on a lady hand and foot. De Tocqueville noticed that American women had little interest in these things. Maybe they were too practical. After all, poems and songs won't plow the field, feed the cows, or put food on the table!

EYEWITNESS ACCOUNT

After traveling to the United States, writer Gustave de Beaumont wrote a novel called *Marie* in which he imagines a conversation about the differences between marriage in Europe and in America.

In Europe, said the traveler, abandoning himself to his poetic feelings, all is dirt and corruption! Women there stoop to sell themselves, and the men are stupid enough to buy them. When a young girl marries, she does not seek a tender soul with which hers may unite, she does not ask for a support to her weakness: she marries diamonds, a title, freedom. Not that she is heartless; she may have loved once, but her beloved was not sufficiently rich. They haggled over her; the man could not throw in a carriage with his price; the bargain fell through. Then, they tell the young girl that love is all foolishness; she believes it, and corrects her mistaken notions; she marries a rich idiot. If she has any soul at all, she pines away and dies. Usually she lives happily enough. Such is not the life of a woman in America. Here marriage is not a business, nor is love a commodity. Two beings are not condemned to love or to hate each other because they are united; they join because they love each other. Oh, how attractive these young girls are, with their blue eyes, their ebon eyebrows, their pure, candid souls! How sweet the perfume wafted from their hair, unspoiled by art! What harmony in their gentle voices, which never echo the passion of greed! Here, at least, when you court a young girl, and she responds, it is a meeting through tender sympathy, and not through cold calculation. Would it not be losing an opportunity for tranquil but delicious felicity not to seek the love of an American girl?

Courtship Among Native Peoples

Native Americans had their own ways of helping the young find each other for marriage. Like the Europeans, most Native tribes had many elaborate customs built into their courtship process. Although many tribes were forced off their land during the 1800s, those tribes that remained intact continued to marry and have children as before.

Money was rare among Native peoples, but gifts and valuables were not. Horses, food, and fine clothes could all be given as gifts by a man who wished to marry a woman. Often these gifts were dropped off at the tent or lodge of the woman's father for his inspection. If her father accepted the gifts, it meant the marriage proposal was accepted. If the gifts were rejected, so was the young man.

Other historians and memory keepers record native traditions such as flute-playing and blanket-wrapping. In flute playing, a man will play a tune for the woman he wishes to marry, and only for her. When other women pass by him, he changes the song. Other traditions include practices as simple as a man standing in the path of the woman he wishes to marry, waiting for her to arrive. When she gets to him, if she passes him by without pausing, it means she rejects his proposal; if she stops, it means she accepts.

One way for a woman to take charge in the Sioux culture was this: if a man showed interest, she could stand outside her tent, wrapped in a blanket, while her parents watched from nearby. If the young man she liked came to her tent, she would open the blanket as an invitation to him. If he stepped inside, it meant that he had declared his intentions to court her for marriage.

Impatient Americans

John Fenimore Cooper, a nineteenth-century American author, made this observation about American courtship: "Without a doubt, when the youth has made his choice, he endeavors to secure an interest in the affections of the chosen fair. . . . These attractions lead to love; and love, in this country, nineteen times in twenty, leads to matrimony." What Cooper noticed is this: American men tend to "win" a woman not by gallantry (outward displays) but by an inward connection: in other words, love. In Europe, the affection that began in public was expected to blossom in a personal, private way once the marriage began. In America, that personal touch was added right at the onset. As with so many things American, the idea seemed to be, "Why wait till tomorrow for something good we can have today?"

As the century progressed, love became more important in America than in Europe, where money and economic considerations continued to be the driving force behind marriages.

To convince his beloved of the depth of his passion, a man sometimes made long and poetic professions of love—or at least this was the romantic ideal.

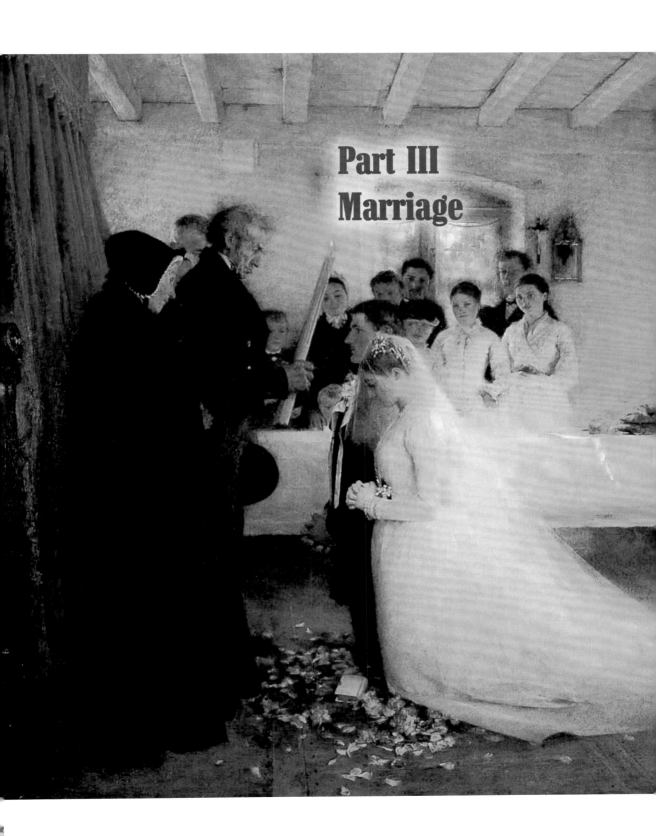

Part III
Marriage

In general, people took marriage very seriously in the 1800s. With divorces far less common, and deaths far more frequent, the marriage vow "till death do us part" had more significance.

In nineteenth-century America, as in almost every society, marriage was seen as an extremely important step in the life of a person. It meant that a person was leaving childhood permanently and entering into adulthood with the intention of having children. Marriage and family were one and the same in the eyes of most people. Few if any people in the 1800s even considered a marriage without children.

How Young is Too Young?

Throughout history, societies have needed to make laws to protect young people from early marriages. In many cases, this meant setting the minimum age of marriage at ten or twelve years old! Shocking as it may sound, pre-teen marriage was not uncommon in many societies.

Things were no different in the United States. Women's rights groups and social reformers, however, began to push for laws to protect the youngest people from early marriages. By the 1880s, most states had set the minimum age at ten or twelve, while one state, Delaware, set it at seven years old!

It was still fairly common in the 1800s for a man to marry a young woman beneath the "age of consent" (the age at which she could legally have sex). In those cases, it was understood that the man would be a protector and guardian of the girl until she reached the proper age. If they had sex before she was of a safe child-bearing age, there would be serious action taken by the community.

Polygamy and Mormonism

In the 1830s and 1840s a man named Joseph Smith founded a new religious movement called the Church of Jesus Christ of Latter-Day Saints (also known as the LDS or "Mormon" church). A part of the church's earliest doctrines was polygamy, a practice in which one man can take many women to be his wives. The LDS church was based in the Utah Territory, but Utah was refused entrance into the union largely because many Americans had heard about the polygamy being practiced there. In 1857, the Utah Mormon War began when the U.S. Army invaded the territory, resulting in a relatively peaceful overthrow of the Mormons. In 1890, the Mormon Church officially rejected polygamy as part of its beliefs.

Utopian Societies and Marriage

But the Mormons weren't the only ones to experiment with polygamy in the 1800s. Various "utopian societies" cropped up in America in the 1800s. These were people who envisioned an ideal society and joined together to create it, usually in a rural setting. They often lived off the land and provided for themselves everything they needed to survive. One such group was called the Oneida Community. The community's founder was a man named John Humphrey Noyes who taught that perfection was attainable in this life. Noyes also believed in what he called "complex marriage" in which one person is "married" to an entire group of people. This was polygamy under a different name, and many people left the Oneida Community in opposition to this practice.

On the other hand, some utopian societies were based upon the principle of celibacy. Quite different from polygamy, celibacy is the rejection of sex for the entirety of one's life. The Shakers and the Rappites, utopian communities of the 1800s, both endorsed celibacy as part of their ideal communities. Both communities wanted to create an ideal society in which men and women were truly equals, and the only way to do that, in their minds, was to reject marriage and sex.

Morman wives and their children.

Slave Weddings

African Americans living in slavery could not usually marry without the permission of their "masters," but slave weddings did occur, especially on larger plantations in which slaves had their own churches. These were not legally recognized marriages, and white owners could separate couples as they pleased. In some communities, however, biracial churches existed, where blacks and whites attended services together. In these congregations, and on the plantation itself, the marriage was recognized as very real. White pastors encouraged the slaves in their congregation to remain faithful to their husbands and wives. On the plantation, some slave owners recognized that by acknowledging and respecting family ties within the slave community, they were keeping the peace.

Unfortunately, the terrible reality is that slave marriages were very rarely given the chance to prosper on the plantation. Often times, a married couple shared a house (usually a one-room cabin) with multiple slaves, which gave them little or no privacy. And even worse, they had almost no say over the upbringing of any children they might have. Ultimately, their children were the property of the slave owner. A slave owner could split up a husband and wife, or a mother and her children, simply by selling one away.

EYEWITNESS ACCOUNT

(Dated to December of 1861, the following is from the diary of a white slave-owner in Camden, South Carolina. The diarist, a white woman, writes down her thoughts while watching a wedding between two of her slaves. The sarcasm and disgust in the tone of the diary entry show how little respect many whites had for the marriage of slaves.)

Oh! the bridal party—all as black as the ace of spades. The bride and her bridesmaids in white swiss muslin, the gayest of sashes—and bonnets too wonderful to be described. They had on red blanket shawls, which they removed as they entered the aisle and seemed loath to put on when the time came to go out—so proud were they of their finery. But it grew colder and colder—every window and door wide open, sharp December wind.

Gibbes Carter arose amidst the ceremony and threw a red shawl over the head of the congregation, to a shivering bridesmaid. The shawl fell short and wrapped itself about the head of a sable dame comfortably asleep. She waked with a snort, struggled to get it off her head, with queer little cries. "Lord ha' mussy! What dish er here now." There was for a moment a decided tendency to snigger—but they were too well-bred to misbehave in church, and soon it was unbroken solemnity. I know that I shook with silent laughter long after every dusky face was long and respectable.

The bride's gloves were white, and the bridegroom's shirt bosom was a snowy expanse fearfully like Johnny's Paris garments, which he says disappear by the dozen.

Native American Wedding Ceremonies

For many Native Americans, marriage was particularly sacred. Some tribes were matriarchal, which means women held leadership positions. Women, children, and family were highly valued. In some tribes, if a man was unfaithful to his wife, he would be publicly whipped by the women of the tribe.

As was the case in many European societies, Natives participated in arranged marriages. If the parents of a young woman accepted gifts or services from a young man hoping to marry their daughter, the young woman had to agree. Once married, the young man usually came to live with his wife's family, or in a small home nearby. The new husband became the servant not only of his wife but also of his wife's mother.

Marriage was taken very seriously, and wedding ceremonies represented a spiritual as well as physical bond. One of the most common and beautiful of the Native American wedding rites is symbolized by the exchanging of blankets. The couple begins the wedding ceremony each wrapped in a separate blue blanket. This symbolizes any loneliness, sorrow, or depression in their lives. Once the ceremony is completed, the couple sheds their blue blankets and a single, white blanket is wrapped around the new husband and wife. The new blanket represents the happiness and peace the new couple will enjoy.

A couple from the Cayuse Tribe of Oregon.

Native American couple on the Crow Creek Reservation.

Interracial Marriages

In the United States today, we take it for granted that any person of any race can marry any other person. However, just as homosexual marriage is being debated today, interracial marriage (the marriage of two people of different races) was debated throughout the 1800s. The fiercest debates were over the marriage of whites and blacks.

You might think that after the Civil War, things would have improved for interracial couples.

In some parts of the American South, a system of intermarriage, called "placage," existed. The marriages were not legal, but rather "common-law" marriages, in which white men took women of African, Indian, and Creole descent to be their wives, sometimes in addition to their white wives.

But in fact the opposite is true. After the Civil War many "anti-miscegenation laws" (laws that ban interracial marriage) were passed! Fearing the new freedom of African Americans, many Western and Southern states were quick to pass laws protecting what they thought of as the "purity" of their race.

Fear of interracial marriage didn't stop with blacks, but extended to Native Americans, Asians, and Hispanics. In some states, laws were even passed that banned people of mixed race (for example, someone with a Mexican mother and a white father) from marrying at all. Interracial marriage and interracial sex were considered felonies. In states without interracial bans, the charges brought against interracial couples were often outright lies, accusing them of adultery or "fornication" (premarital sex).

In 1884 Frederick Douglass married Helen Pitts, a white woman (seen here seated). Both their families were outraged, as were both the white and black communities in Washington D.C., where they lived. Douglass' response was, "This proves I am impartial. My first wife was the color of my mother, my second is the color of my father."

Marriage on the Frontier

Preachers could be hard to find on the frontier. In fact, many of the most important elements of a wedding—a cake, a congregation, a church, and a pastor—were nowhere to be found for many pioneers. But frontier people did their very best to document the wedding. Many couples took the only photograph of their lives on the day of their wedding. Others saved whatever money they had to pay for a preacher to travel the distance. Still others put up even more money to have the preacher carry word of their marriage back to town, where it would be recorded by the state.

A wedding could take place at home just as easily as in a church. In this painting by John Lewis Krimmel, daily life goes on around them as the loving couple are married and the bride's mother cries.

Life was often very hard on the frontier, but people found love and happiness wherever they could.

Elaborate marriage certificates were popular on the frontier. A married couple would receive a beautiful certificate from the preacher who married them and these certificates were often passed down for generations. Many certificates became family heirlooms. For the very poor, frontier weddings were very simple affairs. A bride's dress had usually been worn by her mother and possibly even her grandmother. If she didn't have a dress, she put on her finest calico, or the nicest everyday dress she owned. Many brides tried to at least find a nice pair of shoes for the occasion, even if it meant borrowing them from a friend, just for the day.

The men wore their nicest suit and had their boots shined for the occasion. Neighbors and wedding guests were most likely to bring food and drink as wedding gifts. Some simply offered to help around the bride and groom's home for a few days following the wedding.

Sometimes a preacher simply couldn't be found for a wedding, and in some of these cases, a common-law marriage was formed. The common-law marriage is quite simple: a man and a woman, living together as husband and wife, are declared married. In many frontier areas, this was viewed as seriously as a real marriage. The times often called for men and women to live and work together, and the common-law marriage allowed them to do just that.

Although the common-law marriage has existed in other places and in other times, the American version was short-lived. It served a purpose on the frontier for a while, but disappeared by about 1900. In some states today, it has returned, but doesn't offer nearly same rights and protections as a fully recognized marriage.

EXTRA! EXTRA!

Elizabeth Cady Stanton and the Seneca Falls Convention

The New York Times
July 21, 1848

Today marks the conclusion of a two-day convention held in Seneca Falls, New York, in which over 300 men and women gathered to write down demands for women's rights.

The demands were organized under the title of "Declaration of Sentiments"—a list of women's rights that includes the right to vote. It's being said that many at the convention wished to remove the right to vote, fearing it would make the declaration less realistic, but Frederick Douglass is said to have argued beautifully for its inclusion in the final product. Readers will

Frederick Douglass believed in equal rights for all people, whether black, women, Native American, immigrant, or any other group.

during, and after any marriage. In particular, the act ensures that married women cannot have their own property seized to pay their husband's debts.

The tide seems to be turning in favor of women and women's rights here in New York, especially in the western part of the state, where many such meetings are being held to challenge the fate of women in this country.

know Douglass as the former slave and famous defender of minority rights.

This all comes on the heels of another victory for women's rights which occurred a little over three months ago right here in the state of New York—the Married Woman's Property Act. As readers may recall the act gave women in New York the rights to their property before,

Elizabeth Cady Stanton often disagreed with Frederick Douglass about who exactly should be allowed to vote, but she was one of his few supporters in his interracial marriage.

Women's Rights and Marriage

Throughout the 1800s, women worked hard for equality with men. As the middle class grew in America, more daughters had more access to education. Learning gave women opportunities to speak out against the injustices they saw around them—injustices against not just women but minorities too.

Many women found a voice for themselves in the world of politics and men by first speaking about the family. They did this largely by addressing the issue of alcoholism. Many of the women we remember today as reformers and women's rights activists began their lives fighting alcohol in the home. Americans recognized that a woman could do very little to protect herself or her children from an alcoholic husband.

But their activism didn't end there. Women reformers pushed for equal property rights, the right to vote, and greater control over their financial affairs. As marriage existed in the 1800s, a woman basically signed her fate into a man's hands on the day she married. His decisions could literally ruin her. If he went bankrupt, she did too. If he beat or abused her, she could do nothing but seek refuge from neighbors and friends.

The growth of the women's rights movement and the changing role of women in American society would have a profound effect on relationships between woman and men, and love and marriage would never be the same. In many ways, the reforms that came to be in the 1800s, thanks to intelligent and courageous women like Susan B. Anthony and Elizabeth Cady Stanton, laid the foundation for the rights and opportunities twenty-first-century women enjoy today.

Susan B. Anthony and Elizabeth Cady Stanton (at right) devoted their whole lives to fighting for women's rights. Cady Stanton was married and had children, while Anthony was single, and the two worked well together. Anthony was able to travel more than her friend, and was more often seen publically, giving speeches that Cady Stanton had helped write. She later said that Elizabeth Cady Stanton "forged the thunderbolts and I fired them."

Think About It

If you think about it, we're all here today because of the courtship and marriages of our ancestors in the 1800s, whatever the customs of their particular heritage were at that time.

While social customs and manners change over time, we can be pretty sure that young people in the 1800s were just as interested in getting to know one another, in "courtship," and in dating as they are today.

From what you've learned in this book, think about what a typical "date" would have been like for a young person living in your town in 1850, and compare it with a typical date in your town today.

- In what ways are the two dates most different? In what ways are they the same?

- Do you think the courting couple in 1850 was having fun? As much fun or more fun than today's couple? Why do you think that?

- Why was it so important that a young person's family be a part of courtship and marriage customs in the 1800s? Is it still important?

- The role of women has changed a lot since the 1800s. How has that made a twenty-first century courtship and marriage different from one in the 1800s?

Words Used in This Book

calico: An inexpensive, brightly printed cotton cloth often used to make clothing in the 1800s.

contraceptives: Methods used to prevent pregnancy.

doctrines: The official beliefs and teachings of a religion.

elaborate: Beautifully designed and decorated in a way that is carefully arranged and detailed.

heirlooms: Things like antiques or jewelry passed down through the generations and usually associated with a family member of the past.

integrated: Fitting in, and completely a part of something.

profound: Serious and important.

traditional: Old and established ways of doing things, usually passed down from generation to generation.

Find Out More

In Books

Casas, Maria Raquel. *Married to a Daughter of the Land: Spanish-Mexican Women and Interethnic Marriage in California, 1820–80*. Las Vegas, Nev.: University of Nevada Press, 2007.

Lystra, Karen. *Searching the Heart: Women, Men, and Romantic Love in Nineteenth-Century America*. Oxford, U.K.: Oxford University Press, 1997.

Tyler, Daniel. *Love in an Envelope: A Courtship in the American West.* Albuquerque, N.M.: University of New Mexico Press, 2009.

On the Internet

A History of Dating and Courtship
www.ehow.com/about_4570730_history-dating-courtship.html

Native American Wedding Traditions
www.manataka.org/page348.html

Slave marriages
www.startum.com/slaveweddings.htm

Susan B. Anthony
www.infoplease.com/ce6/people/A0804198.html

Victorian Courtship
www.victoriaspast.com/Courtshipdance/courtshipdance.html

Index

Picture Credits

To the best knowledge of the publisher, all images are in the public domain. If any image has been inadvertently uncredited, please notify Harding House Publishing Service, 220 Front Street, Vestal, New York 13850, so that credit can be given in future printings.

About the Author and the Consultant

Zachary Chastain is an independent writer and actor living in Binghamton, New York. He is the author of various educational books for both younger and older audiences.

John Gillis is a Rutgers University Professor of History Emeritus. A graduate of Amherst College and Stanford University, he has taught at Stanford, Princeton, University of California at Berkeley, as well as Rutgers. Gillis is well known for his work in social history, including pioneering studies of age relations, marriage, and family. The author or editor of ten books, he has also been a fellow at both St. Antony's College, Oxford, and Clare Hall, Cambridge.